Re-Membering the Body

Re-Membering the Body

The Witness of History, Theology, and the Arts in Honour of Ruth M. B. Gouldbourne

Edited by
Anthony R. Cross and Brian Haymes

PICKWICK Publications · Eugene, Oregon

RE-MEMBERING THE BODY

The Witness of History, Theology, and the Arts in Honour of Ruth M. B. Gouldbourne

Copyright © 2021 Wipf & Stock Publishers. All rights reserved. Except for brief quotations in critical publications or reviews, no part of this book may be reproduced in any manner without prior written permission from the publisher. Write: Permissions, Wipf and Stock Publishers, 199 W. 8th Ave., Suite 3, Eugene, OR 97401.

Pickwick
An Imprint of Wipf and Stock Publishers
199 W. 8th Ave., Suite 3
Eugene, OR 97401

www.wipfandstock.com

PAPERBACK ISBN: 978–1–5326–7705–2
HARDCOVER ISBN: 978–1–5326–7706–9
EBOOK ISBN: 978–1–5326–7707–6

Cataloguing-in-Publication data:

Names: Cross, Anthony R., editor. | Haymes, Brian, editor.

Title: Re-membering the body : the witness of history, theology, and the arts in honour of Ruth M. B. Gouldbourne / edited by Anthony R. Cross and Brian Haymes.

Description: Eugene, OR: Pickwick, 2021 | Includes bibliographical references and index.

Identifiers: ISBN 978–1–5326–7705–2 (paperback) | ISBN 978–1–5326–7706–9 (hardcover) | ISBN 978–1–5326–7707–6 (ebook)

Subjects: LCSH: Gouldbourne, Ruth M. B. | Baptists—History. | Baptists—Doctrines. | Baptists. | Baptists women.

Classification: BX6232 C76 2021 (print) | BX6232 (ebook)

Typeset by Luna Seymour.   Manufactured in the U.S.A.

Contents

Contributors   v

Ruth—A Father's Appreciation
Derek Murray   ix

A Personal Note
Peter C. Erb   xxv

Introduction
Brian Haymes and Anthony R. Cross   xxix

Chapter 1
The Letter, the Spirit, and the Letter Again: Reflections on
2 Corinthians 3 and the Work of Biblical Interpretation
Sean F. Winter   1

Chapter 2
The Trauma of Hearing: Listening, Poetry, and the Parable of the Sower
Simon Perry   17

Chapter 3
Proverbs: A Misogynist Text?
Ernest C. Lucas   29

Chapter 4
Women and Ministry, Once More
Stephen R. Holmes   48

Chapter 5
"Co-operation Not Separation": British Baptist Women and Suffrage
Karen E. Smith   67

Chapter 6
Emily Georgiana Kemp, FRSGS: "Her central interest was in living Christianity"
Janice O'Brien   95

Chapter 7
Was Writing about Prayer in the *Baptist Magazine*, 1850–70, Gendered?
Linda Wilson   124

Chapter 8
"I Received Guidance from Above": A Story of an Estonian Female
Preacher, Ilse Katvel
Toivo Pilli   140

Chapter 9
"She Did What She Could": Some Historical Observations on
Following Jesus as a Single Woman
Lina Toth   159

Chapter 10
More Light, Truth, and Transitions? Gender Dysphoria as a Moral Case
Study for the "Further Light" Clause
Michael J. Peat   179

Chapter 11
"Spend and Be Spent": The Nature of the Ministry
Anthony R. Cross   205

Chapter 12
Pastoral Prayer
Brian Haymes   219

Chapter 13
"I Have A Vision": Assessing the Impact of Martin Luther King Preaching
at Bloomsbury Central Baptist Church
Simon Woodman   237

Chapter 14
Shakespeare and Spirituality
Paul S. Fiddes   257

Chapter 15
Intimations of Transcendence: A Legacy of "The Scottish Colourists"
Richard L. Kidd   278

Selected Works of Ruth Gouldbourne   297

General Index   299

Contributors

Anthony R. Cross is an Adjunct Supervisor, The International Baptist Theological Study Centre, Amsterdam, The Netherlands.

Peter C. Erb is Professor Emeritus, Wilfrid Laurier University, Waterloo, Ontario, Canada, and is Theological Advisor at Schwenkfelder Library, Pennsburg, Pennsylvania, USA.

Paul S. Fiddes is Professor of Systematic Theology, University of Oxford, and Principal Emeritus and Senior Research Fellow of Regent's Park College, Oxford, UK.

Brian Haymes is a Baptist Minister, ordained in 1965, served in two British Baptist Colleges and local pastorates the last being Bloomsbury Central Baptist Church, London, UK.

Stephen R. Holmes is Principal of St Mary's College, and Head of Divinity, University of St Andrews, UK.

Richard L. Kidd is a Baptist Minister, and a former Principal of Northern Baptist College, Manchester, UK.

Ernest C. Lucas is Vice-Principal Emeritus, Bristol Baptist College, and Associate Research Fellow, Spurgeon's College, London, UK.

Derek B. Murray is a Baptist Minister, ordained in 1958, served in three pastorates, and in the Scottish Baptist College. Most recently he was Whole Time Chaplain at St Columba's Hospice Edinburgh, UK.

Janice O'Brien is a Professional Researcher, specializing in the India Collection and Twentieth-Century Military Records, and also a member of The Baptist Historical Society.

Michael J. Peat is Free Church Chaplain, University of Bristol, and Research Fellow at Bristol Baptist College, UK.

Simon Perry is Chaplain and Tutor at Robinson College, University of Cambridge, UK.

Toivo Pilli is Director of Baptist Studies at The International Baptist Theological Study Centre, Amsterdam, The Netherlands.

Karen E. Smith is Honorary Senior Research Fellow, School of History, Archaeology and Religion, Cardiff University, Cardiff, UK.

Lina Toth (formerly Andronovienė) is Assistant Principal and Lecturer in Practical Theology at the Scottish Baptist College in Paisley, Scotland,

UK, and Adjunct Lecturer and Supervisor/Promotor at The International Baptist Theological Study Centre, Amsterdam, The Netherlands.

Linda Wilson is an Honorary Research Fellow at Bristol Baptist College, Bristol, UK.

Sean F. Winter is the Head of College at Pilgrim Theological College within the University of Divinity, Melbourne, Australia.

Simon Woodman is the Minister of Bloomsbury Central Baptist Church, London, and the Baptist Chaplain of King's College, London, UK.

Ruth—A Father's Appreciation

Derek B. Murray

It is a privilege to write about my elder daughter, Ruth, of whom I am proud and by whom at times I feel humbled, and this will not be a neutral essay! It is, I suppose, a compliment for any minister when a child follows in his footsteps, and when, in the theological climate in Scotland in the 1980s and a daughter announced her call to the ministry, this gave rise to quite severe misgivings. There were in the first half of the twentieth century two brave women who were recognized as pastors in small churches in Scotland, but since then opposition to women's ordained ministry had become a sort of orthodoxy. (Now, in 2020 there are two women in pastoral charge and a few others in assistant or chaplaincy roles and the climate has changed.) In 1983, Ruth visited the Scottish Baptist College and was welcomed by Dr Gordon Martin, the Principal at the time, but she and three others who approached him at the same time were warned that there would be no prospects of service in Scotland in the foreseeable future. So how did she succeed in following her calling, and where did it come from?

When Ruth was ordained in Bloomsbury Central Baptist Church in 1987, I was invited to preach, and I presented her with a Greek New Testament that had belonged to my great uncle Andrew who was killed in the First World War. When she was inducted as minister in the same church in 2006, I gave her his Vulgate New Testament. This young man was studying for the ministry and has always been spoken of in my family with pride and sorrow. My father treasured a letter from his commanding officer, and he was a sort of family legend. The Testaments were given to me by my grandfather, his older brother, and that grandfather is important in the story. During the Welsh Revival of 1904–6 there was a parallel movement in a previously rundown Edinburgh church, Charlotte Chapel. Founded by the eminent Christopher Anderson in 1808, it met in an old building which once housed the congregation which is now in St John's Episcopal Church at the west end of Princes Street. A new minister, Joseph Kemp, had come in 1901 and revival came a few years later. My grandfather, Peter Boyd Murray, who had been a somewhat nominal member of St Cuthbert's parish church, was swept into the movement, although he was not baptized until the first baptismal service in the new building which was opened in 1912. In later years, he became an elder and at his death in the 1963 was the senior elder of the 1,000 strong congregation.

His eldest son was my father, David, who at his death in 2005, was also the senior elder in the same church, having led the Bible class for many years and having been a much-loved gospel soloist in churches and mission halls around

Edinburgh. So Ruth entered a goodly heritage, and one of her names, Boyd, is inherited from her great-great grandmother, Helen Boyd, mother of Peter. My father was a master baker, the third in family succession, and the family firm, Murray Bakers Ltd, was well known on the south side of Edinburgh and beyond.

My mother, Alice Mabon, came from a Jedburgh family. Her mother and aunts had come to Edinburgh to work as maids in big houses, and some, including my mother and her mother, had joined Charlotte Chapel. My mother died suddenly and unexpectedly in 1941, a few weeks before I was due to start school (the same school that my father, his brothers, and our cousins attended), and I have only a few memories of her. My father and I went to live in my grandparents' big flat overlooking the Bruntsfield Links, and a year or so later my father married a nurse from Aberdeen, Phyllis Donald, whose family were deeply involved in the Gordon Evangelistic Mission, which was in a downtown area of the city. She had been baptized in Elim Hall, a Brethren Meeting, while training as a nurse in Glasgow, and in Edinburgh became a member of what we always called "The Chapel." Ruth's heritage on her father's side was firmly middle class, Baptist and fervently evangelical.

Her mother, Giles Guthrie, was from a different background. Her father and many ancestors were coal miners and farm servants from the Lanarkshire town of Larkhall, near Hamilton. Charles Guthrie worked and studied hard, being promoted, step by step, he claimed, from holding the pit ponies to manager of Fleets Colliery near Tranent in East Lothian, moving many times in the process, so that Giles went to a number of schools, finally settling in Preston Lodge in Prestonpans. Her father, before I knew the family, had suffered a severe heart attack and was working in a Coal Board Office. West country miners and Edinburgh businesspeople are quite different tribes, and Mr Guthrie, although he was an elder in the Church of Scotland, was not a Baptist so that, after very careful thought and prayer, Giles was baptized in Charlotte Chapel not altogether with her parents' approval. She and I had met at Edinburgh University, through the Evangelical Union, and fell in love just as I began to study at the Baptist College. Then suddenly we found ourselves in a strange situation. Giles had been born with mild cerebral palsy, or, as it was then called, spastic paralysis, and my parents, and especially my stepmother, were adamant that she could not become a minister's wife. I was sent to various well-known Baptists who solemnly tried to make me see reason. After Giles died in January 1995 a short autobiography was found on her computer, and Faith Bowers included an extract in the Baptist Union of Great Britain booklet *Complete in Christ*.

> An undergraduate with cerebral palsy found the church loving and welcoming, apparently without reservations—until she fell in love with a ministerial student. Then "very many older Christians took it upon themselves to make it clear to us that it could not possibly be God's will for a minister to marry someone with a physical handicap. I was thunderstruck. I knew the Lord had accepted me and I

could not understand why his people should not. And yet these were mature Christians who were telling us we were wrong.... We both grew up a lot, emotionally and spiritually, over the course of the next few months, when we prayed and talked and prayed again, and eventually accepted that we were not going our own way and disregarding the leading of the Spirit, but that marriage was indeed God's plan for us."[1]

One kindly doctor, a former President of our Union, told me that I would get a call to my first church as I was still single, but that if I married Giles I would not be called to another. And we proved him wrong. We were never aware of any misgivings in the three churches we served, and her mother's strengths have been reflected in Ruth. When it became clear that Giles would not recover from breast cancer, late in 1994, Ruth wrote her a letter, thanking her for her love and example. She shared memories of her life at home and later university, of hospitality freely given to friends who came to visit or stay, of holidays, and the gift of freedom, for prayers and "the way you made it possible for faith to be part of my experience. It was so much part of the bedrock of your life it became easy and natural for me." "And now I have to let you go, and it scares me and makes me so sad. But you've loved and taught me well and so I know—or at least I hope—that the kind of person you have enabled me to be will not fall apart but I will live my life with my version of the faith, grace, dignity and bloody-mindedness that make you so special."[2]

Giles was an only child and when her father took ill in 1971 both her parents moved in with us in our fortunately large manse in Kirkcaldy. Quite soon her father died, but Gran was with us for the next eighteen years, and in her own way had a good influence on us all, including Ruth's younger sister Ann. She was a link with a very different world, whose earliest memory was of the church pulpit draped in black in mourning for Queen Victoria.

Ruth's relationship with my family was less close and my father could not approve of her becoming a minister. A deaconess role would be more appropriate, he wrote to her. But with delightful inconsistency he was pleased that she became a tutor at Bristol Baptist College, and somewhere in the archives of the Baptist Historical Society there is on tape a long conversation she had with her grandfather about the ministry in Charlotte Chapel of Dr Graham Scroggie, my father's mentor and friend for so many years.

Ruth was born on 5 July 1961, in a maternity hospital near Paisley, the town in which I had been since late 1958 the first minister in a church extension charge, and she was immediately taken to the heart not only of the church but of the nearby community. Florins would be put beneath the pram pillow, and when, just before we left for Glasgow, the College Principal, Dr A.B. Miller, conducted a dedication service the church was full.

---

[1] Costie, *Complete in Christ*, 12.

[2] Letter from Ruth Gouldbourne. No details available.

We moved to Glasgow when I was appointed to the staff of the College. We were no longer surrounded by church folk, but Queen's Park Church provided transport for Giles, Ruth and then Ann, born in October 1964, while I was often preaching in a great variety of churches. A crèche was set up by the widow of a previous College Principal in the church kitchen. In our home there was as yet no car or television, but we did have a small dog, and we lived a few yards from the entrance to Pollock Estate, one of Glasgow's many lovely parks.

In March 1966 we moved to Kirkcaldy when I became minister of Whyte's Causeway Baptist Church. The manse was near the church in the town centre, and Ruth was duly enrolled in the West School, where she received all her primary education. Next door was a family with girls the same age as ours, and Ruth is still in contact with her friend of those days. At the right age she joined both the Girls' Brigade in our church and the Brownies in the Old Parish.

While we were in Kirkcaldy, Giles, who already had her MA, took advantage of an offer from Moray House College of Education in Edinburgh to qualify as a teacher of modern languages, and we bought our first car for £50. We also acquired our first TV (bought by my grandparents for the Coronation) and the girls watched Dr Who with the TV doors shut and from behind the sofa! We began in 1971 the adventure of camping holidays in Germany and France and laid the foundation for later travels. It was on the first of these trips that a seed was sown. In the collection of Anabaptist Stories, *Coming Home*, Ruth wrote, "On this day, which was unbearably hot, I was standing with my father in the middle of the town square waiting for my mother and sister to return from some shopping. 'Look up at that spire' said my father. 'Do you see those cages? That was where the captured Anabaptists were hung on display.' ... My father told me as much of the story as a ten-year-old could pay attention to and I started to wonder just what kind of people these could be that everyone hated and feared so much."[3]

In 1973, we moved to Edinburgh and into the large manse in the New Town which had recently been acquired by the church in Dublin Street. Ruth had completed her primary education, and the very Edinburgh question arose, which secondary school would she attend? I maintain that you have to have grown up in Edinburgh to understand its many layered school system. As I had been at a fee-paying school and Giles had not this was an interesting point. We had to choose between paying fees and having holidays. The local secondary school had recently moved from junior secondary status by adding a fifth and sixth year, and we duly sent Ruth there, to Drummond High, where after she made friends, no easy task as the other children had come from local feeder primary schools, she settled well. She once told us that she was known as "the girl who did not swear." There was a small Scripture Union meeting in

---

[3] Gouldbourne, "What makes the Anabaptists so Annoying?" 61.

school, and a larger all-Edinburgh SU Saturday group where she met others from Christian homes and there was a small Bible class in the church. At the school she met Indian and Chinese fellow students, and had, especially in the last three years, the benefit of small classes and good teachers. She duly became Dux, a Scottish word for the best pupil in the school. She took up two ecclesiastical interests in these years—bell-ringing with her friend the Anglican University Chaplain's daughter whom she met at Bristo Baptist Church Guides, and brass-rubbing. Her sixth-year studies dissertation was on J.R.R. Tolkien's *The Lord of the Rings*. We had been introduced to Tolkien in Glasgow by a rather unlikely friend, Dom Robert Petitpierre, Anglican Benedictine monk of Nashdom, and noted exorcist, whom I had met at a conference and invited to stay with us for a holiday. This may also have influenced Ruth towards her later ecumenical adventures.

In 1979, Ruth chose to go to St Andrews University to study English Language and Linguistics, and she spent four years in David Russell Hall of residence. In the first week or so she met Ian Gouldbourne, a Mathematics and Statistics student from Liverpool, and soon brought him home to visit. She also met Hilary Forbes, an Astronomy student, who was her bridesmaid when in 1984 she and, to quote her, the "infinitely patient Ian" were married in the Chapel of St Columba's Hospice, where I was then part-time Chaplain. Ruth had graduated MA in 1983, having been much involved in the Baptist Church, the Christian Union, and the Gilbert and Sullivan Society. She remembered that the careers teacher at Drummond had suggested the ministry when she was sixteen, but that had seemed unthinkable then. When she was younger she had considered theology as rather a waste of time, she told me, but after taking a course on Theology for Arts Students she had a change of mind and with a view to ministry somewhere spent the year before her marriage at New College in Edinburgh while Ian took the civil service examinations and lived in London. This was not her happiest year as she and Ian were separated by 400 miles, but she gained new experiences as a waitress in a stately home and by working in one of Edinburgh's better tartan shops during vacations. She also built up a clientele as a baby-sitter in the New Town. Her calling grew stronger and, in an interview with Andy Goodliff, she said that "the insight and bloody-mindedness of my parents, and the openness and exploration of the church in which I grew up, and the taking-it-for-grantedness of my husband all combined to make what was impossible possible, that and being welcomed by another Union."[4]

At New College she enjoyed her first Theology year and carried off one or two prizes, including one in Hebrew to confound a (male) fellow student who did not believe women could learn that language. In 1984, she married Ian and set off to live in a flat in Chiswick, entering King's College in the Strand and thoroughly enjoying her studies, gaining a First-Class Honours BD in

---

[4] Gouldbourne, "Reflecting on Ministry (3)."

1986. By taking a few extra classes she was entitled to add AKC (Associate of King's College) to her name. Ian had been attending Bloomsbury for some months and Ruth settled in, being inspired by Barbara Stanford and Howard Williams. Since her training had not been with the denomination, she was directed to spend a year at Spurgeon's College, and emerged to serve for a further year as an assistant minister at Bloomsbury, where she was involved in hospital visiting and pastoral work with Barbara and started a group for students and other young people. Her comment on this year was "Barbara taught me to laugh instead of being angry, and how to love and have time for everybody because that is what God does."[5]

In 1988 Ruth was called as part-time assistant minister at the historic Bunyan Meeting Free Church in Bedford, to work with the Rev. Peter Prothero and to study, slowly, for her PhD. She and Ian bought a flat near the main railway station and quickly made new friends in and beyond the church. Bunyan Meeting is aligned both with the Baptist Union and the Congregational Federation and has always, since its seventeenth-century beginnings practised both infant and believers' baptism. There were then three branch churches, so Ruth had a varied experience of Sunday worship. During her time in Bedford her sister, Ann, who had gained a degree in Classical Studies in Newcastle, sat the civil service examination, and came in due time to Luton. So that we had both daughters in Bedfordshire.

While at Bunyan Meeting one of Ruth's contributions to Sunday worship was to lead the intercessory prayers after the sermon. This she did extemporaneously and well. Her first colleague in Bloomsbury, Simon Perry, writing years after the Bedford experience, characterized her intercessory prayers as "incisive, heartfelt, politically engaged and sensitive to the present."[6] And at Bunyan and its mission churches and indeed elsewhere in Bedfordshire, she practised her preaching skills, met with her fellow ministers, including our family friend and distant relative, Sandy Duncan, who was minister at Sundon Park in Luton, and was wisely mentored by Peter Prothero.

In 1994, we went as a family to the Baptist Historical Society Summer School at Aberystwyth, which we thoroughly enjoyed. One afternoon, Giles and I noticed Ruth and Roger Hayden, notable historian, and a trustee of Bristol Baptist College, walking together on the Promenade and eating ice cream. We did wonder what was happening and soon we learnt that Ruth had been offered the position of Tutor in Church History and Theology at that College.

A new chapter in her career began. She accepted the post, moved to a College house in Bradley Stoke and with Ian began the search for a new home

---

[5] Gouldbourne cited by Bowers, *Bold Experiment*, 412.

[6] Perry, "Prayers of Intercession."

which they found in Clifton, a double upper flat in Pembroke Road, near the College when it was in Woodland Road and equally near its new site close to the Clifton Downs. In the College she was given a large study, where she kept College material at one end and her PhD material at the other. The room was reputed to be the one in which Albert Schweitzer slept on a visit to Bristol. Her colleagues were Dr Brian Haymes until he moved to London in 2001, to be succeeded by Dr Chris Ellis, and Dr Ernest Lucas. She taught Church History and Doctrine in the College and also in Trinity College and was amused to find herself lecturing on ecclesiology to Anglicans. Supervision of students working for higher degrees became a continuing feature of her work. Ian and Ruth opened their home to students and others for meals and meetings and from time to time quite lengthy student stays. Ian rose in his profession and eventually became responsible for Ministry of Defence offices in London and Bath.

Ruth was appointed Chaplain to the College, and to fit herself for this position she gained a Diploma in Counselling from the University of Bristol. As part of that course she had to counsel clients and she continued doing this work alongside her ministry in London. She and Ian joined the historic Broadmead church, and while Ruth was often conducting services in a wide range of churches, near and far, Ian became a deacon and for a time joint secretary. He was also involved in the Western Association.

Meanwhile the work on the PhD continued. Her subject was "Theology and Gender in the Writings of Caspar Schwenckfeld," and a revised version was published in 2006 as *The Flesh and the Feminine*. Schwenckfeld was one of the creative thinkers of the Radical Reformation, and in studying his work and especially his attention to the insights of women Ruth had found a subject that matched her own ideas and convictions. Her PhD supervisor, Dr Lyndal Roper, commented on the book that "This is church history at its best. Gouldbourne makes the complex ideas of this misunderstood reformer accessible, and in the process, sheds new light on the Reformation."[7]

Her PhD had been awarded in 2000 at an outdoor ceremony at the Royal Holloway College of London University and was the result of a demanding search for knowledge. Ruth (and Ian) travelled to Pittsburgh, Pennsylvania, where the contemporary Schwenckfelder community maintains a library, and Ruth also spent time in Augsburg where I was able to join her for a few days and see autograph letters of the great man. She was greatly encouraged by Peter Erb, an expert on the Radical Reformation. And she was now the Rev. Dr Ruth M.B. Gouldbourne, an achievement of which we are proud!

And then in 2006 came an invitation to Bloomsbury Central Church. Brian Haymes had retired, and Ruth was known to the church. She hesitated and agonized over the call, but finally she accepted and was inducted to the pastorate along with Simon Perry as joint ministers. A letter arrived at the

---

[7] Lyndal Roper, back cover endorsement to Gouldbourne, *Flesh and the Feminine*.

Bristol College which asked for details for *Who's Who?*[8] She assumed this was a student trick, but it turned out to be genuine, and so she is enshrined in that work of reference.

In her list of interests Ruth put "theatre." In my upbringing the theatre was a forbidden worldly pleasure, but things change! In the church at Dublin Street, amongst several "brilliant individualists," to quote someone who knew the congregation well, was Tom Fleming, son of a previous minister and well-known Scottish actor and commentator on royal occasions in his time. In the 1950s he was the first actor to portray Jesus on television, in the film *Jesus of Nazareth*. And Mr Tom, as Ruth and Ann called him, was, despite work taking him all over the world, a staunch supporter of the church and the manse family. Going to see and hear him in plays, one man shows, following his commentaries on the Festival Tattoo, just meeting him must have had some effect on Ruth. And Tom's church of choice in London was Bloomsbury. In later years, after I had become a full-time hospice chaplain, and the church had moved to its former mission hall at Canonmills, Tom, now doing less travelling, was the leader of the corporate ministry from 1989–2007, and occasionally Ruth was invited to take a service.

Brian Cooper, one of our supplementary ministers, covered the Edinburgh Festival for the *British Weekly*, the *Baptist Times* and the *Stage*. He had stayed with George McLeod and his wife, and when they, with advancing years, were no longer entertaining, Brian came and lived in our front room. He was a source of free tickets to various Fringe shows, and occasionally he asked Ruth to write a criticism. From time-to-time actors rang the doorbell to be interviewed, and on one occasion a man who was presenting a one man show based on John Bunyan's *Grace Abounding* came and performed his interpretation at our morning service. When Ruth moved to London it was to a church in Theatreland which had rooms which were hired for auditions and rehearsals. So it is not surprising that she enrolled for a part-time MA in Shakespeare Studies at King's College. She thoroughly enjoyed the course and duly graduated, "with merit" in 2017. Ian took early retirement and volunteered with the St Mungo Homeless Charity and the Globe Theatre. He also did important work for the church, especially when there was a major redevelopment project.

Dublin Street Church had joined the Baptist Union of Great Britain in the 1950s when the Scottish Union withdrew from the World Council of Churches, in order to be within the mainstream ecumenical movement, so it is not surprising that Ruth has had no difficulty co-operating with other churches in all her posts. When our local Edinburgh churches were discussing the document *Baptism, Eucharist and Ministry*,[9] I remember her, still a

---

[8] Anon., "Gouldbourne, Rev. Dr Ruth Mary Boyd."

[9] Gouldbourne, "Ecclesiology and Gender."

student, arguing with our neighbour, Father Mark Dilworth, OSB, keeper of the Scottish Catholic Records, on the subject of believers' baptism. She has gone on to represent the British Union on a WCC Commission which met in Crete in 2009, and locally in London she was active in a ministerial breakfast group and served as Chair of Westminster Churches Together. More recently she has become Vice-Moderator of Churches Together in Britain and Ireland and has been active in local church groups in Cheadle Hulme, when she moved in 2018 to Grove Lane Baptist Church. While she was in London she was the Visitor for the London Mennonite Centre, until it closed.

Over the years Ruth has continued to read, study, research, write and lecture. In 1997 she was invited to give the Whitley Lecture, which she delivered in various venues with the title *Reinventing the Wheel*.[10] This lecture looked at the place of women in the early Baptist movement in England, their place in ministry, and recent developments, with many quotations from seventeenth century and more recent works. The first outing of the lecture was in the Scottish Baptist College and the quotations were read during the lecture by her friend Sheena, which certainly enlivened the occasion. In 1998, she delivered the Hughey Lectures,[11] on a similar theme at the International Baptist Theological Seminary, Prague, an institution which was to become particularly important for her.

In 1993 she contributed an article to the *Baptist Ministers' Journal*, "Identity and Pain," in which she told part of the story of three informal consultations of women in ministry, and described the strength drawn from finding each other and sharing common anxieties and problems.[12] One result was a deputation to the Tutors' and Principals' Conference, which raised training issues and issued in guidelines for ministers during pregnancy and also revised guidelines for settlement. This was only one of the networks in which Ruth took part. There were for several years meetings of Baptist women pastors from all over Europe, including, to her delight, a Baptist Bishop from Georgia. Most recently she contributed an article, "A short history of Baptist women in ministry" to the Spring 2019 issue of *Baptists Together*.

In 2003, Ruth was appointed to the Board of IBTS, Prague. She was a Senior Research Fellow, and lectured, supervised and examined for the Seminary for many years. From 2007 until 2013, she chaired the Board, and when she moved on a tribute, signed by Keith Jones, Parush Parushev and Lina Toth, stated that she "showed an amazing ability to chair some intense and complex meetings of the Trustees and cope with a wide range of Trustees drawn from different traditions of governance, and to get the work done within the time for enabling people to get early Saturday evening flights

---

[10] Gouldbourne, *Reinventing the Wheel*.

[11] Gouldbourne, "Ecclesiology and Gender."

[12] Gouldbourne, "Identity and Pain."

home."¹³ Lina told me that she admired Ruth's emotional intelligence and another trustee remarked on Ruth's unique style of chairing a meeting. Her last act for IBTS was in 2013 to chair the search committee to find a successor to Keith Jones. The choice of the Committee was her fellow Scot, the Rev. Dr Stuart Blythe.

In August 2012, while IBTS's move to Amsterdam was being discussed, Ruth wrote "one of the joys of being Baptist is living with the provisional nature of all institutions and the capacity to reshape how we do things to meet changing situations."¹⁴ Certainly, ministry in Central London brought many changing situations. The church has a strong core of members and also many, particularly younger people, who came and moved on. For several years interns came from the USA and added both to the variety and to the skills available in the church. Some remain in touch.

Ruth preferred to be known as co-minister of Bloomsbury, first along with Simon Perry and then with Simon Woodman. Dawn Savidge joined the team in Ruth's last years and was encouraged to be involved with the complex needs of the neighbourhood. There was work with homeless people which attracted help form various quarters, including a well-known retired boxer who would call and ask for Ruth and give her a contribution. Refugees and asylum seekers were helped by the church, and Ruth made occasional appearances in court as an advocate. Life was never dull! I happened to be visiting in July 2012 when the service concluding the Gay Pride March was held in Bloomsbury, hosted by Affirm, the Baptist LGBT group. The area of the church was full. Ruth preached (the text was "be kind to each other") and presided at communion. She explained that the order of service would be Baptist, with folk being served in the pews, and the congregation, some with T Shirts proclaiming Catholic and Gay and others who were Anglican, succeeded in sharing a very moving service. She is a Patron of Accepting Evangelicals and put her beliefs into practice.

When the church discussed equal marriage there was potential conflict with the Baptist Union and the London Baptist Association. The official line seemed to be "each church has freedom to interpret the will of God, but we would rather you did not endorse equal marriage." The church seeking to be inclusive did agree to be open to offering to conduct such ceremonies, but it was an uncomfortable time for her. A few years later the church I belong to, Crown Terrace in Aberdeen, invited her to talk about equal marriage and her account was sympathetically received. I asked her what had led her to her acceptance of Gay Rights and Gay people and she reminded me of several folk we had known well in Edinburgh, my cousin Alan, Lecturer at the Edinburgh College of Art, dancer with the Royal Danish Ballet, restaurateur, and a

---

[13] Andronovienė, Parushev and Jones "Thank you, Ruth, and well done!"

[14] Anon., "Proposal to Move IBTS to Amsterdam."

neighbour of our manse, and of Edward, AIDS activist and cousin on her mother's side, both very different, but taken for granted among our friends.

Another contentious matter arose some years previously when an annual Christmas visit of a Palestinian Christian choir was attacked in various periodicals, and, as she described it in her interview with Andy Goodliff, "I dealt very badly with a bullying Zionist group and let them win, when we came under pressure not to allow the event."[15] The choir visit was cancelled, and I remember that the whole affair made her quite unwell. Ruth has always been able to admit when she has been wrong and been very sure when she knows she is right.

Publications in books and journals are important for any scholar and Ruth, while teaching or pastoring, has produced a steady flow, from the Whitley Lecture in 1997 to *Baptists Together* in 2019. In the 2003 volume, *Biographical Dictionary of Evangelicals* she contributed two biographies, of Menno Simons and Balthasar Hubmaier reflecting her enthusiasm for the Anabaptists.[16] The book based on her PhD thesis was published as *The Flesh and the Feminine* in 2006, and in 2008, after a long gestation period, a co-authored book, *On Being the Church: Revisioning Baptist Identity*, which she wrote with Brian Haymes and Anthony R. Cross. In 2011, she and Anthony Cross co-edited *Questions of Identity*, in honour of Brian Haymes, and she contributed an essay on "Story-telling, Sacraments and Sexuality," which brought together several of her interests. In 2013, she published in *Interfaces: Baptists and Others*, a paper on "Episcope without Episcopacy," which she had given at the International Conference on Baptist Studies in Melbourne in 2009. This possibly reflected the influence of teaching and listening at Trinity, Bristol, and certainly her interest in seventeenth-century Baptist history. Book reviews in the *Baptist Quarterly*, *Anvil* and other publications added to her interests and library. In the *Baptist Ministers' Journal* for July 2015, she chose her Desert Island books, the writings of Walter Wink on *The Powers*, E.F. Benson's *The Complete Lucia Victrix*, and *The Collected Works of John Donne*,[17] an indication of a catholic taste in literature!

She has been at least twice on Radio 4. During a programme on Thomas Newcomen, the inventor, she explained his work as a Baptist minister, and in an August 2012 edition of "Beyond Belief" she, Dianne Tidball and Peter Morden discussed various contemporary issues in Baptist church life.

Possibly the most controversial paper she has produced was the Beasley-Murray Lecture for 2010 delivered at the BUGB Assembly in Plymouth and provocatively titled "In Praise of Incompetence." "What," she asks, "is a

---

[15] Gouldbourne, "Reflecting on Ministry (3)."

[16] Gouldbourne, "Balthasar Hubmaier (1480–1528)," and "Menno Simons (1496–1561)."

[17] Gouldbourne, "Desert island books."

minister?"[18] What does ordination mean? Is ministry functional or sacramental? Is ministry doing or being? Is the minister a competent functionary or "a walking sacrament?"[19] The suggestion that incompetence might be a virtue, that ministry occurs at the very edge of (or even beyond) competence was spelled out. "In those moments when the preacher comes face to face with the mysteriousness of Scripture, when having used all the tools of analysis, criticism rhetoric and all the other skills we develop, there is finally the confrontation with the Living Word, that invites us to speak what cannot be spoken, and trust that the Living Word will communicate, there is a moment of ministry." She goes on to describe the moments of grace in interaction with the mystery of another person.[20] Not everyone agreed with her thesis in this lecture and it gave rise to interesting discussions and will go on doing that.

At the Baptist History Conference in 2019, Ruth who has long served on the Baptist Historical Society Committee, spoke about Barbara Stanford, whose archive she has inherited, and her influence on her and many others. We may expect more on that subject. Marie Isaacs also had been an unofficial mentor, and Ruth has for many years had a spiritual director, whom she has visited regularly. Ian has been a constant support and, when he retired, he took over shopping, cooking and general care. This suddenly changed in early 2018 when he suffered minor strokes which left him subject to some anxiety and occasional epileptic "turns," requiring trips to Accident and Emergency Departments in several hospitals. He is now much recovered, but Ruth found herself caring for him, and the move to Cheadle Hulme in the summer of 2018 has been beneficial, for now, for the first time since primary school days, Ruth has a garden, and there are members of Grove Lane church living quite close to the manse which is next to the church. She is also able to do some teaching at the Northern Baptist College. They loved London, but there the manse was not near any of the widely scattered church folk. And now they have a dog!

With so many commitments it might seem that there is no time for hobbies. In Bedford, she developed a keen interest in rugby football. Apart from a wide range of reading, of theology, history, poetry, Shakespeare, Wodehouse, detective novels and a sprinkling of Alexander McColl Smith, Ruth manages to find time to write a blog, produce an annual Christmas play, some stories from which are now in the new anthology of women's worship, *Gathering up the Crumbs*,[21] do cross-stitch, knit, build tiny doll's houses, and

---

[18] Gouldbourne, "In Praise of Incompetence," 170.

[19] Gouldbourne, "In Praise of Incompetence," 170.

[20] Gouldbourne, "In Praise of Incompetence," 182.

[21] Gouldbourne, "Depressed Donkey," "Haughty Camel," "House-proud Cow," and "Sheep's Story."

keep in touch with many friends made over the years and kept, for she has a gift for friendship, and a keen sense of humour, which occasionally shines out in lectures, and she has never, in over thirty years in England, lost her distinctive Scottish accent. "Skating with Auntie Ruth" has been an occasional pleasure for Alice and Amy, her teenage nieces in Edinburgh.

In June 2000, Ruth, with the help of Donald Wilks, a Methodist minister, married Lorna and me in the new Chapel of St Columba's Hospice. For many reasons this was a very moving occasion, and later, when I asked her how she was able to do this, she replied "professionalism." That occasion, and reading at her mother's funeral stand, out for me as times of family love and unity.

There is another. In 2008, I celebrated my jubilee in the ministry, and on a Sunday in October all my immediate family joined me in worship in Crown Terrace church, then in vacancy. The Rev. Muriel Knox, a member of the church and a hospital chaplain conducted the service and then, totally to my surprise, Ruth preached. The text was "She has done what she could" and I think that verse sums up Ruth's life so far!

Bibliography

Andronovienė, Lina, Parush Parushev and Keith G. Jones. "Thank you, Ruth, and well done!" IBTSCentre Amsterdam. https://blog.ibts.eu/2013/10/30/thank-you-ruth-and...

Anon. "Proposal to Move IBTS to Amsterdam: The Core News." 30 August 2012. IBTSCentre Amsterdam. https://blog.ibts.eu/2012/08/30/proposal-to-move-i...

Anon. "Gouldbourne, Rev. Dr Ruth Mary Boyd." *Who's Who* Online. https://doi.org/10.10 93/ww/9780199540884.013.U151366

Bebbington, David W. and Martin Sutherland, ed. *Interfaces: Baptists and Others*. Studies in Baptist History and Thought. Milton Keynes: Paternoster, 2013.

Bowers, Faith. *A Bold Experiment: The Story of Bloomsbury Chapel and Bloomsbury Central Baptist Church 1848–1999*. London: Bloomsbury Central Baptist Church, 1999.

Costie, Joyce. *Complete in Christ: People with Physical Disabilities in the Life of the Church*. Edited by Faith Bowers. Didcot: Baptist Union of Great Britain, 1996.

Cross, Anthony R., and Ruth Gouldbourne, eds. *Questions of Identity: Studies in Honour of Brian Haymes*. Centre for Baptist History and Heritage Studies, 6. Oxford: Regent's Park College, 2011.

Gorton, Catriona, Claire Nicholls, *et al.*, ed. *Gathering up the Crumbs: Celebrating a Century of Accredited, Ordained, Baptist Women in Ministry in the UK*. London: Baptist Union of Great Britain, 2020.

Gouldbourne, Ruth M.B. "Balthasar Hubmaier (1480–1528)," and "Menno Simons (1496–1561)." In *Biographical Dictionary of Evangelicals*, 314–15 and 424–26. Edited by Timothy Larsen. Leicester: Inter-Varsity Press, 2003.

———. "The Depressed Donkey," "The Haughty Camel," "The House-proud Cow," and "The Sheep's Story." In *Gathering up the Crumbs*, 91–94, 94–96, 97–100, and 100–103. Edited by Gorton, Nicholls, *et al.*

———. "Desert island books." *Baptist Minister's Journal* 327 (July 2015) 5–7.

———. "Ecclesiology and Gender: Radical Reformation, Baptist Beginnings, and Baptists Today." The Hughey Lectures 1998, delivered at IBTS, November 1998. https://www. ibts.eu/research/hughey-lectures

———. "Episcope without Episcopacy: Baptist Attitudes to the Bishops in Seventeenth-Century England." In *Interfaces*. Edited by Bebbington and Sutherland, 29–46.

———. *The Flesh and the Feminine: Gender and Theology in the Writings of Caspar Schwenckfeld*. Studies in Christian History and Thought. Milton Keynes: Paternoster, 2006.

———. "Identity and Pain: Women's Consultations 1987–92." *Baptist Ministers' Journal* 243 (July 1993) 8–10.

———. "In Praise of Incompetence: Ministerial Formation and the Development of a Rooted Person." In *Truth That Never Dies*. Edited by N.G. Wright, 168–84.

———. "Reflecting on Ministry (3)." 3 July 2014. andygoodliff: church, world and the Christian life. https://andygoodliff.typepad.com/my_weblog/ministry//Gouldbourne

———. *Reinventing the Wheel: Women and Ministry in English Baptist Life*. The Whitley Lecture 1997–1998. Oxford: Whitley Publications, 1997.

———. "A short history of Baptist women in ministry." *Baptists Together* (Spring 2019), 6–8.

———. "Story-telling, Sacraments, and Sexuality." In *Questions of Identity*, 239–52. Edited by Cross and Gouldbourne.

———. "Theology and Gender in the Writings of Caspar Schwenckfeld." PhD diss., University of London, 2000.

———. "What makes the Anabaptists so Annoying?" In *Coming Home*, 61–62. Edited by Kreider and Murray.

Haymes, Brian, Ruth Gouldbourne and Anthony R. Cross. *On Being the Church: Revisioning Baptist Identity*. Studies in Baptist History and Thought, 21. Milton Keynes: Paternoster, 2008.

Kreider, Alan, and Stuart Murray, ed. *Coming Home: Stories of Anabaptists in Britain and Ireland*. Kitchener: Pandora, 2000.

Perry, Simon. "Prayers of Intercession." Simon Perry Blog. simonperry.org.uk/intercessions/4537489529

Wright, Nigel G. ed. *Truth That Never Dies: The Dr. G.R. Beasley-Murray Memorial Lectures 2002–2012*. Eugene: Pickwick Publications, 2014.

A Personal Note

Peter C. Erb

Dear Ruth:

It has now been well over twenty years since I first met you in discussions on your proposed doctoral thesis on Caspar Schwenkfeld von Ossig. I recall then attempting to convince you to take on writing the "life" of the reformer and your wise response that nineteen folio volumes of his works, even though they now appeared in a modern edition, would be too great a task for a such a degree. You were correct, of course, but that did not keep you from working through all the whole *Corpus*[1] and completing a comprehensive and fine dissertation.

Your study focuses on the place of women in this reformer's life. But it does much more than this. It provides the reader with a full sense of Schwenckfeld's religious position as well. You close your book with a clear summation of his Christian view, a view which you have detailed in the earlier chapters, and then close with a general, but highly applicable statement: "Caspar Schwenckfeld did not set out to write a theology at all. Rather, impelled by a desire both to live himself and to enable others to live lives which were shaped by the calling of God in Christ, he started from a position of pragmatism and ended with a fully shaped, though not always coherent world view."[2]

This statement marks Schwenckfeld's approach to Christian life generally and notes, in particular, his approach to the scriptures. On first reading your dissertation I was pressed, the reason for which I can no longer ascertain for certain, to review in detail his annotations on the newly published Worms Bible of 1529.[3] This Bible stayed in Schwenckfelder hands until after 1632,[4] and eventually found its way into the collection of an English Quaker, Francis

---

[1] Corpus Schwenckfeldianorum. 19 vols. Leipzig: Breitkopf and Hartel, 1907–61). Hereafter CS, volume and page number.

[2] Ruth Gouldbourne, *The Flesh and the Feminine: Gender and Theology in the writings of Caspar Schwenckfeld*. Studies in Christian History and Thought. Milton Keynes: Paternoster, 2006, 228.

[3] Biblia beyder Altt und Neuen Testaments Teutsch . . . M.D. XXIX. Gedruct inn der Keserlichen frey statt Wormbs bey Peter Schoefern imm jar nach den geburt unsers Herren. M.D. XXIX. For Schwenckfeld's annotations see CS 18:606ff.

[4] On the ownership. see CS 18:602. Katharina Streicher in Ulm, Johann Heyd von Daun, Daniel Friedrich, and Daniel Sudermann, who died in 1632.

Fry (1803–86),[5] who travelled to Germany several times after 1852 and who collected Bibles extensively, particularly English versions. I must admit that I took little interest in the English ownership of Schwenckfeld's copy until I met you.

Schwenckfeld annotated his version of the Worms Bible carefully, and paid special attention to the Psalms. He must have purchased it shortly after its publication, and made extensive notes to it between 1530 and 1535.[6] At the very beginning of Genesis, the first words that Schwenckfeld writes in the margin are, "The Scriptures always speak of spiritual things, those things, indeed, through corporal images to shadows [ad umbra: in Schwenckfeld's terms, 'to faith appearances'],"[7] and he follows this with a reference to Psalm 25:10, "the path of the Lord, goodness and truth,"[8] a reference seemingly to his earlier comment. He then writes, "The Hebrews call justice the highest rectitude and highest goodness of morals"[9] before entering, after a brief note, a quotation from Hilary of Poitiers' *Commentary on the Psalms*, Psalm 118 (Vulgate), 73–80 (yodh), the creation cycle. In particular, he was drawn to the following section of the commentary. His marginal note is to Hilary's text as follows:

> fit enim ad imaginem Dei. Non Dei imago; quia imago Dei est primogenitus omnis creaturae: sed ad imaginem Dei, id est, secundum imaginis et similitudinis speciem. Divinum in eo et incorporale condendum, quod secundum imaginem Dei et similitudinem tum fiebat: exemplum scilicet quoddam in nobis imaginis Dei est, et similitudinis institutum.

Human beings are made, according to Hilary, "*toward* the image of God (ad imaginem Dei), not [as] the image of God, since the image of God is the first-former of every creature; rather [human beings are made] *toward* the image of God, that is according to the image and similitude. The divine is built in it and is incorporeal. One becomes then according to the image and similitude of God, namely, the example which is the image of God in us and instituted in us." In a short passage which follows this, Schwenckfeld notes (in

---

[5] For details on Francis Fry, see the Oxford Dictionary of National Biography Online.

[6] See CS 19:603.

[7] Scriptura semper loquitur de spiritualibus rebus ea tamen per Imagines corporales ad vmbras. CS 18:607.

[8] Vie domini Bonitas et veritas, CS 18:607.

[9] Hebrej Iusticiam summam morum rectidudinem et absolutam bonitatem vocant, CS 18:607.

A Personal Note

a passage which is not fully readable) that this relates to "the first origin of man."[10]

How greatly Hilary influenced Schwenckfeld's thought is still not clearly understood. Certainly, Schwenckfeld read Hilary as supporting his own peculiar position on the nature of Christ's body,[11] but it is not surprising that he should quote Hilary first in his reading of the scriptures. The passage he chose sums up the direction of his theology as it would be developed over the years following his exile from Silesia and his "wandering" thereafter.

Early in your book, Ruth, you point out that "by examining the theology of Caspar Schwenckfeld in terms of belief about gender" we will be opened to an examination of his work "in a new and fruitful way."[12] It was while considering your comment here and other aspects of your book, I thought of some words I had written on Schwenckfeld some years ago. I commented then that "the demand of Schwenckfeld's theology for a unified Christian philosophy and practice, for a transcendent hope and a present imminent conclusion, becomes ever more necessary. The possibility of a new earth, brought about in the life of the humiliated and suffering Saviour, is based on the coextensive knowledge of new heavens made real to us in the touch of our glorified Lord, who draws us increasingly nearer to our goal, the deification of our image after the image of God, *ad imaginem dei*."[13] I did not, of course, mean that Schwenckfeld's theology was the basis for such a "Christian philosophy and practice," but rather that it, along with many other Christian interests, looked *toward* such a basis.

Although we have not remained in close contact over the last years, I have been touched in a number of cases in which I have heard of or read your work in the church. This has been true, not only of your writing (which is easily at hand to me), but also of your work within the church, your role as a pastor. In several cases, for example, I have heard of your commitment from Christians who met you because of their Anabaptist associations. In one case, an individual from Kitchener-Waterloo, my own residence here in Canada, reflected to me on an insight he had gained from a short comment you had made at a gathering in London. Interestingly he had forgotten your name at the moment, but still recalled the importance for him of the conversation!

---

[10] As edited from Schwenckfeld's Bible in CS 18:607–608, the passage reads, Fit homo ad Imaginem non Dej Imago. Imago Dej eft primogenitus omnium creaturarum Sed ad Imaginem i. e. secundum Imaginem—incorporale continet? Hilar: PL 116 (118?) Item Quod secundum—non dej et ipsum quoddam dej eft et—Institutum. habet prima hac origo hominis— —quod— — — — autem tractarem? faciamus — — — (P-1)

[11] See above all the extensive use of Hilary in Schwenckfeld's great Confession, CS 7:451ff, published in 1540. Note above all, CS 7:604–20 and 852–62.

[12] Gouldbourne, *Flesh and the Feminine*, 52.

[13] Peter C. Erb, *Schwenckfeld in his Reformation Setting*. Valley Forge: Judson, 1978, 88.

Although it may appear to you at times, as you work within the immediate patterns of your church community, that your life as a pastor is limited, it remains important to remember that limitations are of the "body" and, yet, that the "body" is important, even for a person like Schwenckfeld who is often charged with a rabid spiritualism. That is why your work is so important. As you point out, "Schwenckfeld gave a particular value to bodies and their meaning. In this, he was doing nothing unusual. The Christian faith which he was exploring, and attempting to explain centres on the belief that in Jesus God became human, and existed in a physical body. Central to the expression of that faith has been the theology and practice of the sacraments, based upon physical actions recognized as having spiritual meaning."[14]

Your comment here on spiritual meaning takes one back again to Schwenckfeld's comment at the beginning of his biblical commentary, "The Scriptures always speak of spiritual things, those things, indeed, through corporal images to shadows." The comment "to shadows," as I earlier pointed out comes from the Latin words "ad umbra," here, in Schwenckfeld's terms, meaning "to faith appearances."[15] But what are these "faith appearances"? For Schwenckfeld they are, above all, noted in Psalm 25:10, "the path of the Lord, [that is,] goodness and truth,"[16] a "goodness and truth" summed up in the highest of human virtues, which "The Hebrews," Schwenckfeld tells us, "call justice, the highest rectitude and highest goodness of morals."[17] Here, right at the beginning of his reflections on the Worms' Bible, Schwenckfeld enunciates his view of "justice," a view which he looked to as offering a middle way between Catholics and Protestants.

With this I leave off for the moment, Ruth, wishing you all the best, assuring you that your work to this point has been shaped in its smallest matters and in its larger, *ad imaginem dei*, toward Christ, our Lord, Jesus of Nazareth. It has been a delight knowing you and your father in Great Britain and then again, with your husband when Betty and I were able to greet you in our home here in Waterloo. With all my best,

Peter

---

[14] Gouldbourne, *Flesh and the Feminine*, 46.
[15] See above, and CS 18:607.
[16] CS 18:607.
[17] CS 18:607.

Introduction

That a *Festschrift* be prepared for one celebrating her sixtieth birthday may seem a little unusual. Such collections of essays, written in honour, usually come at retirement of a scholar's life so that, with their work largely done, appraisals can begin. If that ever were a guideline for practice there is nothing fixed or final about it. When the editors of this volume began exploring the possibility of such a project, we found an immediate and enthusiastic response. Other scholars, clearly in gratitude for Ruth Gouldbourne's work, were eager to explore her contribution, continuing and unfinished though it may be. Everyone the editors approached, without exception, agreed to the proposal and stated their eagerness to contribute.

One feature of this *Festschrift* may be unique. There have been occasions when children have offered studies in honour of an illustrious parent, but in this case, happily, we have a father as contributor to a volume honouring his daughter. Others will share our delight at our opportunity to begin the volume with Dr Derek Murray's informative and personal essay.

Frankly, as the idea of this book was shared, the editors realised that we could have too much on our hands, an over-abundance of those eager to be associated and contributing. All who know Ruth will need no explanation for that fact. Indeed, this introduction reflects the many private comments made to us about the subject. Hence, we focus here on some characteristics, some reasons why over and above her scholarship, we and others express our admiration of Ruth and our gratitude for her.

Ruth believes in and readily practices collegiality. We have had direct experience of working with Ruth, in writing a book, teaching courses, sharing study and research groups. What makes her such a great colleague is her willingness to put her knowledge at the disposal of others, to mutually edify, not to score personal points. Any notes of stridency are completely missing when she speaks. The search for truth is far too important than any personal pride of place in an argument. Ruth has the gift of listening, really listening, not least in those debates where important issues are at stake. If she thinks she has to correct a colleague then that is done with gentleness. Of course, she does have clear, strongly held opinions. She is ready to bear witness, though she does not welcome the "fights" in church and society into which she has sometimes been pressed. She is courageous, prepared to challenge public and denominational policies when necessary, arguing and living her case while seeking not to give offence to any.

We hold her to be one of the most genuinely Baptist people we have met. She is loyally critical of the denomination. Where she believes some wrong turns are being taken she will say so and act appropriately, sometimes prophetically. But she will do this in that attitude of mind that claims that the Lord has yet more light and truth to reveal so, in modesty, we had better keep listening and learning lest in our over confidence we overstep the mark of humble discipleship. She acknowledges that she can be wrong, that what she needs is forgiveness. So space is made for others; her ears and mind becomes focused and attentive. She knows that there are forms of the faith too confident to be true. She knows this, not least, because she bears the scars.

There is a proper modesty in all real theologians. They will not turn their all too human interpretations into gods of their own making which, on threat of hell, they require others to worship. This is the way of idolatry which Ruth has learned to recognize and repel. The result is an openness of heart and mind, a humility and readiness for confession and development that is a ministerial competence not all desire, let alone achieve. She lives and believes in the holy catholic church, the communion of saints, the forgiveness of sins, the resurrection of the body, and the life everlasting. She lives trusting in the love of God, the grace of our Lord Jesus Christ, and the fellowship of the Holy Spirit.

The editors and contributors of this volume offer Ruth Gouldbourne this book, *ad majorem Dei gloria*, in gratitude for a friend, a teacher, an example of discipleship, one of God's ministers, a gift to us all.

Brian Haymes and Anthony R. Cross
February 2021

CHAPTER 1

The Letter, the Spirit, and the Letter Again: Reflections on 2 Corinthians 3 and the Work of Biblical Interpretation

Sean F. Winter

τὸ γὰρ γράμμα ἀποκτέννει, τὸ δὲ πνεῦμα ζῳοποιεῖ
For the letter kills, but the Spirit makes alive (2 Cor 3:6).

Cursus verbi dei vivi, liber est, non haeret in visibilibus . . . sed totus in invisibilibus quiescit, quanquam per visibilia nobis adumbratur
The living word of God is not etched in the visible, but rests entirely in the invisible, though visible to us as a shadow.[1]

The following reflections will not be about Caspar Schwenckfeld and yet, for an essay in honour of Ruth Gouldbourne, the temptation to begin in the sixteenth century has been too inviting to ignore. In that turbulent period of theological creativity and certainty, Schwenckfeld was by no means the only person debating at length about the relationship between the word (or Word) and the Spirit (or spirit). His specific and heated debate with Flacius Illyricus about that relationship serves us well, however, as a point of entry for the following study, which will focus on the early Christian text that first placed the terms "letter" and "Spirit" into some kind of tensive relationship.[2]

For Schwenckfeld that tension was such that the letter (construed mainly as the written text of scripture) was very obviously relegated to a secondary position under the pressure of strong appeal to the necessity of the Spirit.[3] As

---

[1] Schwenckfeld, "Letter to Conrad Condatus," 596. Translation mine.

[2] The contrast between "letter" and "Spirit" seems to have been a Pauline invention, developed initially as a part of an series of arguments about the legitimacy and purpose of Paul's ministry in 2 Cor 2–4, where the formula of 2 Cor 3:6 launches a rich trajectory of reception history. Paul reused the antithesis in Rom 2:29 and 7:6 to related but distinctive purposes. See Wolter, "'Spirit.'"

[3] For Schwenckfeld this seems to have been the direct result of his involvement in eucharistic controversies in Luther's circle in the 1520s.

a result, in Schwenckfeld's thought concepts that might be otherwise held in creative tension arguably collapse into unhelpful antithesis. E.J. Furcha's brief summary of Schwenckfeld's position serves to clarify the issue at stake:

> If we were to sketch Schwenckfeld's position in a sentence or two, we might say that the nobleman sensed a tendency in the theology of the Word which Illyricus held toward binding the living creature and recreative Word of God to externals. Over against this threat he asserted that Scripture and the preached word are authoritative only insofar as they are authenticated by the witness of the Holy Spirit.[4]

Ruth herself concurs with this basic classification of Schwenckfeld as "a Spiritualist, one who valued spirit over letter."[5] And it was to this prioritization of the Spirit in relation to scriptural interpretation that Flacius Illyricus took offense: "spiritual exegesis fits scripture like a fist fits into an eye," he apparently stated.[6] Or, in words that more explicitly pick up the biblical contrast that underlies the reformation debates, "the word is God's whether it is on stone, tablets, paper, parchment, or the human memory, registered, composed, written, or spoken by the human voice."[7] Despite this critique, and as is so often the case, different readings of Schwenckfeld's views of the relationship between the inner and outer word, the letter and the Spirit are possible, reflecting the ambiguity of his own writings.[8] What looks on the surface like a clear theological signpost, turns out on closer inspection to point indirectly to a more nuanced and complex landscape.

The tension that caused Lutherans to fall out with Spiritualists in the sixteenth century goes all the way back to the first centuries of the Common Era; to the earliest patristic reception of Paul's language in 2 Corinthians 3:6.[9] Indeed, as the following reflections make clear, it is a tension that is built into the very structure of Paul's argument in that first-century letter. So, as might be expected from the present author, this is actually an essay about Paul, and about us: about the Pauline formulation of the Spirit/letter tension in 2 Corinthians, and about the way that it might continue to shape our own understanding and practice of biblical interpretation.

---

[4] Furcha, "Key Concepts," 160–73, here p.161.

[5] Gouldbourne, *Flesh*, 3.

[6] Ilić, *Theologian*, 116. The discussion on 115–18 helpfully summarizes the debate.

[7] Ilić, *Theologian*, 117.

[8] See the discussion in McLaughlin, "Spiritualism," 282–98. For the broader picture see Murray, *Biblical Interpretation*, 125–57.

[9] On the *Nachleben* of 2 Cor 3:6 in patristic and contemporary sources, see the essays in Fiddes and Bader, ed., *Spirit and the Letter*.

The Spirit and the Letter in 2 Corinthians 3

2 Corinthians 3 opens with a contrast between two kinds of "letter." Paul compares himself (and perhaps co-workers in his apostolic mission) to those who need "letters of recommendation" (συστατικῶν ἐπιστολαί) to legitimate their message and their claim to the Corinthians' loyalty (3:1). Instead, Paul insists emphatically that the Corinthians themselves are the only letter required: "*you* are our letter" (ἡ ἐπιστολὴ ἡμῶν ὑμεῖς 3:2). As a "living epistle" the Corinthian community makes Christ visible to the world. The composition of this letter is the result of Paul's inscriptional activity with raw materials: the Spirit, and humanity or what Paul calls the "tablets of the fleshly heart" (ἐν πλαξὶν καρδίαις σαρκίναις 3:3).[10]

This initial comparison is not a strict antithesis. Paul still composes a letter, albeit a "spiritual" one. That letter still functions to establish and legitimate Paul's apostolic credentials and, as such, provides a basis for Paul's self-commendation.[11] But the emphatic contrast in 3:3 (*not* on stone tables, *but* on tablets of the fleshly heart) seems to provoke Paul to further reflection about the basis for apostolic confidence (πεποίθησις 3:4) and competence (ἱκανός 3:5). While it is difficult to trace the exact reasons why Paul's argument unfolds in 2 Corinthians 3 in the way that it does, it is clear that 3:4–6 effects a transition from questions about the legitimacy of Paul's ministry towards an account of the covenantal framework within which that ministry takes place. Paul's description of that framework in 3:6 intensifies the contrast of 3:3:

3:3	A letter (ἐπιστολή)	not with ink Not on stone tablets	but with the Spirit but on tablets of the fleshly heart
3:6	A covenant	not of the letter (γράμμα) The letter kills	but of the Spirit the Spirit gives life

In these two verses the Greek terms for "letter" differ. In 3:6 Paul is not referring the community as the "letter of Christ," but of the "letter" inscribed into the stone tablets of the Mosaic covenant (3:7). They are connected in that

---

[10] I am skipping over any number of textual and syntactical debates in this summary. Two things are important, however. First, it is the Corinthian community as a whole that is the "letter of Christ" that in turn is to be "read by all." Secondly, the image here is not of Paul writing a private letter on papyrus, but of him engraving (ἐγγεγραμμένη, used twice in 3:2–3) a letter in the form of a public stone monument, conveying official news. Thirdly, Paul's use of the term "flesh" in relation to this imagery reminds us that, for Paul, while the spiritual and material are not the same thing, they are closely interconnected. In 2 Cor the flesh and the suffering body is the site of the Spirit's transforming work (see, e.g., 2 Cor 4:7–12; 5:1–5; 6:4–10).

[11] See Hafemann, "'Self-Commendation,'" 66–88.

both refer to inscriptional activity by God: the tablets of stone given to Moses which were "written with the finger of God" and the new covenant ministry of the Spirit given to Paul. Yet, the work of the Spirit stands, on the face of it, in antithetical relationship to the Sinai covenant. The nature of the transition from one antithesis (relating to Paul and his "opponents") to another (that of the old and new dispensations of salvation history) is relatively clear. At which point, almost everything else about the meaning and coherence of Paul's argument starts to go foggy.[12]

So instead of trying to adjudicate the many alternative construals of the argument and rationale for 2 Corinthians 3:7–18 where Paul unpacks the relationship between the old and new covenant, I would like to make a very basic observation about the relationship between 3:1–6 and 3:7–18. On the one hand, Paul's statement in 3:6, that the letter kills but the Spirit gives life, is, as we have seen, the conclusion to reflections on the relationship in 3:1–6 between different kinds of "letter" and the work of the Spirit in his ministry and in the Corinthian community. On the other hand, 2 Corinthians 3 continues with Paul's extensive reflections on Moses, Sinai, glory, and the veil in 3:7–18. There is obviously a connection between the two passages, because the association between the letter and death, and the Spirit and life from 3:6 is immediately picked up in 3:7–8 and expanded in 3:9–11. Thus:

3:6	A covenant	not of the letter	but of the Spirit
		The letter kills	the Spirit gives life
3:7–11	A ministry	letters of death	of the Spirit in glory
		of condemnation	of justification
		Set aside	permanent

The point I wish to emphasize is that Paul makes this argument (about the giving way of the "script" of the Mosaic covenant to the greater glory of the ministry of the Spirit) *by means of an exegetical treatment of a portion of the Mosaic law*.[13] The Spirit that leads to the setting aside of the "letter" takes

---

[12] The complexities of 2 Cor 3:7–18 and their relationship to 3:1–6 will not be rehearsed here because, initially, those questions are accompanied by a complex history of scholarship but also because, honestly, after many years of wrestling with the issues, I do not really think I yet fully understand what is going on in the text. Plenty of people think that they know precisely what Paul is doing here, however. See, e.g., Hafemann, *Suffering and the Spirit* and *Paul, Moses and the History of Israel*; and Duff, *Moses in Corinth*. I have taken a stab at proposing a possible reason for the confusion: namely that Paul here is incorporating a pre-existing sermon into his apologetic and polemical strategy in 2 Cor, see Winter, "'Daring Synagogue Sermon?'" The subsequent years have done little to build my confidence in that proposal.

[13] The translation of γράμμα as "script" is helpfully made by Richard Hays in his study of this passage, Hays, *Echoes*, 130. While Hays is right to note that the term does

Paul, whose new covenant ministry is *of* the Spirit, back to the interpretation of the letter again. Or, noting that Paul's overall argument ends with a decisive claim about the nature of the Spirit's work in the community (see 3:17–18), we can say that Paul here affirms the primacy of the Spirit by means of his engagement with the letter. In 3:14–15 Paul seems to be critical of one way of "reading Moses," characterized by hardened hearts and veiled minds. But the solution to this problem is not to stop reading Moses. Instead, one turns to the Lord and the Spirit removes the veil in order to enable renewed reading. In short, those who, from the time of Origen onwards, have insisted that this passage is as much about hermeneutics as it is anything else are surely correct. We are invited to think about what it might mean to move from the letter to the Spirit and back to the letter again?

More starkly, we can state the issue in this way. The phrase "letters on tablets of stone" is itself an allusion to a specific text: Exodus 31:18.[14] Yet, Paul undertakes the task of demonstrating that these "letters" now associated with death have given way to the ministry of the Spirit and life *by offering an interpretation of another passage from Exodus*. It is worth pausing to take a look at what precisely Paul does with that section of text, before moving to consider what all this tells us about Pauline and our own hermeneutical convictions.

Without any claim to comprehensiveness, I note four interpretative strategies at work in Paul's "midrash" on Exodus 34.[15] First, while the key text that is being explored is Exodus 34:29–35, which narrates Moses' descent from Sinai and his communication of the commandments to the Israelites with "the skin of his face shining" (34:30), Paul reads that episode in its wider

---

not refer straightforwardly to "Scripture" (for which Paul uses the term γραφή) there is still substantial irony in the shift from the negative assessment of the Mosaic "ministry of death, inscribed on stone tablets, to the constructive exegetical attention made to the scriptural witness to the Sinai event and Moses' status as mediator. In the end, the old covenant that is "read" with a veil is the same old covenant that Paul here reads in the direction of freedom. Hays' discussion is essential reading on the complexities of this passage and has provoked a number of the reflections in this essay.

[14] Exod 31:18 LXX refers to πλάκας λιθίνας γεγραμμένας τῷ δακτύλῳ τοῦ θεοῦ "stone tablets written by the finger of God." In 2 Cor 3:3 Paul effectively detaches the object of writing (stone tablets) from the instrument (finger/Spirit of God cf. Luke 11:20 for the equivalence).

[15] The use of the term midrash has gone out of fashion when thinking about Paul's interpretation of scripture, but cf. the older descriptions of Windisch, *Zweite Korintherbrief*, 112, and Hanson, "Midrash." I use the term less in the technical sense of formal exegetical procedure, and more in the functional sense of biblical interpretation aimed at "actualization that brings the text from the past into the present for religious purposes," so Gignilliat, *Paul and Isaiah's Servants*, 9. For another account of Paul's interpretative work in 3:7–11, see Harris, *2 Corinthians*, 276–80.

narrative context. In particular, Paul's focus on the key term "glory," δόξα, draws on the earlier ascent and theophany tradition in Exodus 24:15–18 and the dialogue between Moses and YHWH that immediately precedes the account in Exodus 34. The request and promise of Exodus 33:18–19 revolve around the revelation of divine glory and it is this theme that Paul picks up and places at the centre of his retelling of the story of Moses' transformed face and, consequently, the inauguration of the Mosaic covenant.[16] Secondly, Paul posits a causal link between narrative details that otherwise, in the Exodus story, are unrelated to each other. Exodus 34:35 states that "the Israelites would see the face of Moses, that the skin of his face was shining; and Moses would put the veil on his face again." Paul argues in 2 Corinthians 3:13 that Moses' veil was to "prevent the people of Israel from gazing" (cf. the emphatic ὥστε of 3:7), a claim that goes further than the text on which it is based. Thirdly, in bringing the motifs of glory and the veil to the foreground of his treatment, Paul passes over a number of details in the text itself: the presence of Aaron; Moses' ability to communicate the commandments, and ignorance in relation to his shining face; the important motif of fear. Finally, Paul seems to add details to the original scene: the notion that the people were "unable" (μὴ δύνασθαι 3:7) to look on Moses' face, for example; a notion related to the motif of hardened hearts in 3:14.

Together, these features combine with more formal exegetical techniques, such as the *qal wahomer* (from the lesser to the greater) argumentation of 3:7–11 and the explicit contemporization of the scriptural text in 3:12, 18, to make it clear that Paul's declaration of the arrival of the "ministry of the Spirit" in which the "veil" is removed, giving way to "freedom," is secured *by means of textual interpretation*. As a result, in 2 Corinthians 3 the relationship between the letter and the Spirit is neither self-evident nor mutually exclusive.

The Shape of Pauline Hermeneutics

If we take these exegetical observations seriously, we can start to identify some of the contours of Spirit-shaped (re)engagement with the letter or text of scripture, as these are set out by Paul. Of course, there may be good reason to be suspicious of, or even to reject, Pauline hermeneutics as a "normative paradigm for intertextual theological reflection."[17] We may regard Paul as too concerned with readings of scripture that legitimate his authority claims, or that provoke the kind of pervasive and pernicious Christian anti-Judaism that we do well to abhor. Nevertheless, those who *do* ascribe some degree of

---

[16] The LXX of Exod 33:18–19 keeps the focus on the revelation of divine glory even more insistently than the MT having YHWH promise that his "glory" (MT: goodness) "will pass before you."

[17] Hays, *Echoes*, 154.

"normativity" to Paul, would do well to note what is going on in his handling of the scriptural text. A close look at what Paul is doing in 2 Corinthians 3 brings three aspects into view.

The first is the invitation to read and interpret in freedom. In his compelling discussion of this aspect of Paul's hermeneutics, Richard Hays notes that this interpretative freedom manifests itself in a number of ways. To begin, it insists on reading the text in the light of new circumstances in a way that "generates novel interpretations that nonetheless claim to be the true, eschatologically disclosed sense of the ancient texts."[18] It is a form of reading that discovers the kerygma not through the formulaic application of hermeneutical rules or techniques, and certainly not by means of the dogged, if still naïve, insistence on perspicuity or notions of literal or plain meaning. The key term for Hays is "allusive": the idea that scripture itself is woven through with evocations of traditions, motifs, and patterns that together render any text we read as already a "complex intertextual matrix." In language that reminded me of Illyricus' quip about spiritual exegesis and punching someone in the eye, Hays writes that "meaning is . . . not so much like a relic excavated from an ancient text as it is like a spark struck by the shovel hitting the rock."[19] 2 Corinthians 3 is an example of exactly that kind of interpretative attentiveness; one not constrained by original intention or sense. Hays writes in relation to our text that

> the true sense of Exodus 34 . . . is actualized in the community of Paul's readers only as a consequence of the hermeneutical transfiguration wrought intertextually in 2 Cor 3:7–18. True interpretation depends neither on historical enquiry nor on erudite literary analysis but on attentiveness to the promptings of the Spirit, who reveals the gospel *through Scripture*, in surprising ways.[20]

I confess that, as I read Paul, I want to press a little harder on the "through Scripture" element of Hays' formulation. The striking thing about 2 Corinthians is that at the very point where Paul might legitimately (within the terms of the argument of 3:1–6) simply have appealed to the authority of the Spirit in relation to the legitimacy of his ministry, he turns aside to ground his claims about the Spirit in implicit claims about textual meaning. Interpretation is done in freedom but, still, it is interpretation that is instrumental for discernment of the promptings of the Spirit.

---

[18] Hays, *Echoes*, 155.

[19] Hays, *Echoes*, 155, citing Jer 23:29, "Is not my word . . . like a hammer that shatters rock?" and the Babylonian Talmud, *Sanhedrin* 34a: "In R. Ishmael`s School it was taught: And like in hammer that breaketh the rock in pieces: i.e., just as [the rock] is split into many splinters, so also may one Biblical verse convey many teachings.")

[20] Hays, *Echoes*, 156 (emphasis added).

This leads to further insights into the role and purpose of Paul's hermeneutical "rock striking," derived from Jane Heath's fascinating account of the way that 2 Corinthians 3:7–18 relates to his overall "visual piety." With a clear focus on Paul's language of "seeing/beholding" in 2 Corinthians 3:18 and its relationship to transformation (τὴν δόξαν κυρίου κατοπτριζόμενοι τὴν αὐτὴν εἰκόνα μεταμορφούμεθα), Heath points out that scholarship tends to assume that understanding Paul's exegesis in the preceding verses is an end in itself, or serves merely to clarify the nature of Pauline polemic and the possible identity of his "opponents."[21] But this is to flatten the language of 3:18 to the point where the language of "beholding" is collapsed into the act of textual reading. It is not exegesis that transforms, but the perception and encounter to which Paul's exegesis points, what Heath calls "the role of the sensorium in perceiving Christ."[22] Noting the connection to a plethora of "invitations to visual engagement" in 2 Corinthians 2:14—5:12 she writes that Paul's rhetoric

> is chiefly oriented neither towards the exegesis of scripture nor towards the apostolic defence against the dazzling, quicksilver opponents, but rather towards enabling the Corinthians to better perceive Christ before God, so as to be transformed from life unto life until the day when they are manifest before the podium of Christ, rather than being transformed from death to death like some.[23]

So, Paul reads Exodus 34 in ways that direct the Corinthians to forms of sense perception that lie the other side of textual interpretation. While the removal of the "veil" does not abrogate the need to engage with the text of scripture, it locates that hermeneutical engagement in a wider discourse of spiritual transformation replete with mystical, ethical and social characteristics.[24]

Again, it is crucial to see that the transformative perception for which Paul appeals in 3:18 is not an alternative to the act of reading, but the consequence of it. The freedom of the Spirit is not a freedom from the work of interpretation, but the presupposition for that work in the "ministry" of justification and glory. In 3:14 Paul speaks of the continuing practice of "reading the old covenant" (ἐπὶ τῇ ἀναγνώσει τῆς παλαιᾶς διαθήκης) and in 3:15 more specifically to the "reading of Moses" (ἡνίκα ἂν ἀναγινώσκηται Μωϋσῆς). In "turning to the Lord" the veil that marked those reading

---

[21] See Heath, *Paul's Visual Piety*, 176–97.

[22] Heath, *Paul's Visual Piety*, 192.

[23] Heath, *Paul's Visual Piety*, 197.

[24] See the insistence that each of these aspects of the "metamorphosis of the beholder" picks up on themes in Paul and in the wider argument of 2 Cor, but are not mutually exclusive, Heath, *Paul's Visual Piety*, 181–87.

practices is removed.²⁵ Yet, *Paul is still "reading Moses*," and expects the Corinthians to read alongside: "we all (ἡμεῖς δὲ πάντες), with unveiled faces . . ."

One might be tempted to think that the text is therefore the "mirror" of which Paul speaks in 3:18, but as we have noted, the clear emphasis on visuality (inverting Israel's visual incapacity in 3:7, 13), the work of the Spirit, and transformation into glory, means that something altogether more experiential is in mind.²⁶ The idea that the "mirror" is Christ himself would be consistent with this view, and makes good sense of Paul's later language about the "glory of God" being now revealed in the "face of Christ" (ἐν προσώπῳ Χριστοῦ, 2 Cor 4:6) rather than the face of Moses. In a suggestive examination of the place of 3:18 in relation to the verses that follow (4:1–18), Heath makes a case for understanding the "mirror" to be the apostles whose "decaying flesh" constitutes a manifestation of the dying of Jesus and thus as "the outward expression of God's revelation and locus of his glorification."²⁷ This leads me to suggest that Paul's hermeneutics do not simply consist in a Spirit directed engagement with the text and, thus, encounter with Christ, but also invites embodied participation in the drama of death and resurrection that stands at the core of Paul's theological vision. Where Heath limits this feature to the embodied experience of the apostles, to which the Corinthians are asked to give their visual attention, my own view is that much of Paul's language invites us to consider the ways that *all* Christian believers (and thus Christian communities) make that death and resurrection drama manifest in ways that invite the attention of the world. It is not clear to me that 3:18 only refers to the apostles who are then described in 4:1–15 in an exclusive way. The ἡμεῖς δὲ πάντες is surely inclusive of the Corinthians and, by implication, all Christians. The first person plurals that follow in 4:1–18 at times seem to refer to the apostles only, but at other times the language is generic enough to permit of an ecclesial, rather than strictly apostolic interpretation.²⁸ To the extent that the embodied manifestation of the dying

---

²⁵ It is likely that the subject of 3:16 is Moses. See the extensive consideration of alternative interpretations in Thrall, *2 Corinthians 1–7*, 268–73.

²⁶ I am here bypassing a host of complex questions relating to the interpretation of 3:18. The discussion in Thrall, *2 Corinthians 1–7*, 282–95, is a helpful a guide to the exegetical decisions that must be made.

²⁷ Heath, *Paul's Visual Piety*, 239. Heath's argument includes a sophisticated appeal to the possible of intertextual relationship between Paul's language and the servant of Isaiah 52–53 to which I cannot do justice at this point.

²⁸ I continue to work on a larger project on 2 Corinthians which makes this point about the deliberative and inclusive focus and aims of the letter as a whole. For another example of the issue, note Paul's appeal to the image of "ambassadors for Christ" in 2 Cor 5:20, on which see Winter, "Ambassadors."

and life of Jesus is rendered "visible," Paul seems to think that the ultimate "beholders" are the "more and more people" of 4:15. This implicit missional appeal rounds off the argument that began in 3:1–3 where we saw that it is the *Corinthians* who are the "letter . . . to be known and read by all" (3:2). Ironically, then, and notwithstanding the complexities of almost every verse in this most difficult of Pauline epistles, we are invited to move from the "letters on stone tablets," to the life-giving Spirit of God, by means of unveiled reading of the text of the old covenant, with a view to becoming a "letter of Christ" in the world. This blend of textual and visual language is a reminder to us that Pauline hermeneutics lie far from the naïve literalisms, unnuanced "christocentrism," or disembodied "spiritualism" that have so often characterized Christian biblical interpretation. Francis Watson summarizes the dynamics well:

> From a Pauline perspective, it is of the nature of the Christ-event to make itself known, and to do so by way of scriptural texts and a proclamation that is nothing other than the authoritative exegesis of those texts. If it is true that for Paul "the scripture must be read in the light of Christ," it is equally true that Christ must be read in the light of the scripture. . . . Paul reads scripture in light of Christ only *in order* to read Christ in the light of scripture; scriptural interpretation *per se* is of no interest to him. And yet, in interpreting the Christ-event, it is genuinely scriptural interpretation that Paul practices.[29]

Hermeneutical Signposts

Freedom, perception, embodiment: Paul's treatment of the relationship between the letter and the Spirit provokes further reflections on contemporary forms of biblical interpretation. Before offering a few comments on each of these themes, however, it is worth reiterating the central claim of this essay in so far as it relates to the continuing place of biblical interpretation within communities of faith. While it is true that many Protestant traditions, historically, have, strongly affirmed the centrality of biblical exposition and engagement for Christian discipleship and corporate worship, it is also true that, in those same traditions, many perceive or promote a basic incompatibility between the search for theological freedom, or the need for spiritual vitality, or the quest for social justice on the one hand, and commitment to the centrality of scripture on the other. Contrary to popular opinion, the fault here lies less with the hermeneutically, spiritually, or socially progressive, and more with forms of *sola scriptura* conviction that confuse the authority of scripture with the authority of a particular set of interpretative decisions *about* scripture. If there is only one permissible interpretation of the

---

[29] Watson, *Paul and Hermeneutics*, 298 (italics original).

text, then arguments about development or change in Christian faith and practice quickly detach from conversations and argument about textual meaning.[30] The effect of this kind of biblical foundationalism is to render scripture lifeless, a letter that all too easily kills.[31] The interplay between letter and Spirit that we see operating in the rhetoric of 2 Corinthians 3 could help us to step away from this zero sum game and encourage forms of genuinely progressive renewal in the life of the church that do not depend on a loosening of ties to the scriptural witness, but that are secured precisely by means of the kind of scriptural interpretation that Paul here practices.

Of course, the letter-Spirit contrast has, since the time of Origen, been used to provide scriptural warrant for various forms of interpretative *freedom*. This initially took the form of providing for the possibility of allegorical interpretation and discerning the "spiritual" meaning located within and behind the "veil" of the scriptural text.[32] As Robert Morgan has argued, however, within Protestant hermeneutics the quest for scriptural legitimation of new theological proposals as well as the significant critique of established tradition meant that Luther and others needed "more textual determinacy than any allegorical web of meanings could provide." In so far as the Enlightenment inherited a preference for literal meaning, and contemporary biblical scholarship has in turn inherited any number of Enlightenment assumptions about textual meaning, the appeal to spiritual meaning "has become marginal in modern Western theology."[33] Morgan then reapplies the terms to his own proposed taxonomy of modern biblical interpretation, arguing that the notion of the "letter" might be used with reference to non-religious biblical scholarship, while "spiritual" interpretation refers to the pole of confessional or faith oriented interpretation. This is one way of proceeding, but all too easily ends up in a situation whereby the constraints of confessional positions (credal, theological, or ideological) inhibit genuine interpretative freedom. More promising, in my view, is to allow for the possibility that the "reversal" of the dominant form of the letter-Spirit contrast found in post-structuralist hermeneutics (broadly conceived) provides us with a model of the

---

[30] The problem is endemic in certain parts of the church. See my discussion of Baptists in Winter, "Persuading Friends."

[31] I have unpacked some of this in my 2007 Whitley Lecture, Winter, *"More Light and Truth?"*

[32] For an excellent summary of Origen's position, see Ludlow, "Spirit." Ludlow makes it clear that Origen never understood spiritual meaning to stand over against literal meaning: "were there no container, there would be no contents," 91.

[33] Morgan, "Spirit," here 47. For the historical narrative see Sheehan, *Enlightenment*. Allegorical interpretation re-enters "western" Christianity at the point where Enlightenment hermeneutics come under critique and, in particular, play a role in some modern accounts of the "theological interpretation of Scripture."

kind of interpretative freedom that we need. Paul Fiddes notes the central insight of this postmodern reversal, based as it is on a broader critique of Western notions of presence:

> A "spirit" that supposedly exists prior to, and outside, the letter thus "kills". Appeal to "spirit" forecloses on the richness of the textuality of the world, and seeks to set up systems to oppress others. The problem with "spirit" is that of domination and anthropocentrism.[34]

For Fiddes, the hermeneutical consequence of this position is to refocus attention on the ways that textual ambiguity and instability provide a playground for all sorts of interpretative work. "The letters of physical signs, with their mutual distinctions and capacity for postponing meaning, are endlessly lifegiving. There is always surplus or excess."[35] Importantly, this is not to place the letter and Spirit back into an inverted zero-sum game but, rather, to overcome interpretative schemas that (mis)use an appeal to the Spirit to enforce patterns of domination and the eradication of difference. It is this polarization which is "deadly."[36]

In my view this opens up the possibility that forms of biblical interpretation that are directed intentionally at the overcoming of this polarity have a strong claim to inherit the "life-giving" and transformative freedom that is the Spirit's true work. This has little to do with confessional positioning or identity, and more to do with the kind of sustained attention to the text that disrupts inherited, "traditional," and sometimes downright lazy assumptions about what the text "must mean." Forms of biblical interpretation often lumped unhelpfully together under the heading of "hermeneutics of suspicion" (feminist and postcolonial approaches to name two) potentially carry these transformative possibilities, as do careful "plain text" readings that serve to remind us that texts do not obviously or invariably bear the meanings we so often attribute to them.

It is this process of discovering the Spirit *in* the letter that makes possible the *perception* of Christ that Paul describes in 2 Corinthians 3:18. The work of biblical interpretation is integral to the cultivation of Christian spirituality: the capacity to behold divine glory.[37] While many biblical scholars will inevitably

---

[34] Fiddes, "Late-modern," here 106.

[35] Fiddes, "Late-modern," 107. The theological rationale that lies behind Fiddes' affirmation of the insights of Derrida *et al.* lies in the formulation, "God has committed God's own self to the text of the world and this commitment is itself the movement of spirit," 130.

[36] Fiddes, "Late-modern," 107.

[37] The Johannine relationship between the revelatory function of the divine *logos* and the consequent potential for believers to "behold the glory of the Father's only Son" in John 1:1–18 is instructive here.

move beyond the work of textual interpretation in their exegetical labours (as I am doing now), it is perhaps the preacher who is most obviously burdened with the task of interpreting scripture in such a way as to make its mediatory role most explicit. Her task, week by week, is not to facilitate an encounter between the hearer and the text, but to interpret the text in such a way as to make it capable of facilitating the encounter between the hearers and the risen Christ, the Lord, the Spirit whose glory is visible in the world. This depends, I think, on preserving, or perhaps in many cases now rediscovering, a commitment to regarding corporate Christian worship, focused on word and sacrament, as the central discipline for the cultivation of "spirituality." It also demands attention to the ways that such worship genuinely orients the church towards Christ, and the pattern of divine glory revealed in Christ's life, death, and resurrection. The transformation of 2 Corinthians 3:18 is corporate in nature: the Corinthian community now "reading Moses" and conforming themselves to Christ so as to become the "letter of Christ" to be read by others. Because spirituality today is so often defined and explained with reference to concepts and practices that have little or no direct relationship to the work of biblical interpretation, it is worth exploring the various ways in which Christian communities can and will find their main source of spiritual nourishment and formation in their engagement with the biblical text.[38]

Which brings us to the importance of *embodiment*: the notion that biblical interpretation as Paul conceives of it, is not something that is simply scrawled onto the page of a letter, or a sermon. It is inscribed onto the suffering bodies of those who grasp that the image of Christ to which they are to be conformed is that of the dying and living one. This suggests that those whose life experience explicitly conforms them to that image will have much to tell us about the meaning and purpose of biblical texts. It also serves to reconnect the church's commitment to understanding scripture to the quest for material, embodied, social justice: the making visible of resurrection life in mortal flesh (2 Cor 4:12).

As an illustration of the congruence of these three features of biblical interpretation that moves from the letter, to the Spirit, to the letter again, I offer for consideration the remarkable work that has been happening in our midst in relation to the church's position on issues of human sexuality and same-sex relationships, including marriage equality. While, of course, it is true that many churches and many Christians remain committed to traditional accounts of the so-called "biblical" vision of sexual ethics, it is undoubtedly the case that many others have developed new understandings, interpretations, and practices. At its best, within the framework of Christian moral reflection, those changes have resulted from a determination to listen seriously to the lived experience of members of the LGBTQI communities, Christian and non-Christian, a willingness to perform the work of spiritual discernment in

---

[38] For some reflections on this theme see my Winter, "Listening."

relation to Christ's presence in those lives and communities, and fresh interpretations of key scriptural texts and trajectories. That interpretative work is not all of a kind. The preachers and Bible study leaders and Christian disciples who have changed their mind on "what the Bible teaches" have been engaged in it. In the scholarly world, I have in mind examples such as Megan Warner's quite brilliant debunking of the idea that Genesis 2:4 provides a normative definition of marriage, or Dale Martin's careful analysis of the meaning of key terms in 1 Corinthians 6:9, as well as Joseph Marchal's sophisticated use of the tools of queer theory in order to recover the experiences of those people other than Paul who lie within and behind his letters.[39]

Interpretative work of this kind reminds us that while the letter can kill, it can also—when read again and considered differently and connected to lived experience—confront us with ways of reading that "makes alive."[40] In this way, discernment of the relationship between the letter and the Spirit remains a perennial and provocative challenge. The interpretative work that emerges out of that discernment is a constant calling and task.

Bibliography

Cross, Anthony R., and Ruth Gouldbourne, ed. *Questions of Identity: Studies in Honour of Brian Haymes*. Centre for Baptist History and Heritage Studies, 6. Oxford: Regent's Park College, 2011.

Duff, Paul B. *Moses in Corinth: The Apologetic Context of 2 Corinthians 3*. NovTSup 159. Leiden: Brill, 2015.

Fiddes, Paul. "The Late-modern Reversal of Spirit and Letter: Derrida, Augustine, and Film." In *Spirit and the Letter*, 105–30. Edited by Fiddes and Bader.

Fiddes, Paul S. and Günter Bader, ed. *The Spirit and the Letter: A Tradition and a Reversal*. London: Bloomsbury, 2013.

Furcha, E.J. "Key Concepts in Caspar von Schwenckfeld's Thought: Regeneration and the New Life." *Church History* 37.2 (1968) 160–73.

Gignilliat, Mark S. *Paul and Isaiah's Servants: Paul's Theological Reading of Isaiah 40–66 in 2 Corinthians 5:14–6:10*. London: T. & T. Clark International, 2007.

---

[39] See Warner, "'Therefore a Man,'" 269–88; Martin, *Sex and the Single Saviour*; and Marchal, *Appalling*.

[40] Because the interpretation of Pauline texts are very much at stake in relation to these contemporary debates, it bears stating that the hermeneutical principles that we have seen Paul taking up in relation to Israel's scriptures are capable (if we consider them at all normative) of being deployed in relation to Paul's letters as scripture (a circumstance that, of course, he never envisaged). Sometimes the most "Pauline" thing that we can do is to read Paul *against* Paul.

Goodliff, A., and Paul Goodliff. *Rhythmns of Faithfulness: Essays in Honour of John E. Colwell.* Eugene: Wipf & Stock, 2018.

Gouldbourne, Ruth. *The Flesh and the Feminine: Gender and Theology in the Writings of Caspar Schwenckfeld.* Studies in Christian History and Thought. Milton Keynes: Paternoster, 2006.

Hafemann, Scott J. *Paul, Moses, and the History of Israel: The Letter/Spirit Contrast and the Argument from Scripture in 2 Corinthians 3.* Milton Keynes: Paternoster, 2005.

Hafemann, Scott. "'Self-Commendation' and Apostolic Legitimacy in 2 Corinthians: A Pauline Dialectic?" *New Testament Studies* 36.1 (1990) 66–88.

Hafemann, Scott J. *Suffering and the Spirit: An Exegetical Study of 2 Corinthians 2:14–3:3 within the Context of the Corinthian Correspondence.* Reprint of *Eugene: Wipf & Stock, 2011.* WUNT 2/19. Tübingen: Mohr Siebeck, 1986.

Hanson, A. T. "The Midrash in II Corinthians: A Reconsideration." *Journal for the Study of the New Testament* 3.9 (1980) 2–28.

Harris, Murray J. *The Second Epistle to the Corinthians.* New International Greek Testament Commentary. Grand Rapids: Eerdmans, 2005.

Hays, Richard B. *Echoes of Scripture in the Letters of Paul.* New Haven: Yale University Press, 1989.

Heath, J.M.F. *Paul's Visual Piety: The Metamorphosis of the Beholder.* Oxford: Oxford University Press, 2013.

Ilić, Luka. *Theologian of Sin and Grace: The Process of Radicalization in the Theology of Matthias Flacius Illyricus.* Göttingen: Vandenhoeck & Ruprecht, 2014.

Ludlow, Morwenna. "Spirit and Letter in Origen and Augustine." In *Spirit and the Letter,* 87–102. Edited by Fiddes and Bader.

Lyons, William J., and Isabella Sandwell, ed. *Delivering the Word: Preaching and Exegesis in the Western Christian Tradition.* Sheffield: Equinox, 2012.

Marchal, Joseph A. *Appalling Bodies: Queer Figures Before and After Paul's Letters.* New York: Oxford University Press, 2019.

Martin, Dale B. *Sex and the Single Saviour: Gender and Sexuality in Biblical Interpretation.* Louisville: Westminster John Knox, 2006.

McLaughlin, R. Emmet. "Spiritualism and the Bible: The Case of Caspar Schwenckfeld (1489–1561)." *Mennonite Quarterly Review* 53.4 (1979) 282–98.

Morgan, Robert. "Spirit and Letter: Mapping Modern Biblical Interpretation." In *Spirit and the Letter,* 47–73. Edited by Fiddes and Bader.

Murray, Stuart. *Biblical Interpretation in the Anabaptist Tradition.* Studies in the Believers Church Tradition, 3. Kitchener: Pandora, 2000.

Schwenckfeld, Caspar. "A Letter to Conrad Condatus entitled: De Cursus Verbi Dei (March 4, 1527)." In *Corpus Schwenkfeldianorum Volume II:*

Letters and Treatises of Caspar Schwenckfeld von Ossig 1524–1527. Edited by Chester David Hartranft. Leipzig: Breitkopf and Härtel, 1911.

Sheehan, Jonathan. *The Enlightenment Bible: Translation, Scholarship, Culture*. Princeton: Princeton University Press, 2005.

Thrall, Margaret E. *The Second Epistle to the Corinthians, Volume 1: Introduction and Commentary on II Corinthians I–VII*. International Critical Commentary. Edinburgh: T. & T. Clark, 1994.

Warner, Megan. "'Therefore a Man Leaves His Father and His Mother and Clings to His Wife:' Marriage and Intermarriage in Genesis 2:24." *Journal of Biblical Literature* 136.2 (2017) 269–88.

Watson, Francis. *Paul and the Hermeneutics of Faith*. London: T. & T. Clark International, 2004.

Windisch, Hans. *Der Zweite Korintherbrief*. 9th ed., Kritisch-exegetischer Kommentar uber das Neue Testament, 6. Göttingen: Vandenhoeck & Ruprecht, 1924.

Winter, Sean F. *"More Light and Truth?"' Biblical Interpretation in Covenantal Perspective*. The Whitley Lecture 2007. Oxford: Whitley Publications, 2007.

Winter, Sean F. "'Ambassadors for Christ' (2 Corinthians 5.20): Ministry in the New Creation." In *Questions of Identity*, 34–49. Edited by Cross and Gouldbourne.

Winter, Sean F. "'A Daring Synagogue Sermon?': Paul's Preaching in 2 Corinthians 3.7–18." In *Delivering the Word*, 24–44. Edited by Lyons and Sandwell.

Winter, Sean F. "Persuading Friends: Friendship and Testimony in Baptist Interpretative Communities." In *The "Plainly Revealed" Word of God?*, 253–270. Edited by Woodman and Dare.

Winter, Sean F. "Listening for the Word of God: Divine Speech, Scripture, and the Task of Interpretation." In *Rhythmns of Faithfulness*, 44–54. Edited by A. Goodliff and P. Goodliff.

Wolter, Michael. "'Spirit' and 'Letter' in the New Testament." In *Spirit and the Letter*, 31–46. Edited by Fiddes and Bader.

Woodman, Simon P., and Helen Dare, ed. *The "Plainly Revealed" Word of God?: Baptist Hermeneutics in Theory and Practice*. Macon: Mercer University Press, 2011.

CHAPTER 2

The Trauma of Hearing:
Listening, Poetry, and the Parable of the Sower

Simon Perry

It was my privilege to serve Bloomsbury Central Baptist Church as associate minister alongside Ruth Gouldbourne from 2006–11. During that time, Ruth was a source of enormous encouragement and support, as well as unofficial mentor. The emphasis on trauma in this piece arises largely from the fact that, during those years, Ruth was extremely gracious in enabling me to face trauma of my own, and extremely courageous in her willingness to enter into the trauma of others. If the element of joy is underplayed in what follows, it is partly because joy without trauma can be delusional, and partly because we are not short of upbeat reminders that joy is a Christian (perhaps even a human) right. At Bloomsbury, Ruth was a mediator of joy and it surfaced most unambiguously in her public prayers. Our habit in leading worship together entailed one of us preaching and the other leading intercessions. To hear Ruth's prayers dovetail with my own sermons was always a humbling experience. Not only was her spontaneity more poetically expressed than my carefully polished rhetoric. More substantively, Ruth's intercessions would "personalize" my all-too-theoretical homilies. In order to do this—Ruth seemed firstly to have immersed herself fully in what I had said, to the extent that she was now seeing the world from my exact location. Secondly, she also knew the congregation so well that she could bring them with her. And thirdly, in so doing her eyes remained riveted on the Jesus Christ we were worshipping. To be heard so fully and complemented so carefully is at once both a profound encouragement and a terrifying challenge, neither of which I fully appreciated at the time. In the years that followed, I have tried to emulate this approach to intercession and the present chapter offers a set of reflections attempting to explain why I have so often failed.

Hear, O Israel
Listen up, Israel: Yahweh our God—Yahweh is one[1] *(Deut 6:4; cf Mark 12:29)*

---

[1] All biblical citations here are the author's own translation.

If an extra-terrestrial being were to observe a Baptist church meeting, they might be forgiven for concluding that listening is the capacity to keep your face-hole shut for just about long enough for your conversation partner to finish their sentence before you cut in with what you were already planning to say in the first place. Hearing, in this drastically limited sense, is little more than verbal tennis—a polite game of taking it in turns to speak. And yet, even this limited capacity to hear is one many of us sometimes lack. In fact, I first met Ruth at a lively meeting held at Baptist headquarters to discuss the nature of church membership—a meeting at which neither of us could get an uninterrupted word in edgeways. It was in conversation over coffee that morning that Ruth and I had opportunity to let off steam with one another on precisely this topic. Listening, we agreed, is a much more demanding endeavour than many of the best-intentioned among us might imagine.

The Baptist church meeting is, in seeking the mind of Christ, an event rooted in serious, mutual, energetic listening. Hearing then, is a discipline that lies at the heart of Baptist identity as it lies at the core of the Judaic worldview. But what does it actually mean for the people of God simply to hear? In the first instance, it can appear to be a straightforward matter of processing information correctly in order to understand. Were human beings as two-dimensional as all that, blank sheets upon which new data can be inscribed, then listening would be nothing more than the acquisition of information that leaves the hearer more enlightened. But, as our extra-terrestrial observer would recognize, to be human is to have a mind already made up, that is, a mindset. A mind long since set, that is, within an ideology which in turn is confined within a historical "episteme." This latter phrase was coined by Michel Foucault to describe a historical epoch that quietly predetermines the way we receive, process and structure our knowledge: how we hear, think and communicate, all at a subconscious level.[2] Many of our earnest endeavours to listen to history are nevertheless plagued by naïve assumptions that we can simply step out of our episteme into the "courts of rationality."[3] Even a historian as distinguished as N.T. Wright, for instance, declares—in his critique of postmodernism—that he would not want to "have my teeth hacked about by a postmodern dentist."[4] On hearing this kind of expression, Ruth—with much greater historical acuity—chuckled, "we are all postmodern, whether we like it or not." The overwhelming, imperceptible ways in which our epistemic context hampers our hearing, are not always fully appreciated. If hearing is to have any bearing on our pre-set minds and the core of our own-most human identity, then what is spoken has multiple lines of near impregnable defences to penetrate. It is for this reason I would like to outline

---

[2] Foucault, *Order of Things*, xvi–xxvi.

[3] Toulmin, *Human Understanding*, 152.

[4] Wright, *God in Public*, 77.

in what follows a manifesto for *radical listening*—radical here in the sense that we might be able to hear not simply the superficial, necessary information we encounter on a daily basis, but to hear God's holy word *from the roots* of our being.

Exposing the roots of anything can be a traumatic experience for those involved, as even a postmodern dentist will confirm. The raw nerves uncovered can lead to unexpected and at times agonizing encounters of pain. Every element of our being, in all its multidimensional complexity, is implicated and exposed in the act of radical listening: the "episteme" that invisibly imprisons us; the ideological convictions to which we inevitably and unwittingly subscribe; the beliefs we consciously treasure; the alternatives we prematurely dismiss; the ethical practices we inhabit; the relational norms we regard as healthy; the fantasies of self-knowledge that bring us comfort; every contingent particularity masquerading as a universal given; and, above all, the smug assumption that lists such as this apply only to others less enlightened than ourselves; everything that makes us who we are, all are brought to the communion table when we engage with the God of scripture. Nothing, no dimension of our humanity is beneath the attention or beyond the scope of *Yahweh our God*, because—as God of creation and of covenant—*Yahweh is one*. That is, no part of our disintegrated world and no element of our fragmented human psyche lies outside the sphere of God's interest or influence. The titanic range and power of forces combining to form our identity thus all come into play in any serious attempt to listen, rendering the act of radical listening a near impossible challenge.

If listening is to be radical in this sense, then to listen well is a life-long pursuit that could prove nothing short of a miracle. It is this insight that led Martin Luther to propound the importance of a "daily baptism."[5] When hearing well, we run the risk that what is precious to us disappears beneath the watery grave never to resurface. Emerging from that grave is not simply a joyous moment of liberation, but potentially also a moment of bewildering, disorientating trauma. If resurrection lies at the heart of Christian belief, and baptism is the personal appropriation of death and resurrection, then Christianity is fundamentally a post-traumatic belief system. In its historical origins (the sequence of events from Golgotha to Garden), in its origins in the life of the believer (baptism as the gateway to Christian life), and in the daily lives of those called to carry the cross (engaging in daily baptism), Christian discipleship is an unavoidably post-traumatic experience. To listen is to expose oneself fully to that disturbing threat of otherness, a moment of profound liberation as well as a moment of unspeakable horror. To listen radically is to have the capacity to be transformed by one's encounter with radical otherness. In this light, it is hardly surprising that not "everyone with ears" is willing to "listen." Most are naturally repulsed by the threat of that which stands over

---

[5] Luther, *Large Catechism*, 4:65.

against us—an aspect of the human condition addressed by Jesus of Nazareth in his first recorded parable.

The Parable of the Sower (Mark 4:1–25; cf Matt 13:1–23; Luke 8:4–18)

Anyone with ears to hear should listen (Mark 4: 9; cf Matt 13: 9; Luke 8:8)

Radical listening does not come naturally. Though humans have the ability to hear, they do not necessarily have the courage, the will, or the determination. Jesus' very first parable alerts the listener/reader to both the difficulty and the responsibility of listening. It is for this reason that in each of the Synoptic accounts, the cluster of material surrounding the Parable of the Sower revolves around the repeated exhortation to listen well. The reading offered below follows Mark's version,[6] taking each section as an expansion of Jesus' plea for radical listening.

LISTEN ATTENTIVELY: MARK 4:3–9

... He said to them, *"Listen attentively!"*

"A sower went out to sow. And it happened that as he sowed, some [seed] fell beside the way, and the birds came and ate it. Other [seed] fell on the rocky patch without much soil, and it sprang up instantly because the soil had no depth. And when the sun rose, it was scorched; and since it had no root, it withered up. Other [seed] fell among thorns, and the thorns grew and throttled it, and it bore no fruit. Other [seed] fell into good soil and began bearing fruit, growing and swelling up and bearing thirty and sixty and a hundredfold." And he said, *"Anyone with ears to hear should listen!"*

In Mark's version both the Parable of the Sower in particular and the parable genre as a whole, are introduced with the simple instruction, "Listen attentively" (lit., "Listen! Look!"). The opening instruction to listen may refer not simply to the words of the parable (*"Listen to what I am about to say!"*) but might just as well constitute the general instruction the parable is designed to explain (*"Be a people who are perpetually ready to listen: [for example] a sower went out to sow ..."*). If this is a parable principally concerned with what constitutes listening—why should it concern the bearing of fruit? Radical listening, as described above, concerns an event that takes place in the depths of one's being. This is precisely the imagery of the parable. Three incremental degrees of failure (no germination, springing up quickly but then withering up, and growing up only to be choked) draw ever nearer to successful fruition. Three incremental degrees of success (thirty, sixty and a hundredfold) then outweigh the losses of wasted seed. As any farmer or biologist will confirm, the failure or fruitfulness of harvest depends not on the seed (there is

---

[6] Though the general interpretation that follows arises from my study of Luke. See Perry, *Gospel According to St Luke*.

negligible variance in its quality) and much more upon the environment in which the seed germinates and begins to grow. In other words, the receptivity of the hearer (in this case, the grade of soil where the seed has fallen) determines the fruitfulness of the seed. If God's people are to be fruitful they will be a people who listen carefully.

In this light it is worth recalling what happened to Jesus when—despite being in his hometown of Nazareth—he delivered an unambiguous address that threatened the episteme treasured by his people (Mark 6:1–6; Luke 4:18–30). If he is to minimize the risk of being arrested, beaten, assassinated or lynched every time he delivers such prophecy, it is best to do so in parables. Such an approach will ensure that the kind of person who would be intent on harming him would not be the kind of person capable of entering into the thought-world of his parable and drawing conclusions that would infuriate them to the point of violence. In the Galilean phase of his campaign, it is best for Jesus if such people will not see and will not understand. As Wright claims, "if too many understand too well, the prophet's liberty of movement, and perhaps life, may be cut short."[7]

LISTEN BUT DO NOT COMPREHEND: MARK 4:10–12

When he was alone, those around him along with the twelve asked him about the parables. And he said to them, "To you has been given the mystery of the kingdom of God, but for those outside, everything comes in parables; in order that 'they may look, but not perceive, and may *listen, but not understand*; so that they may not turn and it be forgiven them.'"

Why would Jesus seek to prevent those "outside" from listening? The "mysteries" of the kingdom, far from being fascinating nuggets of gnostic wisdom, concern rather the unfolding of God's plan for Israel. The coming of God's kingdom would be mysterious largely because—for better or worse—it took unexpected form.[8] Mark's earliest readers may already have seen Jerusalem's beloved Temple reduced to a gargantuan mass of smouldering rubble,[9] leaving countless Jewish people wondering how on earth present

---

[7] Wright, *Jesus and the Victory of God*, 237.

[8] This is how "mystery" is conceived in prophetic tradition (Dan 2:28,44; cf Amos 3:7), in Pauline rhetoric (cf 1 Cor 2:1, 7; Eph 3:2–6: Col 1:26–27; 2:2–3), and in later apocalyptic writings (e.g., I Enoch 63; 103:7; IV Ezra 12:36). With overwhelming regularity in such sources, mystery describes the tension created when present experience (be it comfort or hardship) seems to contradict God's imminent plan for Israel (be it judgment or blessing).

[9] For the Jewish people of the first century the obliteration of the Temple in 70CE was a disaster whose magnitude is difficult for the modern reader to appreciate. The wars of rebellion in the late first century (rather than the alleged "delayed parousia") may well be the principle reason the Synoptic Gospels were committed to writing. After all, the Roman war machine was grinding its destructive might through the

circumstances could possibly be an expression of Yahweh's eternal plan. How could God's kingdom have come, when his Temple, its shrine and the Holy of Holies all lay beneath the debris of a failed national rebellion? This was by no means the first time that desolation had been brought upon Jerusalem in accordance with Yahweh's will, nor was it the first time people had refused to interpret the disaster as Yahweh's will. If Jesus had indeed foreseen that disaster was destined to befall God's people, and that his people refused to see it, he might well have recalled the instruction Isaiah received at his commissioning:

> He said, "Go and tell this people: 'Be always hearing, but never understanding; be always seeing, but never perceiving. Make the heart of this people calloused; make their ears dull and shut their eyes. That way, they might not see with their eyes, and hear with their ears, and understand with their hearts, and turn and be healed.'"
> Then I said, "For how long, Lord?" And he replied: "Until the cities lie decimated without inhabitant, until the houses are abandoned and the fields desolate, until the Lord has sent everyone far away and the land is obliterated (Isa 6:9–12).

Such a passage might indeed have found tragic relevance in the Jerusalem of Mark's day. Jesus cites an abbreviated paraphrase (a targum) of it to explain why his teaching to others is filtered through parables. The phrase continues to puzzle interpreters because it begs the question of why Jesus would want to communicate in order to remain unheard. So long as we regard Jesus' parables merely as a means of conveying correct information, the sentiment will never make sense. However, if a parable is better understood as an ideological explosive device, it is designed not only to "teach" but to reach into the psyche of those who listen well. As a compact, hard-hitting micro-narrative, the parable is designed to shake listeners to their core, displacing one worldview with another. Such an event has long been recognized as a disturbing, violent and potentially traumatic encounter. It may be for this reason many choose to see (the story at a surface level) but not see (its radical and subversive implications); to hear (the elements of the story that confirm their ideology) but not hear (any elements that threaten their precious ideology).

ANYONE WITH EARS TO HEAR SHOULD LISTEN: MARK 4:13–23

> And he said to them, "Do you not understand this parable? Then how will you understand all the parables? The sower sows the word. These are the ones beside

---

village communities where, it is widely supposed, different forms of Gospel tradition were treasured and orally remembered. It was in precisely this period that these traditions are thought to have taken the written form with which we are familiar. See further Perry, *Gospel According to St Luke*.

the way, where the word is sown: when they hear, Satan immediately comes and takes the word that is sown in them. And likewise, these are the ones sown on rocky patch: when they hear the word, they immediately welcome it with joy. But they have no root of their own and are short-lived. When distress or persecution comes about on account of the word, they instantly fall away. And others are those sown among the thorns: these are the ones who, having heard the word, but the concerns of the day, and the delusion of wealth, and the attraction of other things come in and choke the word, and it bears nothing. And these are the ones sown on the good earth: they hear the word and receive it and bear fruit, thirty and sixty and a hundredfold."

He said to them, "Is a lamp brought in to be put under the basket, or under the bed, and not on the lampstand? For there is nothing hidden that will not be made known, to be disclosed; nor anything secret that will not come to light. *Anyone with ears to hear should listen.*"

Jesus responds to the disciples' request by expanding upon (rather than fully interpreting) the parable. The identity of the sower, and of the different groups represented by different types of environment are not given, connections the disciples are still expected to draw for themselves. Commentators have been quick to draw their own connections of course, taking the parable's explanation as addressing (with suspicious foreknowledge) the missionary struggles faced by early Christian communities.[10] However, there is nothing in Jesus' explanation to suggest that the fruit described refers to the quantity of converts won over to the Christian cause. Since each section of this parable tradition climaxes with an exhortation to radical listening, it is far more likely the thrust of the parable concerns ethics rather than evangelism. That is, Jesus is tracing the pathways that run from "hearing" to "doing," from receiving the word to bearing fruit. The three failed attempts to produce fruit—be it due to Satan, to disaster or to distraction—rest neither upon those external forces, nor upon any deficiency in the seed. The same seed that failed to take root in three other patches of ground proved its worth by the production of an increasingly bumper crop. The reason for such superabundance was the receptivity of the environment, that is, the good

---

[10] This has led the majority of scholars in the Jülicher–Jeremias tradition to conclude that this entire section originates not on the lips of Jesus but in early Christian teaching. The main exegetical grounds for this conclusion concern language that is almost exclusive to the Epistles—e.g., *pleasure* (ἡδονή, Titus 3:3; Jas 4:1, 3; 2 Pet 2:13), *short-lived* (πρὸς καιρὸν, 1 Cor 7:5), *cares* (μέριμνα, 2 Cor 11:28; 1 Pet 5:7). Neither does the language of this passage read as though it was translated from an underlying Aramaic. In and of themselves, however, these concerns cannot bear the weight of assuredness often accompanying the claim that this short passage is a creation of the early church. Such a claim owes at least as much to the particular assumptions of modern historiography as it does to exegesis of the text within its own episteme. Attempts to identify a pre-Markan origin to this passage remain largely speculative.

(καλός) earth. When the good heart is receptive, so the logic runs, it will undergo the entire process of bearing fruit by its steadfast fidelity to the word.

The final aphorisms concerning light and revelation over against concealment and darkness are by no means disconnected from the Parable of the Sower—not least because Jesus rounds them off by drawing attention back to the exhortation with which he opened the parable. The aphorisms here, though general by definition, serve a specific purpose in the present discourse: to highlight for the disciples both the necessity and the urgency of hearing. Within the Markan context, the lamp most likely refers to the process of listening. To allegorize the imagery, we may follow the main body of the parable in which the active agent stands for God who lights the lamp just as he plants the seed. The lamp is not intended to remain concealed, even as the seed is not intended to remain hidden in the soil. Inevitably and inexorably, a light—once burning—will manifest itself, just as seed in good soil will bear fruit. The Markan challenge thus appears to be that Jesus's hearers allow themselves to be illuminated, otherwise they might as well remain beneath a bed or a bucket. Israel is the nation that hears God (e.g., Deut 6:4–9; 11:13–21) and it is only in so doing that Israel might in turn fulfil its commission as a light to the nations (Isa 49:6).

The imagery of the lamp thus moves naturally from that of sowing seed as it expounds the inevitability of that which is hidden becoming publicly manifest. If Israel is primordially the nation that hears, then sooner or later the hidden process of hearing will manifest itself in public life. Regardless of one's public reputation or profession, that which a person truly values in private will ultimately be revealed in public. In the second instance, attention is drawn back to the "mysteries" mentioned at Mark 4:11, presently revealed to the disciples but accessible to others only in cryptic parables. God's saving purposes, though in a sense hidden, will finally flood into public consciousness as a lamp once lit and placed on a stand will flood into a darkened room.

Hence, Jesus concludes the discourse with a reminder that he is addressing the process of listening. In sum, he has firstly recognized that listening is and has always been a core identity marker of the people of God. He has secondly acknowledged, however, that so many find listening so impossible, due to failure to listen in the first instance (seed on the rocky patch), failure to listen in the depths of one's being (seed in shallow soil), or failure to listen to the right voice (seed choked by thorns). Thirdly, he has promised that radical listening will inexorably manifest itself in the fruitfulness to which Israel is called.

Poesis as Fruition

> I will place my Torah in their midst and inscribe it on their hearts,
> and I will be their God and they will be my people (Jer 31:33).

Poiesis (ποίησις) is the process of creativity and cultivation, of bringing into being or, alternatively stated, of bearing fruit. When the Synoptics' Baptist urged his listeners to "bear fruit" (Matt 3:8; Luke 3:8) he used the verbal root (ποιέω) of poiesis. Though, as any basic lexicon will show, ποιέω can be translated simply as "to do" or "to make," in the cultural climate of modern pragmatism such a translation can also be misleading. Listening, as outlined above, describes the means by which the word of one person "finds expression" (ποιέω) in the life of another. Consideration of poesis can thus help to articulate what it means to listen radically. It is, after all, possible to listen while keeping the other at arm's length, that is, to listen hypocritically. If poesis has a nemesis, it is hypocrisy—a negative habit which helps to highlight the positive practice of poiesis.

Interpretive preoccupation with the consequences of hypocrisy (being guilty of what I condemn in others) often detracts from the essence of hypocrisy (living by a script which is fundamentally external to who I really am). Originally, hypocrite simply meant "one who replies" (Pindar, *Fragments* 140b), but came to refer to an actor (Plato, *Republic* 2.373b; *Letter of Aristeas*, 219) and gradually acquired the negative connotations of play-acting, pretending and lying (Josephus, *Bellum judaicum* 2.587). In Jesus's day a hypocrite was not simply a liar, but more precisely a person whose adherence to Torah had become the mere enactment of a script that was external to that person's true being. Hypocrisy need not be regarded as a scathing denunciation, since it summarizes aptly the "deontological"[11] pattern of ethics in which morality is attained by observing an external body of principles, laws, values or duties. By contrast "virtue ethics" focuses more upon the primal internal formation of a person's character. In Judaism, the process by which that formation might take place is obedience to Torah which, according to Jeremiah, Yahweh would engrave into the hearts of his people (Jer 31:33; cf., Heb 8:10). The fruits of a person's character would then be the outworking of their rootedness in Torah. By contrast, if Torah remains external to a person's true nature, no amount of well-meaning moral exertion will yield good fruit.

Neither the Torah of Judaism nor the teaching of Jesus present themselves as collections of ethical principles adherents must first understand and subsequently apply. Scripture is no set of external rules disciples must put into practice, which is why the traditional flat-footed progression from *hearing* to *doing* must be carefully reconsidered. It can circumvent the trauma of radical listening and obviate the necessity for poesis. Disciples are by no means expected to hear Jesus give a sermon and then go away and "do" by applying

---

[11] Originating with Immanuel Kant and referred to here as "duty ethics." Its clearest articulation can be found in Kant's 1785 work, *Groundwork of the Metaphysic of Morals*.

such high-sounding moral principles as the Golden Rule.[12] It is certainly not splitting hairs to insist that this dynamic of "bringing into being" be factored into the translation of ποιέω. Unlike simply "doing" what they are told like post-Kantian moral-applicationists ("duty ethics"), if Jesus' followers take his words to heart ("virtue ethics"), they cannot help but bear (ποιέω) the fruit of his teaching.[13]

Poesis, however, also concerns the process by which we assimilate the words of another. It is perfectly possible to cultivate either duties or virtues derived from an idolatrous image of Jesus. In order for genuine poesis to take place, then the living word of the other must first access the beating heart of the hearer. This is the implication both of the Torah being written on the heart, and of the seed/word germinating in the good earth/heart. As outlined above, this cannot be done while keeping the "other" at a safe distance. God's menacingly holy word has multiple levels of human defences to penetrate before it accesses the core of one's being—but that is where the word must take root if poesis is to take place. Poiesis ensures that the route from hearing to doing does not bypass the human heart. For Jeremiah, it is Yahweh himself who is concerned with ensuring his law is first inscribed on the human heart—an activity that happens within the context of committed personal relationship: "I will be *their* God and they will be *my* people." Both *virtue* and *duty* evaporate in the sheer intensity of this all-encompassing consummation of one's full-blown personal allegiance.

Liturgical Listening: Repentance, Confession, Intercession
Produce, therefore, fruits worthy of repentance (Luke 3:8)

Poiesis, as required by the Baptist, was linked to repentance, that is, the capacity to change one's mind. As outlined above, changing one's mind in any substantive way is no easy task given that the human mind is already made up. The defences surrounding the mind include the myth that the mind itself can be readily changed, freed, or transformed. To change one's mind, however, is a task that generally involves far more than one's mind. It implicates our

---

[12] Although ironically the application of the Golden Rule (Matt 7:12; Luke 6:31) is often taken as an example of deontological ethics, that is, an ethic based upon duty. The first formulation of Kant's Categorical Imperative states (Kant, *Practical Philosophy*, 73 [4:421]) that one should "act only in accordance with that maxim through which you can at the same time will that it become a universal law." While it is clearly derived from the Golden Rule, Kant's own attempts to distinguish between them are justified. Kant wants his disciples to *act*; Jesus wants his to *love*.

[13] The logic of Augustine's ethical maxim (*Homilies*, 176): "love and do as you like." In other words, if your prior ethos is formed in loving communion with God, you do not require a list of moral regulations by which to live. The latter practice can be construed as attaching artificial fruit to a rootless tree.

relationships, our history, our future, our allegiances, our commitments, our beliefs, our worldview, our politics, our economics, our entire episteme. In this light, the virtue of "open-mindedness" vaunted *ad nauseum* by the prophets and priests of secular liberalism is a fantasy that could take root only in an episteme of delusional self-righteousness. It is that same episteme that twists tolerance (the refusal to listen) into an unquestionable virtue—despite it being thoroughly incompatible with open-mindedness. Tolerance, after all, retains the unacknowledged assumption of the superiority of my informed opinion over against that of an unenlightened other, without the hardship of engaging seriously with that other. (No justice movement from slave abolition, through women's suffrage and civil rights to transgender inclusivity ever fought in order for underprivileged or oppressed groups to be merely tolerated.) The tolerance of secular liberalism has long-since proved an obstacle to justice, evidence of political failure, and a smokescreen designed to conceal my refusal to listen well enough to have my mind changed. In stark contrast, the Greek verb generally translated as repentance can carry the mind (*nous*) beyond (*meta*) its current configuration, but that move can also prove to be traumatic. This is because the compulsion to repent can irrupt as a liturgical hurricane that leaves you engulfed, uprooted, relocated and disoriented. Poesis, as described above, refers to the process by which a seed sown in the mind can result in a terrifying epistemic shift (the enforced relocation of the mind), or stated more positively, blossom into the fruits of the changed mindset (i.e., the μετανοίας).

Only by means of such repentance is confession possible. Confession speaks of radical continuity between what is in the heart and what is spoken out. Its literal meaning is "to speak the same" (ὁμολογέω), as explained in the Pauline phrase, "if you confess with your mouth that Jesus is Lord, and trust in your heart that God raised him from the dead, you will be saved" (Rom 10:9). In this sense, confession is the opposite of hypocrisy (living by an authoritative but external code) and constitutes the verbal dimension of bearing fruit. As Luther famously translated Luke 6:45, "When the heart is full, the mouth overflows."[14]

Hence, we return to intercession. Ruth's intercessions are indeed poetic, but not only because of her love of language and ability to be spontaneously articulate. Poetic in the sense of poiesis—that someone has taken to heart what they have heard. In the context of a worship service where intercessions follow on from a sermon (delivered by someone else), it was my experience that Ruth had thoroughly entered into the narrative of that sermon and heard it profoundly well. But when it comes to intercession, hearing is necessarily multi-directional: hearing the God to whom we pray, the congregation with whom we pray, the world for whom we pray. If to intercede is to engage in the

---

[14] "Wes das Herz voll ist, *des gehet der Mund über*." Bornkamm, "Luther's Translation of the New Testament," 214.

priestly practice of representing God to the people and the people to God, then every one of the monstrously difficult disciplines described above thus comes into play. You cannot represent those you cannot hear. And the more faithfully you represent them, the more fully you have entered into their world, and they into yours. Intercessions are poetic when they are the liturgical overflow of a listening that has penetrated the depths of your being, that is, when they are the fruit of radical listening.

Bibliography

Augustine. *Homilies on the First Epistle of John*. The Works of Saint Augustine: A Translation for the 21st Century. Trans. by Boniface Ramsey. Ed. Daniel E. Doyle and Thomas Martin. New York: New City, 2008.

Bornkamm, H. "Luther's Translation of the New Testament." In *Luther: A Profile*, 210–17. Edited by H.G. Koenigsberger. London: Palgrave Macmillan, 2014.

Foucault, M. *The Order of Things: An Archeology of the Human Sciences*. London: Routledge, 1989.

Kant, Immanuel. *The Groundwork of the Metaphysic of Morals*. New York: Harper and Row, 1964.

———. *Practical Philosophy*. Trans. by Mary J. Gregor. Cambridge: Cambridge University Press, 1996.

Luther, M. *Martin Luther's Small and Large Catechisms*. St Louis: Concordia, 2019.

Perry, S. *The Gospel According to St Luke*. Black's New Testament Commentaries. London: Bloomsbury, forthcoming.

Toulmin, Stephen. *Human Understanding: The Collective Use and Evolution of Concepts*. Princeton: Princeton University Press, 1972.

Wright, N.T. *God in Public: How the Bible Speaks Truth to Power Today*. London: SPCK, 2016.

———. *Jesus and the Victory of God: Christian Origins and the Question of God: Volume 2*. London: SPCK, 1996.

CHAPTER 3

Proverbs: A Misogynist Text?

Ernest C. Lucas

In their preface to *The New Revised Standard Version* of the Bible the translators explain that they used inclusive language whenever possible in order to avoid the linguistic sexism which arises from the bias of the English language towards the use of the masculine gender. This is an understandable and laudable concern. They admit, however, that this concern sometimes stood in tension with other legitimate concerns that translators have to consider. This tension can result in some debatable decisions. Unlike most other modern English translations of the Bible, some of which share the concern to use inclusive language, the, NRSV uses the word "child," rather than the more formal-equivalence translation "son," of the person who is addressed by the parent in the series of "lessons" in Proverbs 1–9. If it was hoped that this inclusive term might make the lessons seem inclusive it is a vain hope. Their content makes it very clear that they are addressed to a son. This is most obvious in the warnings against giving way to the sexual enticements of evil women (2:16–19; 5:1–23; 6:24–35; 7:1–27) and the encouragement to "rejoice in the wife of your youth" and to be intoxicated with her delights (5:15–19) instead. It is also clear, especially in Prov 4:1–4 (even in the, NRSV) that the parent addressing the son is a father.

There is no way to disguise the fact that Proverbs is a male-centred book. This is most obvious in Proverbs 1–9, but is also clear in the rest of the book. Here women appear only as wives, mothers or sexual temptresses. Some women, understandably, find this a stumbling-block when reading the book. But does the book go beyond being male-centred to being misogynistic? Some argue that it does. They point to fact that women are often portrayed in a negative light. In addition to the four warnings against the sexual enticements of evil women referred to above, there are two others in Proverbs 22:14 and 30:20. There are several proverbs about the quarrelsome wife (19:13; 21:9.19; 25:24; 27:15), but nothing similar is said about husbands. Proverbs 11:22 says, "Like a gold ring in a pig's snout is a beautiful woman without discretion." Feminine charm and beauty are said to be "deceitful" and "vain" in Proverbs

31:30. How strong is this argument that the Book of Proverbs is a misogynist text? What can be said in response to it?[1]

The "Forbidden" Woman

We will begin by considering the evil woman depicted in the four lessons in Proverbs 1–9 referred to above. Two particular Hebrew terms are used to describe her: *zarah* (ESV, "forbidden") and *nokriyyah* (ESV, "adulteress"). These occur in parallel in Proverbs 2:16; 5:20; and 7:5. The basic meaning of these words is "strange" and "foreign" respectively. Because both are somewhat ambiguous in meaning there has been much debate about what they signify regarding this woman. *Zar* (fem. *zarah*) can refer to an ethnic foreigner (Isa 1:7), but in most of its uses it refers to someone who is "out of place" in some way: for example, lay Israelites doing what only priests should do (Exod 29:33; Num 1:51) or someone outside the family (Deut 25:5). In Proverbs 14:10 and 27:2 it means someone other than oneself. *Nokri* (fem. *nokriyyah*) does often refer to what is ethnically foreign (Exod 2:22; 1 Kgs 11:1). It can, however, be used in a more general sense of what is "alien" or "other" (Isa 28:21; Jer 2:21). In Proverbs 27:2 it is used in parallel with *zar* to mean someone other than oneself.

Proverbs 2:17 ("... who forsakes the companion of her youth and forgets the covenant of her God") refers to "her God" rather than Yahweh and some see this as evidence that the woman is not an Israelite. However, Mal 2:14 ("... the LORD was witness between you and the wife of your youth, to whom you have been faithless, though she is your companion and your wife by covenant") is a very close parallel to this verse and speaks of marriage as a covenant to which Yahweh is witness.[2] So, the phrase "the covenant of her God" may be used here because marriage as a covenant is in view, and be preferred to the phrase "covenant of Yahweh" because that would normally be taken to refer to the Sinai Covenant. Alternatively, since the noun "god" can be used in Hebrew as a mark of superlative degree, the phrase can be translated as "her sacred covenant" (NRSV).

Boström[3] argued that the woman belongs to the fertility cult of a foreign goddess and is trying to lure the man into sacral prostitution. Against this, there is nothing in these lessons to suggest this, and if this is her aim then she would be *fulfilling* "the covenant of her God" not *forgetting* it. Clifford[4]

---

[1] Much of what follows draws on, and develops, material to be found in Lucas, *Proverbs*. Biblical quotations are from the ESV unless indicated otherwise.

[2] Hugenberger, *Marriage as a Covenant*, 296–302.

[3] Boström, *Proverbiastudien*, 103–55.

[4] Clifford, *Proverbs*, 27.

suggests that the figure of the Forbidden Woman is based on a type-scene found in epics in which a goddess deceitfully offers a hero love or marriage as something which will transform his life. However, what is offered to the man in Proverbs is not marriage that will transform his life but one night of pleasure. Unlike the hero in the epics, he does not refuse the offer, but accepts it. Blenkinsopp[5] argues that the background to these lessons is the issue of marriage to foreign women in post-exilic Judah (Ezra 9–10; Neh 13:23–27; Mal 2:10–16). However, the warnings in the lessons are clearly warnings against adultery, not against marriage to a non-Israelite.

The most obvious thing that is said about the woman in the lessons is that she is being unfaithful to her husband (2:17, in the light of Mal 2:14; 6:26, 29; 7:19–20). Therefore, the simplest explanation of why she is *zarah* and *nokriyyah* is that she is "out of place," "off limits," "beyond the pale," both socially and morally because she is someone else's wife. This is the justification for the way the ESV translates the Hebrew words. Given the setting of the lessons as the teaching given by a father to a son, the most obvious background for understanding the figure of the forbidden women is the age-old temptation to adultery. But why should this warrant the repeated severe warnings against her allure? The answer is to be found in the significance of adultery in ancient Israel. Wright[6] argues that there is an important socio-theological reason for the commandment against adultery in the Ten Commandments. Although the land was the primary symbol of the covenant relationship between Yahweh and Israel, the family provided the most important realization of that relationship. The existence of Israel as a covenant community in the land depended on the stability of the family for both socio-economic reasons and for a theological reason. Because adultery was a threat to that stability, and so to the whole social order of the covenant community, it was totally unacceptable. It had to be removed by the death of both the man and the woman involved (Deut 22:22).

Because the primary concern of these lessons is the threat that male promiscuity poses to the family and society, their horizon is limited. If men heeded the exhortations to be faithful in marriage a major cause of adultery and prostitution would be removed. However, there is no explicit protest here, or elsewhere in the book, against the wider exploitation of women which may lead to prostitution. This can rightly be seen as an important lack in the book's teaching. However, it does not make it a misogynist text. There is no suggestion that all women are like the forbidden woman. Indeed, what is said about the wife in Proverbs 5:15–19 and about some other female figures in the book makes this clear.

---

[5] Blenkinsopp, "Social Context."

[6] Wright, "Israelite Household," 102.

Feminist scholars differ in how negatively they view these lessons. Brenner[7] argues that in parts of Proverbs 1–9 the speaker is not the father, as usually assumed, but a female voice. However, she does not see this as a positive thing. In her view this female voice has internalized male patriarchal values, which it seeks to protect. In particular she sees the female voice supporting male ideology by recommending control over female sexuality. Bellis, however, takes a different view. She regards the voice which warns the son to avoid the Forbidden Woman as countering the "infamous double standard" which tolerated a degree of male promiscuity in Israelite society. She therefore says that this voice "is not necessarily any more an internalized and androcentric one than the voice of twentieth-century feminists who challenge the remnants of the same double standard today."[8] The only difference is that the speaker in Proverbs tries to undercut the double standard by limiting male sexual freedom whereas some modern feminists wish to increase female sexual freedom. Which approach one adopts depends on one's view of what an egalitarian sexual ethic should be. She points out that Brenner and some other writers are wrong to assert that the teacher is trying to control *female* sexuality. Rather, the teacher is trying to control *male* sexuality. Bellis also argues that in the context of ancient Israelite society enforcement of monogamy was more in women's self-interest than in men's.[9] It should also be noted that, contrary to what some feminist writers assert,[10] the father, if he is the teacher, does not have any problem with feminine sexuality in itself, as his advice about enjoying sexual relations with one's wife in Proverbs 5:15–19 shows.

Evil Men

Many modern readers of Proverbs will have some sympathy with Yee's comment regarding the figure of the Forbidden Woman, "The personification of all that is evil and destructive is, indeed, a disturbing one."[11] However, it is not true to say that *all* that is evil and destructive is personified in this female figure. It is a weakness in the work of most of those who have written about the Forbidden Woman that they have taken the lessons warning about her more or less as isolated texts. They have not tried to understand them in the context of Proverbs 1–9 as a whole. As a result, they have not recognized that she has a male counterpart, or male counterparts, in these chapters, men who

---

[7] Brenner, "Proverbs 1–9," 125–26.

[8] Bellis, "Gender and Motives," 82.

[9] Bellis, "Gender and Motives," 83–86.

[10] E.g., Newsom, "Woman and the Discourse," 153.

[11] Yee, "I Have Perfumed," 66.

personify various aspects of evil and destructiveness which are not found in the Forbidden Woman.

The first lesson in Proverbs 1–9 is a fairly lengthy warning against involvement with a gang of male "sinners" (1:8–19). Apart from the nature of their activities their maleness is indicated in the Hebrew text by the grammatical forms of the verbs, pronouns and possessive suffixes. Some of the things said about them have resonance with what is said later about the Forbidden Woman. Like her they use enticing speech and other enticements to snare the son into joining them. The father warns him that giving in to their enticements will lead to death, which is what he says later about the enticements of the Forbidden Woman. Their feet lead them into evil, just as hers lead her astray. They lie in wait for victims, just as she does.

It seems that a deliberate patterning is being set up here, as is borne out by a feature of the lessons which is rarely noticed. This is that warnings about evil men closely precede all but the last of the passages about the Forbidden Woman. The first passage about her is preceded by an admonition to seek wisdom because this will give deliverance from evil men, who are described in a strong and vivid way (2:12–15), as well as from the Forbidden Woman (2:16–22). The use of the verb "delivered" in vv. 12 and 16 links the two portraits of evil male and female characters. It is unfortunate that the desire of the, NRSV translators to use inclusive language hides this deliberate juxtaposition of evil men and an evil woman, despite the explicit use of the nouns for "man" in the Hebrew of v. 12 and of "woman" in v. 16. Concentration on gender inclusiveness in the language, the words, destroys the gender inclusiveness with regard to evil people that is there in the structure of the passage. Another vivid warning against evil men (4:14–19, the grammatical forms of the Hebrew nouns and verbs make clear that the father is speaking of men) comes shortly before the second warning about the Forbidden Woman (5:1–23). The use of the words "path" and "way" in Proverbs 4:14 and Proverbs 5:5–6 link the two portraits. The final two passages about an evil woman (6:24–35) and the Forbidden Woman (7:1–23) are preceded by another portrait of a "wicked man" (6:12–15). The fact that the first thing said about both the wicked man and the evil woman relates to their speech links the male and female portraits together. Once again, the inclusive language of the, NRSV hides the explicit use of the noun "man" in Proverbs 6:12 and so hides the intended gender inclusiveness of the portraits of evil people.

These portraits of evil men give the lie to Yee's comment that the Forbidden Woman personifies "all that is evil and destructive." They share some evil traits with her, especially the use of deceptive, tempting, speech, but also have evil traits that she does not. In the opening portrait they tempt the son in areas that she does not. They offer the opportunity to play the role of Sheol, regarded in ancient Near Eastern thought as a mythical power and not just a destination after death, rather than becoming its victim. They tempt him to be the oppressor rather than the oppressed and to wield power over people. They offer wealth of the kind that personified Wisdom offers later on. Moreover, they propose a "get-rich-quick" way of obtaining it. There is something similar in the portrait of the evil men in Proverbs 4:14–19. They lie awake at night thinking about how to oppress people and fund their lifestyle by wickedness and violence. It is often said that money, sex and power are the three great motivations to doing evil. The Forbidden Woman tempts the son in only one of these areas. The evil men tempt the son in the other two areas. The comment by Weeks that "What they offer is more tempting, but they offer it less temptingly"[12] than the Forbidden Woman is a subjective judgement with which not everyone might agree. It all depends on what someone finds most alluring. The prominence given to sexual temptation in the lessons is probably to be explained by the reason discussed above, the socio-theological significance of adultery within the Sinai Covenant.

Recognizing the importance of evil men in Proverbs 1–9 undermines the claim of some feminist interpreters[13] that there is in Proverbs an expression of a patriarchal mentality which sees woman as the quintessential "Other." Fox is right to reject this as a mind-set that is foreign to Proverbs in which "there is indeed an essential Other: evildoers (and some kinds of fool) of both sexes. . . . *This* Other is beyond influence and redemption, possessing an inverted and incorrigibly perverse set of values. Women are not the 'other' in such a radical sense."[14]

Personified Wisdom

Camp, another feminist scholar, is less disturbed than Yee is by the figure of the Forbidden Woman. This is because of Camp's appreciation of the literary factors at work in the Book of Proverbs. She does not see the figure as a stereotype of a real person or a class of persons but as an imaginary construct which is intended to provide a contrast to Woman Wisdom. She also says that it is necessary to recognize the "wisdom tradition's predilection for organizing and patterning perceptions in antithetical terms, especially its moral judgments of good and evil, and for depicting these judgments in vivid and memorable vignettes."[15] This makes the point that concentrating on the figure of the Forbidden Woman in isolation ignores the important fact that there is a balancing feminine figure in Proverbs 1–9, Woman Wisdom, who personifies all that is good and life-giving. The strict antithesis of Woman Wisdom in

---

[12] Weeks, *Instruction and Imagery*, 146.

[13] E.g., Maier, "Conflicting Attractions."

[14] Fox, *Proverbs 1–9*, 259 (italics original).

[15] Camp, *Wisdom and the Feminine*, 116–17.

Proverbs is Woman Folly, a personified figure who appears only in Proverbs 9:13–18. She, however, shares many of the characteristics of the Forbidden Woman. Like her, she is "loud" (9:13a; 7:11), lacks knowledge (9:13b; 5:6), invites men to secret meals (9:16–17; 7:15–20), and consorting with her leads to death and Sheol (9:18; 2:18; 5:5; 7:27). It seems that she is the Forbidden Woman in another guise.

The nature and origin of the personification of Wisdom as a female figure in Proverbs 1:20–33; 8:1–36; 9:1–6 has been the subject of extensive debate. Several foreign deities and mythological figures have been proposed as prototypes for this personified figure of Wisdom. We will survey some very briefly.

Kayatz[16] has argued that Ma'at was the prototype for the figure of personified Wisdom in Proverbs 8. Ma'at was the Egyptian goddess of justice/truth (which were a unified concept in ancient Egyptian thought). Fox[17] has critiqued this proposal. He points out that none of a list of characteristics shared by Ma'at and Woman Wisdom that Kayatz gives are characteristics exclusive to Ma'at. They are shared by other gods, and not only Egyptian ones. Although the concept of *ma'at* was deeply embedded in Egyptian religion, Ma'at as a goddess was never popular or well-known. There is no recorded speech by her. Unlike some other Egyptian deities, she was never well-known outside Egypt. She is not a credible prototype for the Israelite figure of Wisdom.

Knox[18] has drawn attention to similarities between Isis and the figure of Wisdom in Proverbs 8. Isis became the most popular goddess in the Near East in Hellenistic times. She was the giver of the first laws and principles and because she had great wisdom she was given the epithet *Sophia* (Wisdom). In several texts she proclaims her virtues and powers in "aretalogies" (hymns in praise of deities). These have some similarities with what Wisdom says of herself in Proverbs 8. Knox suggested that Proverbs 8 was composed as a response to the attractions of Isis worship. However, it was only in the late third century BCE that Hellenistic Isis religion began to spread widely and the aretalogies are not attested before the first century BCE. This is too late for it to have had an influence on even the latest redaction of the Book of Proverbs.

An unusual form of the Hebrew word "wisdom" occurs in Proverbs 1:20 and 9:1 (*khokmoth* instead of *khokmah*). Albright[19] argued that this is one of a

---

[16] Kayatz, *Studien zu Proverbien 1–9*.

[17] Fox, "World Order and Ma'at."

[18] Knox, "Divine Wisdom."

[19] Albright, "Goddess of Life and Wisdom" and "Some Canaanite–Phoenician Sources."

number of "Canaanitisms" in Proverbs 8 and 9. He suggested that a Canaanite goddess of wisdom lies behind the figure of Woman Wisdom in Proverbs. Whybray[20] has critiqued Albright's arguments in some detail. There are many fewer "Canaanitisms" in Proverbs 8 and 9 than Albright claimed and in particular the case for *khokmoth* being a Canaanite feminine singular form is inconclusive. Moreover, there is no evidence that there was a Canaanite goddess of wisdom and no Canaanite wisdom literature has survived. In addition, Fox[21] points out that Woman Wisdom in Proverbs shows none of the characteristics of the known Canaanite goddesses. In particular she is not sexually aggressive or desirable, nor does she represent the realm of vegetation and fertility.

In Proverbs 8:30a Woman Wisdom describes herself using the Hebrew word *amon*, which occurs only here in the Hebrew Bible. Its meaning is uncertain and puzzled even the earliest translators of the Hebrew Bible into other languages. The most common translations into English fall into two groups, "workman/craftsman" (e.g., ESV, NRSV) or "nursling/darling child" (e.g., KJV, REB). Clifford[22], like many modern scholars, regards the word as a loanword from the Akkadian *ummanu*. He argues that the figure of personified Wisdom in Proverbs 1–9 is derived from Babylonian mythology in which pre- and post-flood sages appear as the bringers of culture to the human race. The word *ummanu* is used of the post-flood sages. So, he argues, in Proverbs 8:30 Woman Wisdom should be understood as saying that at the creation of the world she stood beside the Creator "as a (heavenly) sage," who mediates to humans the knowledge they need in order to live in the way their Creator intends they should. This provides a plausible understanding of the role of Woman Wisdom in Proverbs 8:22–31, but it does not account for other aspects of personified Wisdom as portrayed in Proverbs 1–9 as a whole.

Personification is used widely as a literary device. It is fairly common in the Hebrew Bible, particularly in poetry. Human actions can be attributed to abstract qualities and inanimate entities. In Proverbs it is not limited to Wisdom and Folly. For example, it is applied to alcoholic drinks, "Wine is a mocker, strong drink a brawler" (20:1). In the case of Wisdom, however, personification is developed to a far greater degree than elsewhere in the Hebrew Bible. Sinnott sees it as a literary creation in which "Wisdom as a personified figure gives bodily form to an abstraction, with its attendant physical imagery, and links the senses with the understanding. The wisdom authors use this convention to convey to their audiences abstract knowledge in an attractive form."[23] This makes the point that the personification of

---

[20] Whybray, *Wisdom in Proverbs*, 83–87.

[21] Fox, *Proverbs 1–9*, 335.

[22] Clifford, *Proverbs*, 23–28.

[23] Sinnott, *Personification*, 21.

Wisdom was a powerful teaching tool, and raises the possibility that this functional motivation may have been the primary cause of it rather than the existence of any specific current prototype for the figure of Woman Wisdom.

Fox points out that "inchoate personification" of wisdom can be found a number of times in Proverbs. "Various metaphors speak about wisdom as if she were a woman without cohering into a consistent woman figure or governing the development of the passage as a whole."[24] He suggests that this "shows that the full-fledged personification of wisdom is an organic literary development in the Book of Proverbs."[25]

As noted above, Camp has considered the literary factors at work in the Book of Proverbs. She, too, thinks that the personified figure of Wisdom in Proverbs 1–9 is an original literary creation rather than an adaptation of some existing goddess or mythological figure. She argues that the figure is based on a variety of roles that Israelite women fulfilled in reality in daily life. On the basis of an examination of these roles that women are presented as fulfilling in narratives in the Hebrew Bible, Camp discerns two main recurrent depictions of the wife in ancient Israel. The first is that of the woman being the manager of the household, which is idealized in Proverbs 31:10–31. Although, in general, women did not have any explicitly recognized authority in the public sphere, the narratives suggest that when a woman was a good manager of her household it gave her some authority and power in the domestic realm. The story of Abigail in 2 Samuel 25:3–42 is a striking example of a wife whose authority in a large and wealthy household equals, or even exceeds, that of her husband. The second image is that of the wife who is able to exercise influence on the decisions which her husband makes in the areas where he has authority, which may include some in the public sphere. The narratives which present this image cover a range of dates and involve women of different social status in a variety of social situations. As a result, Camp endorses a statement made by Otwell that it seems "likely that the motif of the wise wife reflected a commonplace reality in ancient Israelite culture."[26]

All the female figures in the Book of Proverbs offer advice of some sort. They are all evaluated on whether their advice is good or bad, not on the basis of other traditional roles that women played in the culture of the time. This leads Camp to point out that, in Proverbs, "where mother imagery occurs, the connotation is neither biological nor theological but rather educational."[27] In a number of places the mother's teaching role in the family is referred to in

---

[24] Fox, *Proverbs 1–9*, 331.

[25] Fox, *Proverbs 1–9*, 332.

[26] Camp, *Wisdom and the Feminine*, 87. The quote is from Otwell, *And Sarah Laughed*, 108.

[27] Camp, *Wisdom and the Feminine*, 81–82.

parallel with that of the father, implying that they have equal authority in passing on wisdom to the children (1:8; 6:20; 10:1; 15:20; 23:22–25). A particularly striking case is that of King Lemuel receiving instruction from his mother (31:1–9). This has no parallel in the extant Egyptian wisdom literature. It is notable that no mother imagery is applied to Woman Wisdom in Proverbs. From this one might infer that the Israelite sages did consider that such imagery was essential for a female figure to have authority in the public sphere. In the light of this Camp says, "In this sense the woman is imaged in the book as a virtual equal of the man."[28] She argues that since it is the teaching role of the mother that contributes implicitly to the figure of Woman Wisdom this figure provides a literary model for women idealized as creative, authoritative individuals who are not defined primarily by their role in human reproduction.

To provide further support for her case Camp appeals to the two stories of the wise women of Tekoa (2 Sam 14:1–24) and Abel (2 Sam 20:14–22). She argues that they provide evidence of "a non-regular but recurrent leadership role for women in pre-monarchic Israel"[29] which, she suggests, probably continued in some form under the monarchy. The "great woman" of Shunem (2 Kgs 4:8–10; 8:1–6) may provide evidence of this. "Great woman" is a literal translation of 2 Kings 4:8b, as in the KJV. The ESV interprets this as referring to wealth rather than social status. Of course, the two would often go together. It is clear that the wise woman of Abel did have a leadership role and both wise women used proverbial language effectively to influence their hearers. In their words and actions both women exemplify the values of justice, well-being, life and "the heritage of the LORD." These are covenant values, and are also upheld by Wisdom (2:20–22; 8:18–21, 32–36; 22:22–23; 23:10–11). Camp does not think that these wise women were a model for the literary creation of Woman Wisdom, but does think that they provided a cultural context for Israel's theological appropriation of a female figure for personified Wisdom who makes claims such as those in Proverbs 8:14–16.

In Proverbs 1–9 the father's exhortations to his son to seek wisdom make frequent use of the language of human love. Wisdom is presented as desirable. This not, however, expressed in terms of physical beauty and attractiveness, but because of her moral qualities and the gifts that she bestows on those who find her. Camp notes similarities between the love language used of Wisdom in Proverbs and the language of the Song of Songs. She also notes that both books use the image of a strong, independent woman seeking her lover. These similarities between the two books leads her to point out that one of the genres of ancient Near Eastern love poetry is self-description. It is used by the woman in the Song of Songs to justify or defend herself (Song 1:5–6; 8:8–10)

---

[28] Camp, *Wisdom and the Feminine*, 82.

[29] Camp, *Wisdom and the Feminine*, 120.

or to provoke the attention and response of her lover (Song 2:1–2). Woman Wisdom's use of self-description in Proverbs 8:6–21 does not refer to physical beauty, but serves the same function as the self-descriptions in the Song of Songs. This suggests that aretalogies, such as those of Isis, are not the only possible Near Eastern source in which to seek the origins of this aspect of the personification of Wisdom in Proverbs 1–9. Camp concludes that, "In their experience of the poetry of human love, then, the Israelite readers found at least one way to appropriate the assertive words of Wisdom in Prov. 8."[30]

It is probable that the feminine grammatical gender of the Hebrew noun "wisdom" suggested the possibility of personification of wisdom as a Woman. It is significant that the Israelite sages saw this as not only possible, but also appropriate, on the basis of various roles fulfilled by women in their society. As a literary construct Woman Wisdom is able to combine different roles that might never be expected to be found together in one human person. In fact, in Proverbs 8 some of the claims of Wisdom go well beyond the purely human. And this, too, was not seen by the sages as inappropriate for a female figure. Camp argues that Woman Wisdom in Proverbs has more than a literary function. She is "an *authoritative religious symbol*, whose function it is to mediate between lived experience and a particular world view."[31] However, talk of Woman Wisdom as a "symbol" may obscure what seems to be an important function of Woman Wisdom in Proverbs. This is suggested by the use of the language of love and commitment to Wisdom, and probably of marriage (4:5–9).[32] By this means Wisdom is presented as more than a "mediator" between God and humans, but as the one who can bring humans into a personal relationship with God, their Creator. The Book of Proverbs cannot be regarded as a misogynist text when such a theologically important element in it is presented as the figure of a woman, based on roles fulfilled by women in Israelite society.

The "Capable" Woman

The Book of Proverbs ends with a poem about a woman who is described by the Hebrew word *chayil*. This word has a number of different meanings in the Hebrew Bible. Most often it has the meaning of "might, power" and is often used in a military context. When applied to an individual in this context it denotes him as being a great warrior, a "man of valor" (e.g., Naaman in 2 Kgs 5:1). It may have the meaning "wealth" (Deut 8:17–18) and so be used to describe someone as "wealthy" (2 Kgs 15:20). It can also mean "able, capable." This capability could be the result of might or wealth, but may arise from

---

[30] Camp, *Wisdom and the Feminine*, 103.

[31] Camp, *Wisdom and the Feminine*, 228 (italics original).

[32] See Lucas, *Proverbs*, 66.

spiritual and moral qualities, as it does in the case of men to whom Moses delegates some of his responsibilities (Exod 18:21). A person's capability in some area may make them the subject of esteem so that they are regarded as a "worthy" person. The only other woman in the Hebrew Bible, besides the subject of this poem, who is described as *chayil* is Ruth, and English versions take it to mean that she is a "worthy woman" (Ruth 3:11). The reason the term is applied to her is the way that she has supported and looked after her widowed mother-in-law Naomi (Ruth 2:11). The use of the term of Ruth is significant because it puts her on a level with her future husband, Naomi's kinsman, Boaz. When he is first introduced in the book he is described as "a man of *chayil*" (Ruth 2:1). English translations are divided over whether the phrase here means "wealthy man" (KJV, REB) or "worthy man" (ESV, NRSV). English translations are also divided over what the phrase "woman of *chayil*" means in Prov 31:10).

The poem in Proverbs 31:10–21 is an acrostic. Each of its twenty-two verses begins with a succeeding letter of the Hebrew alphabet, progressing from *aleph* to *taw*. This form may be used as an aid to memory. It may also be used in order to imply a sense of completeness, that the subject of the poem has been covered (at least notionally) from A to Z. The acrostic structure puts some limitations on the development of a thematic structure in the poem. Wolters argues that it does, in fact, have a three-fold structure typical of a hymn.

- An introduction in which the subject of praise is introduced (31:10–12).
- The body of the hymn in which the subject's praiseworthy attributes and deeds are described (31:13–27).
- The conclusion, which includes an exhortation to join in praise of the subject (31:28–31).

This, however, is not a liturgical hymn, but fits into the tradition of Hebrew heroic poetry.[33]

As well as occurring as a description of the woman at the beginning of the poem (31:10) the term *chayil* occurs as an *inclusio* in v. 29 in the phrase *'asu chayil*. Wolters notes that elsewhere this regularly means "to do valiantly" in a military context. Hence he translates the phrase *'eshet chayil* in v. 10 as "a valiant woman." In support of seeing this as a heroic poem he notes other words and phrases in it that have a military connotation. For example, *chayil* itself can mean "strength" and is given this meaning in Proverbs 31:3. It is notable that the woman's strength is referred to in vv. 17, 25, though using different words. The word which is translated as "gain" in v. 11b by the ESV and other English versions normally means "spoil, plunder," and the word

---

[33] Wolters, *Song*, 9–12.

translated as "food" in v. 15 usually refers to "prey." The poem concentrates on what the woman does, not her appearance or feelings. This is a feature of heroic poems. Wolters makes a plausible case for seeing this as a poem in the heroic mould that, unusually, praises a woman who behaves valiantly in the "battle of life" and copes with its demands successfully. It is certainly not a misogynist text.

Some readers[34] do see at least a hint of misogyny in the apparent condemnation of feminine charm and beauty in v. 30. However, here one needs to remember Camp's advice, quoted above, to recognize the use of vivid, antithetical comparisons as a feature of the wisdom literature and not to misunderstand them. In fact, this feature is a strong version of a common feature of Hebrew literature in general, which is a tendency to use hyperbole and, in particular, to say "x not y" when the context indicates that the actual sense is "x rather than y." So, the purpose of v. 30 is not to condemn feminine charm and beauty, but to make the point that they can be ephemeral and even deceptive and that the most important attribute a person can have is that of being someone "who fears the LORD." The fact that the father commends the charms of "the wife of your youth" to his son (5:19) in language which is similar to the erotic language of the Song of Songs shows that the sages in ancient Israel had no problem with feminine charm and beauty in themselves. Wolters argues that the poem in Proverbs 31:10–31 "constitutes a critique of the literature in praise of women which was prevalent in the ancient Near East." Whereas this was preoccupied with the physical charms of women from a purely erotic perspective, the song in Proverbs glorifies the woman's "good works which for all their earthliness are rooted in the fear of the LORD."[35]

The woman who is the subject of the poem works hard to make sure that her household is well-fed (31:14–15) and well-clothed (31:21). She produces the materials (31:13, 19) for the garments and furnishings which she makes (31:21–22). Some of these she sells (31:24) and uses the profits (31:18a) to establish a vineyard (31:16). She is generous to the poor (31:20) and a wise and kind teacher (31:26). Her husband trusts her as the manager of the household and business ventures (31:11) and she supports his place and role in the community (31:12, 23). Both he and her sons extol her all-surpassing capabilities as a valiant woman (31:29). It is not clear whether vv. 30–31 are a continuation of their praise or, as seems more likely, a comment by the poet.

As a result of a study of the history of the interpretation of this poem Wolters concludes, "Generally speaking, the following thesis can be defended: from the earliest extant records of biblical interpretation up to the Protestant Reformation of sixteenth-century Europe, the Song of the Valiant Woman was overwhelmingly understood in allegorical terms. Since then, it has usually

---

[34] E.g., Carmody, *Biblical Women*, 783.

[35] Wolters, *Song*, 13.

been interpreted 'literally' as the portrait of an exemplary woman."[36] In the allegorical interpretations the woman was variously taken to represent the Torah, the human soul, wisdom or the church. In recent decades scholars have generally taken a more nuanced approach to the interpretation of the poem than a simple non-literal (allegorical or symbolic) or literal division.

Since the Reformation many commentators have taken the stance expressed by Scott that the poem portrays "the virtues and accomplishments of an ideal wife and mother, mistress of the household of a prominent man."[37] One might be inclined to see this as an unattainable "ideal," but the author of the poem presents it as something that is rare but attainable (31;10, 29). It is of the nature of "ideals" that they seem somewhat superhuman. Yoder has compiled evidence to show that the woman in the poem "is arguably a composite of real women. She embodies no *one woman*, but rather the desired attributes and activities of *many*."[38] Feminist scholars bring fresh perspectives to the interpretation of the poem. Some regard it with ambivalence. Thus, Brenner says of the woman, "she lives to advance male interest and male well-being. In so doing, however, she ultimately subverts the male order by becoming its focal point and essential requisite. . . . The price of her implicit victory is explicit complicity with the system, . . . thus male dominance is preserved while being overcome."[39] Many feminists, however, choose to emphasize the positive portrait given in the poem, the woman's business acumen, strength, wisdom and independence. Camp, for example, argues that the woman completely overshadows her husband and that "the female image in Prov. 31 defines not only the home itself but also indicates the proper identity and character of the public domain as well, namely one that finds its bearing in home and family."[40] Some argue that the poem has been, and is, an empowering text for women. In Valler's view this has been the case in Jewish tradition because it "highlights the actuality of a liberal conception of woman and womanhood among the sages."[41] Despite being a domestic picture it has enabled people to think of women acting beyond that limited sphere. Masenya regards the picture of the woman in the poem as an ideal to be emulated by

---

[36] Wolters, *Song*, 60.

[37] Scott, *Proverbs*, 22.

[38] Yoder, "Woman of Substance," 446 (italics original). Her evidence is drawn from the Persian period, but she does not establish that it could not be just as valid for other periods of Judean history.

[39] Brenner, "Proverbs 1–9," 129.

[40] Camp, *Wisdom and the Feminine*, 92.

[41] Valler, "Who is *'eshet Chayil* in Rabbinic Literature?" 96–97.

Northern Sotho woman in Africa today, saying, "though the text does have oppressive elements, it also contains liberative or life-giving elements."[42]

Even though the woman in the poem is meant to be seen as a human person, she does share characteristics with personified Woman Wisdom. Both are more precious than jewels (8:11; 31:10) and bring wealth (8:18, 21; 31:11). Each is the mistress of a household (9:1; 31:15, 21, 27) with maidservants (9:3; 31:15). Both provide food (9:5; 31:14) and produce "fruit" (8:19; 31:16). They both impart wisdom (8:6–11; 31:26). Each has honour (8:18; 31:25, 28–31) and strength (8:14; 31:17, 25). The Capable Woman's works praise her in the city gates (31:31) and Woman Wisdom takes her stand and declares her worth in the gates (8:3). It does not follow, however, that the two figures are to be identified with one another. Rather, as Fox puts it, "The Woman of Strength is not a figure for wisdom. While Lady Wisdom personifies wisdom, the Woman of Strength *typifies* it."[43] In fact, in the poem the Capable Woman typifies wisdom because she *incarnates* some of its characteristics. She can be seen as filling out the picture of the "the wife of your youth" (5:18–19) and so as a strict antithesis of the Forbidden Woman, who incarnates some of the characteristics of Woman Folly (9:13–18), the antithesis of Woman Wisdom.

Scholars have often noted that the phrase "the fear of the LORD is the beginning of (instruction in) knowledge (wisdom)" occurs in significant places in the Book of Proverbs. It forms what is often called the "motto" of the book in Proverbs 1:7a. It occurs next in Proverbs 9:10, forming an *inclusio* which marks Proverbs 1–9 as a unit. Then it occurs in 15:33a, which is close to the middle of the book (the Masoretes mark Prov 16:7 as the middle of the book based on the number of verses) so binding the sentence literature with the lessons of Proverbs 1–9. Some also note that the phrase "the fear of the LORD" occurs in the commendation of the woman in Provervs 31:30 and see this as forming an *inclusio* for the whole book with Proverbs 1:7a. Camp, like a number of recent scholars, sees Proverbs 31:10–31 as forming an intentional "bracketing" of the Book of Proverbs since the figure of the woman in the poem resonates with the figure of Woman Wisdom in Proverbs 1–9.[44] Fox sees more than structural bracketing here, "The poem does not so much form an end-bracket to the book as a culmination and recapitulation, drawing together in the woman figure the virtues it teaches throughout the book."[45] In the Hebrew Bible "wisdom" refers to a variety of physical and intellectual skills. In the Book of Proverbs its meaning is more focused on what might be

---

[42] Masenya, "Proverbs 31:10–31," 63.

[43] Fox, *Proverbs 10–31*, 911.

[44] Camp, *Wisdom and the Feminine*, 179–208.

[45] Fox, *Proverbs 10–31*, 916.

described as "life-skill," the ability to cope in the best way possible with the demands of life.[46] The Capable Woman of the poem exemplifies this kind of wisdom very well. It is surely significant that the sages in ancient Israel were at ease in presenting this wisdom incarnated in a female form. This poem is not an expression of misogyny.

Reading the Book of Proverbs

Although the Book of Proverbs is a male-centred text, written and compiled by male sages for men, probably young men starting to make their own way in society, we've seen that some feminist scholars find within it messages that are affirming, even life enhancing, for women. Moreover, evidence has been presented to counter, hopefully convincingly, the claims that it is a misogynist text. Nevertheless, it is understandable that such an obviously male-centred text might be a stumbling-block to some readers, of both genders, especially for those who regard it as part of scripture. This is not a unique problem when it comes to reading and understanding texts. Any reader wishing to have a good understanding of a text has to expend some effort to understand what might be called the "world-view" of the author and the original intended readers. That worldview is influenced by many factors, such as historical setting, cultural situation, ethnicity, gender, language. Any or all of these may create a barrier to understanding for a reader who does not share that worldview. Christians, who accept the Bible as containing a revelation inspired by God, have particular reason to take this task seriously when reading the Bible. At the centre of their faith is the belief that God has been most fully revealed through incarnation in a particular person who lived in a particular historical and cultural situation, had a particular ethnicity and gender, and spoke a particular language. "The word (message) became flesh and dwelt among us" (John 1:14). To understand Jesus' teaching properly requires some understanding of the worldview he shared with his hearers. For example, for a first-time modern reader of the Gospels the meaning some of his parables is unclear because they presuppose an understanding of social customs that seem bizarre today, or historical and economic situations that were specific to Palestine at that time. What is true of Jesus and the Gospels is true of every book in the Bible. Readers who want to apply the message of these books to their lives and situations today have to face the hermeneutical task of what might be called "world-view transposition" of the message. This involves trying to understand the text's worldview, then imaging themselves in the place of the original addressee(s) in order to understand the message and only then consider how it might apply to their situation today in a different historical and cultural setting.

---

[46] Lucas, *Psalms*, 80–81.

A few examples may help here. It is arguable that Brenner's view, referred to above, that the poem of the Capable Woman is subversive of male dominance but only at the cost of complicity with the patriarchalism of the culture, is flawed because she has not put herself fully into the mind of the ancient Israelite young man to which the poem is addressed. Van Leeuwen, who seeks to do this, says, "If Israelite males, like men throughout history, were sinfully prone to demean women as 'the weaker sex,' the praise of woman here is designed to alter errant male perceptions of women. The heroic terms of strength usually applied to men are here given to a woman so her splendour and wisdom may be seen by all."[47] So, he sees it as more thoroughly subversive of patriarchy than Brenner does. Male readers of the poem need to consider what it might mean to be a Capable Man who "fears the LORD" and incarnates the attributes of wisdom presented in Proverbs. In this a first step would be to study Psalm 112, which is an acrostic poem about a man who "fears the LORD," and take that as a template for transposing into their modern situation. Significantly, it does not major on current "macho" male qualities, but on moral and spiritual qualities which are similar to those displayed by the Capable Woman of Proverbs. Women reading the father's warnings to his son about the Forbidden Woman can transpose it into their situation by replacing the honey-lipped woman by the sweet-talking man on the prowl for a one-night stand. A feminist scholar, Bellis, provides an example of how this might be done in "A Letter to My Daughters."[48] These examples are pointers to how the wisdom of the Book of Proverbs can be appropriated today as wisdom for the whole people of God, both women and men.

Abbreviations

AJSL	*American Journal of Semitic Languages and Literature*
ESV	English Standard Version
KJV	King James Version
JANESCU	*Journal of the Ancient Near Eastern Society of Columbia University*
JBL	*Journal of Biblical Literature*
JTS	*Journal of Theological Studies*
NRSV	New Revised Standard Version
REB	Revised English Bible
TynBul	*Tyndale Bulletin*
VTSup	Supplements to Vetus Testamentum

---

[47] Van Leeuwen, *Proverbs*, 264.

[48] Bellis, "Gender and Motives," 90–91.

WMANT   Wissenschaftliche Monographien zum Alten und Neuen Testament

Bibliography

Albright, W. F. "The Goddess of Life and Wisdom." *AJSL* 36 (1929) 258–94.

——— "Some Canaanite-Phoenician Sources of Hebrew Wisdom." In *Wisdom in Israel and the Ancient Near East: Presented to H.H. Rowley*, 1–15. Edited by M. Noth and D. W. Thomas. VTSup 3. Leiden: Brill, 1955.

Bellis, Alice Ogden. "The Gender and Motives of the Wisdom Teacher in Proverbs 7." In *Wisdom and Psalms*, 79–91. Edited by Athalya Brenner and Carole R. Fontaine. A Feminist Companion to the Bible (2nd series). Sheffield: Sheffield Academic Press, 1998.

Blenkinsopp, Joseph. "The Social Context of the 'Outsider Woman' in Proverbs 1–9." *Bib* 72 (1991) 457–73.

Boström, Gustav. *Proverbiastudien: Die Weisheit und das fremde Weib in Sprüche 1–9*. Lund: Gleerup, 1935.

Brenner, Athalya. "Proverbs 1–9: An F Voice?" In *On Gendering Texts*, 113–30. Edited by Athalya Brenner and F. van Dijk-Hemmes. Leiden: Brill, 1993.

Camp, Claudia. *Wisdom and the Feminine in the Book of Proverbs*. Sheffield: Almond, 1985.

Carmody, Denise L. *Biblical Women: Contemporary Reflections on Scriptural Texts*. New York: Crossroad, 1989.

Clifford, Richard J. *Proverbs*. The Old Testament Library. Louisville: Westminster John Knox, 1999.

Fox, Michael, V. *Proverbs 1–9*. Anchor Bible. New York: Doubleday, 2000.

——— *Proverbs 10–31*. Anchor Yale Bible. New Haven: Yale University Press, 2009.

——— "World Order and Ma'at: A Crooked Parallel." *JANESCU* 23 (1995) 37–48.

Hugenberger, Gordon P. *Marriage as a Covenant: A Study of Biblical Law and Ethics Governing Marriage Developed from Malachi*. VTSup, 52. Leiden: Brill, 1994.

Kayatz, Christa. *Studies zu Proverbien 1–9*. WMANT, 22. Neukirchen-Vluyn: Neukirchener Verlag, 1966.

Knox, Wilfred L. "The Divine Wisdom." *JTS* 38 (1937) 230–37.

Lucas, Ernest C. *Proverbs*. Two Horizons Old Testament Commentary. Grand Rapids: Eerdmans, 2015.

——— *The Psalms and Wisdom Literature*. Exploring the Old Testament, Volume 3. London: SPCK, 2003.

Maier, Christl. "Conflicting Attractions: Parental Wisdom and the 'Strange Woman' in Proverbs 1–9." In *A Feminist Companion to Wisdom Literature*, 92–108. Edited by Athalya Brenner. Sheffield: Sheffield Academic Press.

Masenya, M. "Proverbs 31:10–31 in a South African Context: A Reading for the Liberation of African (North Sotho) Women." *Semeia* 28 1997) 55–68.

Newsom, Carol A. "Woman and the Discourse of Patriarchal Wisdom: A Study of Proverbs 1–9." In *Gender and Difference in Ancient Israel*, 142–60. Edited by Peggy L. Day. Minneapolis: Fortress, 1998.

Otwell, J.H. *And Sarah Laughed: The Status of Women in the Old Testament*. Philadelphia: Westminster, 1977.

Scott, R.B.Y. *Proverbs, Ecclesiastes*. Anchor Bible. New York: Doubleday, 1965.

Sinnott, Alice M. *The Personification of Wisdom*. Aldershot: Ashgate, 2005.

Valler, S. "Who is *'eshet Chayil* in Rabbinic Literature?" In *A Feminist Companion to Wisdom Literature*, 85–97. Edited by Athalya Brenner. Sheffield: Sheffield Academic Press, 1995.

Van Leeuwen, Raymond C. *Proverbs*. New Interpreter's Bible, 5. Nashville: Abingdon, 1997.

Weeks, Stuart. *Instruction and Imagery in Proverbs 1–9*. Oxford: Oxford University Press, 2007.

Whybray, R.N. *Wisdom in Proverbs*. London: SCM, 1965.

Wolters, Al. *The Song of the Valiant Woman: Studies in the Interpretation of Proverbs 31:10–31*. Carlisle: Paternoster, 2001.

Wright, Christopher J.H. "The Israelite Household and the Decalogue: The Social Background and Significance of Some Commandments." *TynBul* 30 (1979) 101–24.

Yee, Gale A. "'I Have Perfumed My Bed with Myrrh': The Foreign Woman (*'iššâ zārâ*) in Proverbs 1–9." *JSOT* 43 (1989) 53–68.

Yoder, Christine Roy. "The Woman of Substance (אשת־חיל): A Socioeconomic Reading of Proverbs 31:10–31." *JBL* 122 (2003) 427–47.

CHAPTER 4

Women and Ministry, Once More

Stephen R. Holmes

Introduction

Ruth Gouldbourne's Whitley Lecture was devoted, at the request of the lecture committee, to considering "women and ministry in Baptist life," a subject she—even then—described herself as "peculiarly qualified" to address.[1] She lists the positive experiences she brings to the topic, before acknowledging that the story is "painful" as well as exciting,[2] although she remains silent about her own experiences of that pain. The lecture explored the mismatch between policy and practice through the twentieth century in the Baptist Union of Great Britain (BUGB): although Edith Gates became the first woman to be called to a Baptist pastorate in 1918, and the Council agreed in 1925 that "Baptists see no objection to women ministers,"[3] in practice for the next several decades women did not become ministers, because deaconesses could do all the same work, but for less money.[4] Again, a stained glass ceiling (surely un-Baptist in every way!) remained in place to the time the lecture was written. As Ruth writes, "We have had no women Superintendents, no woman has been head of a department of the Union,"[5] and "although there are no rules or regulations to prevent women from taking posts in association life, it just does not seem to happen somehow ... women are made unable to take responsibility or leadership."[6]

---

[1] Gouldbourne, *Reinventing the Wheel*, 5.

[2] Gouldbourne, *Reinventing the Wheel*, 6.

[3] Quoted in Gouldbourne, *Reinventing*, 27.

[4] Gouldbourne, *Reinventing*, 28, reports that there were five female ministers in 1965, but thirty-eight deaconesses serving as pastors of churches in "the mid–60s," 26. See also the telling quotation from Gwenyth Hubble, 28.

[5] Gouldbourne, *Reinventing the Wheel*, 29.

[6] Gouldbourne, *Reinventing the Wheel*, 29. This passage comes from Neil Hall's research, *Waiting in the Wings*, details of which are unknown.

I cannot, of course, bring any of the experience Ruth brought to the subject in her lecture; nor can I bring the trained historian's skill in narrating lived experience that she displays in enviable abundance there. Although I have been involved in some activism down the years, I suppose my main contribution in this area has been some interventions concerning theological arguments: what reasoning motivates those who oppose the ministry of women, whether through upholding formal rules, or through less formal frustration? Is this reasoning valid?

I base this essay on the claim that, while there is a pressing need for the activism to continue, there is only one interesting question left in the theological debate.[7] That question is: why, given it is now clear that the biblical text does not regard gender as a barrier to ministry in any direction,[8] did earlier readers of the text not see this? I will offer an answer in four sections: some very brief justification for the assumption underlying the question, and a sketch of some possible routes for looking for an answer; an argument that all contemporary readings of the biblical texts on gender and ministry are novel; a demonstration that, historically, the "better," and/or more counter-cultural, a reader, or a reading community, was, the more likely they were to regard gender as indifferent to ministerial office; and an exploration of some work in the history of ideas concerning gender which offers a plausible answer to the question posed. I will suggest that the lines of evidence taken together suggest that the reason that (most) earlier readers saw patriarchy in the biblical text was an inability to escape their cultural context enough to discern the plain teaching of that text.

The Failure of "Complementarianism"

I take it that, to any serious student of the debate, the failure of arguments for a male-only ministry is now evident, although I make no attempt to demonstrate that here, partly for reasons of space, and partly because rehearsing the arguments at any length would be no way to write in Ruth's honour. The story needs telling more completely (something I aspire to do in the not-too-distant future) but, quickly, over recent decades a series of

---

[7] This essay is admittedly programmatic, and represents not so much a detailed argument—although I trust I offer enough evidence of each point that a fair-minded reader will be convinced—but a prospectus for a longer piece that I intend to write when time allows.

[8] I phrase it like this in recognition of Schüssler Fiorenza's criticism of "androcentric scholarship [that] defines women as 'the other' . . . and reduces us to 'objects' of male scholarship," quoted in Gouldbourne, *Reinventing*, 37, citing Elizabeth Schüssler Fiorenza's "Breaking the Silence: Becoming Visible," in *Women Invisible in Theology and Church*, by Elizabeth Schüssler Fiorenza and Mary Collins (Concilium, 182. London: SCM, 1985), page not given.

different arguments have been offered for the position, each of which has been abandoned by its leading partisans when it was clearly untenable. The last candidate (pending the offering of another) fell in 2016. There is no plausible remaining argument for the position.

In roughly chronological terms, there was a narrow exegetical argument, based on an appeal to certain verses in 1 Corinthians 11 and 14, and 1 Timothy 2, and claiming that there was an evident biblical prohibition on female ministry on the basis of these verses. While there is still scholarly dispute over the proper interpretation of some of these texts, there is a broad consensus that they cannot bear this sort of weight. The second argument offered was a broader exegetical one, seeking to find a repeated pattern of gender relations in scripture—in essence a claim that the patriarchal order that the Pauline texts gestured to was a creational ordinance witnessed to by scripture. To simplify a fairly involved debate, this failed because the arguments either proved too little, or too much even for (most of) their proposers to stomach. Finally, a rather bizarre (to anyone who actually understood ecumenical doctrine) trinitarian argument leveraged a reading of 1 Corinthians 11:3 in an attempt to locate the desired patriarchal order not in creation, but in the eternal divine life of the Trinity. It did not take much historical knowledge to see that the doctrine of the Trinity being proposed was demonstrably anti-Nicene,[9] and so this argument also fails, assuming we desire to remain within the historic Christian church. This argument was played out dramatically in public in blog posts through the summer of 2016, and then again at the 2016 meeting of the Evangelical Theological Society.[10]

Of course, the arguments did not fall into neat historical periodizations—nothing ever does. The strange trinitarian argument is very recent: Kevin Giles, who is a veteran of these debates, suggests it was first offered by Knight in 1977, and I suppose him to be right.[11] The other two arguments demand more careful history, as we shall see. The first arose fairly gradually from around 1920, and increasingly from around 1960, as cultural assumptions about gender differences were questioned, and so the historical reading was found inadequate. The second goes deeper in a sense: assuming the normalcy of patriarchy, it was natural to try to read it into the Bible; we have to question whether the assumption of patriarchy was found in the Bible or brought to it, however, a question I shall discuss below.

---

[9] I made the argument in a journal article, Holmes "Classical Trinitarianism and Eternal Functional Subordination."

[10] Giles, *Rise and Fall*, 35–47.

[11] Giles, *Rise and Fall*, 9. In an earlier article with a similar title Knight did not develop his distinctive ideas about 1 Cor 11:3. See Knight, "New Testament Teaching," 86.

If all this is right, then, as I have indicated, the only question remaining is, why did earlier readers of the biblical text not see this? Several possible reasons would be plausible. It may, first, be that we are reading what is in effect a different Bible at some key point: text-critical advances, or better philology, may mean that there are earlier arguments we can now safely ignore, or new arguments that we now can construct that were not available to earlier readers. Both these things are in fact to some measure true: there are good text-critical reasons to be cautious about the authenticity of the, fairly crucial, verses 1 Corinthians 14:34–35,[12] and there are some genuine advances in our understanding of technical vocabulary that strengthen the case that various women Paul names in his letters were people he regarded as fellow ministers of the gospel.[13] While certainly part of a cumulative case, these shifts are not of themselves, however, weighty enough to explain the change.

Second, we might interrogate the proposed traditional readings, asking if they are indeed faithful repetitions of the exegetical moves of earlier generations of readers, or if they are in fact just as innovative as revisionist readings, albeit without reversing the final conclusion. This will be the burden of my second and third sections below. Finally, we might look for changes in cultural assumptions brought to scripture that change the natural reading of texts; this will be the burden of my fourth section, before I offer a conclusion.

The Novelty of "Complementarian" Readings of Scripture

In his *Lettres Provinciales*, Pascal mocks the French Dominicans and the French Jesuits of his day for agreeing to raise the use of a certain term ("le pouuoir prochain" ["proximate power"]) to be a test of orthodoxy, although they were both completely open about the fact that they meant entirely

---

[12] In the MS tradition there is both uncertainty as to whether these verses should be between vv. 33 and 36, or placed after v. 40 (where they are in the Western MS tradition), and a minor tradition of MSS lacking these verses entirely. Scribal marks in Codex Vaticanus and Codex Fuldensis indicate that the anonymous scribe of Vaticanus, and St Victor of Capua, who ordered the amendments to Fuldensis, had textual evidence that these verses were in some way difficult. There are several other arguments, leading probably the majority of recent New Testament scholars to conclude that the verses are an interpolation. For a summary of the evidence with extensive reference, see Payne, *Man and Woman, One in Christ*, 225–67. See particularly the list of recent scholars who have argued that the verses are an interpolation on text-critical grounds, 226–27 n.39.

[13] The key word here is συνεργος, which recent study has shown to be a formal title Paul uses for coworkers, and which is used of Euodia and Syntyche in Phil. 4:2–3 (and of Priscilla, Aquila, and Timothy in Rom. 16:3, 21, indicating the status of the title). See, e.g., Ellis, "Paul and His Co-Workers," esp. 440–41.

different things by that term.[14] In a similar way, we cannot accept that wildly variant readings of a biblical text agree just because they reach the same point of final application.

Given this, the fact that recent "complementarian" readings of certain texts come to the same conclusions as older readings does not mean they are interpreting the text in the same way. They may be, but the point can be investigated and meaningfully challenged. Andrew Bartlett makes the point forcibly, arguing, with a battery of citations, that

> The traditional majority Christian view was robustly patriarchal. Women were inferior to men, both in rank and in nature. Men were the leaders in all spheres of life. As compared with men, women were regarded as inherently defective, being less intelligent, more prone to sin and unfit for the kind of leadership which men were able to provide. They were not in God's image in the same full sense as men.[15]

He goes on to point out, first, that this view is incompatible with the New Testament teaching, and, second, that "few devout Christians, at least in Westernized countries, now hold the traditional view."[16] "Traditional" interpretation grounds patriarchy in the sure knowledge of male superiority, and finds in the biblical text applications of this generally-known principle; "complementarian" interpretation is forced to try to find some sort of gender differentiation in the biblical texts. It fails so to do. New "complementarian" interpretations have to establish from the texts that it is appropriate to differentiate ecclesial roles on grounds of gender; the older interpretations assumed that role differentiation on grounds of gender was a universal human norm, which biblical texts merely confirmed, applied to ecclesial roles also. The weight the texts had to carry to establish gendered ministry was incommensurably less under the traditional interpretations.[17] Recent "complementarian" readings have to ask far more of the few texts on which they rely, and it has become evident that those texts cannot give what the recent readings need from them.

The "narrow exegetical" argument I identified above fell fairly quickly on these grounds. It pointed to a small handful of texts that seemed to assert male-only ministry. As we shall see below, readings of these texts that predate the twentieth century assumed that some measure of imbalance in the natural capacities of the two sexes is an evident fact of experience, and so these texts

---

[14] Pascal, *Texte Primitif*, 8–11.

[15] Bartlett, *Men and Women in Christ*, 29.

[16] Bartlett, *Men and Women*, 33.

[17] In the next section I shall offer close readings of several older commentators, and this point will become very evident.

were, traditionally, read as being fairly uninteresting notes that a universal and common human order—patriarchy—should apply in the church as well. Absent the ability to assume that patriarchy was a given, they had to become justifications, not examples, of a male-only ministry. This move was radically innovative, and, it has clearly failed.

Similarly, the "broad exegetical" argument relied on a (more numerous) series of biblical texts that had traditionally been read as confirmatory examples of a "truth" already known, that there was a difference in capacity between the genders. The radical new reading, that probably only gained real traction in the 1960s,[18] sought to find in these texts sufficient evidence to establish a creational difference in gender roles. Clearly, the level of proof needed to establish something is rather higher than the level of proof needed to confirm something known from elsewhere; it is now clear that, whether the texts offered the latter or not, they most certainly could not offer the former.

I have commented already on the novelty of the strange "trinitarian" (in fact, Arian) argument concerning eternal functional subordination and its supposed implications for gender roles on the basis of 1 Corinthians 11:1–3, and on its failure. If what I have claimed above is right, then the point is now clear on the basis of the three preceding arguments: "complementarian" readings of scripture are novel repudiations of the tradition, not continuations of it.

I have made a series of claims about "traditional" readings; these now need to be substantiated. I am not going to detail the sad history of Christian patriarchy, citing writer after writer who asserted, often in the most offensive ways possible, the inferiority of women: that work has been done, and those vile opinions do not need repeating here. Rather, I want to turn to some of the most celebrated, or more counter-cultural, biblical interpreters in history, and show that their commitment to hearing biblical truth led them to struggle with, albeit generally unsuccessfully, their inherited patriarchy.

The Witness of History

From at least[19] the Reformation to the beginning of the twentieth century, there is a clear correlation in British and North American Christian history at

---

[18] That is, and as we shall see, an early modern writer might come to the text with the evident "fact" of male superiority before him, and so read the text in ways which supported that "fact;" locating the first reader to come to the text unconvinced of a prior account of gender capacities and found a justification for such an account within the text is harder, but the 1960s would be my best guess for his (almost inevitably . . .) historical location.

[19] I suspect that the point could be driven back into various biblicist reforming movements in the Middle Ages, but I have not done enough work yet to assert so in print.

least[20] between the extent to which a biblicist[21] movement sets itself against the prevailing culture, and its willingness to embrace the ministry of women. Put simply, movements which visibly value the Bible above cultural mores are more likely to be unconcerned about gender in their accounts of qualifications for ministry. While there are hints of this in Elizabethan Separatism, it is in the middle years of the seventeenth century that it becomes very obvious. Katherine Chidley rose to be a major advocate of Independency, a powerful controversialist, a church planter, a successful evangelist, and a political agitator on behalf of the Levellers.[22] Early Baptist churches were open to the teaching and prophetic ministry of women.[23] The Society of Friends, in their attempt to not merely recreate, but to live in the apostolic age, welcomed the ministry of women equally to that of men, and produced some remarkably powerful controversialists, notably Margaret Fell,[24] whose exegetical work informed Evangelical proponents of the ministry of women well into the nineteenth century.

The Independents and Baptists fairly soon embraced a degree of respectability, and accepted the patriarchal norms of their age, while the Quakers were stronger in the courage of their biblical convictions. With the dawning of the Evangelical Revival, however, patriarchy was once again subject to biblical critique. The influence of lay leaders such as the Countess of Huntingdon is well known, as is John Wesley's willingness to license female preachers. Wesley, it is true, based his (slowly won) openness to women preaching on the doctrine that God was performing an extraordinary work in Methodism, and so that more usual norms were suspended,[25] but nonetheless he encouraged women such as Sarah Crosby, Sarah Ryan, Mary Sewell, Grace Walton, Ann Cutler, and Mary Bosanquet-Fletcher to preach.

---

[20] Again, I suspect that the point is more general, but lack the data to demonstrate this adequately.

[21] That is Separatist, Puritan, or Evangelical.

[22] Her ODNB entry might thus far be the best introduction, though she deserves a far more extensive treatment that treats her as a Separatist theologian, not as a proto-socialist or a proto-feminist (both latter descriptions are true, but they visibly grow out of her theological convictions, and so cannot be the primary lenses to narrate her life and thought). Gentles, "Katherine Chidley."

[23] See Freeman, *Company of Women Preachers*.

[24] For the key primary text, see Fell, *Women's Speaking Justified*. For a helpful commentary, see Thickstun, "Writing the Spirit."

[25] See Chilcote, *John Wesley and the Women Preachers of Early Methodism*.

After Wesley's death Methodism fractured into Wesleyan and Primitive streams.[26] The Wesleyans sought respectability and embraced patriarchy, forbidding female preaching in 1803;[27] led by Hugh Bourne, the "Prims" were more adventurous. Bourne had benefitted personally from the ministry of Mary Bosanquet-Fletcher, and was committed to belief in the ministry of women and men indifferently.[28] He was a wheelwright by trade, and a Wesleyan Methodist lay preacher until, somewhat ironically, being expelled for disorderly evangelism in 1808. With William Clowes he founded the Primitive Methodist Connexion, which thrived in the UK until it reunited with the Wesleyans to form the current Methodist Church in 1932.[29] Bourne's tract defending the ministry of women is largely a remarkable example of plain-sense Bible reading, although it begins with a fairly classic Evangelical appeal to evangelistic success as proof of the appropriateness of a practice: "If . . . the Lord owns their [i.e., women who preach] labours by turning sinners to righteousness, we do not think it our duty to endeavour to hinder them . . ." (173)

Bourne then turns to Joel 2:28, quoted in Peter's Pentecost sermon in Acts: "sons and daughters shall prophesy." A word study on "*navi*" (prophet) leads Bourne to assert that "a prophet was simply one who was employed in the service of God" in various capacities, including preaching (174). He thinks his point is established, and turns to a series of objections which it seems had been raised in conversation by a friend; each is answered quickly by biblical

---

[26] There were several other smaller, or shorter-lived streams, most of which were at least as open as the Primitive Methodists to the ministry of women. These include the Independent Methodists, the Bible Christians, and the Magic Methodists (so-called because of charismatic/pentecostal tendencies), as well as other very small groups. There is evidence that the Magic Methodist preacher, Nancy Foden, influenced Bourne's thinking before the 1807 Mow Cop camp meeting that is generally regarded as the beginning of the Primitive Methodist tradition. See Graham, *Chosen by God*, 17–18.

[27] There were dissenting voices; e.g., Zachariah Taft, who was married to Mary Barritt (sometimes Barrett), a noted preacher, who had published her own *Memoirs of the Life of Mrs Mary Taft*. He published a defence of women's preaching in reply to a magazine article in 1809 (*Reply to An Article*), and then in the 1820s a series of biographical sketches of female preachers, as well as his *Scripture Doctrine of Women's Preaching*.

[28] He wrote a tract defending this position, *Remarks on the Ministry of Women*, in 1808. No copies are extant, but the text is reproduced in Walford, *Memoirs of the Life and Labours of Hugh Bourne*, 172–77. Further references to this text are parenthetical and in line to save a profusion of footnotes.

[29] The movement spread internationally, and the history is different in different places, but the story is generally of pan-Methodist reunion in the first half of the twentieth century.

example. God authorized Miriam, Deborah, and Huldah to be prophets. Anna in the temple prophesied, as did Mary and Elizabeth. Jesus sent the woman of Samaria to be an evangelist, and after his resurrection sent Mary to "preach Jesus and the resurrection . . . to the apostles themselves. Thus our Lord ordained her an apostle to the apostles, a preacher to the preachers, and an evangelist to the evangelists" (175).[30] The New Testament accounts of the apostolic church are replete with examples of women who prophesy, that is, preach, and/or who work as evangelists: Philip's daughters, Priscilla, Euodia and Syntyche (175). Paul gives instructions in 1 Corinthians 11:5 on how women are to dress when they preach; says Bourne, "This is rather decisive. He here lays down rules and regulations for this very thing . . ." (175).

Finally he turns to the question "Is not women's preaching interdicted by apostolic authority? 1 Cor. xiv. 34. 1 Tim. ii. 11." His response is rather beautifully blunt, and worth quoting extensively.

> It is rather harsh to suppose that an apostle interdicted what had been the practice of the church of God in all ages, what had been personally sanctioned by our Lord himself, and what even the same apostle had just been establishing by giving rules for it. 1 Cor. xi. 5,6,7. The question then, is, "What are we to understand by these scriptures?" I shall not endeavour to give you on this any opinion as my own; for having never studied them very closely, I could not in conscience do it. (175)[31]

The remainder of the tract is taken up with rebutting various objections.

Bourne's argument was simply to point to all the female prophets, preachers, and evangelists in scripture, to Jesus' own appointment of at least two of them, to Paul's instructions on how women should preach, as simply compelling evidence that this was a normal practice in the apostolic church, explicitly sanctioned by Jesus and the apostles. Given this, he is simply indifferent to the challenge texts: whatever they mean, they cannot forbid what was routine in the life of the earliest churches, and explicitly sanctioned by Jesus himself.

---

[30] I assume the repetition of Thomas Aquinas's title, "apostle to the apostles" is coincidental, as it seems almost inconceivable that Bourne read Aquinas, and it is hard to see a plausible chain of transmission. For the phrase in Aquinas, see his account of the three privileges given to Mary Magdalene in lecture 3 on the resurrection in his commentary on John, "Tertio officia apostolicum, immo facta est apostolorum apostola . . .," §2519.

[31] Bourne in Walford, *Memoirs of the Life and Labours of Hugh Bourne*, 176, goes on to suggest that he has been told that these texts speak of church order, and comments, "if women must ordain or set apart the men for the ministry, it would be usurping authority, for the greater would be blessed of the less." This is revealing, and I will return to it.

The denominational commitment to egalitarian ministry that Bourne bequeathed to the Primitive Methodists lasted into the middle of the nineteenth century, but not beyond. That said, the Wesleyan/Methodist influence is decisive for the next set of stories. The nineteenth-century holiness traditions, shaped by Phoebe Palmer, were virtually all open to the ministry of women and men indifferently. Palmer herself was a lifelong Methodist, who began her own, remarkable, preaching ministry in 1838 in her hometown of New York.[32] Her famous "shorter way to holiness" was based on the exhortation that "naked faith" in scripture promises was the heart of the matter: assurance came from believing the promises, not from any experience or feeling.[33] Lowrey suggests that in this context her approach to the Bible was proto-fundamentalist, moving away from Wesley's insistence on using reason and experience to make sense of the biblical text.[34]

History records that 25,000 people were converted under her ministry, and she spent four years promoting her ideas in the UK. Among her eighteen books one, *The Promise of the Father*, defends the ministry of women. She starts by acknowledging the propriety of normal gender divisions: "We believe woman has her legitimate sphere of action, which differs in most cases materially from that of man . . ." (1). That said, "facts show it is in the order of God that woman may occasionally be brought out of the ordinary sphere of action . . . the God of providence will enable her to meet the emergency with becoming dignity, wisdom, and womanly grace" (1–2). It is hard to tell whether she was sincere in these opening comments, given how forceful and pointed the remainder of the book is;[35] the "promise of the Father" of the title is Joel's prophecy that the Spirit will be poured out, and so both daughters and sons will prophesy, which Palmer also understands to mean preach. She offers many examples from Evangelical history of female preachers being used powerfully to bring salvation, but the heart of her argument is always exegetical; if much more expansive, it is not very different from Bourne's brief tract. Women's preaching and leadership was simply routine in the apostolic churches, and so should be in churches now; this is so evident from so many texts of scripture that, whatever a couple of verses in Paul might mean, they cannot be denying this reality.

---

[32] The best biography is probably still White, *Beauty of Holiness*.

[33] Lowrey, "Fork in the Wesleyan Road," offers a careful reading of Palmer's account of sanctification, and how it differs from Wesley. On Palmer's theology more generally, see Heath, *Naked Faith*.

[34] Lowrey, "Fork in the Wesleyan Road," 190–92.

[35] The occasional poetry, in particular, can be almost brutal. E.g., Palmer, *Promise of the Father*, 16: "Not she with traitorous kiss her Saviour stung; / Not she denied him with unholy tongue: / She, while apostles shrank, could danger brave, / Last at his cross, and earliest at his grave."

Palmer's holiness teaching inspired the birth of many new Christian movements, one being the Salvation Army. Like other holiness traditions, the Army has always had both male and female leaders and preachers. Catherine Booth wrote a defence of Palmer's ministry, which served as a defence of every woman's ministry, *Female Ministry; or, A Woman's Right to Preach the Gospel*.[36] The superscription of the book was Joel 2:28, and the argument followed Palmer's in large part. Booth, however, made no gestures towards conventional ideas of women's weakness or proper station: nurture, and particularly education into subservience, created the visible differences in capacity between the sexes, not nature—and certainly not providence. She recruited, trained, and deployed thousands of women as ministers of the gospel over the course of her life.[37]

Many other examples could be offered, but the point here is that, from the 1640s to 1900 or so, commitment to women's ministry was a distinctive of biblicist and counter-cultural traditions. Chidley, like other Separatists, risked her life to practice what she understood to be authentic New Testament Christianity; seventeenth-century Baptists and Quakers were, in different ways, attempting to model, or to be, the apostolic church. Bourne protested against the cultural compromises of Wesleyan Methodism in the name of a simple Bible Christianity. Palmer can be described as a proto-fundamentalist. Booth led a radically counter-cultural missional movement.

There are counterexamples, of course; the rise of the Brethren in the nineteenth century is one of the more obvious. But it seems abundantly clear from Anglophone Protestant history, at least, that, in general, the more a given movement rejected its culture and took its stand on the Bible, the more it was likely to welcome the ministry of women.

What of individual exegetes? The same point applies. For reasons of space, I will demonstrate this with a couple of examples only, John Calvin, who is without question one of the truly great biblical commentators in Christian history, and Matthew Henry, whose place as a preacher's commentator was once unchallenged, and is still fairly secure. I will look here only at commentary on the key verses that play in to debates about gender and ministry.[38]

---

[36] Booth, *Female Ministry*. The original edition was published in 1859. Booth, *Female Ministry*. The original edition was published in 1859.

[37] For a rapid summary of the work see Murdoch, "Female Ministry." Murdoch also makes some sobering historical points of the sort Ruth made in her Whitley Lecture: the theory did not always translate into practice.

[38] Calvin's surprisingly feminist commentary is visible elsewhere, for instance on Matt 19:9–10, where Jesus denies the general right of a man to divorce his wife. Calvin criticizes the horror of the disciples by pointing to the lot of married women, who had no right of divorce at all.

On 1 Corinthians 11:3, Calvin immediately offers a comparison with Galatians 3:28, acknowledging an apparent contradiction. He resolves this by making a distinction between "Christ's spiritual kingdom," in which there is no distinction of persons, and "external human society" in which "civil order" and "distinctions of honour" are necessary.[39] Therefore, he insists *coram Deo*, concerning spirituality and conscience, Christ is the head of man and woman alike (*absque discrimine*); "decorum" however demands inequality in society.

This interpretation informs his account of 1 Corinthians 14:34–35,[40] which text he first insists relates only to "what is becoming" in "a rightly-constituted assembly." That is, he believes that there will be contexts where it is necessary for a woman to speak, but in the ordinary course of things this should be forbidden. He accepts that there might be a degree of puzzlement as to why the "subjection" of women demanded by "the law" should result in a ban on speaking; his response is to insist that to teach is to take a superior position, and so logically incompatible with subjection. He defends the public subjection of women as simply common to human experience, but also something natural: female rule, he suggests, would be broken and deformed (*vitiosam turpemque esse gynaecocratian*).

Calvin makes the same points in interpreting 1 Timothy 2:11–15. Women should be quiet and not teach because God has committed the teaching office to men only. Examples such as Deborah do not overturn this because they represent extraordinary divine acts, which must be accepted as such, but which do not change the ordinary course of things. (This argument I take to be equivalent to the exception Calvin offered in his exposition of 1 Corinthians 14.) Teaching, Calvin suggests, is necessarily an exercise of authority, and so women are forbidden from teaching because women are "made by nature to obey." For this reason, he again suggests that female rule is "monstrous."

He finds support for this point as the text moves on to appeal to the creation narrative. Although the reference is merely to the order of creation, Calvin acknowledges that this appears weak (Christ came after John the Baptist, but was above him, he observes) and so reaches back into Genesis to find a better answer. The woman was created to be an "inferior help added to the man" (*viro addiderit adiumentum inferius*), and this demonstrates "the eternal and unbreakable appointment of God." Calvin imagines that Eve found freedom and joy in her submission before the fall, but the text insists that her servitude was made an imposition by the curse which followed the fall.[41]

---

[39] *Calvini Opera* (hereafter *CO*) XLIX (= *Corpus Reformatum* [hereafter *CR*] LXXVII, 474). (Translations from the Latin here and elsewhere are my own.)

[40] *CO* XLIX (= *CR* LXXVII) 532–34.

[41] *CO* LII (= *CR* LXXX) 275–79.

Calvin wrote his commentaries in the middle decades of the sixteenth century;[42] we could trace the interpretation history of these verses down through the years; if we did, we would merely find the same themes emerging repeatedly. One further example will serve to make the point: the famed Puritan commentary by Matthew Henry (1662–1714), which remains in print and is still used by many more conservative preachers to the present day.[43] Henry in fact died before completing the commentary, and the published comments on the Pauline texts were completed by others after his death, based in part on his notes; the commentary has been universally received as a whole, however, so this need not concern us.

When he addresses 1 Corinthians 11:3, the commentator is first concerned to clear up a potential christological misunderstanding, and then to stress that the apparent parallelism conceals real difference.[44] "Christ" here should be read not as the divine Logos, but as "Christ in his mediatorial character and glorified humanity." As such, he is both the "head of the whole human kind" and "has a superior." The concern here is both soteriological and trinitarian. The salvific union of believers with Christ as the head of the church is necessarily a union with the human nature, because it must (in the then-common federal theology) parallel the Adamic covenant in which Adam is the federal head of all humanity. The trinitarian concern is fairly simple: the three divine persons are co-equal, and so language of "headship" cannot meaningfully apply to the eternal triune relations.[45]

The commentary then turns to "the head of the woman is the man," and insists that the apparent parallel is potentially misleading: "The man is the head of the two sexes: not indeed with such dominion as Christ has over the kind or God has over the man Christ Jesus . . . ." Women should be in "subjection," it argues, because that "is the situation in which God has placed her," although it is not clear at this point whether this is understood as "placed" in creation, and so to do with a difference in nature, or "placed" by command. However, in the commentary on v. 8 the point is settled: woman was created lesser than man, although "superior to the other creatures here

---

[42] According to the author's prefaces the commentary on 1 Cor is dated 1546, and that on 1 Tim 1556.

[43] I am using a modern printing, but will refer to the commentary merely by textual references, as it may be found in many editions in print and online. M. Henry, *Commentary*.

[44] M. Henry, *Commentary*, on 1 Cor 11:1–16, §II. Quotations following are from this section.

[45] It will not surprise any theologically literate reader that Matthew Henry's commentary offers absolutely no support for the tedious and ill-informed modern arguments defending an incoherent mess that gets called "eternal functional subordination," and making claims about gender norms on the basis of that.

below," and so the subjection is a result of different natures. The rest of the discussion addresses the implied permission in the text for women to pray or prophesy, suggesting that "inspiration" might suspend certain natural orders.

This interpretation is confirmed in passing in the comments on 1 Corinthians 14, although most of the discussion is about the nature of teaching. The commentator asks rhetorically, "what is more indecent than for a woman to quit her rank, renounce the subordination of her sex . . .?" and insists that "The natural distinctions God has made, we should observe."[46] As in Calvin, we see appeals to a natural order, and to public decency.

The appeal to public decency is relatively straightforward: in a culture where gender norms prohibited public roles for women, the reputation of the gospel depended on a certain conformity to such norms. Calvin's distinction between the egalitarian "spiritual kingdom" of Christ and the patriarchal "public order" demonstrates this point. The natural order argument looks different: somehow our commentators assume that women are inescapably inferior in some sense to men, and so should properly submit. The reason given in the 1 Timothy text is, as Calvin notes, rather strange: order of creation does not ordinarily imply order of authority, after all, in the first chapter of Genesis, the placing of the creation of humanity last in order is clearly intended to emphasize the importance of humanity. However, neither commentator struggles with the assumption that women are in some ontological sense necessarily inferior to men, and that this natural difference justifies role differences.

This point is crucial. Both commentators assume a natural difference between men and women, and so find suggestions of a role difference simply plausible. Neither offers any argument that the natural difference is taught by scripture—Calvin's struggles with the creational appeal in 1 Timothy 2 demonstrate this clearly; he sees Paul making an exegetical argument for the natural difference he knows to be there, but sees also that the argument is unbearably weak; he never questions that the natural difference is there, however, only wondering how it should be defended.

If there is anything surprising here, it is Calvin's suggestion of an egalitarian "spiritual kingdom." I have noted before that Calvin is often surprisingly feminist in his biblical interpretation. I presume (given no other plausible explanation) that this is simply because he listened hard to the scriptural text, which denies the patriarchy of his culture (and ours). According to the texts, in Christ gender should cease to be an organizing category, and this is demonstrated in the accounts of female ministry in the New Testament epistles; Calvin was too good a reader not to see this, and too faithful an exegete to ignore it. His appeal to "decorum" as a reason to reject the inevitable implication rings rather hollow and is simply incompatible with his later defence of female subjection as natural, which is clearly based on a

---

[46] M. Henry, *Commentary*, on 1 Cor 14:34–35.

belief in a natural difference between women and men. Henry's *Commentary* is more consistent, assuming at each point that there is some constitutional inadequacy in the woman that makes her, whoever she may be, incapable of fulfilling certain roles in the church.

Apart from an interesting inconsistency in Calvin, then, we see that these two early modern commentators on the text assumed that to be female was to be deficiently human, and that the deficit here, whatever it may be, justified the barring of certain tasks—specifically, teaching and leadership—to women. We could spend considerable time in early modern biblical commentary and find this same point rehearsed again and again. Calvin, as an attentive reader of scripture, betrays an awareness that the Bible denies that women are deficiently human, and also denies by example that women are barred from various offices;[47] his response to this at his best is to invoke a merely sociological reason for the absence of female ministry—"decorum"—although elsewhere he surrenders to the assumptions of his culture.

We can see the same assumptions of female deficiency even in the defences of female ministry we considered above. After all his arguments, Bourne reads 1 Timothy 2 as denying the ability of a woman to ordain a man, since "the greater would be blessed of the less."[48] Whether she believed them or not, Palmer began her book on female ministry by paying lip-service, at least, to assumptions about the natural inferiority of women. Booth was more robust, insisting that differences were the result of nurture, not nature—her need to make this argument demonstrates that she was well aware of the prevailing assumption of natural differences, however. We need to ask where these assumptions about natural difference come from, and whether they have any basis in scripture or theology.

Cultural Assumptions about Sexual Difference

Thomas Laqueur has argued in his seminal book *Making Sex* that broadly in Western intellectual history a "one sex" model of humanity has been, fairly recently, replaced by the "two sex" model assumed by contemporary Western culture. In a "one sex" model, the natural difference between woman and man is not an innate difference of two different sexes, but due to a deficiency: women are imperfect males—or, to put it differently, men are properly human, women only deficiently so. In a "two sex" model women and men embody different but equal ways of being human.

Laqueur begins his account with a historical tale of male sexual violence told by a French physician in the eighteenth century. A young monk arrives at an inn, where he finds his hosts grieving the apparent death of their daughter,

---

[47] He is clear, e.g., that Junia is a female apostle.

[48] See n.31 above.

who is due to be buried the next day. They ask him to keep vigil over the body. He rapes the "dead" girl that night and flees; the funeral is interrupted by her awakening; she is restored to the family and is soon found to be pregnant. This case puzzled French physicians of the day, since they believed that the internal organs of the woman were the same as the external organs of the man, and that orgasm was necessary for both parties for pregnancy to occur; how could her sexual ecstasy have passed unnoticed? Eighty years later the same case was re-narrated by another physician to prove that the female orgasm was not necessary to conception.[49]

The first analysis is an example of the "one sex" model: there is a parallel between male and female anatomy; if male orgasm is necessary to conception, then so must female orgasm be. If male and female anatomy are parallel, however, it seems that one must be normative and the other deficient. For much of European intellectual history, that is, there was an unquestioned assumption that a woman was a deficient man. This was the import of the "one-sex" model.

The deep roots of the "one sex" model are in classical antiquity: Galen and Aristotle.[50] Debate continues on precisely what each author thought;[51] but the reception history seems fairly clear, and is summed up in Laqueur's account of a "one sex" model. Such an account claims that sex differences are disabilities. A woman is a disabled man. If one assumes this, then, in the face of an apparent exegetical suggestion that women are incapable of performing certain functions in the church, it is very easy for biblical interpreters to infer that this was due to the deficiencies of being female.

The significance of this observation is clear from the historical investigations above. Bourne assumes, and Palmer at least pays lip-service to, the assumption that to be female is to be lesser in some way than being male. Henry's *Commentary* finds a consistent line on gender differences and church office by stressing precisely this point. Calvin is such a good reader of scripture that he hears the biblical challenge to this point when it is made, but he elsewhere assumes the point nonetheless. These various readers were all conforming to the best scientific account of sexual differentiation their age had to offer, and so we should not be overly critical of their positions—but we must assert that the account of sexual differentiation they assumed is simply wrong, and so their exegesis stands in need of correction. This is as true of Hugh Bourne's strictures about ordination as it is of Henry's *Commentary*'s refusal of the ministry to women.

---

[49] Laqueur, *Making Sex*, 1–3.

[50] Laqueur, *Making Sex*, 25–33.

[51] See, e.g., D.M. Henry, "How Sexist is Aristotle's Developmental Biology?" and Connell, "Aristotle and Galen on Sex Difference and Reproduction."

I propose that this shift in cultural understanding of sex difference is an adequate answer to the question that is controlling this essay: if it is now clear that the New Testament does not debar women from any and every office and role in the church, why did earlier readers not see this? We may answer: because they were assuming a "one-sex" model, and so that women were in some sense deficiently human. In this they were drastically wrong, but they were also repeating the deep cultural assumptions of their day. Only a profound commitment to reject culture in favour of scripture, found in the Quakers, some early Baptists, the Primitive Methodists, Phoebe Palmer, and Catherine Booth, or a profound commitment to read and repeat the truth of scripture, found supremely in the examples I have been considering in John Calvin, could effectively challenge these deep cultural assumptions.

We now know, of course, that the "one sex" model was utterly wrong: women are women, not deficient men. God created us male and female, and pronounced the creation "very good." Our sex differences are not due to imperfect gestation; they are due to chromosomes.[52] With this recognition in place, the argument of this essay is now complete: several proposed exegetical arguments that would bar women from the preaching ministry have all failed. They have each failed because they asked texts that had been read on the assumption of female inferiority to demonstrate female inferiority, and none of the texts could do that. If readers in previous generations read the texts as barring women from the preaching ministry, that is because they wrongly assumed female inferiority, the best of them, like Calvin, saw this, and offered convoluted defenses of the status quo.

At the same time, biblicist movements that were aggressively determined to test every position by the one canon of scripture, and were uncaring of social mores, repeatedly came to the conclusion that scripture taught that God calls women and men indifferently to the preaching ministry, and to every role within the church. If (some, as we have seen repeatedly) earlier readers of the Bible could not see this clear teaching of scripture, it is only because they were letting pagan and erroneous accounts of gender control their reading. Biblically faithful exegesis will recognize and celebrate the ministry of women.

Bibliography

Aquinas, Thomas. "Tertio officia apostolicum, immo facta est apostolorum apostola . . ." *Sup. Evan. S. Ioan. Lect.* §2519.

Bartlett, Andrew. *Men and Women in Christ: Fresh Light from the Biblical Texts*. London: IVP, 2020.

---

[52] Of course, we must be cognizant in such discussions that there are people who are born intersex. There is not space here for a full consideration of this reality, but I do not think that this recognition changes the argument I am advancing.

Booth, Catherine. *Female Ministry; or, A Woman's Right to Preach the Gospel.* 2nd ed. London: Morgan & Chase, 1870.

Chilcote, Paul W. *John Wesley and the Women Preachers of Early Methodism.* American Theological Library Association Monograph Series, 25. Metuchen: Scarecrow Press, 1991.

Connell. Sophia M. "Aristotle and Galen on Sex Difference and Reproduction: A New Approach to an Ancient Rivalry." *Studies in History and Philosophy of Science* 31.3 (2000) 405–27.

Ellis, E. Earle. "Paul and His Co-Workers." *New Testament Studies* 17.4 (1970) 437–52.

Fell. Margaret. *Women's Speaking Justified and Other Pamphlets.* Edited by Jane Donawerth and Rebecca M. Lush. Binghamton: Centre for Medieval & Early Renaissance Studies, 2018.

Freeman, Curtis W. *A Company of Women Preachers: Baptist Prophetesses in Seventeenth-Century England.* Waco: Baylor University Press, 2011.

Gentles, Ian J. "Katherine Chidley (fl. 1616–1653)." ODNBO.

Giles, Kevin G. *The Rise and Fall of the Complementarian Doctrine of the Trinity.* Eugene: Cascade, 2017.

Gouldbourne, Ruth M.B. *Reinventing the Wheel: Women and Ministry in Baptist Life.* The Whitley Lecture, 1997–1998. Oxford: Whitley Publications, 1997.

Graham, E. Dorothy. "Chosen by God: The female itinerants of early Primitive Methodism." PhD diss., University of Birmingham 1986.

Heath, Elaine A. *Naked Faith: The Mystical Theology of Phoebe Palmer.* Cambridge: James Clarke, 2009.

Henry, Matthew. *Commentary on the Whole Bible.* 6 volumes. Grand Rapids: Hendrickson, 1991

Henry. Devin M. "How Sexist is Aristotle's Developmental Biology?" *Phronesis* 52.3 (2007) 251–69.

Holmes, Stephen R. "Classical Trinitarianism and Eternal Functional Subordination: Some historical and dogmatic reflections" *Scottish Bulletin of Evangelical Theology* 35.1 (2007) 90–104.

Knight, George W. "The New Testament Teaching on the Role Relationship of Male and Female with Special Reference to the Teaching/Ruling Functions in the Church." *Journal of the Evangelical Theological Society* 18.2 (1975) 81–91.

―――. *The New Testament Teaching on the Role Relationships of Men and Women.* Grand Rapids: Baker, 1977.

Laqueur, Thomas W. *Making Sex: Body and Gender from the Greeks to Freud.* Cambridge: Harvard University Press, 1990.

Lowrey. Kevin T. "A Fork in the Wesleyan Road: Phoebe Palmer and the Appropriation of Christian Perfection." *Wesleyan Theological Journal* 36.2 (2001) 187–222.

Murdoch, Norman H. "Female Ministry in the Thought and Work of Catherine Booth." *Church History* 53.3 (1984) 348–62.

Palmer, Phoebe. *The Promise of the Father; or, A Neglected Speciality of the Last Days*... Boston: Henry V. Degan, 1859.

Pascal, Blaise. *Texte Primitif des Lettres Provinciales.* Paris: Hachette, 1867.

Payne, Philip B. *Man and Woman, One in Christ: An Exegetical and Theological Study of Paul's Letters.* Grand Rapids: Zondervan, 2009.

Taft, Mary. *Memoirs of the Life of Mrs. Mary Taft; formerly Mrs Barritt, written by herself, with a portrait.* London: J. Stevens, 1827.

Taft, Zacharias. *A Reply to an Article Inserted in the Methodist Magazine, for August 1809, entitled Thoughts on Women's Preaching.* Leeds: printed at the Bible-Office by G. Wilson, 1809.

Taft, Zachariah [sic]. *The Scripture Doctrine of Women's Preaching: Stated and Examined.* York: printed for the author by R. and J. Richardson, 1826.

Taft, Zechariah [sic]. *Biographical Sketches of the Lives and Public Ministry of Various Holy Women* ... 1825–27. Reprint. 2 vols. Peterborough: Methodist Publishing House, 1992.

Thickstun, Margaret Olofson. "Writing the Spirit: Margaret Fell's Feminist Critique of Pauline Theology." *Journal of the American Academy of Religion* LXIII.2 (1995) 269–79.

Walford, J. ed. *Memoirs of the Life and Labours of the Late Venerable Hugh Bourne.* Edited by ed. W. Antcliff. Cambridge: Cambridge University Press, 2011.

White. Charles Edward. *The Beauty of Holiness: Phoebe Palmer as Theologian, Revivalist, Feminist, and Humanitarian.* Grand Rapids: Francis Asbury Press, 1986.

CHAPTER 5

"Co-operation Not Separation:" British Baptist Women and Suffrage

Karen E. Smith

Among the most significant events in modern British history was the reform of the electoral system when the "Representation of the People Act" was passed by Parliament in 1918. This reform extended the right to vote, to men aged over twenty-one, whether or not they owned property, and to women aged over thirty who resided in a constituency or occupied land or premises with a rateable value above £5, or whose husbands did. It also extended the local government franchise to include women aged over twenty-one on the same terms as men. Ten years later, in 1928, the "Representation of the People (Equal Franchise) Act" granted the right to vote to all women aged over twenty-one, regardless of any property qualification.[1] The story of the long journey of the campaign for women's enfranchisement has been described by Elizabeth Crawford as an effort to trace a journey "not only into citizenship but also into a society which that citizenship has progressively feminized."[2] Crawford's study of this grand cause has primarily focused on the work of suffrage societies—often categorized as "militant" and "nonmilitant"—and viewed within a social and political context. While these terms help define the action of some people within the group, they do not take into account other motivations for involvement in the suffrage cause.

In a study that examined the role of theology in the suffrage movement, which focused primarily on the Anglican organization, the Church League for Women's Suffrage (CLWS), which was formed in 1909, Robert Sanders demonstrates how the distinction between "religion" and "politics" easily collapsed when suffrage is also seen as a spiritual struggle. Noting theological themes such as the incarnation and the realization of the kingdom of God, combined with an emphasis on mission and evangelism, Saunders claims that the CLWS provided a new way of thinking about the roles of women and men. In fact, he argues that churches did not simply respond to "changing

---

[1] "UK Parliament website."

[2] Crawford, *Reference Guide*, ix.

ideas about sex and gender," in society; rather, they were themselves "sources of new thinking about the roles of men and women."[3]

The CLWS was, of course, the first of other religious groups—Catholic, Jewish, and Free Church—that formed to promote the cause of women's suffrage. The Free Church League for Women's Suffrage (FCLWS) that organized in 1910, stressed that it stood for the advocacy of enfranchisement of women on the same basis as men. Membership was open to men and women of Free Church principles and they claimed that their "methods" were religious and educational.[4] To promote their cause, the FCLWS published a newspaper, the *Free Church Suffrage Times* (*FCST*) between 1913 and 1915 before changing the name to the *Coming Day* (later the *New Day*) between 1916 and 1920.

From the beginning some Baptist men and women supported the FCLWS. However, for the most part, Baptists in England do not appear to have joined or helped to organize Free Church Suffrage Groups. This seeming lack of involvement may have led to Ernest Payne's conclusion that Baptist churches "generally showed no inclination to welcome or even to take seriously the claim for women's suffrage."[5] More recently, Colin Cartwright has noted the involvement of Baptist women and men in the movement for the enfranchisement of women, but still maintained that their voices were "muted" and suggested that their involvement was part of a rise in "spiritual militancy."[6] Yet, a closer look at Baptist life tells a different story. For while Baptist membership in suffrage groups may have been limited, many Baptists were in effect not only very actively engaged in seeking to promote greater opportunities for women to serve, but they also promoted woman's suffrage, albeit through established denominational organizations. In doing so, the women worked with and gained the support of men within the denomination. Indeed, noting the work of Baptist women and men together through the denomination, in 1913 the *FCST* commented approvingly,

> This is as it should be. We suffragists believe that it is to the advantage of our common humanity that as far as possible the attack on evil should be made by our united forces. It is by co-operation, not separation, that real progress will be made.[7]

---

[3] Saunders, "Great and Holy War," 1475.

[4] Crawford, "Free Church League for Women's Suffrage," 232.

[5] Payne, *Baptist Union*, 151.

[6] Cartwright, "'Enfranchisement of Baptist Women'?".

[7] *FCST* 1 July 1913, 5.

Over the last thirty years, while serving as a pastor and a teacher, Ruth Gouldbourne has drawn attention to the need to reflect deeply on issues of context and theology within the church, and she has encouraged Baptists to remember and celebrate the long but often "hidden history" of Baptist women in Britain.[8] She has also worked within the denomination in the service of Christ, and, in so doing, she has demonstrated the importance of working cooperatively with others. In this volume that seeks to honour Ruth, and to give thanks for her scholarship and ministry, this essay will seek to examine the way that, by working cooperatively within the denomination, some earlier Baptists contributed to the full enfranchisement of women. After a brief overview of both the social context in which the suffrage movement was born, as well as the theological underpinning for shared life together among Baptists, this essay will argue that far from being silent, many Baptists cooperated together to encourage greater involvement of women in society and in the church in general, and more specifically, to give women the right to vote.

The Issue of Female Enfranchisement in Britain: The Changing Political and Social Context

A study of the development of women's suffrage within British society has suggested that while even in the eighteenth century some women may have considered themselves deserving of enfranchisement, "the development of enfranchisement as a goal—and increasingly as the ultimate mark of individuation and public recognition of women—took place slowly in the nineteenth century and must be seen in context as emerging from a period of hotly contested parliamentary reforms."[9]

The first petition for women's suffrage presented to Parliament in 1832 by Henry Hunt, MP, was by Mary Smith of Stanmore in Yorkshire, and argued that "every unmarried female, possessing the necessary pecuniary qualifications should be entitled to vote for members of parliament (*sic*)."[10] (At this point, of course, universal suffrage was not accepted even for men.) Harriet Taylor Mill's essay, *The Enfranchisement of Women*, written perhaps in collaboration

---

[8] Gouldbourne, *Reinventing the Wheel*, 31–45.

[9] Chalus and Montgomery, "Women and Politics," 218.

[10] Kathryn Gleadle, *The Early Feminists: Radical Unitarians and the Emergence of the Women's Rights Movement, 1831–51* (Basingstoke: Palgrave Macmillan, 1995), 71, cited in Chalus and Montgomery, "Women and Politics," 218; and Anon., "Orator Hunt and the First Suffrage Petition."

with her husband, John Stuart Mill, was published in 1851.[11] After her death in 1858, John Stuart Mill presented a petition to Parliament for woman's suffrage in 1866 and in 1869 he published his now famous treatise, *The Subjection of Women*. From this time on until it was granted, woman's suffrage would become "a perennial, if at times intractable, parliamentary problem."[12]

While political reforms were important, there were also other issues which affected the changing attitudes toward the vote for women. Practically, in the nineteenth century, an emphasis on education and the growth of industry opened new doors of opportunity. Some women went to university and training colleges and prepared to be teachers, nurses, doctors, and accountants. Others became authors and illustrators as they contributed to a burgeoning number of newspapers and magazines. As industry developed, women developed skills as glove, hat and corset makers, lace makers, weavers, clay workers, house and kitchen maids, paper makers, pin makers and a host of other jobs.[13] In short, with the changing social and economic context, there was not only more opportunity for, but also a growing acceptance of, women working outside the home.

The home, of course, was still a prominent feature of the Victorian era. Among Nonconformists in general, and for Baptists in particular, it appears that even as education and work opened up new vistas for women, the Puritan ideal of the home continued to be promoted from the pulpit and in religious publications.[14] At the same time, in the nineteenth century Baptist women gradually found opportunities for service outside the domestic sphere through involvement in mission work, social reform and philanthropic activities. Many were active in societies which formed to help the poor, widows, orphans and other disadvantaged people. Seeing alcoholism as a major cause of social ills, Baptist women also had a prominent place in the temperance movement.

Reflecting on the development of the contribution of Baptist women within this wider context, it is notable that there are two historical parallels between the Baptist emphasis on mission and evangelism, and the growing efforts to recognize the contributions of women. In 1792, William Carey wrote his *Enquiry into the Obligations of Christians to use Means for the Conversion of the Heathen*, which sparked the growth of a world mission effort and, in that same year, Mary Wollstonecraft published her remarkable pamphlet on the *Vindication of the Rights of Women*. Moreover, around the

---

[11] For a discussion of the similarity between the ideas found in her work and the later publication of *The Subjection of Women* by her husband, see Miller, "Harriet Taylor Mill."

[12] Chalus and Montgomery, "Women and Politics," 219.

[13] Ward, *Female Occupations*.

[14] See Smith, "Baptists at Home," 101–22, and "Nonconformists, the Home and Family Life," 285–304.

same time that J.S. Mill was pressing for greater freedom for women in 1866, Baptist women in 1867 organized the Ladies Association for the Support of Zenana Work and Bible Women in India (the name changed to The Baptist Zenana Mission or BZM in 1897) which—until it was amalgamated with the Baptist Missionary Society (BMS) in 1914—was successfully run almost entirely by Baptist women. To note these parallels between Baptist mission efforts and the moves within secular culture for the rights of women is not, of course, to suggest that Baptist women were directly influenced by the writings of Wollstonecraft or Mills. However, it is to highlight the fact that as the issue of the rights of women was being discussed in society more widely, so Baptist women were taking an active role in mission work and seeking societal reform. Their involvement in these activities, especially in the temperance movement, led many women and men to reflect on the need for woman's suffrage in order to be able to bring about social change. Moreover, since they were taxed on an equal basis with men, many women argued that taxation and representation go together and therefore women should be allowed to vote.

As women began to take on more roles within society as a whole, in the context of church life, often they were still restricted by the perceived scriptural injunctions that women should remain silent in the church and that men were to be the head of the household. The use of religious mandates to maintain societal order and to silence women in the male dominated church and society, has led some scholars to suggest that women were at the very least victims of a Puritanical emphasis on "female subordination" or, worse still, they were "passive agents of a repressive code."[15] Yet, to view women in this way seems to treat religious belief as a matter of tradition or an accepted code of conduct, and neglects other theological and spiritual motivations which may have shaped the response of women in the church. Moreover, for Baptist men and women it omits the important emphasis on cooperation together within covenant community.

Consenting to "Walk Together":
Covenant Life as the Foundation for Cooperation

At the heart of Baptist life is the understanding that the church is made up of men and women who have been called by God to be in relationship with one another and with God. While for women the opportunities to speak publicly were limited, their voices were never silent.[16] In fact, when they emerged in the seventeenth century, Baptists were castigated by their opponents for

---

[15] Davidoff and Hall, *Family Fortunes*, 114–18; cf. Saunders, "Great and Holy War," 1474.

[16] For information on seventeenth-century Baptist women, see Smith, "Holy Living and Holy Dying."

allowing "swarmes . . . of all sorts of illiterate mechanic (*sic.*) Preachers, yea of Women and Boy Preachers."[17] As evidence among others, a lace-woman, Mrs Attaway, was said to have been speaking publicly.[18] Whether or not Mrs Attaway or members of the congregation would have described her as a preacher is debatable. However, there is evidence that during the period of the Commonwealth, there were a number of women who were associated with the Fifth Monarchy Movement who openly spoke out when they believed that they had a "a word of prophecy." After the restoration in 1660, Curtis Freeman has claimed that women no longer spoke of prophecies, which suggests that their original urgent calls for change may have been related to political as well as theological issues. Moreover, Freeman suggests that as "the Baptist movement became organized and institutionalized many egalitarian expressions of the early days dissipated."[19] While this may have been true in terms of opportunities for public preaching or "prophesying," evidence suggests that women did continue to take part in congregational life. In fact, while statistics are very difficult to assess, arguably, women were in the majority in seventeenth-century Baptist communities of faith.

Exploring the reasons for the continued appeal of Baptist life to women, Rachel Adcock has suggested that women who were "seeking greater liberty and purity of worship" were attracted by congregational order.[20] This may be true; however, while freedom of speech and conscience were important to early Baptists, there is no evidence to suggest that women were part of Baptist congregations simply because they were seeking opportunities for them to preach or pray publicly. Rather, what may have been more important to both men and women was the fact that as descendants of the Puritan Separatist tradition, Baptists believed that the church was a "gathered" community of faith made up of men and women who had been brought together by God to worship and serve.

Their commitment to work together may be found in covenant agreements that stressed the need for cooperation with one another. Both men and women signed or made their mark on the covenant agreements which pledged holiness of life, as well as a firm commitment to bear with one another's weaknesses, failings and infirmities as well as pledging to meet together for worship and to support the minister. Women were active in church life and gave spiritual and financial support, even at times using their homes as "conventicles" or meeting places for congregational worship.

---

[17] Edwards, *Gangraena*, 29 and "Epistle Dedicatory," n.p.

[18] Edwards, *Gangraena*, 30–31.

[19] Freeman, *Company of Women Preachers*, 39, and "Visionary Women Among Early Baptists."

[20] Adcock, *Baptist Women's Writings*, 14.

Of course, while they emphasized "life together" in a "gathered" community, Baptist women and men did not share equally in the life of the church. In many congregations, women were expected to "keep silent" in worship and when they were allowed to speak the conditions were often prescribed. For instance, the *Broadmead Records* first mention a deaconess in 1662 and then indicate that in 1678/9 deaconesses were recognized in the church. However, they had to be sixty years of age and also agree not to remarry before they were "set apart by fasting and prayer to speak a word to their souls, as occasion requires, for support or consolation to build them up in a spiritual lively faith in Jesus Christ."[21]

With the Act of Toleration in 1689, Baptists, as well as other Dissenters, were given the freedom to worship, though they were not given civil equality and remained, in effect, second class citizens until the Test and Corporations Acts were repealed in 1828. Still, Baptist congregations continued to flourish and women played their part in congregational life. This is not to deny that the restrictive Puritan model of the "ideal woman" and the cultural norm of women being relegated to the home and their faith to the private sphere were often proclaimed from pulpits. Yet, Baptist women found ways to express their faith. They wrote hymns and poems, taught Sunday school, and developed new approaches to education, as well as contributing to social and philanthropic causes.

When the Particular Baptist Society for the Propagation of the Gospel was formed in 1792 (later named the Baptist Missionary Society) women were involved in the mission cause, though not always recognized for their work.[22] Women who were serving in BMS mission stations were not appointed and paid a salary as missionaries, but were there as the wives of the men who were the appointed missionaries. The BMS was also wary of appointing single women to the mission field. So, when an appeal came to British Baptist women to send women to minister to women who were secluded in zenanas in India, in 1867 the Ladies' Association for the Support of Zenana Work and Bible Women in India was organized (the name changed to The Baptist Zenana Mission [BZM] in 1897).[23] The BZM was run by women and proved to be an important way for them to use their gifts in the service of Christ. While it was, in effect, a separate organization to the BMS, they cooperated with the BMS until they were amalgamated as an auxiliary organization of the BMS in 1914. Women also took an active part in social reforms within the community, and by 1890, the deaconess movement—which gave many

---

[21] Hayden, *Records of the Church of Christ*, 51, 208; cf. Underhill, *Records of the Church of Christ*, 397–98.

[22] See Smith, "Role of Women in Early Baptist Missions."

[23] See Smith, "Women in Cultural Captivity," 105.

women a recognized sphere of service within the denomination—was officially established.²⁴

Acknowledging the fine work that women were doing through the BZM, it is not surprising that in 1908 when J.H. Shakespeare, General Secretary of the Baptist Union of Great Britain from 1898–1924, wanted to create a sustentation fund to provide financial support for ministry, he realized that he needed the support and fundraising skills of the women. Hence, at his suggestion, another women's group, named the Baptist Women's League (BWL), was formed.²⁵

Working within denominational organizations like the BZM and the BWL throughout the nineteenth and early twentieth centuries, Baptist women confidently sought to use their gifts to work for change. While female suffrage was never openly stated as a goal of these movements, many women could readily see how "having the vote" could provide them with the opportunity help change society and therefore fulfill their service for Christ. However, it seems that some Baptist women did not feel they needed to form a separate organization in order to work for suffrage. Rather, their focus was on service. As Margaret Hardy, a member of Florence Road Baptist Church and community leader in Brighton, claimed in 1913, "The Woman's Movement is a religious movement, it is the expression of desire in the heart of woman to serve her day and generation with her highest powers."²⁶

The pattern of women having opportunities to serve in organizations which were recognized under a denominational "umbrella" could be seen as a way that men were able to keep a measure of control (or at least oversight) over the work, while women adhered to the role of the "submissive woman." However, a closer examination of the lives of Baptist women seems to tell a different story. Indeed, far from ignoring the issue of suffrage or choosing to remain silent while others spoke out, it may be argued that Baptist women addressed issues of inequality, though often in ways that would not threaten the male-

---

²⁴ Randall, *English Baptists*, 44; and Bowers, "For God and the People," 473.

²⁵ For a discussion of Shakespeare's support for Baptist women, see Smith, "Forgotten Sisters," 178; and BU Council report year ending 1911, 42. Angus Library, Regent's Park College, Oxford.

²⁶ *FCST* 1 November 1913, 77. Margaret Hardy, MBE, JP (1874–1954), was elected in 1928 as a councilor for the Borough of Brighton and in 1933 she was elected as the first female Mayor of Brighton. She was a member of the Florence Road Baptist Church where she taught Sunday school and served as president of the local Sunday School Union. In 1920 she served as the national president for the BWL. In WWI she volunteered to go to France as part of the YMCA Women's Auxiliary and worked long hours offering respite to soldiers with intellectual, social, moral and spiritual needs. In 1922 she served a year as the President of the National Free Church Women's Council. In the same year she became a magistrate. Robertson, "Biographical Sketch of Margaret Hardy," n.p.

dominated hierarchal structure. By using the existing structures, women tried to cooperate with men who were Baptist pastors and leaders to bring about change. In short, Baptist women worked through the groups already established in the churches, such as temperance, BZM and BWL, to work for political, social, and ecclesial equality between men and women, and specifically to achieve suffrage for women.

Temperance and the Question of Women's Suffrage

Women and children were often the victims of poverty and crimes that were linked to the excessive consumption of alcohol such as gambling, prostitution and public disorder. Hence, after the British Association for the Promotion of Temperance was established in 1835, very quickly temperance was linked to women's suffrage, since greater representation was needed if societal change was to take place.[27] While initially Quakers took the lead in meetings, many Baptists joined the temperance crusade and groups in churches, such as the Band of Hope (f.1847), encouraged sobriety. Baptist ministers often took part in temperance meetings which discussed the importance of giving women the vote. For example, on 19 March 1872, Thomas Wilkinson, a Baptist minister in Tewkesbury, chaired a temperance meeting that presented a signed petition in favour of women's suffrage.[28] He was also present in 1876 at a public meeting "in support of the Bill for Extending the Parliamentary Suffrage to Women Householders,"[29] and continued working for the cause and became the corresponding member from Tewkesbury to the Bristol Suffrage Society.[30]

Of course, Baptists participated in temperance gatherings around the country, which put the support of suffrage at the top of the agenda. In 1881, for example, a meeting in advocacy of women's suffrage was held at the Temperance Hall in Shipley and chaired by the pastor of Rosse Street Baptist Church, the Rev. T. Easton. While a motion in favour of woman's suffrage was passed,[31] it was not without opposition. One person argued that women should not be allowed to vote because men who were married would effectively be given two votes since "the woman would always vote as her

---

[27] See Smith "Balfours and the Burns," 444–55.

[28] Crawford, *Regional Survey*, 135.

[29] *TRAG* Saturday 18 November 1876, 1.

[30] Crawford, *Regional Survey*, 135.

[31] The motion stated, "That in the judgment of this meeting the Parliamentary franchise should be extended to women who possess the qualifications which entitle men to vote, and who, in all matters of local government, have the right of voting." *STE* Saturday 12 November 1881, 4.

husband directed."³² This sexist view was over-ridden and support for the motion was no doubt aided by the fact that Alice Elizabeth Cliff Scatcherd, a well-known advocate for woman's suffrage attended the meeting and spoke for half an hour drawing attention to the close link between the woman's franchise and social reform, insisting

> the right to exercise the franchise at Parliamentary elections was claimed for all the women householders and ratepayers, because such women are as fully entitled to vote as men, and are as capable of exercising the right; and because women suffer injustice by unfair laws which if they had a vote, they would have the power of removing.³³

This emphasis on the vote and social reform was also central to the arguments made by Baptist women, Clara Balfour (1808–78) and her daughter, Cecil Balfour Burns (1829–97), who were outspoken activists for both the temperance and suffrage movements. Both women favoured total abstinence and travelled widely giving speeches, chairing temperance meetings and promoting woman's suffrage as a means for achieving social reform. In 1876, Cecil Burns³⁴ is credited with writing, "A Few Words to Temperance Women on the Women's Suffrage Question". Likewise, in 1878, she contributed to a series of leaflets prepared by the Woman's Suffrage Society.

Cecil was married to the Baptist minister, Dawson Burns (1828–1909), and both were respected by fellow Baptists for their work as temperance campaigners. So it is not surprising that in 1889 she was invited to speak at the Baptist Assembly on the topic, "Women's work in the Church." While many of those attending the meetings may have expected her to speak of the accepted roles of women in the church at that time, surprisingly Cecil took advantage of the opportunity to give an address to the assembly that was later published as "Woman's Official Position in the Church." Reprinted by her husband in a book entitled, *Memorial Leaves: A Selection From the Papers of Cecil Burns*, the address began with the question, "What, at the present time, is the recognised position of women, beyond their mere membership, in nearly all our religious communities?"³⁵ She then made the point that in the early church the position of women was very clear in that they were "regarded, and approved of, as 'servants,' or 'deaconesses.'"³⁶ Then, carefully, Burns gave an

---

[32] *STE* Saturday 12 November 1881, 4.

[33] *STE* Saturday 12 November 1881, 4. Scatcherd was married to Oliver Scatcherd, a textile factory owner at Morley, near Leeds. Crawford, *Reference Guide*, 618–20.

[34] At the request of her maternal grandmother, she received the name Cecil, one given to boys rather than to girls. Burns, *Memorial Leaves*, 7.

[35] Burns, *Memorial Leaves*, 51.

[36] Burns, *Memorial Leaves*, 52.

exegetical survey of texts that might be used to argue against women serving in the church and suggested that there were different interpretations of the texts. While she did not suggest that women might be pastors, she did argue for the formation of groups that women could oversee within the church. In particular, it seems that she felt that the biblical office of deaconess should be reinstated. Her point was that the gifts of women needed to be recognized and utilized by the church, especially if the church was serious about evangelism. She concluded,

> The whole subject of women's position and women's work in the Church is deserving of serious consideration. Many naturally shrink from according to women certain names and offices in the Church, because such names and such offices have died out. Does not this repugnance arise out of a conformity to custom, rather than from unbiased judgment? If the truths of the Gospel are to be more broadly scattered . . . nothing should be lost to the Church that could in any form conduce to the enlargement of her borders, and the spread of her influence, so that by all and every means, she may indeed become the fair Evangelist of the world.[37]

While an animated discussion followed the address, at the time it was reported by Sarah Tooley,[38] a Baptist and journalist, that the discussion

> marks an epoch in woman's history within Nonconformity. Each delegate who spoke was in favour of a greater prominence being given to women in Church life; without a single dissentient voice it was accepted as a plank in the Baptist Forward Movement, now being inaugurated that women should be allowed, nay encouraged, to pray publicly in the prayer meetings, to conduct services, to form themselves into guilds as nursing sisters, and even to enter the pulpit itself, if they have the gift of tongues.[39]

Acknowledging that it would take time for these measures to be enacted in the churches, nevertheless, it was believed that "a wider sphere of usefulness is now the privilege of women. If they have a message to tell, they may tell it out as a man does."[40]

The remarks made in the *Women's Penny Paper* illustrate how the issue of the rights of women (expressed at the time through the call for suffrage) and the theological parlance of the service of women in the church were easily

---

[37] Burns, *Memorial Leaves*, 63.

[38] Tooley was the wife of a Baptist minister and later became very active in the Women Writers' Suffrage League which was founded in 1908. Doughty, "Tooley [née Southall], Sarah Anne (1856–1946)."

[39] Tooley, "Women at the Baptist Union," 75.

[40] Tooley, "Women at the Baptist Union," 75.

aligned. As the writer suggested, it did, indeed, take some time for women to find both a place in the "wider sphere of church life" and to be given the vote. Yet, as time went on and as suffrage for women became a more focused issue in society, so among Baptists there were more direct appeals for women to have the vote in order for them to serve Christ, especially as they addressed social ills in society.

However, while suffrage and social reform, were closely linked, it should be noted that the issue of woman's suffrage was never simply about addressing social problems. As Cecil Burns indicated so clearly, for many Baptist women the real issue was having the freedom to use their gifts in service for Christ. With that goal—the desire to serve Christ—in mind, in the late nineteenth century some Baptist women began to push even harder against the boundaries of the accepted spheres of women's service within the church at home and abroad.

BZM and the Formation of Spheres of Service

Formed in 1867, the BZM provided an important means through which British Baptist women could extend their sphere of service even as they continued to work cooperatively within denominational structures. While it has been suggested that the women who worked with the BZM were "unable to criticize gender inequalities, in British society" this was not entirely the case.[41] While initially, Baptist women were "captive to culture" and in their work in the zenanas perpetuated an emphasis on domesticity and the woman's place in the home, as their work progressed and gained notice it appears that women used opportunities to point out the inconsistencies of treatment of British women in England. For example, in 1891 Ellen Farrer,[42] a medical doctor appointed by the BZM to serve in India, was asked to speak at the Baptist Assembly in Manchester. On that occasion, she took the opportunity to point out that women who were trained and sent as missionaries abroad were not afforded the same opportunities for service at home. She claimed that

> most Christian people are now prepared to acknowledge that there is a wide field for women as medical missionaries in foreign lands, especially in India, where many of our less fortunate sisters must suffer and even die for want of medical aid worthy the name unless they can be attended by a doctor of their own sex, but it is not yet so generally recognised that there is an opening for women in a similar capacity at home. There is an old objection, still so frequently raised against the study of medicine by women, that I cannot pass on without a word

---

[41] Lauer, "Opportunities," 222.

[42] For Ellen Farrer, see Anderson, *Mission for Medicine*.

upon it—viz., that this study must destroy the finer qualities which constitute true womanliness.[43]

Farrer then argued that it was inconsistent for people "to hold that for a woman to be a doctor in this country she must be unwomanly but are willing for women to train to be shipped off to India or China either as medical missionaries or as secular practitioners."[44]

As well as missionaries like Farrer speaking in favour of greater opportunities for women, there were also women at home who worked for change in attitudes toward women. For example, Emily Georgiana Kemp (1860–1939),[45] who served as President of the BZM in 1913, was a very strong advocate for the rights of women and the need for women's suffrage.[46] Kemp's parents, George Tawke Kemp (1810–77) and Emily Lydia Kelsall Kemp (1827–1904) were founder members of Bloomsbury Baptist Church in London before moving to Rochdale to pursue their business in the woollen trade.[47] In Rochdale, they were part of the West Street Baptist Church and very strong supporters of the BMS. Emily's sister, Emily Jessie Kemp, was first appointed by the BZM as a missionary to India. Due to ill health, she returned to Britain after three years. Later, when the BZM refused on health grounds to approve a second appointment as a missionary, she, along with another sister, Florence, went to China and served under the auspices of the China Inland Mission. The sisters both married (Florence married Evan Henry Edwards and Emily Jessie Kemp married Thomas Wellesley Piggot) and, with their husbands, served as missionaries in China. Sadly, the Piggots died in 1900 during the Boxer Uprising.[48] Unlike her sisters, Emily Georgiana never married[49] and never served on the mission field, though she took an active part in the BZM and gave generously to mission work. In addition to visits to India, and later China, she also travelled on behalf of the BZM (at

---

[43] Farrer, "Women's Work among the Sick and Poor," 8.

[44] Farrer, "Women's Work among the Sick and Poor," 10. Steinbach, *Women in England*, 75, has noted that medicine was considered to be a career option for which women were unsuited.

[45] See the chapter by Janice O'Brien in the present volume.

[46] *FCST* 1 October, 1913, 2.

[47] Emily Lydia Kelsall Kemp's sister, Sarah, was married to Samuel Morton Peto who was instrumental in organizing the "bold experiment" that became Bloomsbury. See Bowers, *A Bold Experiment*, 41–42.

[48] Bickers, "Pigott [née Kemp], (Emily) Jessie (1851–1900)."

[49] In a light-hearted comment she claimed she had never married because her Governess from Switzerland was "a rabid man-hater, and prayed continually that none of us might have the misfortune to get married." Kemp, *Reminiscences of a Sister*, 12.

her own expense) to visit other mission stations and later wrote of her observations and illustrated them in several published works.[50]

Kemp attended Somerville College in Oxford from 1881 to 1883 and not surprisingly she was outspoken in her support for women.[51] In 1913, Kemp wrote an article for the *FCST* which claimed that, unlike women in China, British women were not allowed to serve freely in the church. While she believed that women missionaries helped to spread the "feminist movement" to India, she lamented that more progress had not been made among women in the church in Britain. She wrote,

> It has not been sufficiently realized yet that the powers of women in Great Britain with regard to spiritual work have but limited scope in the churches of all denominations—with the sole exception of the Friends. Those women who have a real vocation as teachers, leaders, preachers, have no natural outlet at home. . . . But this is not the case in the foreign field, where there is far greater freedom of action and stimulus to original and initiative work. Where the Church is not fettered by tradition woman naturally and instinctively takes her place alongside of man in Church-work as well as fellowship.[52]

Kemp then called for more women to go out as missionaries in order to teach the women there to use their influence for good.

> Throughout the length and breadth of the country women are beginning to know their power and longing to exercise it. It is still largely in the hands of the missionary to influence and direct the new movement: she can give noble ideals of life and character, and a wide choice of study to the eager student. She has an opportunity of service and of making history which has never before been offered to her, in the training of high-class women in the East. It is mainly in two directions that this work can be most fruitful—in normal and medical school work; for in this way the women of the East can be fitted to undertake the training of their sisters, who will ultimately—and, indeed, it may be in a comparatively short time, especially in China—take it out of foreign hands.[53]

The next year, Kemp wrote a letter to the editor of the *FCST* in which she decried the fact that churches were still too slow to accept the gifts of women. Her complaint seems to arise from her attendance at a meeting for

---

[50] Minute Book of the Zenana Mission, No. 1, Committee meeting 13 July 1877, n.p.

[51] *Somerville College Register* (1879–1971), n. p.

[52] E.G. Kemp, FRSGS, "The Feminist Movement in the East and its Relation to Foreign Missions," *FCST* 1 September 1913, 6.

[53] Kemp, "Feminist Movement," *FCST* 1913, 6.

missionaries where the men far outnumbered the women on the platform. The letter read,

> DEAR SIR,—Can you find space for the following? There was an interesting gathering of missionaries held in the Memorial Hall, Farringdon Street, on Friday, January 16th, under the auspices of the Free Church Council, and by the kind invitation of Mr. and Mrs. Evan Spicer. Many denominations were represented, and after tea a sympathetic address was given by Dr. Garvie. The platform crowded, first with secretaries of societies, next with missionaries on furlough. There was one noticeable feature in both cases—not a single woman on the platform, except the hostess, though there were women secretaries present, and many women missionaries. One society boasting only a single missionary unless my ears misled me—was represented; whereas a society with eighty-eight women missionaries was entirely ignored. Every speaker was a man, and some of them pointedly enumerated the women fellow-workers, evidently conscious of the slight put upon them. The Free Church Council is very much behind the times in its attitude towards women, and this is a glaring illustration. How long are we expected to put up with it? And do the leaders consider that they are rapidly alienating the sympathy of some of the ablest and the most spiritually minded women in Nonconformist circles? The women of the Baptist Churches are being freely used as instruments for collecting money for the Sustentation Fund, and those who have successfully won their services will, it is to be hoped, see that they take an equal part in the distribution of that fund. Women are notoriously better spenders of public funds than men. At the present time the spiritual activities of women are seriously cramped by the narrow-minded policy of our Free Churches. It is a matter that claims our serious attention as to what are the right steps to take to alter this. It is injurious to our better nature that we should always be thrusting ourselves forward, but at present this seems the only way of obtaining the privilege of service—to giving our best for the common good. We have no doubt there is some better reason than jealousy which prevents men using the gifts of women in the pulpit or platform. This is sometimes said, but we do not believe it. We should like to find out the true reason. In the meantime, we must continue ceaselessly to protest against the present deplorable waste of woman's spiritual energy. That should be spent instead in the service of God and man. Yours, &c., E.G. KEMP[54]

Kemp's emphasis on the freedom of women to serve abroad and at home was also a theme that emerged in some of her books. Significantly, however, she did not base her argument on recognition of the "rights" of women. Rather, her focus on women using their gifts was grounded in the theological and spiritual idea that men and women were called to follow Christ. In her *Reminiscences of a Sister*, she spoke of her mother who did much to help care for others in the community and claimed,

---

[54] *FCST* 1 February 1914, 15.

The present feminist movement has had its foundation well and truly laid in many parts of the country by such women as my mother, who quietly and unostentatiously have been empire builders of the best kind, and who have striven with no small measure of success to bridge the social gulf which alas! still divides class from class.[55]

To celebrate their sixtieth anniversary, the Women's Missionary Auxiliary (formerly the BZM) commissioned Kemp to write a history of the work of women in missions between 1867 and 1927 which she entitled *There Followed Him Women*. Illustrated with her own artwork depicting various scenes from her many visits to mission stations over the years, in the book she also highlighted the fact that the women who served were not only as capable as men, but they were, like men, called to follow in the way of Christ.

Kemp believed that women were equal to men and should be allowed to live as equals. An independent spirit, she remained active in Baptist life[56] and contributed generously to Baptist work. In January 1912, she bought and presented to the BMS the manor house that became Carey Hall and was used as a women's missionary training college.[57] While she remained in membership in Bloomsbury Baptist Church, later in life she became a member of the World Council of Faiths, an interfaith movement which was founded in 1936. When that body was to meet in Oxford in 1937, she approved the plans for the building of, and provided the funding for, a Chapel of all Faiths at Somerville College.[58]

Toward a New Order:
The BWL and the Cooperation of Churches and Ministers

When the BWL was founded in 1908 women had a new platform on which to work co-operatively with men in the denomination. However, some felt there was a danger that women would merely be used for fundraising and their other gifts to the church would be overlooked. At the Baptist Union meeting in Manchester held at the Free Trade Hall in 1913, Ethel (Annakin) Snowden was invited to speak on the theme, "A Woman's View of the Church." Snowden, had grown up attending a Congregationalist church, but

---

[55] Kemp, *Reminiscences of a Sister*, 28.

[56] As an adult, she returned to Bloomsbury in London. While in Rochdale, she was active in West Street Baptist Church, and as a student in Oxford she taught Sunday school class at New Road Baptist Church. Whitehead, *Rochdale Baptists*, 30; and Amey, "Giving and Receiving," 370–71.

[57] Martin, *Fifty Years of Carey Hall*, 14; and Amey, "Giving and Receiving," 371.

[58] The theme for the conference was "The World's Need of Religion". See Braybrook, *Wider Vision*, 50.

as a young woman had gone to Liverpool to train as a teacher. While there she attended Pembroke Baptist Chapel and came under the influence of the pastor, Charles Aked,[59] who had recognized her gifts as a public speaker and she became a popular speaker with Baptists.[60] A member of the National Union for Woman's Suffrage (NUWSS) and a vice-President of the FCLWS, she wrote a number of books advocating for the vote for women, including, *Women and the State* (1907) *The Woman Socialist Movement* (1907) and in 1913, the same year that she was invited to speak at the Baptist Assembly, she published *The Feminist Movement*.

At the 1913 Baptist Assembly meeting, she left no doubt that if women were to remain in the church men and women together needed to recognize the gifts of women. A newspaper account of Snowden's remarks said that "she regarded the invitation to speak as an acknowledgment that among religious bodies the old days of patronage of woman were at an end, and that now they were to take their places side by side with men, not as inferiors but as comrades."[61] Then, pointing out the valuable work that women had already made to society as a whole, Snowden argued that

> unless the churches were prepared to be fair to women and to open the doors of the fullest opportunity to them, respected their wishes and their opinions as it had used their money and their humbler talents, and protested more loudly and clearly against the unspeakable wrongs to women, then she was as certain as she was standing there that the critical women of the present, and their more critical daughters of the future, would certainly forsake the Church, as their husbands, fathers, and sons were, alas, in such numbers beginning to forsake it.[62]

At Baptist Union meetings the next year a big celebration was held in the Royal Albert Hall in London in order to give thanks for the success of the efforts toward the Sustentation Fund. At a session that was reportedly "crowded from stalls to gallery," Ethel Snowden again spoke and highlighted the contribution of women in the church by saying that the church of all ages owed much to women. Then she posed several direct questions:

> Were the Churches now going to repay their debt? Would the Churches sanction and appoint women deacons? Women on every Committee? Women in the pulpit? And would they support women's claim for citizenship in the State?[63]

---

[59] Smith, "Charles Frederic Aked (1864–1941)."

[60] Smith, "Call for a Just Peace," 113–14.

[61] *FCST* 1 November 1913, 2.

[62] *FCST* 1 November 1913, 2.

[63] *FCST* 1 June 1914, 6.

Since this meeting was celebrating the success of the Sustentation Fund, some who heard Snowden's remarks felt that she should not have mentioned the issue of women's involvement. This criticism, however, was apparently countered by pointing out that the Baptist Union meeting was "one of thanksgiving for women's services as well as men."[64] On the following Tuesday, at the same Assembly meeting, Margaret Hardy of Brighton addressed the meeting immediately after a speech from John Clifford and reaffirmed the importance of the church recognizing the "wisdom of womanhood" and also allowing women to use their gifts freely. Hardy said that men had

> been filled with—shall we call it?—such a sense of self-sufficiency, that they have attempted their great things without us, which explains why so many of them have been so imperfectly done.[65]

Hardy, as noted earlier, believed that the question of women using their gifts was not just a political issue, but a spiritual one. This belief was echoed by many other notable Baptists. In 1914, for instance, Baptist minister, Ivory J. Cripps, claimed that the "Woman's Question in all its aspects is fundamentally a spiritual question." Indeed, he argued it was "the chief spiritual issue" of that time.[66] Eloquently, he then argued that if women were not allowed to participate fully in the churches, they would eventually leave. As he put it,

> How is it possible to keep it out of our Churches, and out of our pulpits? . . . [T]he whole thing is ultimately a spiritual issue, which must concern us in our purely spiritual mission. . . . [T]he Woman's Question brings up the Christian ethic and ideal in their most elementary form. The very heart of the Gospel, and its greatest contribution to human progress, is its discovery of the individual, of the intrinsic worth and value of every human soul.[67]

This emphasis on the equal value of every person male or female was an important theological statement which would underpin the insistence that women should be allowed to preach and to serve in the same way as men in the churches. One of the strongest proponents for the equality of women was, of course, John Clifford (1836–1923), who not only served as President of the FCWSL, but he also regularly spoke on behalf of the suffrage cause. In February 1915, a Free Church League Suffrage service was held in

---

[64] *FCST* 1 June 1914, 6.

[65] *FCST* 1 November 1913, 2.

[66] *FCST* 1 May, 1914, 5.

[67] *FCST* 1 May 1914, 5.

Westbourne Park Baptist Church where he served as minister and it was said that suffrage was "endorsed and urged in no uncertain terms" by him. It was reported that

> Dr. Clifford's prayer was very uplifting. It contained the expression, Thou Who art our Father, Thou Who art our Mother, and addressed God as the Catholic Spirit Who regarded not sex, a catholicity we have not granted nor expressed.[68]

While not all Baptist ministers were as bold in their feminist theological leanings, increasingly a number of pastors spoke out in favour of women being allowed to contribute to church life in any way. At a BWL meeting held at Bloomsbury Baptist Church in April 1915, F.C. Spurr claimed that "A fair reading of history shows that the Church has never wholly ignored woman's true role in life; but unhappily it has never wholly recognized it."[69] Noting that some of the names of the great saints of the church were women, he lamented that the church had "recognized the exceptional woman, but not the ordinary woman."[70] He then spoke of all of the injustices against women claiming that the church had allowed women to be degraded economically by not supporting fair wages. Moreover, he stated bluntly that the church had degraded women morally, claiming,

> The double standard of morality still prevails. The man may sin and sing, the woman may sin but she must suffer. To the male sinner society will still open its doors; to the woman there is left only too frequently, the dirty pathway that leads to hell. Not yet has woman received her full rights of maternity, and her full rights of release when marital bondage has become unendurable and impossible. To an alarming extent there still persists the wicked idea that after all woman was created to be man's toy, man's tool.[71]

Given the way women had been treated, Spurr concluded that it was not surprising that the time should come when women would speak out. He claimed that education had revealed to "her capacities" and "her rights." He concluded,

> With this demand of woman to employ her capacities and to exercise her rights the Church must sympathize. Woman must be no longer a plaything, flattered for her beauty, sought for the pleasure that she gives. She must be recognized as a woman in the full content of that term. It is her right. ... Women are in a majority in the Church. Women do some of the best work in Churches. It

---

[68] *FCST* 1 February 1915, 1.

[69] *FCST* 1 May 1915, 4.

[70] *FCST* 1 May 1915, 4.

[71] *FCST* 1 May 1915, 4.

should be recognized officially and esteemed. Every gift should be used, since all gifts are of God. Women are already on the Council of the Baptist Union. Why should not they be represented on the council of every local church? The future needs woman's work more than ever.[72]

As the support for increasing the spheres of woman's service in the church gained support, there was concern that some women were impatient with the slow response on the part of some ministers and churches. In 1916, the BWL annual meeting was at Kingsgate Chapel when Isabel Russell James spoke to a "large and enthusiastic gathering" and pleaded for "breadth of outlook and magnanimity of temper to the new range and value given to women's work in this time of sacrifice and service."[73] The Rev. S.W. Hughes, closed the meeting with what was described as "an earnest tribute to the power and influence of women as an enrichment of the Church's life."[74]

While there were attempts to open some doors for women to serve in the church, there was a growing awareness that other doors remained firmly shut. In the *FCST* in December 1916, a lengthy article was devoted to the lack of women deacons in most Nonconformist churches. While some churches such as Ferme Park Baptist, had elected women to the diaconate as early as 1906,[75] others had not. This article insisted that there was "no formal obstacle to the use of women in any capacity in our Free Churches, no bishops' ban nor ecclesiastical embargo." The article stated unequivocally that these churches were free to choose women and should do so.[76] The writer suggested that the real problem was not "prejudice or aversion," but "inertia" on the part of women in the churches. The article concluded with a challenge to the women,

> If women made up their minds to be deacons, they would become deacons, and as they are in a large majority no power on earth could prevent them. They have only to work for their admission to the diaconate with the same zeal they have worked for their admission to professions and trades, and every church would

---

[72] *FCST* 1 May 1915, 5.

[73] *FCST* 15 May 1916, 5.

[74] "Memoirs of Ministers and Missionaries," *The Baptist Handbook* (1955), 328. Samuel William Hughes (1874–1954) succeeded John Clifford as pastor of Westbourne Park Baptist Church from 1915 to 1932. He then became the Secretary of the National Council of Evangelical Free Churches in 1932 and then Secretary of the Free Church Federal Council from 1939 until his retirement in 1946. On his death, the *Times* recognized him as "one of the great Nonconformist leaders" of the twentieth century.

[75] *BapArg* 10 (1906), 12, noted that three women had been elected to the diaconate at Ferme Park Baptist Church.

[76] *CD* December 1916, 1.

soon have some. One, surely, need not argue its advisability. When we think that the larger half of our churches is of the feminine gender, that churches deal with children, with the sick and the poor, that women in normal times have often more leisure than men and are available at all times of day, that they are for the most part more religious than men, he would be a bold man who would argue against us. . . . There is nothing against women in the diaconate. Everything for it. But it is for women themselves to get there.[77]

How effective this article might have been is difficult to say. However, it was reported in January 1917 that at least one church, Jesmond Baptist Church, Newcastle-on-Tyne, had unanimously elected two women as deacons.[78] At any rate, after 1917 the move to allow women to preach and to serve as deacons seems to have grown. Admittedly, this may have been due to the fact that because of the war there were fewer men in the churches and women were contributing in many different ways. Clearly, however, there was a continuing desire to involve women in the life of the church. For example, it was reported in February 1917 that Mrs Graham-Barton had invited a speaker to Kingsgate Baptist Chapel, Holborn, who addressed the topic "Woman's Awakening" to a "large and appreciative audience."[79] Her husband who was the pastor of the church, Alexander Graham-Barton, was an ardent supporter of suffrage and he reportedly paid for a copy of *The Coming Day* (formerly the *FCST*), to be given to every member and arranged for further copies of the paper to be offered for sale every month.[80]

In March 1917, the *CD* reported that the "psychological moment" had arrived for carrying the message to Christian bodies and a number of meetings (with women speakers)—some which were men's meetings—had been arranged in the churches. Baptist churches in London included Westbourne Park, Kingsgate, and Holloway Road.[81] In June 1917, at an annual business meeting, the FCLWS approved a resolution of the Hackney branch that women preachers should form a fellowship "with the object of their being available to preach as and when there shall be opportunity."[82] By September 1917, the *CD* reported that there was a growing demand for "our list of women preachers."[83] Among those who had been invited to Baptist churches were a Mrs Wheatley, who was invited to lead services at Victoria Street

---

[77] *CD* 15 December 1916, 1.

[78] *CD* 15 January 1917, 2.

[79] *CD* 15 February 1917, 9.

[80] *CD* 15 February 1917, 9.

[81] *CD* 15 March 1917, 3.

[82] *CD* 15 June 1917, 3.

[83] *CD* 15 September 1917, 3.

Baptist Church, and Mrs Stephens, who had been preaching and speaking for the BWL, also for the BMS. The report in the *CD* claimed,

> These services have been fruitful of much good and augur well for the future of women's ministry. Mrs. Wheatley, who is convenor of the Women Preacher's Fellowship, conducted the services at Victoria Street Baptist Church, Windsor, on August 12th. In the morning she preached upon "The Heavenly Vision"; and in the evening upon "The Vision Materialised." Mr. Reavell (church secretary) writes: "The visit of Mrs. Wheatley was greatly appreciated by the church and congregation. It is the first time our church has had a woman preacher, and we hope to have others whenever the opportunity presents itself."[84]

By October 1917 it was reported that "interest and support of women preachers grows with astonishing rapidity."[85] Upon receiving the list of women preachers, John Clifford replied,

> DEAR MRS. WHEATLEY,—Your letter is most welcome. It is another sign of the dawn of the better day. I rejoice and hope your work will be very fruitful. With best wishes for your God-inspired venture.
> —I am, Sincerely yours, JOHN CLIFFORD.[86]

Conclusion

On 25 April 1918, when Baptist women crowded into Kingsgate chapel to welcome their new BWL President, Mrs Charles Brown,[87] they had another cause to celebrate as well. For by an Act of Parliament which was given Royal assent on 6 February 1918, the right to vote was given to some women who were over the age of thirty. While that right would not be extended to all women until 1928, the passage of this bill marked a milestone in the long struggle for women's suffrage. Significantly, it was noted that Brown delivered her address "from the pulpit" as she expressed gratitude "for the increased power given to women in the use of the vote." She claimed that it was "a sacred duty for those who were qualified to use this new weapon for beneficial reforms." She then urged the women to "leave old grooves and prepare for the coming days."[88]

---

[84] *CD* 15 September 1917, 3.

[85] *CD* 15 October 1917, 5.

[86] *CD* 15 October 1917, 5.

[87] *CD* 15 May 1918, 3. Charles Brown was minister at Ferme Park from 1890 to 1925.

[88] *CD* 15 May 1918, 3.

Brown's emphasis on using the vote for societal reform, as well as calling for women to become involved in service to Christ in new ways, seems to sum up the key issues for many Baptist women and men who supported the suffrage cause. The issue of suffrage, as it first emerged, was seen by many as a necessary step in order to address social ills. In other words, initially, while the issue of the "rights of women" was important to some, it does not seem to have been the primary motivating factor for Baptist women in their efforts to achieve the vote. Rather, they were seeking the vote in order to enlarge their sphere of service. Working through the temperance groups, the BZM and BWL, Baptist women found effective, though still limited, spheres of service for Christ, albeit in ways that did not threaten the male hierarchy. These groups, of course, should not be seen as nascent feminist groups organized for the purpose of supporting suffrage or women's rights. Their focus was on both men and women serving Christ through the church.

While many Baptist women and men celebrated the move to grant the vote to women as an act of equality, it is telling that there were those who were somewhat ambivalent and perhaps not completely at ease with more women serving on an equal basis with men in the church. For example, at the same BWL meeting when the granting of suffrage was celebrated, it appears that a deaconess from Bloomsbury Chapel, Sister Dorothy, was fearful that this move might mean that women might lose the influence they had in service in the church. She urged the women to "retain their individuality" and not become "second-hand men," and claimed that what mattered was "character" and "atmosphere not activities."[89] Then, in an acknowledgement that because of the war women were increasingly needed in the church, she argued,

> If the Church wanted to win the young women of to-day it must get back to the conception of the Church as "The Bride of Christ." The words "Jesus, Lover of my Soul" might have a tremendous significance for the many women who would of necessity have to remain single. A close, intimate personal relationship with Christ would alone satisfy the deep longings of the individual soul.[90]

The story of the deaconess movement, their spirituality, and their attitudes toward suffrage is a topic for other research. Suffice it to say that the deaconess movement (somewhat akin to a monastic movement) had provided a special sphere of service for women which gave them status and allowed them the freedom to speak and to minister to others in the name of Christ. While in many ways this sphere of service continued to preserve the Puritan emphasis on "the ideal woman" it had, at the same time, provided some women with an opportunity to serve in ministry within the community. For

---

[89] Sister Dorothy Gotch served at Bloomsbury in 1915. Bowers, *Bold Experiment*, 270.

[90] *CD* 15 May 1918, 3.

those women, and others within the churches, perhaps it was unsettling to think of leaving "old grooves" and preparing for something new.

Finally, it should be noted that in 1918 when the vote was granted to some women, J.H. Shakespeare published *The Churches at the Cross-Roads* in which he warned the church not to ignore the gifts of women to the church. Dedicated to Isabel (Riley) James, who had helped organize the BWL, and her father A.F. Riley, Shakespeare not only paid tribute to the work of women in the church, but claimed again that "in Christ Jesus there is and can be no distinction" between men and women and that "sex in itself can be no bar to position and service." Indeed, as Shakespeare put it, "Only at its peril can the Church make itself the last ditch of prejudice in this respect or forget that its problems will be best solved by men and women working together."[91]

The desire to cooperate together was, of course, one reason why many Baptist men and women worked through denominational organizations to effect change for women. Arguably, this desire may have reflected misplaced loyalty to a denomination that was controlled by men or an inability of women to throw off the ties of cultural captivity. Even so, their efforts to work within temperance groups, the BZM and BWL, also reflects a spirituality that was deeply rooted in the Baptist understanding of "life together" in service for Christ.

Bibliography

Books and Articles

Amey, Basil. "Giving and Receiving: New Road and the Baptist Missionary Society." In *Protestant Catholic Church of Christ*, 351–78. Edited by Chadwick.

Anon. "Orator Hunt and the First Suffrage Petition." "UK Parliament." https://www.parliament.uk/about/livingheritage/transformingsociety/electionsvoting/womenvote/parliamentary-collections/1866-suffrage-petition/the-first-petition/

Anderson, Imogen Siobhan. "A Mission for Medicine: Dr Ellen Farrer and India 1891–1933." PhD diss., Durham University, 1997.

Adcock, Rachel. *Baptist Women's Writings in Revolutionary Culture, 1640–1680*. Farnham: Ashgate, 2015.

Bickers, Robert. "Pigott [*née* Kemp], (Emily) Jessie (1851–1900)." Oxford Dictionary of National Biography Online.

Bowers, Faith. *A Bold Experiment: The Story of Bloomsbury Chapel and Bloomsbury Central Baptist Church, 1848–1999*. London: Bloomsbury Central Baptist Church, 1999.

---

[91] Shakespeare, *Churches at the Cross-Roads*, 9–11.

———. "For God and the People: Baptist Deaconesses 1901–1905." *Baptist Quarterly* 43.8 (October 2010) 473–93.

Braybrooke, Marcus. *A Wider Vision: A History of the World Congress of Faiths.* Oxford: Oneworld, 1996.

Burns, Dawson. *Memorial Leaves: Selection from the Papers of Cecil Burns.* London: Ideal Publishing Union, 1898.

Carey, William. *An Enquiry into the Obligations of Christians, to use Means for the Conversion of the Heathens. In which the Religious State of the Different Nations of the World, the Success of Former Undertakings, and the Practicality of Further Undertakings, are Considered.* Leicester: Ann Ireland, J. Johnson, T. Knott, R. Dilly, and Smith, 1792.

Cartwright, Colin. "'The Enfranchisement of Baptist Women'? A Brief History of the Baptist Women's League and the Women's Suffrage Movement in England and Scotland," *Baptist Quarterly* 49.4 (2018), 146–64.

Chadwick, Rosie, ed. *A Protestant Catholic Church of Christ: Essays on the History and Life of New Road Baptist Church, Oxford.* Oxford: New Road Baptist Church, 2003.

Chalus, Elaine and Fiona Montgomery. "Women and Politics." In *Women's History, 1700–1850*, 217–59. Edited by Hannah Barker and Elaine Chalus. London: Routledge, 2005.

Crawford, Elizabeth. *The Women's Suffrage Movement: A Reference Guide, 1866–1928.* London: Routledge, 2001.

———. *The Women's Suffrage Movement in Britain and Ireland: A Regional Survey.* London: Routledge, 2006.

Davidoff, Leonore, and Catherine Hall. *Family Fortunes: Men and Women of the English Middle Class, 1780–1850.* Revised ed. London: Routledge, 2007.

Doughty, Terri. "Tooley [née Southall], Sarah Anne (1856–1946)." Oxford Dictionary of National Biography Online.

Edwards, Thomas. *Gangraena: The first and second part of Gangræna, or, A Catalogue and discovery of many errors, heresies, blasphemies and pernicious practices of the sectaries of this time, vented and acted in England in these four last years also a narration of divers stories, remarkable passages, letters: an extract of many letters, all concerning the present sects: together with some observations upon and corollaries from all the fore-named primisses.* London: T.R. and E.M. for Ralph Smith, 1646.

Farrer, Ellen. "Women's Work among the Sick and Poor." Papers read at the Autumn Assembly of the Baptist Union held in Manchester on Thursday 8 October 1891. In *The Training of Women for Christian Work.* London: Alexander and Shepheard, 1891. (A draft of this address may also be found in the papers of Ellen Farrer, The Angus Library, Oxford).

Freeman, Curtis W. *A Company of Women Preachers: Baptist Prophetesses in Seventeenth Century England.* Waco: Baylor University Press, 2011.

———. "Visionary Women Among Early Baptists." *Baptist Quarterly* 43.5 (2010) 260–83.
Gouldbourne, Ruth M.B. *Reinventing the Wheel: Women and Ministry in English Baptist Life*. The Whitley Lecture 1997–1998. Oxford: Whitley Publications, 1997.
Hayden, Roger. *The Records of the Church of Christ in Bristol, 1640–1687*. Bristol: Bristol Record Society, 1974.
E.G. Kemp. *Reminiscences of a Sister S. Florence Edwards, of Taiyuanfu*. London: Carey, 1919.
———. *There Followed Him Women*. London: The Baptist Missionary Society, 1927.
Lauer, Laura "Opportunities for Baptist Women and the "Problem" of the Baptist Zenana Mission, 1867–1913." In *Women, Religion and Feminism in Britain, 1750–1900*, 213–29. Edited by in Sue Morgan. Basingstoke: Palgrave Macmillan, 2002,
Martin, Hugh. *Fifty Years of Carey Hall 1912–1962*. Selly Oak: Council of Carey Hall, [1962].
Mill, Harriet Taylor. *The Enfranchisement of Women: Essays on Equality, Law, and Education*. In *Collected Works of John Stuart Mill*: Volume XXI, 393–416. Edited by J. Robson. Toronto: Toronto University Press, 1984. https://oll.libertyfund.org/title/mill-the-collected-works-of-john-stuart-mill-volume-xxi-essays-on-equality-law-and-education
Mill, John Stuart. *The Subjection of the Rights of Women*. In *Essays on Equality, Law, and Education: Collected Works of John Stuart Mill*: Volume XXI, 259–348. Edited by J. Robson. Toronto: Toronto University Press, 1984. https://oll.libertyfund.org/title/mill-the-collected-works-of-john-stuart-mill-volume-xxi-essays-on-equality-law-and-education
Miller, Dale E. "Harriet Taylor Mill." In *The Stanford Encyclopedia of Philosophy* (Spring 2019). Edited by Edward N. Zalta. https://plato.stanford.edu/archives/spr2019/entires/harriet-mill/
Payne, Ernest A. *The Baptist Union: A Short History*. London: Baptist Union of Great Britain, 1959.
Randall, Ian M., *The English Baptist of the Twentieth Century*. A History of the English Baptists, 4. Didcot: The Baptist Historical Society, 2005.
Robertson, Dan, "Biographical sketch of Margaret Hardy." *100 Pioneering Women in Sussex*. Brighton Museum. https://brightonmuseums.org.uk/discover/2020/05/21/brightons-first-female-mayor-margaret-hardy-mbe-1874-1954/
Saunders, Robert. "'A Great and Holy War:' Religious Routes to Women's Suffrage." *The English Historical Review* 134.571 (2019) 1471–1502.
Shakespeare, J.H. *The Churches at the Cross-Roads: A Study in Church Unity*. London: Williams and Norgate, 1918.
Smith, Karen E. "The Balfours and the Burns: Baptists battling the power of strong drink." *Baptist Quarterly* 45. 8 (2014), 444–55.

———. "Baptists at Home." In *Challenge and Change: English Baptist Life in the Eighteenth Century*, 101–22. Edited by Stephen Copson and Peter J. Morden. Didcot: The Baptist Historical Society, 2017.

———. "A Call for a Just Peace: Ethel Snowden in Wales, 1916–17." In *The First World War and Baptist Life and Thought*, 110–23. Edited by Larry J. Kreitzer. Oxford: Regent's Park College, 2014.

———. "Charles Frederic Aked (1864–1941): 'A Fighting Parson' for Social Reform." *Baptist Quarterly* 50.1 (2019) 3–18.

———. "Holy Living and Holy Dying: The Response of some British Baptist Women to 'Come Out' from the World." In *Come out from Among Them, and Be Ye Separate Saith the Lord: Separationism and the Believers' Church Tradition*, 85–101. Edited by William H. Brackney. Eugene: Pickwick Publications, 2019.

———. Nonconformists, the Home." In *T&T Clark Companion to Nonconformity*, 285–304. Edited by Robert Pope. London: Bloomsbury, 2013.

———. "The Role of Women in Early Baptist Missions." *Review and Expositor* 89.1 (1992) 35–48.

———. "Women in Cultural Captivity: British Women and the Zenana Mission." *Baptist Quarterly* 42.2 Part 1 (2007) 103–13, and 42.3 (2007) 245–48.

Snowden, Ethel. *The Feminist Movement*. London: Collins, 1913.

———. *Women and the State*. In Anne Constance Smedley, *Women: A Few Shrieks! Setting forth the necessity of shrieking till the shrieks be heard*. Letchworth: Garden City, 1907.

———. *The Woman Socialist Movement*. London: G. Allen, 1907

Steinbach, Susie. *Women in England, 1760–1914*. London: Weidenfeld and Nicolson, 2004.

Tooley, Sarah. "Women at the Baptist Union." *WPP* 59, 7 December 1889, 75.

"UK Parliament." https://www.parliament.uk/about/living-heritage/transformingsociety/electionsvoting/womenvote/overview/thevote/

Underhill, E.B., ed. *The Records of the Church of Christ, Meeting in Broadmead Bristol, 1640–1687*. London: Hanserd Knollys Society, 1857.

Ward, Margaret. *Female Occupations: Women's Employment 1850–1950*. Newbury: Countryside Books, 2008.

Whitehead, A. *The Rochdale Baptists 1773–1973: A Short History*. s.l.: s.n., 1998 [1973].

Wollstonecraft, Mary. *Vindication of the Rights of Women: With Strictures on Political and Moral Subjects*. London: J. Johnson, 1792. https://oll.libertyfund.org/title/wollstonecraft-boll-33-mary-wollstonecraft-a-vindication-of-the-rights-of-woman-1792

Manuscripts and Minute Books

Somerville College Register, 1879–1971, Somerville College, Oxford
Zenana Minute Book, Angus Library, Regent's Park College Oxford
BU Council Report, 1911, Angus Library, Regent's Park College Oxford

Newspapers and Other Sources

The Baptist Argus	*BapArg*
Free Church Suffrage Times (*The Coming Day*)	*FCST* (*CD*)
Shipley Times and Express	*STE*
The Tewkesbury Register, and Agricultural Gazette	*TRAG*
Women's Penny Paper	*WPP*

CHAPTER 6

Emily Georgiana Kemp, FRSGS:
"Her central interest was in living Christianity"[1]

Janice O'Brien

Introduction

On the southern side of Somerville College's main quad sits an edifice of monumental proportions. Instantly recognizable as a religious building, a visitor might wonder how it came to belong to an Oxford college which is not affiliated to a religious denomination. The heavy external doors, with square cut, classical Greek lettering set above them, give the impression of a mausoleum. Nikolaus Pevsner described the exterior as "bleakly classical" and the interior as "unloved-looking."[2] This writer disagrees: indeed, the immediate impression of the interior is one of light and of a beautiful luminescent quality often found in Nonconformist chapels. There is an inherent dignity in the simplicity of design. A wide nave, bordered with wooden panelling and stalls, leads to a stained-glass window. Radiant colours of blue, red, gold and green, cause the glass to glow richly against the plain white plaster walls. The subject of the window is Christ resurrected, stately and resplendent in rays of glorious light, set against a formal pastoral background suggestive of the "Gateway to the Knowledge of Life."[3] Two female figures stand beneath Christ, the one holds a lamp denoting Truth, her companion holds a mirror denoting Learning.[4] The names of notable Somervillians are recorded on memorials: Cornelia Sorabji, Constance Mary Coltman, Dorothy L. Sayers, Vera Brittain, Indira Gandhi, Iris Murdoch, Margaret Thatcher, to name a few.

Dedicated in 1935, the Chapel only reached completion following a tense period of misunderstandings, recriminations and compromises which surely affected the health of the two women who were pivotal to the decisions

---

[1] Farnell, ed., *Helen Darbishire*, 11.

[2] Sherwood and Pevsner, *Oxfordshire*, 251.

[3] Somerville College, *Chapel Leaflet*, 1937.

[4] Somerville College, *Chapel Leaflet*, 1937.

concerning design, materials and furnishings: Helen Darbishire, Somerville's Principal, and Emily Georgiana Kemp, former student and donor of the Chapel.[5]

Following Emily Kemp's death on Christmas Day 1939, the ensuing obituaries were generous in length and infused with gratitude. The *Baptist Times* dedicated an entire column, finalizing with the words, "Many good causes will be the poorer for her death but the memory of her determination and devotion will long be an inspiration."[6] With the passage of time, her contribution to the Baptist denomination and the many causes she supported are forgotten. Her books are not readily available, her Asiatic legacy of paintings, fabrics and artefacts, gifted to the Ashmolean, is not on public view.

Somerville College Chapel alone stands as a visual memorial to this remarkable woman. The aim in this chapter is to offer an introduction to the life and work of Emily Georgiana Kemp. Her family were of enormous importance and inspiration to her. I have, therefore, included those significant family events which plausibly shaped some of her choices.

Beginnings

Emily Georgiana Kemp was born on 23 May 1860 in Rochdale, Lancashire. The youngest daughter of George Tawke Kemp and Emily Lydia née Kelsall, hers was a privileged childhood. Kemp, originally a silk manufacturer from Essex,[7] had joined in business with his father-in-law, Henry Kelsall, woollen and flannel manufacturer, a few years prior to Emily's birth. Respected for fairness and favourable working conditions, Kelsall and Kemp sought to better the lives of their workers, a number of whom were fellow members of Rochdale's West Street Baptist Chapel.[8] Emily's parents had started their married life in Tavistock Square, London. Mrs Kemp's sister, Sarah Ainsworth Kelsall, had married Samuel Morton Peto in 1843.

Kemp and Peto were the inspiration behind Bloomsbury Baptist Chapel, Peto in his practical capacity of civil engineer and Kemp as a founding member. Bloomsbury Chapel, as it was then called, encapsulated the Christian philanthropic ideals of the two families, ministering to the slum dwellers around St Giles-in-the-Fields, alongside the wealthy inhabitants of the neighbouring leafy squares.[9]

---

[5] For further discussion of Kemp, see the chapter by Karen E. Smith in the present volume.

[6] EAP, "In Memorium: Miss E.G. Kemp, F.R.G.S."

[7] *City of London Freedom Admissions.*

[8] Kemp, *Reminiscences*, 12.

[9] For the definitive history of the founding of Bloomsbury Chapel, see Bowers, *Bold Experiment.*

In 1860, when Emily was born, the Kemp family consisted of four daughters, Emily (Jessie) born 1851, Ellen (Constance) 1852, Susannah (Florence) 1856 and Lydia Peto 1858. A son, George, was added to the family in 1866. The siblings were to remain close throughout their lives. Emily particularly looked up to and found spiritual inspiration in Florence. Following Florence's death in 1916, she wrote a biographical tribute, *Reminiscences of a Sister, S. Florence Edwards of Taiyuanfu*. From this source we read of a happy, outdoor childhood, where the children were less restricted than other Victorian children of their social standing.

From early years, the Kemp children were immersed in the concept of mission, be it on home ground in and around Rochdale, or from the stories recounted by missionary friends and family in far-away lands. The family home "Beechwood," together with the Kelsall grandparent's home, "The Butts," served as beacons for those who shared the same ideals in both religion and politics. Richard Cobden and John Bright were frequent visitors and both held political meetings in the Kelsall and Kemp warehouses. In June 1861 Cobden addressed 5,000 from Messrs Kelsall & Kemp's warehouse.[10] Christian unity and ecumenism ere also of the utmost importance to the family. Emily describes an early memory demonstrating this:

> The great event of the year to us youngsters was the missionary dinner given by our grandparents on the occasion of the annual meetings in the town and district, to which were invited the neighbouring ministers of all denominations, for the family were always anxious to promote Christian unity, and made systematic efforts in that direction. How well I remember the preparations for the dinner!—the beautiful mahogany table, with its cut glass and silver reflected in the shining surface, and above all, the noble decanters of sherry and port, of which no small amount was consumed. After a very lengthy dinner, beginning at four o'clock, the whole party adjourned to West Street Baptist Chapel for the missionary meeting—by far the most interesting services that ever took place there in those days, and to which we went with great alacrity.[11]

School-days were not cheerful memories for Emily. She followed Constance and Lydia to Miss Dransfield's school in Champion Hill, London. She found the days monotonous and religion only broke the monotony with attendance at the Metropolitan Tabernacle—where she would have heard Spurgeon preach—and the Moody and Sankey meetings which were held in London, during their 1873–75 British tour. For Emily, the spiritual atmosphere of the school was "painfully exotic" with "religious experiences

---

[10] Mattley, *Annals of Rochdale*, 31.

[11] Kemp, *Reminiscences*, 11.

almost *de rigueur*."¹² Schooldays finally ended, and Emily followed Florence and Lydia to a type of finishing school in Cannstadt, Germany.

New Ventures

George Tawke's health was failing in the early 1870s and in 1874 the entire family spent the winter in Cannes on account of his health. Two years later, he and Mrs Kemp, plus two daughters (Jessie and the other was either Emily or Constance),[13] travelled to Egypt with hope of a restoration of health, but, to the enormous grief of the family, he died at Debod on the Nile in March 1877. The newspaper obituaries made much of his philanthropy and the innovative design of his factories at Middleton, where special regard was given to ventilation and gardens. The *Chelmsford Chronicle* obituary reported that Kemp had gifted £10,000 for the founding of a Baptist institution in Rome.[14] Kemp was a friend of Garibaldi: it is interesting to conjecture a connection here.[15]

The Kelsall grandparents had pre-deceased Kemp and consequently the running of Kelsall & Kemp now fell, to a degree, onto the shoulders of Mrs Kemp. Emily was to write later that the Feminist Movement had its foundations well and truly laid by women such as her mother.[16]

Other family changes occurred during this period. Jessie had longed since childhood to serve as a missionary and now the opportunity arose for her to work in Delhi under the Rev. James Smith of the Baptist Missionary Society (BMS), and Miss Bertha Thorn of the Baptist Zenana Mission (BZM). Jessie was a resounding success at the mission, however, physical sickness determined that after three years-service she returned home.[17] Florence was also looking towards missionary service. The disgrace of Britain's part in the opium trade and all the subsequent miseries affected Florence deeply. She now persuaded Jessie that China would be better suited to her health. A cousin, Dr Robert (Harold) Schofield, who, together with his wife, was attached to Hudson Taylor's China Inland Mission (CIM) provided the opening.

---

[12] Kemp, *Reminiscences*, 18.

[13] Florence and Lydia were in Germany, see Kemp, *Reminiscences*, 24.

[14] "Death Announcement." Kemp's will, proved Manchester 1877, mentions property situated in the Piazza San Lorenzo, Lucina, Rome. The BMS had overseen the purchase of a property at the same address in 1875 which became the headquarters of the Apostolic Christian Baptist Church. The Rev. James Wall pastored the church in 1875. See "BAPTISTS AT ROME

[15] Kemp, *Reminiscences*, 30.

[16] Kemp, *Reminiscences*, 28.

[17] Kemp, *Reminiscences*, 32.

Schofield was the first medical missionary to work in the opium riddled province of Shansi.[18] The Schofield's task was building up the mission dispensary in Taiyuanfu, the capital of the province.[19] At that time the BZM were not sending single women to the interior of China, so the two sisters went out in 1882 under their own auspices. However, before going, Florence needed clearance from Hudson Taylor because she did not believe in the doctrine of eternal punishment. Emily attributed this to Florence's extremely sensitive character.[20]

Emily, meanwhile, was embarked on an exciting adventure of her own. Her published work resonates with a deep love and knowledge of literature and it was to academia that she turned her attention in 1881 when she was accepted as one of the first students at Somerville Hall, Oxford.[21]

Life in the university city was perhaps more restricted than she was accustomed to, but she was finally branching out on her own rather than following in the wake of her gifted sisters. Lectures were segregated and chaperones had to be present. A strict dress code was aimed at making the women as inconspicuous as possible. Emily was firmly told that walking to a garden-party wearing a white flannel tennis dress and carrying a racquet and shoes was unacceptable and "considered to be aping the men."[22] Reprimands aside, drawing from Helen Darbishire's *In Memoriam to Emily Georgiana Kemp* (1940), the impression of Emily's Somerville days are of one who entered fully into the student life and she was remembered for her "energy," "vigour," "gifts and enthusiasms." The *Memoriam*, also records that Emily was looking ahead to training as a medical missionary.[23]

With her studies at Somerville completed in 1883 Emily offered to join Florence in Taiyuanfu, the reason being that unforeseen changes had occurred at the mission. In August of 1883 Harold Schofield had succumbed to Typhus fever. A further change just before Dr Schofield's death was cause for celebration. A dashing Anglo–Irish missionary, Thomas Wellesley Pigott, had captured the heart of Jessie who had nursed him through a deadly fever. The couple were ideally suited: both were single minded in serving the Lord in China and had dedicated themselves to Christian service from childhood.[24] Following the marriage, Florence went to live in the nearby girls' school and

---

[18] I have adhered to the contemporary spellings Kemp used in her published works.

[19] Schofield, *Memorials*, 162–67.

[20] Kemp, *Reminiscences*, 22.

[21] Bryant, ed., *Somerville College Register* (1881). (The *Register* is arranged by year.)

[22] Adams, *Somerville for Women*, 120.

[23] Farnell, ed., *Helen Darbishire*, 10.

[24] Pigott, *Steadfast*, 115.

worked more closely with the Chinese. This arrangement left her rather isolated and the family in Rochdale were anxious for her well-being.

Florence was really appreciative of Emily's offer, but she emphasized that Emily should only come if she felt called to the work. She urged Emily to seek advice from their mother, "the wisest of earthly counsellors, and He to whose unerring wisdom you submit all, will, I know not suffer you to take a wrong step."[25] Emily did not go and the family anxieties ceased in 1885 when Florence married Schofield's replacement, Dr Eben Henry Edwards. When the couple had their first child in 1886 it was Constance who went out to help Florence.[26]

Between 1883 and 1888 Emily was involved to some extent with the Oxford University Extension Programme. She did secretarial work and financially supported students through the scheme.[27] In the autumn of 1888, she enrolled at the London School of Medicine for Women. Jessie had also studied there while on furlough in 1885. Medical studies did not go well for Emily. The winter session of 1888–89 examination results record that she was third from last in Anatomy with a score of 172 out of 570. Her summer session results of 1889 were also poor with scores of 40 out of 100 for Chemistry and 17 out of 100 for Physiology.[28] Were health problems the cause or had Emily embarked on a subject which held no interest for her? Darbishire spoke of a physical weakness which was a life-long problem and prevented Emily from attaining her goal of being a medical missionary.[29] This is difficult to understand given Emily's later explorations to remote corners of Asia.

In 1891, Emily began a period of study at the Slade School of Fine Art.[30] Under the tutorage of Alphonse Legros[31] and other leading professors she blossomed as an artist, and in particular developed her style in the medium of watercolour. Her artistic talent proved of enormous value in providing illustrations for her later publications and in enhancing her lectures with lantern slides.

---

[25] Kemp, *Reminiscences*, 38.

[26] Kemp, *Reminiscences*, 46.

[27] Bryant, ed., *Somerville College Register* (1881). See also "Peeps from Tom Tower."

[28] *London School of Medicine for Women: Student Admission*.

[29] Farnell, ed, *Helen Darbishire*, 10.

[30] Bryant, ed., *Somerville College Register* (1881).

[31] Legros painted portraits of both Emily and Lydia. The portraits were gifted by Emily to the Ashmolean Museum, Oxford. See *Will of Emily Georgiana Kemp*.

China

With studies at the Slade completed in 1893, Emily finally set forth on her first visit to China; leaving London on 25 August, she embarked on the steamship, *Glenartney*.[32] This was to be her first experience of life at an overseas mission station. Perhaps she hoped to reach a decision about her personal calling for missionary service. The plan was that she would act as temporary governess to the children of Florence and Eben—George, John and Marjorie (the first child, Henry, had died in 1887). The Pigotts had moved to Shouyang some eighty miles north of Taiyuanfu, leaving Eben and Florence in charge of the dispensary. Both couples had severed their ties with the CIM following differences of opinion with Hudson Taylor. From 1892, the Pigotts and Edwards were responsible for their own independent mission, known as the Shou-Yang Mission. CIM staff continued at the mission until 1896 when Hudson Taylor withdrew the remaining staff.[33]

Emily's first book, *The Face of China*, published in 1909, describes the year spent in Shansi, 1893–94, together with a subsequent visit in 1907–8. Her first impressions make a compelling narrative, the pages spill over with descriptions of people and places. There is humour, too, for she was always ready to see the humorous side of events as well as the tragic. A seasoned traveller since childhood, Emily apparently took all the discomforts associated with travel in her stride. On this first voyage to China, she had the companionship of two BZM ladies, Agnes Kirkland and Lucy Shalders. Upon reaching Hong Kong, the ship was caught up in the tail of a typhoon and "carried for forty-eight hours wherever it pleased to take us. . . . Most of the time we were without food, and could not even get a cup of tea; whilst we found it hard work to cling to a seat."[34] The drama passed and very quickly Emily is enthusing over the beauty of the bay and the harbour which she thought surpassed all the renowned harbours of the world. At Shanghai she parted from her friends and embarked on a coastal steamer feeling a little disconcerted to discover she was the only female passenger.

Sailing slowly up the Peiho on a week-long voyage, the passing scenery was novel and at times shocking. "One dreadful object kept recurring again and again—a tall pole on the river-bank with a basket on top, containing a criminal's head."[35]

At Tientsin, Emily was met by Florence and Eben, and together the three travelled the long and arduous route to Taiyuanfu. Once settled at the mission, she passed her time with the children and painting the everyday

---

[32] *Port of London: Outwards Passenger Lists.*

[33] Kemp, *Reminiscences*, 64–65.

[34] Kemp, *Face of China*, 1.

[35] Kemp, *Face of China*, 73.

scenes. Her brush went to work; temples, pagodas, street scenes, people in everyday and ceremonial dress, all were skilfully observed and recorded. Although, she was enchanted by China, she wrote that she was always conscious of a certain hostility toward foreigners, "a deep-rooted smouldering aversion which might at any time burst into flames."[36] Emily taught fourteen English children in the Sunday school and years later she remonstrated, "Many of these happy youngsters were to share their parents' terrible death by the sword ... I find it difficult to listen patiently to those people who run down missionaries as seekers of soft jobs."[37] Emily had to curtail her visit when the Sino–Japanese war broke out in the summer of 1894.

The Pigott family returned home on furlough in 1896 and during their absence from China the situation against foreigners escalated. A new governor had been appointed to Shansi, Yü Hsien, who was known to be particularly hostile towards foreigners. Was it safe to return? Family discussions centred around the question, but such was the Pigott's dedication to the Chinese Christians that they were determined to return. The only child of the couple, William (Wellesley), might have stayed behind but the boy was devoted to China and his father wanted them to return as a complete family.[38] Florence, Eben and children left China for furlough in 1899.[39]

In June 1900, the situation in China became grave as the Boxer rebels converged on Peking. Fired with a hatred of western influence and Christianity, they intended to kill all foreigners and Chinese Christians. The Legation Quarter was held under siege as Qing government soldiers aided the rebels. An Eight-Nation Alliance was quickly formed and rushed to the rescue. As the family in Rochdale waited anxiously for news, the killing and destruction began to rage through Shansi, encouraged by Yü Hsien and the Qing Empress Dowager, Cixi. With years of discontent compounded by opium addiction, successive famines and severe floods, Shansi was easily ignited.

In the evening of 27 June, a hostile crowd gathered around the Taiyuanfu hospital compound. Fire was kindled at the gates and looting began. Nine missionaries, servants and a few Chinese schoolgirls were in the compound. As the fire spread, they knew it was imperative to force an exit. Dark had fallen when the little band sought to pass through the howling mob. Edith Anna Coombs, a friend of Emily's from Somerville days, was in charge of the schoolgirls.[40] Two of the girls had been undergoing the painful process of

---

[36] Kemp, *Reminiscences*, 61.

[37] Kemp, *Reminiscences*, 59.

[38] Pigott, *Steadfast*, 165.

[39] Kemp, *Reminiscences*, 82.

[40] Edith Anna Coombs, a Congregational minister's daughter from Edinburgh, had been a member of J.H. Jowett's congregation at Carr's Lane Chapel, Birmingham,

having their foot-bindings removed and could not easily walk. Edith, seeing they were missing, went back for them. She stumbled in the dark, the girls were snatched from her arms and she was pushed into the flames of the bonfire. Her companions were oblivious to her plight. As she struggled from the fire, the mob threw furniture on top of her and so died the first Shansi martyr.[41] Thirty-five years later, Emily arranged that the first memorial to be placed in Somerville Chapel would honour Edith Coombs. In all probability it was Emily who had financed the training and arrangements for Edith to work at Taiyuanfu.

Escape was impossible, all foreigners were at the mercy of Yü Hsien. At first the missionaries were allowed to stay with their colleagues who had homes outside of the medical compound, but on 7 July, Yü Hsien ordered all the Taiyuanfu missionaries to move to a house under his supposed protection. Two days later, the missionaries, twenty-six in number, including nine children, were ordered to the Yamen (government office); there the group were paraded in front of Yü Hsien before he ordered their execution by the attending soldiers. At the same time, five Roman Catholic missionaries, seven Sisters-of-Mercy and all the faithful Chinese servants were slain.

Meanwhile, the Pigott family and their group, seven in total, including thirteen-year-old Wellesley and two little girls, Mary and Ernestine, daughters of Mr and Mrs Atwater of the American Board Mission at Fen Chou Fou, had arrived at Taiyuanfu from Shouyang on 8 July.

When the terror struck Shouyang, they had placed themselves under the protection of the local magistrate, but at some point it was decided either by the magistrate or by the mission group that they should proceed to Taiyuanfu. The terrible journey was taken in mule-carts with Tom Pigott and John Robinson (Wellesley's tutor) wearing wrist-chains, supposedly for their own protection in case of a Boxer ambush. At every opportunity on the route Tom Pigott preached the gospel. Upon arrival at Taiyuanfu the men and women were separated. The following afternoon they were summoned to the Yamen. In the courtyard they passed the massacred bodies of their friends, and at the orders of Yü Hsien they suffered the same fate. The decapitated bodies were thrown on the rubbish heaps outside the city walls. In total, 159 foreigners were killed in Shansi and untold numbers of Chinese Christians were tortured and killed.[42]

It would be September before the family in Rochdale had their worst fears confirmed; Edwards immediately left for China but due to the situation had to wait for admittance into Shansi. Finally, one year to the day of the

---

before leaving for China. He wrote a tribute to her which was published in *Fire and Sword*, 220.

[41] Edwards, *Fire and Sword*, 64–65.

[42] Edwards, *Fire and Sword*, 69–82. See also Pigott, *Steadfast*, 228–40.

massacre, he and seven other missionaries entered Taiyuanfu as guests of the new governor. Christian services including a public funeral were arranged, attended by Chinese dignitaries and with full Chinese ceremonial, the remains of the martyrs were laid to rest.[43]

Not wishing to burden the people of Taiyuanfu with extra taxes and because he wanted to demonstrate Christian love in practice, Edwards refused the indemnity for the loss of ten buildings belonging to the Shou-Yang mission.[44] The overall indemnity agreed for Shansi was allotted to fund a university at Taiyuanfu. The Rev. Dr Timothy Richard was the architect of the plan and it was agreed that he should have control of the administration for ten years.[45]

Florence joined her husband in due course and together they set about rebuilding the mission hospital. Whether the appalling tragedy affected Emily's decision regarding a missionary career or whether it was health or perhaps even her personal views on how mission might be styled, it appears that from this point she determined that her missionary role would be in the sphere of an active observer, encourager of co-operative work among missionary organizations and initiator of cross-cultural friendships.

Mission

In the autumn of 1902, Emily visited India and later recollected the experience in *"There Followed Him Women"* (1927), published to mark the sixtieth jubilee of the Women's Missionary Association of the BMS (WMA).[46] Her introduction to life in India was, in her own words, "thoroughly depressing."[47] The sights and sounds interested her and particularly it being the occasion of the great Delhi Durbar, but the barriers of caste and the situation of women were difficult issues for Emily. As a guest of Miss Bertha Thorn at the Mission House, much of Emily's time was taken up with visiting schools and hospitals; often she would know the person in charge, an old school friend now running a school for unwanted children or an

---

[43] Edwards, *Fire and Sword*, 131–38.

[44] Edwards, *Fire and Sword*, 155.

[45] Richard, *Forty-Five Years*, 299–301.

[46] In the same year Emily Kemp was elected to honorary membership of the BMS. She had first been elected on to the BZM Committee in 1895. She also served on the Medical Committee. See *Baptist Missionary Society 138th Annual Report*, 36.

[47] Kemp, *"There Followed Him Women,"* viii.

Indian friend from Somerville days, working as a Lady Dufferin doctor,[48] struggling to break down barriers of superstition and ignorance.

A visit to Benares was particularly repugnant. Emily wrote, "I never saw such a repulsive, hateful place in my life."[49] To look on a woman lying in front of a temple god was "unendurable."[50] She found it incredible that the British government were "restoring the temples and allowing indecent processions through the streets."[51] A visit to the burning ghat filled her with such horror that she nearly fell over a corpse in her desire to escape and she flatly refused to see any more. Irritation is evident over Annie Besant who "after a spell of Buddhism ... has formed a [Hindu] college, goes about lecturing, and is received by some leading British officials!"[52]

In 1904, the BZM asked Emily and Miss Edith Angus to visit Delhi and sort out "certain knotty problems."[53] She undertook the task and indeed visited India on several occasions to visit missions, but India never claimed her heart in the way China did.

"*There Followed Him Women*" is a fitting tribute to the women who served the BZM and the WMA. Emily's belief was that women have a special duty to be the "Christ-bearer to all humanity" and first and foremost to other women. She wrote,

> God gave to humanity the greatest of all gifts through a wonderful girl. ... Christ chose as the herald to humanity of the greatest message of His human life that Mary who had been delivered by Him from the seven-fold power of evil. To her He said: "Go and tell ... I am risen." ... The angels told the women to go and tell the news, but it needed the Christ Himself to send Mary as His messenger to His disciples and to the world.[54]

A considerable amount of her thought, energy and wealth was directed towards empowering women to be all that God intended for them.[55]

---

[48] Lady Hariot Dufferin, Vicereine of India 1884–88, established hospitals for women and children.

[49] Kemp, *"There Followed Him Women,"* 37.

[50] Kemp, *"There Followed Him Women,"* 38.

[51] Kemp, *"There Followed Him Women,"* 37–38.

[52] Kemp, *"There Followed Him Women,"* 38.

[53] Kemp, *"There Followed Him Women,"* 26.

[54] Kemp, *"There Followed Him Women,"* 13.

[55] Little is known of Emily's suffrage affiliations. She was probably a subscriber to the National Union of Women's Suffrage Societies (NUWSS). Her name is listed in *Common Cause*, the NUWSS newspaper, on 8 September 1910 as one who donated to the Trafalgar Square NUWSS demonstration of 9 July 1910.

The Kemp family were barely assimilating the Taiyuanfu tragedy when it became apparent that the health of Mrs Kemp, the dependable matriarch of the family, was failing. The theologian, Marcus Dods, friend and confident to Emily, wrote several letters to her around this period. In April 1904, he wrote,

> If I began about your experience of "cutting off the right hand" I would become tedious. Besides, these matters are better talked of than written about. But I may say that this world is unintelligible except on the hypothesis that it is for our schooling, and that he that sows in tears is the likeliest to have sheaves worth gathering. It is truly a *death* we must pass through, a quitting of our hold on all that once seemed life to us. . . . But it is impertinent in me to suggest what you already know and practice so much better than your affectionate friend . . . .[56]

Later in October of the same year, Dods visited Emily, Constance and Lydia in Rochdale and wrote, thanking them:

> . . . I cannot be too grateful to yourself and your sisters for giving me so good and profitable a time. I am beginning to look upon Rochdale as a home of rest where everything tends to resuscitate what is good in one. . . . If medals are given for saving life, should not medals also be given to those who renew the best life in us ?[57]

A further letter followed in November of 1904.

> And what I chiefly hope for you is that you may construct, out of outward circumstances to which ordinary people would succumb, the rich and influential character Christ destines for you. Is it not a better preparation for India, after all, than the sunshine of Bordighera?[58]

Mrs Kemp died soon after this letter was written. She had left Rochdale in November with the intention of wintering in Bordighera, but had taken ill at Dover and died there in December.[59]

The loss of Mrs Kemp was felt acutely not only by the family but by the people of Rochdale where she was dearly loved for the many good causes she had initiated.[60]

George was now head of Kelsall & Kemp. He had already carved out a distinguished career in politics and the army as well as being a celebrated

---

[56] Dods, *Later Letters*, 109.

[57] Dods, *Later Letters*, 138.

[58] Dods, *Later Letters*, 51.

[59] *Foreign Office: Probate Records.*

[60] "Funeral of Mrs Kemp."

cricketer.[61] He had married Lady Beatrice Egerton[62] in 1896, both were ardent campaigners for women's suffrage.

Early in 1906, the family were alarmed by reports of unrest in China and fearful for Florence and Eben in Taiyuanfu, George contacted the Foreign Office outlining his fears.[63] To have a repeat of the earlier tragedy was unthinkable. In spite of the risk, the Edwards's continued their work and the situation calmed down.

Perhaps it was Marcus Dods who persuaded Emily to return to China, for in 1907 she and a friend, May Meiklejon MacDougall, set off on a six-month exploration of China.[64] Emily's subsequent publication, *The Face of China*, is dedicated to Dods, "To whose suggestion and encouragement it owes its existence." May MacDougall was a stalwart travelling companion. The daughter of a Scottish surgeon, she was some fifteen years younger than Emily. Her 1918 *Women's Royal Naval Service* record indicates that she "is able to act independently and shows initiative."[65] The ideal travelling companion for Emily's adventures. Dods wrote to Emily *en route* in August 1907.

> Be sure to write up your diary day by day, and don't disappoint your publisher and the public who wait to get some experience of unknown China.... I have an impression your travels are going to be note-worthy and will afford an opportunity for the utilisation of your gift of drawing and painting. And what fun you two will have.[66]

The adventure took the two women through the provinces of Shantung, Chili, Hupeh, Szechwan, and Yunnan. In contrast to the 1893–94 visit, Emily experienced no hostility and in Tientsin and Taiyuanfu the travellers were treated as honoured dignitaries. The frontispiece of *The Face of China* is a self-portrait of Emily, dressed as a female travelling scholar, complete with Buddhist pilgrim staff and horn spectacles. The narrative suggests that this was indeed the dress the women wore.[67] Emily found travel a sheer pleasure;

---

[61] George was elevated to the peerage in 1913 and took the title, Lord Rochdale. See "Obituary."

[62] Beatrice, Lady Rochdale, walked from Carlisle to London on the *Great Pilgrimage* (June–July 1913) in support of women's suffrage. She was already a local hero for her philanthropic work in and around Keswick where she and George had a country house (Lingholm). See Robinson, *Hearts and Minds*, 164–66.

[63] *Foreign Office: China*.

[64] There is a note in Kemp, *Face of China*, 87, which suggests Emily was in China in September of 1904.

[65] *Admiralty: Women's Royal Naval Service*.

[66] Dods, *Later Letters*, 270–71.

[67] Kemp, *Face of China*, 236.

she was very adaptable to whatever arose and, considering the luxury she was accustomed to, the privations frequently experienced on her travels were accepted as part and parcel of the whole experience. In Tali Fu, Yunnan Province, an official rest-house proved to have a number of uninvited guests:

> The next night we were not so lucky, and had the most riotous party of rats in the loft above us that I have ever encountered. Their revels brought down no inconsiderable portion of the ceiling on our heads, and finally the rats themselves came down in a sort of stampede upon us, showing no respect whatever for the British face or form.[68]

The following morning saw the women setting off with their bearers; the discomforts of the night were soon forgotten as they climbed upwards through pine woods and crimson rhododendrons; higher still, they turned to gaze back at the long range of snow-capped mountains and revelled in the sheer beauty of it all.[69]

Emily had a collectors eye for textiles and items purchased on her travels were often used to illustrate her lectures.[70] In Peking, she purchased, with some difficulty, an item she clearly intended to wear, "a black spotted leopard-skin coat lined with lovely blue silk, on which I had set my heart."[71] And at a military review she was so taken by the tiger uniform of the *Tiger Braves*, that she not only painted a portrait of a soldier clad in his yellow and black striped uniform, complete with the mask like cap designed to suggest all the ferocity of the tiger, but also ordered an exact replica of the costume.[72]

The journey covered a wide geographical area and enabled Emily to grasp a much wider appreciation of Chinese culture than her 1893–94 visit. She was eager to observe the new schools and universities (with the assistance of missionary friends) brought about by the reforms the Qing government implemented after 1901. Such was the pleasure of the entire adventure that upon crossing the frontier into Burma both women thought they would like to turn around and go all the way back.[73] *The Face of China*, published in 1909,

---

[68] Kemp, *Face of China*, 242.

[69] Kemp, *Face of China*, 243.

[70] A number of the costumes and textiles were gifted to the Ashmolean Museum, Oxford. See *Will of Emily Georgiana Kemp*.

[71] Kemp, *Face of China*, 99.

[72] Kemp, *Face of China*, 85.

[73] Kemp, *Face of China*, viij [*sic*].

brought mixed reviews,[74] but was on the whole a triumph for Emily and earned her place among her contemporaries at the geographical societies.[75]

Emily and May set off on a further adventure in February 1910. This took them on a four-month journey through Manchuria and Korea. Emily was also eager to see the changes occurring in these regions but confessed to having a "profound anxiety" over how these changes were affecting the local cultures.[76] Russia and Japan were steadily strengthening their hold on China's borders, namely Manchuria and Korea. She needed to go and see for herself what the impact of this was.

Travelling via the Trans-Siberian Railway to Harbin, they were once again enriched in their travels by the local knowledge of missionaries who arranged visits to schools and colleges. In Korea they particularly enjoyed a Sunday visiting the many churches in Pyongyang. Emily thought that the Korean Christians were "much more capable of self-government, and forming a national church, than would be conceived possible by those who have not seen this wonderful people."[77]

Six months later, Korea was annexed by Japan, and many of Emily's anxieties concerning national culture were realized. The final part of the journey through Turkestan was not part of the original plan, but on finding a railway link they decided to apply for permission through the British Embassy at St Petersburg. Delighted to obtain permission, the women travelled on, and were particularly enchanted by Samarkand, which Emily described as "the most wonderful city I have yet to come across in my wanderings."[78] She did, however, deplore the condition of women in this part of Central Asia.[79] The entire journey was immortalized, complete with Emily's water colours, in *The Face of Manchuria, Korea, and Russian Turkestan,* published the same year. A second book associated with Emily was published in English in 1910, *Buddhism as a Religion* by Heinrich Hackmann. Emily translated the original work from German into English.

It is easy to speculate that Emily's interest in Eastern religions indicates that her adherence to the central doctrines of Christianity were somehow weakened; whereas, as an observer of other cultures and particularly those of

---

[74] See, for instance, "Face of China."

[75] Emily was admitted as a Fellow of the Royal Scottish Geographical Society in 1907. (Information received via a telephone conversation with the archivist of the Society in 2019.) There is a reference in *Face of China* to her FRSGS, therefore, it was not granted as a consequence of the 1907 journey. See *Face of China*, 43.

[76] Kemp, *Face of Manchuria*, vij [*sic*.].

[77] Kemp, *Face of Manchuria*, 82.

[78] Kemp, *Face of Manchuria*, 213.

[79] Kemp, *Face of Manchuria*, 229.

China, it was surely profitable that she had an understanding of those cultures and religions? Her concept of constructive mission was based on the theory of gospel teaching without westernizing a culture, save to liberate it from harmful customs and ignorance. She wrote in 1910,

> the churches in which they worship must have a home like feeling, so that nothing may suggest to them that Christianity is a foreign religion. When all is said and done it came from the East and not from the West, so that its externals at least should have as little western colouring as possible.[80]

Carey Hall and the Roof of the World

If Emily's enthusiasm for cross-cultural mission was untiring, so too was her energy for ecumenism. In 1911, she gave her attention to a project which would unite the two in the concept of Carey Hall, United Missionary College. The origins of the College began in 1906 when a group of women from the London Missionary Society (LMS), the BZM and the Women's Missionary Association of the Presbyterian Church of England explored the idea of setting up a training centre for women missionaries. Following the 1910 World Missionary Conference in Edinburgh, to which Emily was a delegate,[81] the planning really got underway and a committee was drawn up in the summer of 1911. Emily was elected Treasurer, Amelia Angus, Chairwoman, Jane Craig, Secretary, and Christina Irvine was to be the first Principal. An invitation was put forward to join the three missionary colleges at Selly Oak, Birmingham, and a manor house was found in the vicinity. In January 1912, Emily bought the house and presented it to the BMS. The house was named after William Carey and so Carey Hall United Missionary College for Women was founded. The first students arrived in September 1912.[82]

The European antagonisms which exploded into the First World War were already coming to a head when Carey Hall was officially opened in November of 1912. Revolution in China had brought about the end of the Qing dynasty and with it the end of 2,000 years of imperial rule. It was against this backdrop that Emily turned her attention toward an adventure which was to prove exhilarating and also her most challenging. Friend, and fellow Asiatic explorer, Sir Francis Younghusband, warned against the plan, which was to cross the Himalayas from Kashmir into "Chinese" Turkestan following the Silk Road. Younghusband knew the route and warned that even for a man the passes were arduous and extremely dangerous. And so it was that in August of

---

[80] Kemp, *Face of Manchuria*, 50.

[81] Kemp, *Reminiscences*, 88.

[82] See Martin, *Fifty Years of Carey Hall*, 8–16.

Emily Georgiana Kemp

1912, Emily and May MacDougall set off from the town of Leh, in the upper Indus Valley, with their guides, to traverse the ancient trade route across the Karakorum range into China. The intrepid pair reached the frontier fort of Shah-i-Dulah on 28 August, the first European women to have reached that remote place.[83] Emily wrote,

> The road had been a hard one, often leading over pathless mountains and up ravines. where cliffs towered above us to a height of 23,000 or 24,000 feet, and the torrents filled with ice-cold water and snow from the melting glaciers had to be crossed some 20 or 30 times in a single day. ... The vast solitude was haunted by the dismal cry of vultures. ... Breathing became difficult, and the cheery spirits of our men failed: faces are skinned and lips become so sore, that even a smile is perforce a painful one. ... It was therefore, with profound satisfaction that we wended our way downwards through a somewhat less austere valley, sweet with the scent of bog myrtle . . . .[84]

From there onwards, the travellers were showered with gifts of local delicacies and, upon reaching Yarkand, were received in the manner of royalty. As the year turned to autumn, they reached Kashgar where they were warmly welcomed, being the first lady guests in twenty-four years, by the British Consul-General, Sir George Macartney and his wife.[85] Emily felt a great admiration for Macartney who, unsupported, had kept his region calm during the Chinese Revolution of the previous year. Emily found plenty of subjects to paint and the two women had a pleasant three week stay. From Kashgar they travelled via Irkeshtam, across the perilous Terek Dawan Pass in the Alay Mountains and finally, to the enormous relief of family and friends, reached the railway terminal at Andijan.

There was hardly time, upon returning home, to fulfil the round of lectures, arrange a meeting with the Foreign Secretary, in order to communicate messages from Macartney,[86] prepare *Wanderings in Chinese Turkestan* for publication and at the same time, embark on a journey to India with Lydia, "in order to secure a first-hand knowledge of the missionary work which is being carried on there, especially amongst the native women,"[87] before the world descended into war.

---

[83] Kemp, *Wanderings*, 3.

[84] Kemp, *Wanderings*, 3.

[85] Kemp, *Wanderings*, 18–22.

[86] *Foreign Office: Private Offices.*

[87] Lydia and Emily gave a lecture on their tour at West Street Chapel in June 1914. See "Misses Kemp in India."

War Work

Within months of war being declared, Emily and May were off to the Haute-Marne district of France to assist in the setting up of a military hospital for French soldiers.[88] Emily roused friends and associates to the cause and Hôpital Temporaire, d'Arc-en-Barrois, became as well known for its volunteer corps made up of renowned artists and writers as for the exemplary medical care practiced there. Kathleen Scott (widow of Robert Falcon Scott), John Masefield, Henry Tonks, Laurence Binyon, were just a few of the names associated with the hospital.[89] Eben Edwards, now returned from China on account of Florence's failing health, volunteered there before serving with the Royal Army Medical Corps (RAMC) and later in the war, the Young Men's Christian Association (YMCA).[90] After a short while, Emily and May left the overall running of the hospital to the Bromley-Martin sisters, Madeleine and Susan, who had also been part of the initial set-up, and took on the running of a convalescent hostel in the village.[91] In 1916, Emily volunteered for eighteen months as a masseuse in the French Military Hospital in Paris. Following this she organized canteens and rest-rooms in the Verdun region.[92] May MacDougall, joined the Women's Royal Naval Service (WRNS) in 1918 and organized hostels for the Royal Navy.[93]

The busy war years were chequered with personal grief for the Kemp family. Florence died in 1916. Emily had been recalled from Paris and spent the final days with Florence. *Reminiscences of a Sister* was published in 1920. Emily wrote, "the fact of spending so many hours in her dear company has been the greatest inspiration to myself and has increased my admiration for the best of sisters."[94] Lydia died suddenly in April 1918,[95] and, in July 1918, Robert Amor Edwards, youngest son of Florence and Eben, was killed in action.[96] His elder brother, George Kemp Edwards, had taken up the medical

---

[88] Anon., "Bloomsbury at the Front."

[89] Binyon, *Dauntless France*, 145–46.

[90] *World War 1 Medal Cards*.

[91] "Hospital Work in France."

[92] Bryant, ed., *Somerville College Register* (1881).

[93] *Admiralty: Women's Royal Naval Service*.

[94] Kemp, *Reminiscences*, Prologue.

[95] Local newspapers reported that several thousand people attended Lydia's funeral procession and internment in Rochdale cemetery. See "LATE MISS L.P. KEMP." Lydia (and Constance) had been very active in local affairs. Lydia was the first woman to stand for local government in Rochdale when she was nominated as an Independent candidate for Castleton North Ward in 1912. See "YESTERDAY'S ELECTIONS."

[96] Kemp, *Reminiscences*, 94.

work at Taiyuanfu and remained there throughout the war. Exhausted by the demands, he died of fever in May 1919. Emily lamented "O TAIYUANFU! Will your deaf ears at last listen to the call of love and sacrifice?"[97] George was the eighth member of the family to be laid to rest in the Taiyuanfu cemetery. She wrote in 1927,

> the city [Taiyuanfu] is "stony ground" for the seed of the Gospel. Drenched with the blood of martyrs, it might be supposed that we should have seen a glorious harvest; but it has not been so. All the more it needs a wealth of loving service to break down this stronghold of Satan.[98]

Soon after *Reminiscences of a Sister* was completed, Emily set off for China and this time she travelled with Florence (Marjorie) Edwards, her young doctor niece who was to take up the work at Taiyuanfu.[99]

China acted as a balm for Emily, she wrote, "Oh, there is a charm in China found nowhere else! You pass out of thronged streets into calm poetic retreats where the turmoil of life is hushed; for a brief spell life stands still."[100] Thirteen Provinces were visited including some time spent with mission friends in Kweichow, who were working amongst the aboriginal tribes there. Apart from Emily's obvious joy of travelling in China again, there was a further reason for this visit. A building was being constructed in Taiyuanfu which was to serve as an institute for women and high-school age girls. It was to be a traditional Chinese structure and Emily was funding it in memory of Florence. While in Kweichow, Emily saw some handsome carved window frames and despite all the difficulties of transportation she determined to have them for the Institute.[101] *Chinese Mettle*, published upon her return, was to be Emily's final book on China. In May 1922, she was invited to Paris to lecture on her travels among the aboriginal tribes of China to the French Geographical Society. She was presented with the Society's medal, the first time the award had been granted to a woman.[102]

---

[97] Kemp, *Reminiscences*, 123.

[98] Kemp, *"There Followed Him Women,"* 85.

[99] In 1907, the Edwards's decided that the work at Taiyuanfu should be under one Mission and accordingly they joined with the BMS and later gifted the Taiyuanfu property to the BMS. See Kemp, *Reminiscences*, 106–107. Eben continued working in China after WWI. He retired back to England in 1926 and died there in 1945. See "Late Dr E.H. Edwards."

[100] Kemp, *Chinese Mettle*, 24.

[101] Emily wrote about the "Edward's Memorial Institute" in *"There Followed Him Women,"* 82–83, but made no mention of the fact that she was the person behind the project. The Institute was formerly opened in October 1923.

[102] "Miss Emily G. Kemp."

Constance died in May 1922. Little is recorded of Lydia and Constance, but they too were remarkable for their selfless work with many local causes and for their support of overseas mission.

Sixty Years and Beyond

At sixty years of age Emily did not visibly slow down. She continued to be a popular speaker on Baptist and Geographical Society platforms. She was elected to Honorary Membership of the BMS in 1927. Her final book, *Mary, With Her Son, Jesus,* was published in 1931. The narrative is remarkable for its depths and insights, although written in a very simple style. The concept for the book came about through a remarkable encounter in the Amazon.

A long desire to visit the Rainforest persuaded Emily in 1929 to accept the invitation of a friend, Captain Buck, to sail on his ship, up the Amazon to Manaus. She was accompanied on the trip by Margaret Ellen Dobson, a long-time servant of the Kemp family.[103] Among the passengers were eight Franciscan nuns, setting off for missionary service in the heart of Brazil. Drawn by their radiant serenity, Emily sought their company and soon it was discovered that seven of their number had died alongside her own loved ones at Taiyuanfu in 1900. Deeply affected by this encounter Emily wrote,

> Naturally, our hearts were deeply stirred as we talked together of those days, and of the work still carried on there by their successors and ours. ... In this atmosphere of Love and Service a great urge came upon me to write in very simple form the story of the wonderful Mary who bore the hope of all the world. It came to me unexpectedly and with overwhelming force.[104]

It was Emily's hope that "Others may find from the narrative some fresh light on their daily path and courage in dark days."[105] It seems plausible that her next major project also came into being at least partially through the Amazon encounter.

Somerville College Chapel

Emily's companion of many adventures, May Meiklejon MacDougall, died in August 1931. So many friends and all of Emily's much-loved sisters had gone before her, and she too was slowing down, but there was one final project.

In June 1932, Emily sent an unsigned letter (enclosing her address) to the Council of Somerville College. The content of the letter outlined her "great

---

[103] *Port of Liverpool: Inwards Passenger Lists.*

[104] Kemp, *Mary, with her Son*, 12.

[105] Kemp, *Mary, with her Son*, 13.

desire to build for the college a beautiful, simple & significant house for the purposes of meditation, prayer & other spiritual exercises." She considered that the youth of the 1930s would be more receptive to the building if it were called a house rather than a chapel, and also that it would be more acceptable to those of other beliefs. She explained that the leading idea would be embodied in a stained-glass window "Dedicated to Christ, Lord & Giver of Life." For she said, "It is Christ alone commands universal reverence and He is the essential of our faith." She would like the house to be called "Christ House." She did not intend there to be an altar, only a raised dais, furnished with table, chairs and a lectern. Emily emphasized that she was anxious to know whether the gift would be acceptable as she wished to make all the necessary plans before her death. Marcus Tod,[106] would, she said, explain her plan to the College in more detail and answer any questions they might have.[107]

Emily received a reply, dated 20 October, from the Principal, Miss Darbishire. The Council were interested, but not without some reservations. They insisted that the building be called a chapel, but allowed that Emily might suggest an inscription. It was also suggested that Emily send the Council an outline of her vision for the building.[108]

As the news spread through the College, feelings against the Chapel became very apparent. On 25 October, the Association of Senior Members informed the Council by letter, that fifty-five of its members thought an undenominational chapel "highly unsatisfactory." It would, they argued, end up "characterless and vague."[109] Vera Brittain was among those who signed the letter. Following a meeting with the Principal on 9 November, the Junior Common Room members presented three petitions indicating fifty-eight objections and thirty supporters for the Chapel, whilst ninety-six members were against the proposed site.[110]

Whether Emily was aware of the heated debates is unclear. She replied to the letter of 20 October on 1 November. Her reply to Miss Darbishire outlines her enthusiastic ideas for the Chapel, and while she emphasizes her

---

[106] Presumably this is Marcus Niebuhr Tod, specialist in Greek inscriptions and a fellow of Oriel College, Oxford. In the end it was Emily herself who outlined the details for the Chapel, but it is conceivable that Tod had a hand in the external Greek inscription on the Chapel. Rather enigmatically, Emily says that Marcus Tod will explain to the Council why she needs to know soon if the gift will be accepted. *Chapel Foundation: Letter*, June 1932.

[107] *Chapel Foundation: Letter*, Kemp to Council, 4 June 1932.

[108] *Chapel Foundation: Letter*, 1 November 1932.

[109] *Chapel Foundation: Petition*, 1932.

[110] Adams, *Somerville For Women*, 182.

understanding that the College will have ultimate responsibility for how the Chapel is used, it must have been apparent to Darbishire that Emily had no intention of being a passive donor. Emily hoped that the Council would allow her to have "A House of Prayer for all peoples" (Isa 56:7) inscribed over the entrance. Her desire was that the Chapel would inspire the students to seek God's will for their lives; the special meaning of the place is, she says, "<u>Life</u>." Here she includes a quote from John R. Mott as way of explanation, "Live, each according to the light you have."[111] Mott quotes the concept in his 1932 publication, *The Present-day Summons to the World Mission of Christianity*:

> We know that, even apart from conscious knowledge of Him, when men are true to the best light they have, they are able to effect some real deliverance from many of the evils that afflict the world; and this should prompt us the more to help them to find the fullness of light and power in Christ.[112]

It was Emily's wish that the Chapel would appeal to students from other cultures, and build upon the work of breaking down prejudices, which, she affirmed, Somerville had always tried to do.[113]

She had, all her life, sought to work for Christian unity and, beyond that, to understand other cultures and faiths. She had personally suffered from war and the horror unleashed in 1900 when one culture was so possessed with suspicion and hatred for another that it sought its destruction. After the First World War, there was a deeper more urgent searching for that which binds humanity. Thomas Phillips' *The Grace of God and a World Religion*, was published in 1928, and Mott, who was at the forefront of the ecumenical movement, wrote,

> Nor has it [Christendom] sufficiently sought out the good and noble elements in the non-Christian beliefs, that it might learn that deeper personal fellowship with adherents of those beliefs wherein they may be more powerfully drawn to the living Christ.[114]

The living Christ was the core of Emily's vision for the Chapel.

In terms of the day-to-day use of the Chapel, Emily thought that there should be included daily prayers, private prayers and meditation, praise and thanksgivings with "frequent Te Deums and Psalms," plus occasional services and addresses. Holy communion, too, if the students desired it, and music,

---

[111] *Chapel Foundation: Letter*, Kemp to Darbishire, 1 November 1932 (emphasis original).

[112] Mott, *Present-Day Summons*, 257.

[113] *Chapel Foundation: Letter*, Kemp to Darbishire, 1 November 1932.

[114] Mott, *Present-Day Summons*, 257.

especially Bach, "because he is so cheering and inspiring," and speakers, those who would be concerned with breaking down "sectarian prejudice." But not "popular cranks like Gandhi" (perhaps her sentiments against Gandhi had something to do with his visit to the Lancashire textile mills in 1931.[115] Emily concludes the letter by giving detailed examples from her experience of educational establishments that have been successful in breaking down sectarian prejudices: Selly Oak Colleges, Serampore College, The Shantung Christian University (Emily was on the Board of Governors[116]) and the Tyndale Biscoe School at Srinagar.[117]

The correspondence between Emily and Darbishire suggests that Darbishire was immensely grateful for the donation of the Chapel and was, on the whole, supportive of the concept, but she had to win over the Council and past and present students. Henry Norman Spalding, Professor of Eastern Religions, also acted as an advisor and negotiated between Emily and the College. George (Lord Rochdale) was the only family member with whom Emily discussed the plan and he supported her throughout. The design and site were finally, after much discussion, agreed between Emily's chosen architect, Courtenay Theobald, Percy R. Morley Horder (who was already engaged on commissions for Somerville), and a third architect agreed upon by both Somerville and Emily, Walter Tapper.[118]

Much of the correspondence between Emily and Darbishire is painful to read. By July 1934, Emily was exhausted by the conflicts over decisions for the interior, and accuses Darbishire of sweeping away things she wanted, one of which was a large room designated for prayer-meetings.[119] The Principal defended herself and reminded Emily that the prayer room had to be cast aside because of rising costs.[120] There was also upset over the inscriptions. Above the entrance, "A House of Prayer for All Peoples" was carved in classical Greek letters, as Emily requested, but she also wanted an inscription inside the Chapel:

---

[115] Gandhi's Indian National Congress Party's policy of boycotting British goods had caused widespread unemployment in the Lancashire textile mills. When Gandhi visited the mill town of Dawen in September 1931 he received a tumultuous welcome, but insisted the hunger and poverty being experienced in Lancashire could not compare to that of India. See "COTTON DEPUTATIONS' QUESTIONS TO MR GANDHI."

[116] Shantung Administration, British Section of the Board of Governors, 1928.

[117] *Chapel Foundation: Letter*, Kemp to Darbishire, 1 November 1932.

[118] Adams, *Somerville for Women*, 182.

[119] *Chapel Foundation: Letter*, Kemp to Darbishire, 19 July 1934.

[120] *Chapel Foundation: Letter*, Darbishire to Kemp, 20 July 1934.

THIS CHAPEL BUILT IN THE YEAR OF OUR LORD 1934 IS
DEDICATED TO JESUS CHRIST THE LORD THE GIVER OF LIFE

MINE HOUSE SHALL BE CALLED A HOUSE OF PRAYER FOR ALL PEOPLES.

The inscription was placed high up on the wall above the vestibule and Emily complained that it was practically unseen. Emily begged for an end to the continual correspondence over the Chapel. Darbishire consented, but was at pains to tell Emily how well the Chapel was coming along.[121]

The dedication service was set for early 1935. Darbishire had agreed to read 1 Corinthians 13:1–13 at the service, but was completely taken aback when Emily presented the Chapel with the *New Testament in Modern Speech*. She wrote to Emily, protesting that her conscience would not permit her to read the chapter in a version she considered inferior to the *Authorised Version*.[122] When the service finally took place in February, neither Emily or Helen Darbishire were well enough to attend. Feelings were still running high over the Chapel and one former student replied to her invitation that she was sorry, but she would never enter the Chapel except for a funeral or memorial service.[123]

In the summer of 1937 Emily was apparently in reasonable health and looking forward to the World Congress of Faiths (WCF) meetings in Oxford. Somerville and Balliol were to host delegates. Sir Francis Younghusband, the founder and leader of the WCF, was a man of a vague, mystical nature, moulded by supernatural experiences in Tibet and by atheist philosophers.[124] However, the literature produced for the WCF was very much concerned with reflecting on that which unites humanity and in particular the 1937 Conference was much concerned with the dangerous situation the world was in, as it stood on the brink of the Second World War.

Emily was particularly delighted that the Chapel would be available for prayer. Full of enthusiasm she designed a leaflet explaining the symbolism of the Reginald Bell stained-glass window, which was for Emily the central feature of the Chapel.[125] She also added the statement that religion was a founding principle of the College. Helen Darbishire acted quickly by asking Spalding to intervene and stop the leaflets being distributed.[126] Once more,

---

[121] *Chapel Foundation: Letter*, Kemp to Darbishire, 18 August 1937.

[122] *Chapel Foundation: Letter, Chapel Foundation: Letter*, 15 January 1935.

[123] *Chapel Foundation: Letter, Chapel Foundation: Letter*, Matilda Snow to Darbishire, 11 January 1935.

[124] *Papers of Sir Francis Younghusband*. See also Younghusband, *Mutual Influence*, x.

[125] Somerville College, *Chapel Leaflet*.

[126] *Chapel Foundation: Letter*, Darbishire to Kemp, 24 July 1937.

there was confrontation between Darbishire and Emily. The former knew the College Council would not endorse the leaflet and she argued that religion did not appear in the statutes until 1925. Darbishire felt that the Chapel was now more widely accepted by the College and therefore wanted to avoid any fresh controversy.[127] Emily apologized that by not signing her name to the leaflet it gave the impression that Somerville had endorsed it, but would not back down on the notion that religion was not one of the founding principles of Somerville; she was after all there in the early days and knew that Somerville's foundations were based on religious toleration and she had personally known the founders.[128]

The Last Word

Emily died at her brother, Lord Rochdale's, home in Richmond, Yorkshire, on Christmas Day 1939. Until a few days before, she had remained in touch with the situation in China, giving to relief and re-construction work as the war with Japan escalated.[129] Helen Darbishire had become accustomed to give an address in the Chapel after the Sunday evening service. On the 14 January 1940, she addressed those in the Chapel with the news that it could now be revealed that Miss Emily Kemp was the donor. She then proceeded to present a memoriam which was constructed to inspire the students, and, especially given the situation of war, instil purpose and courage. If there was any hint of the confrontations over the Chapel, they were graciously veiled: "what she [Kemp] intended to do she did, in spite of warning, in spite of opposition, she had too, a strong sense of humour and that inestimable gift, the power to enjoy, a zest for life and all the manifestations of life ... Her central interest was in living Christianity."[130]

Emily's will included legacies to many of her devoted causes including, Carey Hall, the BMS, Regent's Park College, Shantung Christian University, and, to Somerville College, "my terra-cotta, 'The Annunciation' by Della Robbia ... subject to the condition that the said terra-cotta 'The Annunciation' shall be placed in the Chapel ... in a position to be approved by my Executors and the Council of the said College."[131]

Helen Darbishire wrote to the executors on 24 January 1940,

---

[127] *Chapel Foundation: Letter*, Darbishire to Kemp, 25 August 1937.

[128] *Chapel Foundation: Letter*, Kemp to Darbishire, 12 August 1937.

[129] Farnell, ed., *Helen Darbishire*, 11.

[130] Farnell, ed., *Helen Darbishire*, 11.

[131] *Will of Emily Georgiana Kemp*.

At a meeting of the Principal and Fellows yesterday it was unanimously agreed that the College will wish to accept the bequest of the Della Robbia terra cotta subject to the conditions defined in the Will, namely that a suitable position should be found for the terra cotta in the College Chapel, such position to be approved by the Executors and by the Council of the College.[132]

On 14 April 1940, the terra-cotta, *The Annunciation,* proclaiming God's great love for humanity, trustingly received by a young woman, was removed from Emily's drawing room in her London residence and placed in the Somerville Chapel by Courtenay Theobald.[133]

Bibliography
Primary Sources

THE BRITISH LIBRARY

Papers of Sir Francis Younghusband: MSS Eur F 197/117–125 (Religious Activities).

LONDON METROPOLITAN ARCHIVES (LMA)

City of London Freedom Admissions: COL/CHD/FR/02.
London School of Medicine for Women: Student Admission: H72/SM/C/01/03/001.

THE NATIONAL ARCHIVES (TNA)

Admiralty: Women's Royal Naval Service: ADM 321/1/192.
Foreign Office: China: FO 371/27/59/493–497.
Foreign Office: Private Offices: FO 800/108.
Foreign Office: Probate Records: FO 917/1496.
Inland Revenue: IR 62/1905.
Port of Liverpool: Inwards Passenger Lists: BT 26/899/26.
Port of London: Outwards Passenger Lists: BT 27/137/2.
World War 1 Medal Cards: WO 372/6/166177.

---

[132] *Inland Revenue.*

[133] The terra-cotta was declared by Oxford conservationists as not an original from the fifteenth century Della Robbia workshop, see https://www.blogs.some.ox.ac.uk. Emily's terra-cotta was valued at £100 in 1940, see *Inland Revenue.* Whether or not Emily believed her piece to be fifteenth–sixteenth century is unknown. It is plausible that with the advantage of her tutorage at the Slade School she executed the terra-cotta herself. The Birkenhead Pottery founded 1894 also went under the title of The Della Robbia Pottery.

NEWSPAPERS
"BAPTISTS AT ROME." *York Herald* 23 March 1875, 4
"COTTON DEPUTATIONS' QUESTIONS TO MR GANDHI," *Lancaster Daily Post* 26 September 1931, 6.
"Death Announcement." *Chelmsford Chronicle* 20 April 1877, 5.
EAP. "In Memorium: Miss E.G. Kemp, F.R.G.S." *Baptist Times* 4 January 1940, 14.
"The Face of China." *Morning Post* 4 October 1909, 2.
"FUNERAL OF MRS KEMP." *Heywood Advertiser* 9 December 1904, 6.
"HOSPITAL WORK IN FRANCE." *Rochdale Observer* 20 October 1915, 2.
"The Late Dr E.H. Edwards." *Rochdale Observer* 25 July 1945, 2.
"THE LATE MISS L.P. KEMP." *Rochdale Times*, 10 April 1918, 2.
"Miss Emily G.Kemp", *Rochdale Observer* 30 December 1939, 7.
"THE MISSES KEMP IN INDIA." *Rochdale Observer* 13 June 1914, 10.
"Obituary." *Rochdale Observer* 28 March 1945, 3.
"Peeps from Tom Tower." *Witney Express* 28 April 1887, 5.
"Trafalgar Square Demonstration." *Common Cause* 8 September 1910, 355–356.
"YESTERDAY'S ELECTIONS." *Rochdale Times* 2 November 1912, 7.

PROBATE SEARCH ONLINE:
www.probatesearch.search.gov.uk (copies of original wills supplied by the Principal Probate Office).

Will of Emily Georgiana Kemp. Proved London 11 March 1940.
WILL OF GEORGE TWAKE KEMP. PROVED MANCHESTER 7 JULY 1877.

SOMERVILLE COLLEGE ARCHIVES; BY KIND PERMISSION OF SOMERVILLE COLLEGE
Chapel Foundation: Letters: SC/TR/BG/CH/8. Petition: SC/TR/BG/CH/7.
Somerville College, *Chapel Leaflet*. s.l.: s.n., 1937.

Secondary Sources

Adams, Pauline. *Somerville for Women: An Oxford College, 1879–1993*. New York: Oxford University Press, 1996.
Anon. "Bloomsbury at the Front." *Bloomsbury Magazine* (January 1915), ii.
Baptist Missionary Society: *138th Annual Report*. London: Baptist Missionary Society, 1930.
Binyon, Laurence, *For Dauntless France: An Account of Britain's Aid to the French Wounded and Victims of War*. London: Hodder & Stoughton, 1918.
Bowers, Faith. *A Bold Experiment: The Story of Bloomsbury Chapel and Bloomsbury Central Baptist Church 1848–1999*. London: Bloomsbury Central Baptist Church, 1999.

Bryant, Hilda, ed. *Somerville College Register, 1879–1959*. Oxford: Oxford University Press, 1961.

Conder, Katherine E, ed. *The World's Need of Religion—Being the Proceedings of the World Congress of Faiths, Oxford, July 23rd–27th*. London: Nicholson & Watson, 1937.

Dods, Marcus, ed. *The Later Letters of Marcus Dods, D.D. 1895–1909*. London: Hodder & Stoughton, 1911.

Edwards, E.H. *Fire and Sword in Shansi*. Edinburgh: Oliphant, 1903.

Farnell, Vera, ed. *Helen Darbishire, Somerville College Chapel Addresses*. London: Blackwell Scientific, 1962.

Hackmann, Heinrich. *Buddhism as a Religion: Its Historical Development and Its Present Conditions*. London: W.C. Probsthain, 1910.

Kemp, Emily Georgiana. *An Artists Impression of Western Tibet and the Turkestans*. London: Central Asian Society Proceedings, 1913.

———. *Chinese Mettle*. London: Hodder & Stoughton, 1921.

———. *The Face of China*. London: Chatto & Windus, 1909.

———. *The Face of Manchuria, Korea, and Russian Turkestan*. London: Chatto & Windus, 1910.

———. *"There Followed Him Women."* London: The Baptist Missionary Society, 1927.

———. *Mary, with her Son, Jesus*. London: Golden Vista, 1931.

———. *Reminiscences of a Sister, S. Florence Edwards of Taiyuanfu*. London: Carey, 1920.

———. *Wanderings in Chinese Turkestan*. London: Wightman, 1914.

Martin, Hugh. *Fifty Years of Carey Hall, 1912–1962*. Birmingham: Selly Oak Colleges. 1962.

Mattley, Robert D. *Annals of Rochdale*. Rochdale: Aldine, 1899.

Mott, John Raleigh. *The Present-Day Summons to the World Mission of Christianity*. London: SCM, 1932.

Phillips, Thomas. *The Grace of God and a World Religion*. London: Carey, 1928.

Pigott, C.A. *Steadfast unto Death: or Martyred for China*. London: Religious Tract Society, 1903.

Richard, Timothy. *Forty-Five Years in China*. London: T. Fisher Unwin, 1916.

Robinson, Jane. *Hearts and Minds: The Untold Story of the Great Pilgrimage and How Women Won the Vote*. London: Black Swan, 2019.

Schofield, A.T. *Memorials of R. Harold A. Schofield*. London: Hodder & Stoughton, 1885.

Sherwood, Jennifer, and Nikolaus Pevsner. *The Buildings of England; Oxfordshire*. London: Penguin Books, 1974.

Younghusband, Francis. *Mutual Influence: A Re-view of Religion*. London: Williams & Norgate, 1915.

Shantung Administration. British Section of the Board of Governors, 1928. http://divinity-adhoc.library.yale

CHAPTER 7

Was Writing about Prayer in the *Baptist Magazine*, 1850–70, Gendered?

Linda Wilson

Introduction

Writing in the *Baptist Magazine* in March 1859, D. Jones of Folkestone claimed that "the sisterhood generally are in possession of some natural advantages over their brethren ... which greatly favor their progress as disciples."[1] His comment was in the context of an article about husband and wife team Priscilla and Aquila, described in the book of Acts as instructing Apollos, a convert from Alexandria. Jones argued that, because her name came first, Priscilla must have taken the leading role in Apollos's training. He proceeded to use this as a launching point to generalize about the nature of male and female spirituality, arguing that "*the predominance of emotion and trust in women's nature confers a manifest facility for receiving and therefore knowing* Christian truth." Women, he believed, have "a quicker intuitive perception of the truth."[2] There are echoes here of the classic work *The Angel in the House* published ten years earlier by Coventry Patmore, in which an idealized woman is described as naturally spiritual,[3] as well as of the common phrase "a fibre more in her heart and a cell less in her brain."[4] One might note in passing that even Catherine Booth, pioneer of the theology and practice of women preachers, who challenged the use of this phrase, believed that women had "a more finely tuned emotional nature," although she used this as an argument in favour of women preaching.[5]

Another insight into the Baptist understanding of the spirituality of women and men came in 1860, the year following Jones's article, when the *Baptist*

---

[1] *Baptist Magazine* 51 (1859), 154.

[2] *Baptist Magazine* 51 (1859), 154 (italics original).

[3] Page, ed., *Coventry Patmore*, 89–90.

[4] This phrase was denounced by the co-founder of the Salvation Army, Catherine Booth, see Booth-Tucker, *Catherine Booth*, 1:117.

[5] Quoted in Walker, *Devil's Kingdom*, 27.

Magazine printed an address to theology students at Madison University by one Professor Harvey. In it, Harvey argued that prayer was an essential part of being a Baptist minister, but that to be their best spiritual selves, men needed to bypass their intellectual selves.[6] In other words, while women were considered to be naturally more spiritual and less intellectual than men, the reverse was true for men, putting them at a disadvantage spiritually. This is the flip side of the ideology epitomized in Patmore's poem, and indeed, it has been argued that Patmore's poem is as much about a crisis of masculinity as an attempt to define a particular version of femininity.[7] The implication of both these articles is that prayer came more naturally to women because they were less ruled by their minds, so, in order to be truly spiritual, men also needed to respond to God with their hearts rather than their minds. Baptist men aspiring to a spiritual life or to pastoral leadership should, therefore, aim to develop the feminine side of their natures because being male was somehow inadequate for understanding and responding to God. Yet at the same time women were considered inappropriate for leadership or public roles. Hence in the article that referred to Priscilla, the author assured his readers that her role was only private, so there was no "violation of decorum or of apostolic rule."[8] The gendered understanding of female and male natures in these Baptist writings could seem contradictory and disadvantaged both sexes.

There are further echoes of Patmore and this gendering of spirituality in an anonymous poem published in the *Baptist Magazine* in May 1870, entitled simply "Home":

> There is a spot of earth supremely blest,
> A dearer, sweeter spot than all the rest;
> Where man, creation's tyrant, casts aside
> His sword and sceptre, pageantry and pride;
> While in his softened looks benignly blend
> The sire, the son, the husband, father, friend;
> Here woman reigns; the mother, daughter, wife,
> Strews with fresh flowers the narrow way of life;
> In the clear heaven of her delightful eye
> An angel guard of loves and graces lie;
> Around her knees domestic duties meet,
> And fireside pleasures gambol at her feet.[9]

---

[6] *Baptist Magazine* 52 (1860), 11.

[7] Christ, "Victorian Masculinity," 146–62.

[8] *Baptist Magazine* 51 (1959), 154.

[9] *Baptist Magazine* 62 (1870), 291.

Presumably the editor of the magazine considered these lines, which endorsed an extremely romanticized view of domesticity, to be both appropriate for readers and broadly representative of the Baptist understanding of gender roles. Idealized male and female roles were clearly delineated in this poem, even though in this era women were active outside the home in a range of philanthropic work and were beginning to agitate for equal rights. Furthermore, this ideology of separate spheres had only ever been an ideal achievable by middle class women, as by its nature such a role was not possible for working class women.[10] Some historians have questioned whether the notion of "separate spheres," and the gender roles associated with that term, is helpful,[11] while others have argued that it had been present much earlier than Davidoff and Hall suggested.[12] Bebbington has rightly noted that attitudes to women's roles among evangelicals was complex.[13] However, this poem along with other articles demonstrates that the ideology of separate spheres contributed significantly to the Baptist understanding of the nature of male and female spirituality in the mid- to late-nineteenth century, especially as reflected in the pages of the *Baptist Magazine*.

In this chapter, I will seek to discover to what extent these gendered attitudes were reflected in Baptist understandings of prayer during the mid-Victorian period. I will draw primarily on articles in the *Baptist Magazine*s of 1850–70 in order to do this, supplementing these texts with other selected material. I will consider several aspects of writings about prayer or recounted experiences of prayer, including private prayer, praying parents, family prayer and corporate prayer.

Private Prayer

Regular private prayer was an essential part of the faith of Baptist women and men. Bebbington has commented that "Prayer was the most obvious way in which evangelicals practiced their faith," noting that all those writing about the subject insisted that individuals should set aside time at least once a day for prayer, preferably first thing in the morning, in addition to family prayers.[14] Similarly, Ian Randall has noted that, historically, evangelicals have

---

[10] The classic work on the development of separate spheres, Davidoff and Hall, *Family Fortunes*, is specifically about the middle classes.

[11] Vickery, "Separate Spheres?"

[12] See, for instance, Shoemaker, *Gender*. For further discussion of women's role at this time, see Wilson, *Constrained by Zeal*.

[13] Bebbington, *Dominance*, 202–3.

[14] Bebbington, *Dominance*, 78–79.

"practiced seriously the life of prayer."[15] The importance of prayer is reflected in the pages of the *Baptist Magazine*. During the years 1850–70 there were a total of twenty-six long articles concerning prayer (although some were separate instalments of one article), as well as several shorter items, book reviews and poems relating to the topic. The expectation of the authors of these pieces, and those giving advice to evangelicals more generally, was that women and men would be equally dedicated to personal prayer. For instance, an article in the *Baptist Magazine* in June 1863 concerning the appropriateness of offering prayer to Christ referred to the prayers of "men and women" and to "any of my readers, young or old."[16] The writer appears to have assumed that his readers' experience of prayer would be the same regardless of gender as well as of age. The assumption noted above that women found it easier to pray is not necessarily reflected in some of this advice. However, in an earlier study I discovered evidence that while prayer was central in the lives of both women and men (at least for those who were significant enough in their own congregations to have their obituaries included in the *Baptist Magazine*), more female obituaries than male ones referred to private prayer.[17] Of course, this raises several questions: was this because women had more time for personal prayer? Was it because women were more likely to be known for their prayer habits than other aspects of their lives? It does seem to support the belief noted earlier that women were considered to be more spiritual, although this was contrary to basic evangelical teaching about the nature of fallen humanity and redemption. There is a tension here between evangelical theology and Victorian culture.

It is interesting to note, however, that some of the writing about prayer seems to be feminized, in that there are suggestions at times that men should take on what might be seen as more female characteristics, such as weakness, when in an attitude of prayer. For instance, in an article of 1860 entitled "Prayer Essential to Ministerial Success," a transcript of a talk given in Madison, USA, Professor Harvey declared that prayer "is the uplifted hand of man's weakness laying hold upon God's strength."[18] A different author, in an article of February in the same year, stressed man's lowly place when coming to God in prayer, which can only be done in humility "through the merits of Christ." Indeed, this author described a person at prayer as "the worm of the earth creeping into the presence of the Eternal to shelter itself beneath the covering wing of infinite mercy."[19] He then gave several biblical examples of

---

[15] Randall, *Evangelical Tradition*, 76. See also Wilson, *Constrained by Zeal*, 112–16.

[16] *Baptist Magazine* 55 (1863), 377.

[17] Wilson, *Constrained by Zeal*, 112–16.

[18] *Baptist Magazine* 52 (1860), 11.

[19] *Baptist Magazine* 52 (1860), 85. Here and elsewhere "man" can be assumed to refer to both men and women unless the context indicates differently.

prayer, all of which are male, but his statement that "Prayer is essential to maintain the life and power of progress of the spiritual life"[20] was surely intended for both men and women, who according to the evangelical gospel were equally in need of the grace and support prayer could offer. This author was quite judgmental in his approach and set high standards: having stressed that grace is the only way to receive salvation, he then expected a high level of engagement with personal prayer as a way of progressing in the spiritual life, which seems closer to a gospel of salvation by works than to one of grace. In some instances, therefore, language about prayer assumes similar characteristics in men and women, and these could be traits often thought of as female.

Other historians have also commented on this. Discussing women's spirituality in an earlier period, 1500–1720, Patricia Crawford noted the complex use of gendered language, suggesting that the "use of female metaphors in religious discussion," such as the church being the bride of Christ, "could place all men in an ambiguous situation in relation to God."[21] Similarly, Robert B. Shoemaker referred to Phyllis Mack's observations that in the seventeenth century men could "depict their intense religious feelings in conventional feminine terms,"[22] and John Tosh, in his important book *A Man's Place*, which focuses on middle-class masculinity and domesticity in Victorian England, wrote that the process of conversion "was alarmingly close to common stereotypes of womanly behaviour."[23] An unusual aspect of this feminization of spirituality can be found in an article of February 1860, by one W. Crowe of Hammersmith, where the author refers to "a human spirit in communion with her God and Father," implying that the soul, whatever the physical being it resides in, is inherently female.[24] However, this was the only instance discovered of this particular approach. There is no indication that this assumption of a quasi-female role in relation to God affected male identity in other ways.

In addition, apart from these few examples, language about the nature of personal prayer in the *Baptist Magazine* does not seem to have been especially gendered. For instance, Rev. J. Jenkinson wrote an article in 1852, "On Restraining Prayer Before God," in which he discussed the reasons why people "restrain" from prayer, in which, apart from some comments about ministers being diverted from praying, and the use of the male pronoun for both sexes, was not gendered in its approach, but appears to assume that the

---

[20] *Baptist Magazine* 52 (1860), 86.

[21] Crawford, *Women and Religion*, 14.

[22] Shoemaker, *Gender*, 210, referencing Mack in his footnote on 211.

[23] Tosh, *Man's Place*, 113.

[24] *Baptist Magazine* 52 (1860), 87.

reasons for lack of prayer are common to all.²⁵ A similar use of unthinkingly male language to refer to all believers, women and men, can be found in an article of 1860 by Rev. C.B. Lewis of Calcutta.²⁶ Suggesting that if prayer has little effect it is because people have not prayed enough or with enough passion and persistence, he insisted that "the whole body of early Christians were men of prayer."²⁷ Here, for men and women, the blame for prayers not fully answered is put on the person praying, another example of the pressure that the evangelical approach placed on individuals. Apart from this example, unanswered prayer is rarely discussed in the pages of the *Baptist Magazine*, or if mentioned, is not really engaged with. A trite comment in the December 1867 edition suggests that God has answered even when people think he has forgotten. The rather simplistic implication seemed to be if that Christians pray for relief of suffering, but that suffering gets worse, that that is God's answer.²⁸ A brief article in December 1867 entitled "The Answer to an Unanswered Prayer" was similar in its approach. Here the author imagined that God's answer to prayer is to cast "us into the furnace of affliction" and thus, like the potter, "moulds us after a loftier pattern into a fairer type of character," and that this in itself, is the answer to the prayer.²⁹ Once again, some of the more difficult issues are sidestepped.

However, in the private diaries of Sarah Thomas we see a rare honesty. Sarah was a Baptist woman living in Fairford, Gloucestershire, whose personal diaries for the years 1860–65 have been discovered and published. Unlike some Victorian diaries, these were never intended for the eyes of anyone else and make revealing reading. Referring to one of her suitors, she wrote, "Prayed earnestly for dear J. I cannot forget him. When, dear Lord, will Thou answer my prayers for him."³⁰ Writing about her servant situation she laments on 29 April, 1860, that "I am very discouraged as I had made this quite a subject of prayer and it seems God has not heard me."³¹ Later the same year, regarding the question of who to marry, she lamented, "My spirits deeply depressed. I pray for guidance and God doesn't seem to hear. I am in great perplexity as I have always cast my troubles on Him who is supposed to hear all people."³² She then went on to blame her own inadequacy, but it is clear

---

[25] *Baptist Magazine* 44 (1852), 749–51.

[26] *Baptist Magazine* 52 (1860), 413–18.

[27] *Baptist Magazine* 52 (1860), 413.

[28] *Baptist Magazine* 52 (1867), 786.

[29] *Baptist Magazine* 59 (1867), 58–59.

[30] Lewis, ed., *Secret Diary*, 16.

[31] Lewis, ed., *Secret Diary*, 18.

[32] Lewis, ed., *Secret Diary*, 53.

that she did question whether God heard her prayers. However, given the different nature of these writings, and the lack of a corresponding male example, it is hard to draw any conclusions about gender differences relating to honesty about unanswered prayer.

Sarah also used prayer to anchor herself and to give a fresh perspective on difficult circumstances. For instance, when struggling over relationship problems, she wrote in her diary, "I have to spend time in prayer, oh, cold and sinful that I am, what should I do without this resort."[33] This personal account indicates the comfort that prayer could be to Baptist women. It has been demonstrated that although there were some assumptions about women finding prayer more natural than men, and some instances where the relationship of men to God was couched in feminized language, most discussion about private prayer in the *Baptist Magazine* and by other writers in Baptist circles or read by Baptists was rarely gendered.

Praying Mothers and Fathers

When it comes to advice about praying for children, however, the situation was rather different. Here, assumptions were made about the role of women and the spiritual power of a mother's prayers. In the period under study, articles about praying mothers can be found in several issues of the *Baptist Magazine*. An article from the 1850 edition is representative of this sub-genre of writing on the subject of the influence of praying mothers. The story was recounted of William, whose mother "was one that served the Lord," and who did her best to train him up well, "watering her efforts with prayer."[34] However, he "developed an aversion to everything good," so she prayed for him more and more until she died. He was imprisoned several times, but after being seriously injured in a fall became repentant and was clearly converted, dying a few weeks later. He knew a lot of scripture off by heart, the legacy of his mother's teaching. The author urged mothers to take encouragement from this example, not to give up in despair if a son is indifferent to religion. "Let such a one know that his mother prays for him ...." The kind of prayer needed should be "real, heartfelt, agonizing prayer." Although the author made it clear that it was the grace of God that could bring about change, so much stress was put on the prayer of the mother that it seems the responsibility for a child's salvation becomes hers. It is significant that, in this article, only mothers are urged to do this. The writer began by saying that he is writing because often, when children do not choose faith, the parent's prayers can seem fruitless, "faith fails and despondency ensues."[35] As in more

---

[33] Lewis, ed., *Secret Diary*, 133.

[34] *Baptist Magazine* 42 (1850), 746–47.

[35] *Baptist Magazine* 42 (1850), 745.

general articles on the subject, noted earlier, there is little engagement with questions of unanswered prayer, the suggestion being that faith needs to be stronger, implying a rather naïve and perhaps immature form of faith, with a need to provide answers to all problems, rather than being willing to live with some unanswered questions.

As well as *Baptist Magazine* articles, some tracts, brief and stylized, and rather cringeworthy to modern readers, contributed to this genre. Some of these tracts were advertised in the *Baptist Magazine*, and several were published by Baptist publishers, so were clearly aimed at a Baptist audience. Baptist women and men are likely to have read these tracts and the sentiments expressed in them would have helped to shape their spirituality and their understanding of the role of mothers and other relatives in praying for children. Presumably, therefore, the understanding about prayer and about gender roles on the part of these writers and publishers was considered by parents, and by the *Baptist Magazine*, to be in line with their belief about the place of Baptist women in this period. These tracts aimed to reinforce aspects of evangelical faith such as the danger of hell and the significance of prayers, and they tended to be rather simplistic. Conversion was the main aim. In these stories such a transformation often occurred just prior to death, as in the example of William cited above. Typically, the individual was rescued at the last moment, and these conversions were attributed to prayer.

Occasionally in these accounts it was a grandmother, not a mother, who was the trigger for such a rescue. A tract called *Grandma's Prayers Answered* focused on a woman who spent a lot of time in prayer, especially for her baby granddaughter, and claimed that although "the dear old grandma died when baby was nine months old, the influence of her prayers seemed to follow the child through life."[36] A few parallel accounts featured a father as the praying figure facilitating redemption. In some of these cases the credulity of the reader is stretched, as a different individual in the story seems to have done more to rescue the black sheep of the family than the person who prayed. For instance, in one tract entitled *A Blind Father's Prayer Answered*, while the blind father's prayer was the focus in the story, it is his daughter, Emma, who seemed to be doing all the work of tracking down the miscreants in the family—in one case narrowly preventing one of her brothers becoming an actor. So this tract, ostensibly about the prayers of a father, seems in practice to be more about the persistent actions of a sister.[37] This is rarely the case with the articles or tracts which feature a praying mother, suggesting that often the woman is the active member of the family, whether by prayer or action.

While this focus on praying mothers can be understood as one aspect of the ideal of the woman as the Angel in the House, it should be noted that this has

---

[36] *Grandma's Prayers Answered*, 1.

[37] *Blind Father's Prayer Answered*, 15.

been a trope found throughout much of the history of Christianity, for instance, in the prayers of Monica, mother of Augustine. The effect, one would think, of these articles and tracts would be as likely to engender guilt, as people wondered if they were praying enough, as to provide encouragement. Some of the arguments are unanswerable and require trust—as the person praying dies before seeing the apparent answers to their prayers. For the purposes of this study, the significant factor is the emphasis on the responsibility of mothers, in particular, to pray, demonstrating a gendered aspect of the nature of prayer where the salvation of children is concerned.

Family Prayers

As Bebbington has noted, daily prayers, including servants and guests staying in the household, "were the focal point" in evangelical households.[38] To what extent was writing about this aspect of prayer a regular part of life for many Baptist women and men gendered? In the *Baptist Magazine*, writers on this topic assumed that it was the responsibility of the man as head of the household both to instigate and lead the prayers. One article about family prayer in September 1862 by Rev. C.M. Birrell set his comments in the context of male responsibility for the upbringing of children. In it, Birrell suggested that family prayers should be held twice a day, and stresses the importance of doing this by saying that "he who expends his strength on other men's vineyards and neglects his own ... reverses the divine order of his duties."[39] This is interesting on two counts: firstly, it is clearly addressed to men, making the assumption that the organizing and leading of family prayers is a male responsibility, and, secondly, it sees the home (the "vineyard") as being of prime importance for men as well as women. This chimes with the analysis of masculinity in this period by John Tosh, who has argued that "The Victorians established the 'common sense' of the proposition that to be fully human and fully masculine, men must be active and sentient participants in domestic life."[40]

As well as the occasional article concerning family prayers, the *Baptist Magazine* reviewed various publications that were intended to facilitate domestic worship. The reviews were usually suspicious of any that included pre-written prayers, or any form of liturgy, Baptists having a strong antipathy to any prayer that was not spontaneous. Ellis notes that Baptists regarded liturgical forms as "tyranny."[41] Even the Lord's Prayer was regarded with

---

[38] Bebbington, *Dominance*, 79.

[39] *Baptist Magazine* 54 (1862), 558 and 560.

[40] Tosh, *A Man's Place*, 197.

[41] Ellis, *Gathering*, 115.

uncertainty, and only gradually came to be acceptable during the period investigated.[42] Small volumes intended to be used in family prayers, which provided set prayers, therefore tended to be dismissed by reviewers. Although in 1867, the reviewer of a book called *The Year of Prayer* thought highly of the author, Dr Henry Alford, Dean of Canterbury, and the "simple and scriptural language," but he disliked the book because of its set prayers: "the use of such a work is almost unknown amongst our readers."[43] The following year, a similar book by Robert Vaughan was dismissed with the words: "even when Dr. Vaughan is the author, forms of prayer fall very short of the rudest outpourings of the heart."[44] Again, in 1869, discussing Bristol writer, David A. Doudney's *Service at Home for the Young Folks in Schools and Families, for Wet Sundays and Winter Evenings*, the reviewer commented that "the prayers are direct and fervent (this we must allow, even if we do not approve of 'forms')."[45] In all these articles and reviews, there is nothing to suggest anyone other than a man, whether head of the house or some other member, should lead these prayers.[46] The expectation, and usual practice was that these would be led by the male head of the household.

However, sometimes women did lead family prayers. Sarah Thomas's diary gives us an example of a female-led household which engaged in family prayer. Sarah, who lived with her younger sister and a servant, and frequently had male guests, led the daily prayers. She found this a struggle at times, noting in her diary entry for Friday 27 January 1860, "This morning had quite a trial to engage in family prayer" and three days later she commented of family prayer "I felt 'twas but a feeble affair so went to prayer meeting in evening."[47] The suggestion here is that she hoped to gain some spiritual sustenance from family prayer, and when she found it lacking turned to her church prayer meeting instead. It is also interesting to note that, in true evangelical fashion, Sarah considered family prayers of prime importance. Elsewhere, her diary indicates that married women could take the initiative in

---

[42] An article in the *Baptist Magazine* 46 in December 1854, 725–29, was very antagonistic to any use of the Lord's Prayer by Baptists, regarding it as only intended for use by the disciples prior to the resurrection, while by the 1869 edition, (volume 61) 1, it was being advocated by the Rev. N. Haycroft as a basis for a useful pattern of prayer.

[43] *Baptist Magazine* 59 (1867), 43.

[44] *Baptist Magazine* 60 (1868), 113.

[45] *Baptist Magazine* 61 (1869), 317.

[46] *Baptist Magzine* 54 (1862), 561, where it is suggested by Birrell that not all in the household might want to participate, but only male pronouns are used when discussing these possibilities.

[47] Lewis, *Secret Diary*, 8–9.

introducing regular prayers into a household. Sarah recorded on 3 January 1862 that she had had "a pleasant evening" with Mrs Burges, adding, "I begged her to have family prayers but she says she can't till after her confinement."[48] Sarah assumed that Mrs Burges was able to decide herself to hold family prayers. The language also indicates how important Sarah thought it—"I begged her."

Women-led family prayers happened not only when the household was entirely female, but when the man of the house was absent, or did not share his wife or daughter's faith.[49] Mrs Harris was one woman who led family prayers when her husband was away from home, as described in her obituary in the *Baptist Magazine* of 1852. She led family prayers in her husband's absence in order to please him, and the result was, apparently, her own conversion.[50] Thus, in practice, Baptist women could sometimes take the initiative in leading family prayers, but it was not considered the norm, and was usually viewed as second best.

Women prayed with each other on other occasions, too, more informally than with family prayers. For instance, when Sarah Thomas was alone in the house with only her servant, Esther, and they heard violent knocking on the door at midnight, once they heard "the vagabond run off" Sarah insisted on giving thanks together before they went back to bed.[51] Sarah also frequently visited people in her village who were ill and needy. She went to see Martha Brown, who, she noted, "looks like a corpse and has dreadful cough." She was afraid of dying, so, "When her mother went downstairs, though timid about it, I prayed with her."[52] Another example, given in the *Baptist Magazine*, is that of Margaret Binns, who prayed when visiting people on their sickbeds, but only those of women.[53] It is likely that there were many such occasions of informal prayer.

Corporate or Public Prayer

Family prayers, as has been seen, were theoretically led by men, but sometimes in practice were led by women. In the larger arena of public prayer in church, however, women's voices were rarely heard during this period. Ellis has explored the central place of prayer in Baptist worship, most clearly expressed

---

[48] Lewis, *Secret Diary*, 111.

[49] See Wilson, *Constrained by Zeal*, 151.

[50] *Baptist Magazine* 44 (1852), 697.

[51] Lewis, *Secret Diary*, 9.

[52] Lewis, *Secret Diary*, 75.

[53] *Baptist Magazine* 45 (1853), 296.

through what was commonly known as the "Long Prayer,"[54] often more than fifteen minutes in length, consisting of "requests both for worshippers and others."[55] He pointed out that the content of these prayers can only be known roughly, as by their nature they were never written down. There is no way of knowing, for instance, whether women and men were equally included in petitions, or whether the way they were represented revealed gender assumptions or expectations. As this was habitually prayed by the minister of the congregation, it was male in expression and the congregation would have expected that such significant public prayers were prayed not just by a man, but by a specific category of man. They could at times be rather dry: a writer in the *Baptist Magazine* in July 1850, signing himself merely "Philos," suggested that public prayers on the part of the preacher were often lifeless, and encouraged people to listen and critique them rather than join in praying.[56] This was perhaps the consequence of the fact that public prayer in Sunday services was clearly selective, and it seems only open to men who were also pastors.

How far was this also true of another staple of Baptist community life, the prayer meeting? Randall has observed that "regular prayer meetings have marked evangelical congregations from the eighteenth century onwards."[57] These were normally held on an evening during the week and provided "an opportunity for lay members to offer spontaneous prayers."[58] But was this opportunity open to women as well as men? Rarely, is the answer: exclusively male participation appears to have been the norm. For instance, at a series of prayer meetings attended by people from dissenting churches in Fairford, Gloucestershire, for a week in January 1860, six or seven "mostly different men" prayed each night.[59] An article by the popular Baptist minister Charles Haddon Spurgeon, the following year entitled, "A Few Remarks Upon Prayer Meetings," is also enlightening, as well as amusing. It is clear that Spurgeon assumed that men would be the ones praying at these gatherings, as several times he referred to men specifically, writing, for instance, about "praying men" who participate in the meetings.[60] He suggested that the spirit of revival has improved these meetings, but lamented the

---

[54] Ellis, *Gathering*, 105.

[55] Ellis, *Gathering*, 106.

[56] *Baptist Magazine* 42 (1850), 407–9.

[57] Randall, *Evangelical Tradition*, 84.

[58] Bebbington, *Dominance*, 79.

[59] Lewis, ed., *Secret Diary*, 8.

[60] *Baptist Magazine* 53 (1861), 556.

... hard-shelled brethren whom no enthusiasm can penetrate, and no arguments arouse [who] continue in their usual petrified condition, mumbling forth prayers which exercise none of the Christian graces, except the patience of those who are doomed to listen to them.[61]

Spurgeon also noted that, despite being opposed to set prayers, people often prayed very similar prayers each time they participated: "We have known some brethren's prayers by heart, so that we could calculate within a few seconds when they would conclude."[62] The assumption is always that it was "brethren" who are participating. Bebbington also refers to long prayers in these meetings by the same people, almost certainly men, which discouraged younger people from attending.[63] It is worth noting that, even if prayers were mostly under five minutes, or ten at the most, as Spurgeon advocated,[64] in prayer meetings of a thousand or more such as he presided over there was very limited opportunity, even for men, to participate. Most people, whether men or women, would have joined in by listening to and quietly supporting the prayers of others and saying "Amen," rather than by praying their own prayers. Opportunities for participation in such large gatherings was inevitably limited.

Many Baptist churches, however, would have had much smaller numbers attending, so in theory more people could participate. However, while women often attended these prayer meetings, it appears that they seldom contributed. Sarah Thomas noted several instances in her diary of attending ecumenical prayer meetings in her village of Fairford, as well as ones at her own Baptist chapel, but there is no indication she ever participated in any of them, despite having a significant role in the village.[65] Another *Baptist Magazine* article in 1861 supports the conclusion that these occasions were male-dominated. An anonymous author responded to Spurgeon's article noted above. His response was entitled, "A Few More Remarks On Prayer Meetings from Another Hand," and stressed that in these prayers a "man's real feelings are expressed," writing of "One man" and "a Christian brother" praying.[66] Whereas, as noted earlier, some mentions of "men" or "man" can be taken in this period to be referring to people of either gender, specifics such as the last two mentions are clearly referring to males only. These articles on prayer meetings in the *Baptist Magazine* assumed that participation was male.

---

[61] *Baptist Magazine* 53 (1861), 553.

[62] *Baptist Magazine* 53 (1861), 555.

[63] Bebbington, *Dominance*, 79.

[64] *Baptist Magazine* 53 (1861), 556.

[65] Lewis, ed., *Secret Diary*, e.g., 8 and 15.

[66] *Baptist Magazine* 53 (1861), 751.

Some churches established female prayer meetings, which gave women the opportunity to participate in semi-public prayer. Even here, however, such involvement was unusual enough to be mentioned in an obituary: for instance, Mrs Birtwistle, who attended a Baptist church in Blackburn, was noted for her participation in female prayer meetings,[67] while Margaret Binns prayed in both female prayer meetings and mother's meetings.[68] Women who were not used to speaking in public would have found it hard to take this step, even in a women-only gathering. The author and hymnwriter Marianne Farningham commented on how difficult it was for women "to pray aloud and before others, and it is certainly not made more easy by fear of criticism."[69] She led a Sunday school class for young women, which at its height numbered nearly 200 participants, Marianne encouraged the girls, aged between sixteen and twenty-four,[70] and sixty to eighty of these participated in a more informal Tuesday evening gathering, where they were encouraged to participate. A member recalled that, on her first visit, ten girls prayed "Simple, earnest, wonderful prayers in their own words."[71] Realizing how difficult it could be for women to pray aloud, she made a point of training these girls to pray in each other's company. There is no indication, however, that this led to the women praying in mixed company. Even more so than in family prayer, therefore, male leaders and male participation were the norm in mixed company. Any exceptions, even rarer here in the third sphere of church life than in the home, were seen as unusual if not an aberration, reinforcing the public/private, male/female dichotomy.

Conclusion

It has been demonstrated that in the years between 1850 and 1869, there was in writing about Baptists and prayer a clear delineation of male and female roles, and of characteristics belonging to men and women, despite some language appearing to feminize men's relationship with God. Although some people were challenging these roles, consciously or unconsciously, in church and society, much of the language in the *Baptist Magazine*, and in a sample of other publications read by or written by Baptists, still upheld this separate sphere ideology. According to these sources, the occasions on which women could pray in public were limited. Women, it seems, almost never participated

---

[67] *Baptist Magazine* 46 (1854), 306.

[68] *Baptist Magazine* 45 (1853), 296.

[69] Farningham, *Will you take it?* 5.

[70] Farningham, *Sunday Schools of the Future*, 102, and *Life*, 116.

[71] Farningham, *Working Woman's Life*, 115. For more on Marianne Farningham, see Wilson, *Marianne Farningham*.

in church services or corporate prayer meetings, unless they were women-only occasions. In the home, there was a different emphasis: the role of men as head of the house was in tension with the perceived nature of women as the more spiritual of the two. Nevertheless, men usually led family prayers unless absent or less interested in religion than the women, or unless it was a female only household. The man's role as leader of his household was thus safeguarded.

Generally, language about the nature of personal prayer does not seem to have been especially gendered. If anything, although only one writer refers to the soul as female, both men and women are put in what might appear to be a female role in relation to God. However, there was an assumption, reflected in various articles, that somehow a mother's prayer was particularly efficacious, although the evidence in the stories recounted was not always convincing. Articles and other writings about prayer, therefore, in the *Baptist Magazine* and elsewhere, reflected a clash between evangelical beliefs about individuals before God, whether men or women, and social assumptions and expectations. Evangelical theology about the nature of humanity, that all are sinful before God and in need of the same redemption, was in tension with the ideology of the time, that women were more spiritual, even naturally spiritual, and should be the guardians of morality and spirituality based in the home. This tension was never satisfactorily resolved during the Victorian period, and does not seem to have been apparent to the Baptist men and women who wrote about prayer at the time, whether privately or for publication. Prayer was a significant and important part of the lives of Baptist women and men in this period, but aspects of it, and the way it was often written about, were clearly gendered.

Bibliography

Baptist Magazine 42–62 (1850–70).

Anon. *Grandma's Prayers Answered*. No. 9. s.l.: Baptist Tract Depositary, n.d.

Amderson, Mrs. *A Blind Father's Prayer Answered*. No. 17. New Series by Mrs Anderson. s.l.: The Tract Depositary, n.d. [Bound, probably by Regent's Park College Library, in a selection called "Tracts by B Authors."]

Bebbington, David W. *The Dominance of Evangelicalism*. Leicester: IVP, 2005.

Booth-Tucker, Frederick St-George de Latour. *The Life of Catherine Booth: The Mother of the Salvation Army*. 2 Volumes. New York: Fleming H. Revell, 1892.

Christ, Carol. "Victorian Masculinity and the Angel in the House." In *A Widening Sphere: Changing Roles of Victorian Women*, 146–62. Edited by Martha Vicinus. London: Indiana University Press, 1980.

Crawford, Patricia. *Women and Religion in England, 1500–1720*. London: Routledge, 1993.

Davidoff, L., and Hall, C. *Family Fortunes: Men and Women of the English Middle Class, 1780–1850*. 2nd edn, London: Routledge, 2002.

Ellis, Christopher J. *Gathering: A Theology and Spirituality of Worship in Free Church Tradition*. London: SCM, 2004.

Farningham, Marianne. *Sunday Schools of the Future*. London: James Clarke, 1871.

———. *Will you take it?* London: James Clarke, 1877.

———. *A Working Woman's Life*. London: James Clarke, 1907.

Lewis, June, ed. *The Secret Diary of Sarah Thomas, 1860–1865*. Moreton-in-Marsh: Windrush, 1994.

Page, F., ed. *The Poems of Coventry Patmore*. London: Oxford University Press, 1949.

Randall, Ian. *What a Friend We Have in Jesus: The Evangelical Tradition*. Traditions of Christian Spirituality Series. London: Darton, Longman and Todd, 2005.

Shoemaker, Robert B. *Gender in English Society 1650–1850*. Harlow: Addison Wesley Longman, 1998.

Tosh, John. *A Man's Place: Masculinity and the Middle-Class Home in Victorian England*. New Haven: Yale University Press, 2007 ed.

Vickery, Amanda. "Golden Age to Separate Spheres?: A Review of the Categories and Chronology of English Women's History." *Historical Journal* 36.2 (1993) 383–414.

Walker, Pamela J. *Pulling the Devil's Kingdom Down: The Salvation Army in Victorian Britain*, Berkeley: University of California, 2001.

Wilson, Linda. Constrained by Zeal: Female Spirituality Amongst Nonconformists 1825–75, Carlisle: Paternoster, 2000.

———. *Marianne Farningham, A Plain Woman Worker*, Milton Keynes: Paternoster, 2007.

CHAPTER 8

"I Received Guidance from Above:" A Story of an Estonian Female Preacher, Ilse Katvel

Toivo Pilli

This article deals with the person and ministry of an Estonian female preacher, Ilse Katvel. It seeks an answer to the question, "What sets Ilse Katvel apart as a preacher and interpreter of faith? And in what ways did she represent uniting elements of Christianity?" Images from nature helped Katvel to render meaning to religious experiences. It might even be said that she practised a grassroots environmental theology. Her charismatic spirituality was atypical. At first sight, her spirituality could be considered Pentecostal, but was instead part of the holiness tradition, and a closer examination would detect similarities even with the Catholic "convent spirituality." The pursuit of a holy life, modesty in living conditions, celibacy, Christ-centeredness, communal relationships, charity, contemplative Bible reading, regular prayer, openness to miracles—such traits characterize a committed Christian life, in some cases even that of a saint, both in the first centuries of Christianity and the Middle Ages, as well as in the recent past. Furthermore, Katvel's connections exceeded the confines of one confession. She did not emphasize denominational distinctions; instead, she lived out the spiritual common ground found in different Christian traditions.

Early Years and Religious Influences

Ilse-Anete Katvel was born on 28 January 1906.[1] Soon, the family moved to Voka village near Toila and Oru in northern Estonia.[2] Ado and Leena, Ilse's parents, who had married in 1903, lived in a rational marriage of mutual respect. The family's stronger party was the mother, who made major decisions, managed the money issues, and raised the children. Their father

---

[1] Katvel, *Rännutee rõõmud*, 101 and 120. Part of the MS has been published in print: Katvel, *Virumaa ärkamise lugu* and *Saaremaa ärkamise lugu*.

[2] Katvel, *Rännutee rõõmud*, 96–97.

earned money for the family.³ Although Katvel's later singleness was undoubtedly due to religious motives, one may nevertheless ask whether some role in her decision not to marry was possibly caused by marriage relationships she witnessed in childhood. There was little intimacy in the family. The union of her parents was not embellished by caresses or enriched by kisses; "there was none of such cosiness and cuddling between these two human beings."⁴

The religious quests of this vibrant girl started at a young age when the family attended services at the Lutheran churches in Pühajõe and Jõhvi. Ilse was bonded with the pastor Jaak Varik by a friendship of trust. These ties never broke even after Ilse joined an Evangelical Christian Free Church, justifying her step because its doctrine and life were "closer to the Word." "It is not enough to go to church and attend Communion if real-life follows a different path," the girl explained with youthful resolution. Pastor Varik did not take offence at the explanation.⁵

Evidently, in 1921 the family came into contact with members of the Christian abstinence society, The Blue Cross, and among them was Aleksander Sildos, head of the Narva Blue Cross Society. The Society in Narva, north-east Estonia, was established in 1920.⁶ The Society's choir organized outings and thereby enlivened "the Moravian and free church activities at several locations in Viru County,"⁷ and Ilse attended their meetings.⁸ Visits by the Blue Cross figures ceased after a while, yet Katvel's journey—from earnest piety to experiential assurance in the faith—continued.

Personal relationships and existential questions played a role in her coming to religious conversion in the Free Church mode. In 1922–23, when moving to Tallinn to learn sewing, the sixteen-year-old girl took graveclothes with her in order that her relatives would have these at hand if needed.⁹ At that time, she primarily attended Lutheran churches, although her aunt had joined an Orthodox church. Unlike her peers, she found no fascination in entertainments; rather, she felt attracted to religious issues and "fellowship with God's nature."¹⁰ Her communication with the Free Churches began in 1927–28, when she was back in Tallinn for further training in sewing, as her

---

³ Katvel, *Rännutee rõõmud*, 17–19.

⁴ Katvel, *Rännutee rõõmud*, 91–92.

⁵ Katvel, *Virumaa ärkamise lugu*, 62.

⁶ [Laks], *Aleksander Sildos*, 40–41. On the Blue Cross, see Bärenson, "Evangeelne karskusselts Sinine Rist," 7.

⁷ Kaasik, "Aleksander Sildose vaimulik tegevus Eestis," 33.

⁸ Katvel, *Rännutee rõõmud*, 167–69.

⁹ Katvel, *Rännutee rõõmud*, 172.

¹⁰ Katvel, *Rännutee rõõmud*, 172.

mother was convinced that a woman needed to practice the trade diligently. She particularly remembered a visit to a Methodist church. The sermons were delivered by Aleksander Kuum and Ferdinand Tombo.[11] Towards the close of the service, a peculiar revival method was used. First, all who were children of God were asked to raise a hand, and then the same invitation was issued to those who were not. Ilse was confused. She did not want to "vote" herself out of the ranks of God's children as she indeed believed in Jesus Christ and the forgiveness of sins. Yet she was not sure whether she could count herself among God's children from the Methodist perspective.[12]

In the following years, Katvel embraced the Free Church concept of conversion as a "well-defined change of life—a repentance of sin and a commitment to Christ as personal Saviour . . . ."[13] The Katvel's home at Voka became a venue for revival services. The first such "farm meeting" was organized by mother and daughter, Elviine and Helmi Juurik, in 1931. A crowd of approximately sixty gathered.[14] Elviine Juurik was active in visiting families, sharing the gospel, supporting the poor, and distributing Christian literature. "She had a soft and beautiful singing voice."[15] She sang from both the Lutheran Church songbook and the popular Pentecostal collection *Võidulaulud* [*Songs of Victory*]. The sermons at farm meetings, the ideas from Christian literature as well as the example of the young schoolteacher, Helmi Juurik, offered Ilse a different, more experiential language to describe her religious pursuits.

Although Ilse Katvel's religious conversion was a process that spanned several years, it included a specific emotional experience. On 24 October 1932, she had what might be called a spiritual breakthrough. She was in the woods collecting spruce pitch when she clearly heard Christ speak. She was reminded of Christ's wounds—the image resonated with the "wounds" inflicted on the trees, from which resin exuded. The experience continued with the words from the Gospel of John, "Yet to all who received him, to those who believed in his name, he gave the right to become children of God" (John 1:12). She later called what followed, "the downpouring of the Holy Spirit." She started to thank God in elation, "it was as if I had gotten wings—so fleet of foot was I when I hurried home." In the following weeks, she was filled with peace and

---

[11] At the time, Aleksander Kuum (1899–1989) was a Methodist pastor in Tartu, while Ferdinand Tombo (1890–1969) acted in the same capacity in Haapsalu. Both were also involved in the youth association "The Epworth League." Toomas Pajusoo, email information, 24 March 2009.

[12] Katvel, *Rännutee rõõmud*, 173–76.

[13] Briggs, "Conversion," in Briggs, ed., *Dictionary*, 122.

[14] Katvel, *Rännutee rõõmud*, 180–83; and Sirel, *Eesti pühad naised*, 95.

[15] Katvel, *Rännutee rõõmud*, 170–71.

joy. She felt compassion for wrongdoers and strove to remedy and expiate her own past wrongdoings.[16]

The religious conversion, the regeneration, produced such moral sensitivity that she sought to rectify, if ever possible, even insignificant past moral mistakes. Katvel recalls, "I remember how the vendor wept when I wanted to pay him for the birthday cards stolen fifteen years ago—to clear the old debt with interest—and I asked for forgiveness for my mischief from him, now an old man. He forgave me readily and rejected all redress. . . . God's blessing descended upon me like dew, and it felt good and light in my cleansed heart as if it had taken a sauna."[17]

On 22 April 1934, Ilse Katvel was admitted to the membership of Narva Evangelical Christian Free Church, which in 1932 had grown out of the Blue Cross movement after distancing from the Moravian Bretheren. The new church was headed by Aleksander Sildos.[18] The Evangelical Christians were open for cooperation with Lutheran and pietistic circles and various Free Churches, emphasizing—at least as an ideal—ethical living over doctrinal differences.[19] This attitude also came to characterize Katvel's activities. The hope for new church members was, "Produce good perfume and bloom as a rose of Sharon in the congregation and in your neighbourhood."[20] It was in the midst of nature that Katvel's religious breakthrough occurred, and it was a metaphor from nature that helped her find her Christian mission for life.

Openness to the Holy Spirit

In the late 1930s, the work of the Holy Spirit assumed increasing importance for Ilse Katvel's spirituality. While doing her chores in the kitchen, she underwent an inexplicable experience, which she later called the baptism of the Holy Spirit. The experience was powerful to the limits of her endurance. "I made several rounds in the kitchen . . . praising, worshiping, and exalting God. Being conquered by the Holy Spirit, I no longer sensed myself, and my happiness and joy flowed over . . . ." Even so, Katvel never veered, either at that time or later, towards any extreme removed-from-reality fanaticism, although her religious practices were at times unconventional. She did not

---

[16] Katvel, *Rännutee rõõmud*, 184–88.

[17] Katvel, *Rännutee rõõmud*, 157–58.

[18] [Laks,] *Aleksander Sildos*, 52–53; and Kaasik, "Aleksander Sildose vaimulik tegevus Eestis," 41–42 and 44.

[19] Laks, *Kakskümmend viis aastat vabakoguduslist liikumist Eestis*, 9–10.

[20] Katvel, *Rännutee rõõmud*, 188.

neglect her everyday duties. "[I] tried to be honest, just, disciplined, and trustworthy, serving my Lord there, too," she writes.[21]

This pneumatologically experiential element helped her to conceptualize spiritual growth, experiencing God. She developed an urgent desire to be obedient to God. She resisted temptations and rebuked Satan to retreat.[22] Her life acquired a certain mystical–ascetic aspect. Living with a pure heart became central. The longing to do God's will became intrinsic to her for life. That will, however, was ascertained by the light of inner intuition, the hearkening of the "voice" of the Holy Spirit, and an unblemished conscience. Similar examples of spiritual alertness may be found across the gamut of Christian spirituality: the biographies of saints, the actions of prophets, the spiritualistic currents of the Reformation, holiness movements, and charismatic modes of faith. The emphasis on the experiential and contemplative aspects of faith over the intellectual and cognitive aspects is often called mysticism, although the term has various shades of meaning.[23]

Occasionally Katvel's steps were inspired by the guidance of the Spirit, even where others would have employed commonsense, which in Christian terms is also a gift of God. Once, while having lunch by the aisle in the dining hall, she heard an inner voice urging her to sit farther away by the window. She protested in her soul that once one sits down by the aisle, where people move about, one should not look for better places. Soon, however, a passer-by spilled an abundance of soup on her new summer coat. To Katvel's mind, the misfortune was caused by her disobedience to the guidance.[24] Still, her mystical attitude was proportionally combined with practicality, striking an effective equilibrium. Her religious sensibility was neither agitated nor neurotic.

Her later Christian life included "singing in the Spirit," albeit she was not usually much of a tune-carrier. It is not quite clear what singing in the Spirit meant, yet it may be assumed to stand for spontaneous singing, which gave rise to both the lyrics and the melody in the process. In the form of glossolalia, the same kind of singing has been attributed to the Pentecostal preacher, Theodor Kreitsberg of Tartu.[25] Singing in tongues of prayer is also mentioned in a 1984 overview of the history of the youth ministry at Kuressaare Baptist church.[26] There is no information on Katvel practicing glossolalia; evidently, what she sang was in Estonian, her mother tongue. It should be noted that

---

[21] Katvel, *Rännutee rõõmud*, 200.

[22] Katvel, *Rännutee rõõmud*, 188–200.

[23] McGrath, *Christian Spirituality*, 6.

[24] Katvel, *Rännutee rõõmud*, 255–56.

[25] Kiil, *Meenutusi nelipühi ärkamisest Eestis*, 50.

[26] Mäemets, *Noored, lähme pühas innus*, 41.

when speaking of the Holy Spirit's work she is, again, using images of nature: the Spirit is like a "breath of wind" (cf. John 3:8) and a "warm revitalizing spring shower."[27]

The intermingling of experiencing the Holy Spirit, an ethical lifestyle, and a Christian commitment is reflected in Katvel's views and the literature that inspired her. Two authors who were particularly influential for her were Evan Roberts and Ivan Kargel. Their writings emphasized the work of the Holy Spirit in moulding the character of a Christian believer. Roberts spoke of identification with Christ's death and resurrection.[28] Kargel taught that the Holy Spirit changes a believer to be more like the Lord, shapes the conduct and mentality, and gives one courage to witness for Christ. Yet this presupposes that a person gives up his or her self, for one's ego stands "right in the way" of God.[29]

Katvel also underlined supernatural identification with Christ, "The Holy Spirit takes of Christ and transfers to us the nature of Him in whom there is everything we need for life and godliness, including faith. We are receptive and grateful that we do not need to seek faith on our own. . . . Woe to us if we forget that faith is God's gift of grace and lives in a pure conscience. . . . Faith is the creation of the Holy Spirit, transferred from Jesus into us, and it is part of the fruit of the Spirit."[30] This key premise of Protestant theology that even faith is ultimately God's gift and grace[31] found a personal expression in Katvel's life in the form of trust, humility, and gratitude. The pneumatological aspect of her approach to faith was closely related to the broader evangelical-revivalist and holiness movement mentalities.[32] Pentecostalist expressiveness influenced her to a lesser extent.

Preaching as a Calling

On 8 December 1937, the Narva Evangelical Christian Free Church certified in writing that Ilse Katvel had been elected as an evangelist. This woman, who was only slightly over thirty years old, went to speak and hold services in Narva-Jõesuu, Kiviõli, Kukruse, Kohtla-Järve, and elsewhere at the church's

---

[27] Katvel, *Rännutee rõõmud*, 250–51.

[28] Roberts, *Pühitsuselu astmed*, 40.

[29] Kargel, *Milline on sinu wahekord Pühavaimuga?* 13–14, 41 and 75–76.

[30] Katvel, *Rännutee rõõmud*, 273.

[31] McGrath, *Reformation Thought*, 113–14.

[32] See Randall, *Evangelical Experiences*, 30–33 and 206–30; Price and Randall, *Transforming Keswick*, 148–87 and 228–58; and Nichols, *Development of Russian Evangelical Spirituality*, 218–32 and 245–49.

outreach locations.³³ She imitated speakers who were more experienced. She developed herself as a religious personality and exerted herself to formulate a meaningful message. This is the prerequisite of all successful speaking; to have a message and to have a personality to render the word reliably spoken.³⁴

Nonetheless, Katvel recognized that the best thoughts often came only after her descent from the pulpit. "Ministering with the Word of God, I have prayed for the Word from the Heavenly Father. Ever and again, it has opened up to me much more richly, clearly, and dearly only after speaking. It is as if I, as a student, have received my flawed school paper from the supervisor with the corrections and improvements."³⁵ However, the awareness of her own limitations acted as an incentive for character development, as a prompt for more diligent Bible reading and interpretation. "I could be grateful for sharing God's holy and living Word even as a duffer, far from being a master of my trade."³⁶ However, she was being too modest here. Her contemporaries remember her as a gripping, metaphorical, and pithy speaker. She had a gift for Bible teaching.³⁷ Once, while preaching on Egypt's plagues, she presented a vivid imagery of frogs, "how they encroached upon the Pharaoh's palace, his bedrooms, even beds . . . ."³⁸ Naturally, preaching was not merely a rhetorical exercise; Katvel was open to the supernatural. "After being baptised with the Holy Spirit, God opened up His Word to me and spoke to me through the Word as well as in a voice. The Lord enabled me for Scripture exposition. I received guidance from above."³⁹

Katvel's first speech before a crowd took place in the prayer house of Narva Evangelical Christians. Extremely shy in her school years, she now felt a peace, and was bold "as one who is in her proper place." She added, "And the Lord did not leave me dumb or disgraced but revealed the Bible events in the form of a picture that He considered necessary for me to communicate fluently."⁴⁰ The skill to visualize the narrative is a valuable gift for a speaker. This method in sermon preparation encompassed contemplative prayer, waiting for the "appearance of the Word." At times, Katvel got inspiration from a previous speaker; at other times, the main ideas of the sermon were

---

[33] Katvel, *Rännutee rõõmud*, 204.

[34] Killinger, *Fundamentals of Preaching*, 187–206; and Pilli, Palamets *et al.*, *Avatult avalikust kõnest*, 7–8.

[35] Katvel, *Rännutee rõõmud*, 204.

[36] Katvel, *Rännutee rõõmud*, 205.

[37] Margus Mäemets, telephone conversation, 30 October 2020.

[38] Herman Mäemets's notes, 6 May 2009.

[39] Katvel, *Rännutee rõõmud*, 201.

[40] Katvel, *Rännutee rõõmud*, 202.

already on her mind. Nevertheless, the determining factor for her was still a close relationship with God and moral integrity.[41]

Nowhere does she criticize the classical, well-structured homily based on in-depth exegesis, which was practiced, for instance, by well-known Estonian pastors Osvald Tärk and Robert Võsu. Her own method, however, was rather an imagery-rich textual exposition, intuitive decisions about words to speak and hearkening of the heart. The effectiveness of this method was supported by the depth of the speaker's personality, it was meaningful as based on a very good knowledge of the Bible. That kind of speaking required earnest commitment. She prepared her sermons carefully, but in her own way. She never overemphasized emotions to cover up a lack of preparation. Her sermons were pithy, full of content, even styled in a matter-of-fact manner, but never drab. They bore on the reality of the listeners' lives and interpreted the Bible in an insightful and refreshing manner.

Katvel served as a preacher for approximately fifty years. After moving to the Saaremaa Island in 1944, she ministered at the Valjala congregation which had a Pentecostal background. The pastor of the congregation, commencing in 1945, was Aleksander Väli. Soon Katvel was elected as a member of the congregation's board, a deacon, and a preacher.[42] In essence, she fulfilled the functions of the second leader, or co-leader, of the congregation. Her work, however, was not confined to just one congregation. She was invited to preach and teach in many places. She was a long-anticipated guest in different churches and at Christian youth summer camps that were semi-clandestine during the Soviet era.[43] Additionally, she was a spiritual counsellor for many. She considered confessional conversations and intercessory prayers as important as preaching.[44]

Although Katvel developed into a mature and original preacher, public speaking was not her only means of proclaiming the gospel. Her perspective on Christian ministry was more holistic than that of many contemporary male preachers. She did not separate spiritual ministry from practical daily labour. She could preach in the worship time and work in the kitchen before or after. "In prayer weeks, I had the opportunity to minister to the people with the Word at quite a few congregations . . . as well as give a helping hand in the household chores. . . . Thus, I ministered to Baptist as well as Methodist people of God."[45] The so-called revival weeks and prayer weeks (with worship

---

[41] Katvel, *Rännutee rõõmud*, 205.

[42] Katvel, *Saaremaa ärkamise lugu*, 81; The Commissioner of Religious Affairs, Valjala "Rahu Saalemi" Church, 17–19 and 22–23.

[43] Mäemets, *Noored, lähme pühas innus*, 19–20.

[44] Katvel, *Rännutee rõõmud*, 374.

[45] Katvel, *Rännutee rõõmud*, 333.

services held on seven or eight consecutive days) were organized, typically once a year, at many Estonian Free Churches in the Soviet era.[46]

Convent Practices without a Convent

On Saaremaa a small circle of devoted friends gathered around Katvel. Jointly and individually they practised "spiritual disciplines," which included consistent prayer, reading the Bible and religious literature, encouraging fellow Christians by mail. The ultimate goal of such a life of devotion was as follows: "God's purpose for us is holy and noble; in the fellowship with Christ, with members of His body, He produces in us likeness to Jesus."[47] The friends were united by the ideal of pursuing spiritual depths. This was like a lay sisters' community without cloister and consecration. Focusing on direct spiritual communion with God, they occasionally leaned into Christ-mysticism. In the history of Christianity, this is nothing unprecedented; women have had a significant role in practising mystical spirituality, often as a reaction to a formalized and rigidly administered Christianity.[48]

Devotion along the lines of convent ideals is also indicated by the fact that Katvel never married. Indeed, in the 1930s marriage was on the horizon. Ilse, however, took her time. When she finally met with the young man she had exchanged letters with for three years, the spell was broken. She wrote, "Although this brother in faith was a decent person in every respect, he was not destined for me."[49] Through inner feelings and prayers, Katvel came to a considered conclusion that she was destined to lead a celibate life. The Christian community became a family for her. She was convinced that upon arrival to the eschatological city of God "we will all be enriched by the love greater than one has ever found in marital bliss down here." Her children were "spiritual children"—people whom she had led to faith.[50]

The resemblance to a cloister-like devotion is also striking in the balance between work and prayer and the openness to miracles. Katvel's life points to the Benedictine principle of *ora et labora*,[51] although she probably never verbalized such a connection. Nevertheless, she discovered that work might serve as an environment of meditation: "I so gladly did . . . a lot of daily work. The Lord was near; I sojourned in a heavenly atmosphere. . . . I was free to contemplate celestial things. . . . The Holy Spirit reminded me of one

---

[46] Kurg, 'Ühe medali kaks poolt," 145–46.

[47] Katvel, *Rännutee rõõmud*, 213.

[48] Küng, *Catholic Church*, 107.

[49] Katvel, *Rännutee rõõmud*, 234.

[50] Katvel, *Rännutee rõõmud*, 236.

[51] Gonzales, *Story of Christianity*, 1:240–41.

A Story of an Estonian Female Preacher, Ilse Katvel 149

scripture text after another."[52] Of course, she did not rely on intentionally accepted rules of spiritual life or a centuries-old structure. She fitted spontaneous convent practices into the framework of daily life and a Free Church modality of faith.

In her own way, Katvel also kept the promise of poverty. She was undemanding concerning her earnings, shelter, and food. She lived, in her own words, "on a missionary's income." She had no secure job; she lent a hand in household chores of fellow Christians or worked at the state farm. She believed that God needed her as "free." Referring to the 1950s, she wrote, "God has so separated me for Himself that I do not even have a flowerpot on the window sill, not a soul of an animal, nothing that may hold me back when the Lord needs me."[53] She accepted "gifts of love" that were sent to her—sometimes food, sometimes items of clothing—but she was definitely "no sponger who whiled away her life in idleness."[54] She only attended to her minimal needs. She worked and helped those in need. She was a "practical person," because, as pastor Herman Mäemets described her, "she sometimes took with her a bag of potatoes [when visiting somebody]."[55] Katvel had learned to share as one who "had nothing" and yet "possessed everything" (2 Cor 6:10).[56]

For a prolonged period, Ilse Katvel lived at Elise Luup's farm at Kõljala, Kõljala, where she had arrived as a worker in 1953 at the housewife's request.[57] She ran the household, tended the cattle, laid the table. Urve Pink, a child in the household, wrote concerning her childhood experience of Katvel, "she had the gift of preparing food from nothing." This was a laudable skill, particularly in the poverty-stricken circumstances of the early collectivization period in the 1940s–50s, when people in Estonia were often "not at all better off than those in Siberia."[58] Despite difficulties in life,[59] Katvel had an affable sense of humour. Urve Pink stated, "She was able to turn her blunders into fun with her good sense of humour. She was able to see everything from quite a different angle than an ordinary person." Once, the housewife had to be away for a few days, and Ilse looked for a cooking pot to prepare food, murmuring

---

[52] Katvel, *Rännutee rõõmud*, 279.

[53] Katvel, *Rännutee rõõmud*, 319.

[54] Katvel, *Rännutee rõõmud*, 303–4.

[55] Herman Mäemets, oral information, 23 February 2009.

[56] Katvel, *Rännutee rõõmud*, 364.

[57] Helju Liiv, notes on 6 May 2009.

[58] Urve Pink, letter to Toivo Pilli, 10 March 2009.

[59] See the disheartening overview of the war-ravaged Voka, her home village, in Katvel's letter to Helmi Juurik, 14 October 1944, in Sirel, *Eesti pühad naised*, 127–31.

to herself, "Why on earth did she have to take that pot with her!" The children had lots of fun overhearing that![60]

Although Ilse Katvel herself did not use the comparison, her religious practices resembled the spirituality characteristics of Christian commitment in a convent setting.

Prayers and Fasting

While helping at the Valjala church on Sundays, Katvel turned her residence into a prayer venue. On a regular basis, the farm hosted half a dozen or more persons, who gathered for prayer, and at times stayed overnight and went straight to work the next morning. These long evening prayers, almost daily, took place for about ten years; sometimes, special prayer times were at night or early in the morning.[61] Later on, Katvel organized group prayers a couple of times per week for approximately twenty more years. The text of the memoirs states, "We prayed in support of the Kingdom work in general, as well as for prayer requests submitted orally or by letter, and whatever prayer was laid on the heart."[62] The prayer community was characterized by a drive for spiritual development and deliberate dependence on God's grace and help.[63] "We understood the need to strictly obey the Holy Spirit, who is our teacher, instilling into us Jesus' divine nature and bonding our old nature with His death . . . ."[64] Most of the members of the prayer group worked the fields of the state farm.

Prayer was not only about experiencing God's presence, but also about warfare against the dark powers of the spiritual realm. Prophesying and glossolalia with interpretation was not unknown to this group of believers. Particularly active in this kind of prayer was Alvine Trei.[65] However, it seems, as already mentioned, that Katvel did not practise glossolalia herself. The group provided pastoral counselling, "Through sister Alvine [Trei], God was able to speak to quite a few people who came to her to discuss their knotty life problems."[66] This community never ruled out the possibility of God's miraculous intervention.

---

[60] Urve Pink, a letter to Toivo Pilli, 10 March 2009.

[61] Helju Liiv, notes 6 May 2009.

[62] Katvel, *Rännutee rõõmud*, 332–33.

[63] Katvel, *Rännutee rõõmud*, 380.

[64] Katvel, *Rännutee rõõmud*, 214.

[65] Urve Pink, letter to Toivo Pilli, 10 March 2009.

[66] Katvel, *Rännutee rõõmud*, 376.

Katvel also prayed for day-to-day matters. Alvine Trei was persecuted on the state farm as the foreman gave her more demanding assignments than others, and she was unable to harvest enough hay for the cattle. Katvel decided to bless Alvine's hay swaths. She pronounced, "I did it in firm faith. God used the blessing to multiply the meagre quantity of hay to such an extent that the cattle in her charge could not fully consume it, and some was left over in spring."[67] Certainly, the blessing was also related to the women's diligent work, but that was by far not an exhaustive explanation for them. They had experienced God's help.

While prayer as a spiritual "exercise" presupposes perseverance, fasting requires an even greater commitment. Although fasting has been understood as partial or full abstinence from food to enhance self-discipline and sensitivity to the spiritual life,[68] Katvel defined fasting in even broader terms. She wrote,

> Fasting is a God-ordained means of grace for spiritual focusing before God. If applicable, one refrains, for a shorter or longer period, from satisfying one's earthly needs, such as eating, drinking, sleep, work and chores, the company of humans, talk about needless things, music or reading, which would otherwise obstruct the fellowship of a praying spirit with God. For we expect a special meeting with God in which He will give His answer to our pleas, guidance in our activities, clarity in issues, light for making decisions, a helping hand or a reassuring message, whether to ourselves or our neighbours. We thirst for our fellowship with God to grow purer, clearer, stronger for the forthcoming trials of faith, hours of ordeal, decisions, elections, work, duties or sufferings, sacrifices, burden-bearing, resisting Satan, suffering injustice, overcoming temptations, or also for the saving of souls, expelling the evil one, release from certain diseases, as Jesus mentioned to his disciples. Matthew 17:18–21.[69]

Such a grassroots theology was supported by biblical examples and, in particular, by Jesus' life.[70]

Spiritual development includes growing in compassion and taking care of those who were suffering.[71] Katvel wrote, "Many die of diseases because fellow members of the human race are indifferent and inconsiderate to their dismal state"[72] (cf. John 5:1–8). Formally, the responsibility for taking care of the elderly and the sick lay with the Soviet government; in reality, however, informal support structures, including the assistance of church members, were

---

[67] Katvel, *Rännutee rõõmud*, 378–79.

[68] Douglas, Elwell and Toon, *Concise Dictionary of the Christian Tradition*, 150.

[69] Katvel, *Rännutee rõõmud*, 360–61.

[70] Katvel, *Rännutee rõõmud*, 352–59.

[71] Katvel, *Rännutee rõõmud*, 279.

[72] Katvel, *Rännutee rõõmud*, 285.

exceedingly important.[73] The prayer group on Saaremaa often combined their care with prayers for healing. Leevi Väli describes how he, as a pre-school boy, was suffering from a severe infection in the middle ear, but the pain receded after Katvel's prayer. "Everyone knew that I would get help when Ilse Katvel came. Before she laid her hands on my ears and prayed, she first warmed them above the stove."[74]

Katvel did not share the view widespread in some charismatic circles in Estonia in the 1970s that if the faith were firm enough, the individual would heal in any case.[75] She left space for God's mystery, even when confident of healing by faith. She was also of the opinion, as were members of Free Churches in general, that when praying for healing, the individual must positively ask forgiveness for all transgressions (cf. Jas 5:13–16), for even small misdemeanours "that are unresolved and not laid under the blood in prayer" may "impede the implementation of the power of Jesus' name." Nonetheless, she was honest enough to admit that not all people would be healed.[76]

Katvel did not pray for people alone. She had compassion for all creation. "God has mercy on any creature, and He has considered it necessary to give life to everyone, be they underground, above the ground, up in the air or in water." She prayed for the healing of a toad which had been wounded. The next year, the landlady found a big toad by a ditch. The toad had a scar on the left shoulder blade. "I was by all means immensely delighted as I gave thanks to the Creator," writes the preacher.[77] While living and working at the farm, Katvel also prayed for the healing of a young pig which had some internal disease. On the other hand, once, during the war, she prayed, out of compassion that a sick horse would die, for there was no hope for healing, nor was there anybody to help to mercy-kill the agonized animal. "I heaved a sigh of relief when it was interred."[78] To find such a Francis-of-Assisi-minded individual in the history of the Estonian Free Churches is somewhat out of the ordinary, but bears witness to the diversity of the Free Church tradition. Despite denominational and historical differences, the various forms of Christian spirituality also have a fair share of common ground, including empathy and closeness to nature.

---

[73] Pilli, *Usu värvid ja varjundid*, 135–36.

[74] Leevi Väli, telephone conversation, 4 November 2020. For other similar stories, see Katvel, *Rännutee rõõmud*, 305 and 376–77.

[75] See Oral Roberts, "Kui tahad saada terveks, siis talita järgmiselt." For views on healing in the Union of Estonian Evangelical Christian and Baptist Churches, see also Pilli, *Dance or Die*, 185–88.

[76] Katvel, *Rännutee rõõmud*, 296.

[77] Katvel, *Rännutee rõõmud*, 311.

[78] Katvel, *Rännutee rõõmud*, 316.

Naturally, one may question the theology of animal-oriented prayers for healing. Yet one thing is clear, Katvel's concept of God's work was far more comprehensive than that of many of her urbanized modernist faith friends. It was natural for her to see prayer encompassing nature in its entirety. Such spirituality originated from peasant culture, the rustic life experience, and the inherent disposition to behold the beauty of nature. Biblical images further fortified this.

Nature Teaches Obedience

Ilse Katvel was one of the few in the Soviet era to endeavour to conceptualize relationships between the creation and the Creator—albeit applying a homemade theology. First, she concluded that nature was God's way of speaking to people. This "reveals to us the awe-inspiring relationship" that the Creator has with the creation, "drawing mankind to join in." Observing nature, a human being understands the importance of obedience, "both the living and the inanimate nature know how to comprehend ever so precisely and plainly what God says and wants, responding immediately thereto."[79] God also calls people through his Word. Both nature and the Word teach us voluntary obedience to God. Second, she was inspired by the Bible and had an eye for the aesthetic value of creation. Jesus often employed images from nature. Magnificent pictures of nature are provided in the Psalms, while the book of Jonah reflects relationships between the creation and the Creator. Nature testifies to God's goodness and grace. The story of Noah is likewise instructive. There was peace on board a ship filled with all kinds of animals; how then can "a child of God" stir up trouble and strife?[80]

Experiences and emotions from nature contributed to spiritual development. "Observing and perceiving God-created nature has invigorated me. God has become great and glorious. My humility, love, trust, vitality, reverence, and boldness to draw closer to the Heavenly Father and Jesus Christ have been enhanced...."[81] Nature exhibits how God cares for people.

> Herbs with healing power have been sown everywhere. They may be berry-bearing junipers on a dry knoll or reddish cranberries by a bog-pool, white-flowered yarrows in the sunlight by the road, burdock roots buried in the earth, coltsfoots by the ditch, valerians, camomile by the fields, Iceland moss on the verge of moorlands.... Walk through the forest in the murmur of nature, and your nerves heal from the technological noise and rush! ... How much more

---

[79] Katvel, *Rännutee rõõmud*, 386.

[80] Katvel, *Rännutee rõõmud*, 388–93 and 398–99.

[81] Katvel, *Rännutee rõõmud*, 388.

then would God enrich His church, which is the body of Christ, with various kinds of spiritual gifts![82]

Also, Hildegard of Bingen, though in a different historical setting, spoke about obedience, the healing powers of nature, and how God's Word is revealed in all creation.[83]

Many biblical texts indicate that creation has a more important function than merely being a means to meet human needs.[84] In Ilse Katvel's simple Bible-inspired theology, nature is an important messenger; it is not primarily corrupt and degraded, which was a widespread view among Estonian Baptists during the Soviet years.[85] Instead, she believes there is a positive symbolism; nature is beautiful and theologically relevant, reflecting the Creator's will concerning everything that exists, including human beings.

Last Years

In the last years of her life, beginning in 1976, Ilse Katvel lived in Tallinn. She wrote, "The apartment where I live in Tallinn has three rooms, and we are three sisters in Christ here . . . ."[86] She continued to be invited to preach and teach in different churches. Despite her Free Church background, she preached at Lutheran churches when requested; for example, in Prangli Lutheran chapel.[87] She maintained her pattern of community life and cooperation with various Christian movements.

Ilse-Anete Katvel died on 25 March 1987.[88] She was buried in the Rannamõisa cemetery. The funeral ceremony took place at Rannamõisa Lutheran Church and pastor Karl Reinaru officiated. A Baptist pastor, Herman Mäemets, tied his thoughts in with the words of the Gospel of John, "I have brought you glory on earth by finishing the work you gave me to do" (John 17:3–4). The pastor of Valjala church, from Saaremaa, spoke about Ilse Katvel as the congregation's ambassador and spiritual mother, "You arose as a mother in Israel" (a reference to Deborah, cf. Judges 5:7).[89] Her influence

---

[82] Katvel, *Rännutee rõõmud*, 400.

[83] Ruut, *Bingeni Hildegardi* Ordo Virtutum, 9, 32 and 35; Heepen, *Keskaja ravitarkused*; Hildegard of Bingen, *Elava valguse sõnad*, 23.

[84] Liht, "Beyond Instrumentalism and Mere Symbolism," 127.

[85] Liht, "Restoring Relationships," 13–14.

[86] Katvel, *Saaremaa ärkamise lugu*, 93.

[87] Sirel, *Eesti pühad naised*, 90.

[88] Ilse-Anete Katvel's funeral songsheet.

[89] Herman Mäemets, notes 6 May 2009.

towards uniting different people and religious movements was manifested even at her burial service.

Summary

Ilse Katvel was a profoundly spiritual, even mystical-charismatic individual. She preached regularly for approximately half a century throughout Estonia, particularly on Saaremaa. Preferring the intuitive and imaginative approach to the rational and systematic method in sermon preparation, she was a colourful representative of that line in the homiletic tradition of the Free Churches. Her sermons grew out of an excellent knowledge of the Bible. She sought in prayer a message for the audience and her words were supported by the maturity of her personality. Perhaps that is why she struck a chord not only with her peers, but also with young people. She had the spiritual gift of teaching and preaching, although the toolbox for her ministry was more diverse.

Although Katvel was unlikely to have thought in this way, it may be said in retrospect that she was characterized by "convent practices without a convent." She practised ascetic living of a particular kind in a Free Church mode. She devoted herself to God and helped her fellow human beings. "It is inexpressibly precious to serve—to be of use to my Lord somewhere. This exceeds all earthly joys," she said.[90] Living for a prolonged period on Saaremaa, she gathered around her a spiritual fellowship. She did the necessary household and farming chores, meditated on the Bible, prayed and fasted regularly with her sisters in Christ. Katvel remained single for life. She did not encumber herself with major mundane duties, but was free to serve different churches. She led a simple life. She accepted donations, but often passed them on generously to others. This inevitably invokes parallels with Francis of Assisi, whose programme was poverty, humility and simplicity, freedom from earthly property, focus on and identification with Christ, accompanied by solidarity with both humanity and all creation.[91]

Katvel endeavoured to understand the relationships between the creation and the Creator. She had an eye for the beauty and an ear for messages coming from nature. Natural images helped her to render meaning to Christian experiences and insights. Nature played the role of context and interpretative instrument at the time of Katvel's religious conversion and also later. She prayed for the healing of not only humans, but also animals if necessary. The images of nature in the Bible and the reality of God's creation above all recalled two things: God's goodness and people's duty to obey God's will.

---

[90] Katvel, *Rännutee rõõmud*, 401.

[91] Küng, *Catholic Church*, 98–101.

Influenced by the early twentieth-century holiness movement, Katvel's spirituality included charismatic openness and expectation for miracles. Nevertheless, she evaded extreme enthusiasm. Affirmation of God's omnipotence led to a sincere conviction that God intervenes in earthly situations. Hence, it is not surprising that Katvel prayed for healing and fulfilled the functions of a pastoral counsellor. Her charismatic personality reminds one not so much of Pentecostal spirituality as of that of medieval saints. Indeed, she valued religious experiences, the "downpouring" of and "filling" with the Holy Spirit. However, God's help for her was manifestation of the sovereign grace of the Almighty, a divine intervention that was revealed in the context of a committed life.

Finally, her activities promoted unity, as she cooperated with people from different denominations. Her spirituality, pursuit of a holy life, which nevertheless was charitable and kind, resonates with the kindred aspirations of various religious movements, not just with the particularities of one denomination.

Bibliography

Literature

Bärenson, Jaan. "Evangeelne karskusselts Sinine Rist" ["The Evangelical Abstinence Society the Blue Cross"]. *Kuulutaja* [*The Herald*] 11 (November 1993) 7.

Briggs, John H.Y. "Conversion." In *A Dictionary of European Baptist Life and Thought*, 122–23. Edited by John H.Y. Briggs et al. Milton Keynes: Paternoster, 2009.

Douglas, J. D., Walter A. Elwell and Peter Toon. *The Concise Dictionary of the Christian Tradition*. London: Marshall Pickering, 1989.

Gonzales, Justo L. *The Story of Christianity:* Volume 1. New York: HarperSanFrancisco, 1984.

Heepen, Günther. *Keskaja ravitarkused: Püha Hildegardi pärand* [*Healing Wisdom of Middle Ages: A Heritage of Hildegard of Bingen*]. Tallinn: Varrak, 2016.

Hildegard of Bingen. *Elava valguse sõnad* [*Words of Living Light*]. Tallinn: Allika, 2016.

Kaasik, Toivo. "Aleksander Sildose vaimulik tegevus Eestis ja tema vabakoguduslike vaadete kujunemine" ["Aleksander Sildos' Ministry in Estonia and the Development of his Free Church Views"]. MA diss., Eesti Evangeelse Luterliku Kiriku Usuteaduse Instituut, 2016.

Kargel, Ivan. *Milline on sinu wahekord Pühavaimuga?* [*What is Your Relationship to the Holy Spirit?*]. Keila: Külvaja, 1931.

Katvel, Ilse. *Rännutee rõõmud* [*Joys of the Pilgrimage*]. Undated typescript. Herman Mäemets' Library.

———. *Saaremaa ärkamise lugu* [*Story of Saaremaa Revival*]. Rakvere: Rakvere Nelipüha Kogudus, 2009.

———. *Virumaa ärkamise lugu* [*Story of Virumaa Revival*]. Rakvere: Rakvere Nelipüha Kogudus, 2009.

Kiil, Evald. *Meenutusi nelipühi ärkamisest Eestis* [*Reminiscences of the Pentecostal Awakening in Estonia*]. Tallinn: Logos, 1997.

Killinger, John. *Fundamentals of Preaching*. Minneapolis: Fortress Press, 1985.

Kurg, Ingmar. "Ühe medali kaks poolt: evangelisatsioon ja misjonitöö" ["The Two Sides of a Medal: Evangelisation and Missionary Work"]. In *Osaduses kasvanud* [*Grown in Fellowship*], 141–53. Edited by Üllas Linder and Toivo Pilli. Tallinn: Eesti EKB Koguduste Liit, 2009.

Küng, Hans. *The Catholic Church. A Short History*. New York: Modern Library Paperback Edition, 2003.

Laks, Johannes. *Kakskümmend viis aastat vabakoguduslist liikumist Eestis, 1905–1930* [*Twenty-Five Years of Free Church Movement in Estonia, 1905–1930*]. Tallinn: [Evangeeliumi Kristlaste Vabakogudus], 1930.

[———]. *Aleksander Sildos: elulugu* [*Aleksander Sildos: A Life Story*]. Typewritten manuscript, 1967. Toivo Pilli's Library.

Liht, Helle. "Beyond Instrumentalism and Mere Symbolism: Nature as Sacramental." *Journal of European Baptist Studies* 2 (2020) 124–39.

———. "Restoring Relationships: Towards Ecologically Responsible Baptistic Communities in Estonia." MTh diss., International Baptist Theological Seminary, Prague, 2008.

McGrath, Alister. *Christian Spirituality: An Introduction*. Oxford: Blackwell, 1999.

———. *Reformation Thought: An Introduction*. Oxford: Blackwell, 1999.

Mäemets, Margus. *Noored, lähme pühas innus: Kuressaare EKB koguduse noortetöö 1970–2005* [*Young People, Let Us Go in Holy Fervour: Youth Ministry at Kuressaare ECB Congregation in 1970–2005*]. Kuressaare: Kuressaare Siioni kogudus, 2007.

Nichols, Gregory L. *The Development of Russian Evangelical Spirituality: A Study of Ivan V. Kargel (1849–1937)*. Eugene: Pickwick, 2011.

Pilli, Toivo. *Dance or Die: The Shaping of Estonian Baptist Identity under Communism*. Milton Keynes: Paternoster, 2008.

———. *Usu värvid ja varjundid* [*The Colours and Shades of Faith*]. Tallinn: Allika, 2007.

Pilli, Toivo, Hillar Palamets et al. *Avatult avalikust kõnest* [*Openly about Public Speech*]. Tartu: Atlex, 2008.

Price, Charles, and Ian Randall. *Transforming Keswick*. Carlisle: OM Publishing, 2000.

Randall, Ian. *Evangelical Experiences: A Study in the Spirituality of English Evangelicalism 1918–1939*. Carlisle: Paternoster, 1999.

Roberts, Evan. *Pühitsuselu astmed* [*Stages of Sanctification*]. Tallinn: Valgus, 1933.

Ruut, Riina. *Bingeni Hildegardi* Ordo Virtutum: *Vooruste mäng* [Ordo Virtutum *by Hildegard of Bingen: Play of Virtues*]. Tartu: Härmametsa talu kirjastus, 2004.

Sirel, Stanislav. *Eesti pühad naised: 20. sajandi misjonärid, prohvetid ja evangelistid* [*Holy Women of Estonia: 20th Century Missionaries, Prophets and Evangelists*]. Rakvere: Rakvere Nelipüha Kogudus, 2013.

Archive Materials

ARCHIVES OF THE UNION OF THE EVANGELICAL CHRISTIAN AND BAPTIST CHURCHES OF ESTONIA (EEKBLA)

Ilse-Anete Katvel's funeral songsheet.
Liiv, Helju. Notes, 6 May 2009.
Mäemets, Herman. Notes, 6 May 2009.
Pajusoo, Toomas. Email, 24 March 2009.
Pink, Urve. Letter to Toivo Pilli, 10 March 2009.
Roberts, Oral. "Kui tahad saada terveks, siis talita järgmiselt" [*If You Need Healing Do These Things*]. Undated typescript.

NATIONAL ARCHIVES OF ESTONIA (RA): THE COMMISSIONER OF RELIGIOUS AFFAIRS

Valjala "Rahu Saalemi" Church, RA, ERA.R–1989.3.291.

ORAL INFORMATION

Mäemets, Herman. Oral information, 23 February 2009.
Mäemets, Margus. Telephone conversation, 30 October 2020.
Väli, Leevi. Telephone conversation, 4 November 2020.

CHAPTER 9

"She Did What She Could:" Some Historical Observations on Following Jesus as a Single Woman

Lina Toth

The very first sermon I heard the Rev. Dr Ruth Gouldbourne preach was one that she delivered as a visiting lecturer at the International Baptist Theological Seminary, which at the time was situated in Prague, the Czech Republic. The sermon, based on the passage in Luke 14:3–9 and following the story of the woman who anointed Jesus, was entitled "She Did What She Could." As a call to appreciate and celebrate people's actions in light of their particular circumstances, the title of her sermon captures something fundamental about Ruth's own approach to life and faith, and so it seems appropriate to use it in the title of this chapter.

In the following pages, I will explore one particular aspect of life which can be considered through the prism of "doing what one can." To situate this in terms of our contemporary concerns, let me start with the following peculiar fact. While in Western societies single people are the fastest growing, and increasingly the most populous, demographic group, it is still not unusual for them to find themselves treated as an oddity, an exception to the rule, whether by accident or due to some special calling in life.[1] Nowhere is this more true than in the context of the church. In many Western countries, single people make up about half of the population—double to their proportion in the middle of the twentieth century.[2] In Christian communities, however, this number is typically lower, and in some contexts significantly so.[3] As I have

---

[1] I explore this issue in detail in two volumes of my own: Andronovienė, *Transforming the Struggles of Tamars*, and Toth, *Singleness and Marriage After Christendom*.

[2] United Nations, "World Marriage Data 2019."

[3] The numbers can vary greatly between urban, youth- and young adults-oriented ministry, and suburban or rural churches. Extensive studies and hard figures are often unavailable, but the lower number of single people in the church compared to that in the society at large, has been sufficiently established. For instance, less than 25 percent of active churchgoers in the United States are single—twice less than in the population at large, Chiu, "A Single-Minded Church." In the United Kingdom, less than a third

argued elsewhere, a firm link has been forged between the church and the (nuclear) family, as a result of which Christian communities typically envision themselves primarily as places for married people and their children. Although things are changing, in too many churches, single people still feel invisible, or less valuable.[4]

Another peculiar feature characterizes the experience of single people in the church context: namely, gender imbalance. Exceptions and denominational variations notwithstanding, the face of the church (and indeed that of many other world religions) is female. "The evidence . . . is cumulative: in enquiry after enquiry, the predominance of women is not only affirmed, but striking."[5] Among single Christians, two women to one man is not an uncommon ratio.[6] As a result, single heterosexual women will often experience their singleness somewhat differently in their own community of faith, compared to other realms of their lives.[7] The norm of being married will be likely felt more acutely, yet opportunities for finding a marriage partner will be significantly limited.[8]

Given the reduced availability of men, a number of these women find themselves to be "involuntarily free": having a longing for a loving, intimate relationship and a nuclear family of their own, and quite likely wrestling with questions of why God is not answering their prayers. At the same time, however, an assumption that every single woman in the church is unhappy is a gross mistake: there will be those who have actively chosen to stay single, as well as women for whom marriage is simply not the highest priority.[9]

---

of practicing Christians are unpartnered, according to one study, "Research cofunded."

[4] E.g., "What do single Christians say about church."

[5] Berger *et al.*, *Religious America, Secular Europe*, 110.

[6] Pullinger, "Where are all the men;" and Stone, "Sex Ratios."

[7] Obviously, gender ratio does not have the same implications for the LGBTQ+ women, whose experience of singleness would be dependent on their own (current) theology of sexuality, and the degree of their church's inclusivity.

[8] These observations are made with an understanding that the categories of *married* and *single* are far from straightforward, especially once we take into consideration cohabitation on the one hand and marital estrangement on the other. For my purposes here, by "single" I refer to women who see themselves as single. Some of them may be in some sort of an intimate relationship, but they would not perceive or describe themselves as "coupled" or "in a relationship." This would include those who may have always been single, as well as divorcees and widows; those who are single parents as well as those without parental responsibilities.

[9] My use of "marriage" in this case is synonymous with "coupledom," and includes any long-term, intimate, and presumably sexual relationship between two people, whether that is religiously or legally sanctioned or not.

Furthermore, interest in getting married is likely to fluctuate depending on one's age and other life circumstances. Yet in the environment which—implicitly at least, and often explicitly—extols the married state and sees it as normative, many single women will experience at least some discomfort or ambivalence about their single status.

Coupledom as the norm, and singleness as an exception, has been deeply etched into our contemporary Christian psyche. However, in the story of the Christian church this has not always been so. In this chapter, I offer two historical episodes that reflect very different ways of single Christian women constructing their life, and, in their own way, "doing what they could" in their particular circumstances. The first one of them comes from the earliest Christian centuries which saw a number of Christian women going against the deeply fixed imperial norm of marriage. The second episode explores the late medieval communities of the Beguines, who carved out ways of flourishing in their own "cities of ladies."[10] In light of these two historical episodes, seemingly so far removed from the concerns of our Western culture today, I will then offer some concluding observations in relation to today's challenges and opportunities facing single Christian women who desire the path of Christian discipleship.

Singleness as a Sign of the Heavenly Age in Early Christianity

Although early Christianity is sometimes imagined as a homogenous group, it was, of course, anything but. Among the various debates that were raging were disputes over different understandings of family and celibacy practices. Any potential changes in the role and the shape of marriage and family touched upon a highly sensitive area of the Roman culture: namely, the centrality of the patriarchal household—the symbol and the key element of the societal order of the day. In such a context, individual conversion to Christianity was a radical, indeed political, act.[11] Christian identity was tightly linked to the vision of a new community, a new kind of a family made of slaves and free people, women and men, Jews and Gentiles. Such a reimagination of human relations drastically clashed with the traditional household order and the centrality of marriage to its maintenance.

Just how central a role marriage played in the maintenance of Roman society is manifest in the fact that imperial legislation required all female citizens aged twenty to fifty, and all male citizens aged twenty-five to sixty, to be married. While there were some loopholes and exceptions, the rhetorical

---

[10] Simons, *Cities of Ladies*.

[11] Cahill, "Christian Social Perspective," 166.

power of the law is striking.¹² Such legislation was primarily aimed at the ruling class, and had to do with the concern of keeping a sufficient level of population growth. However, it was presented as a moral concern about the deterioration of family values in the Roman Empire—in other words, it was about returning to the mythical ideal of a harmonious and prosperous family life, and so making Rome great again.¹³

It is no wonder that Christian churches, seeing themselves as new-order families, soon found themselves in the most direct confrontation with the established system. Some of them found the perceived clash going too far and unnecessary. Indeed, certain Christian writings reflect eagerness to convince Roman society that Christians were not as radical as rumour had it, and that they were not really the haters "of the human race."¹⁴ The *Letter to Diognetus* sought to demonstrate that as far as human relations went, Christians were, in fact, just "like all others;" "they marry, as do all [others]; they beget children, but they do not destroy their offspring. They have a common table, but not a common bed."¹⁵

The majority of early Christians were most likely married, but what is striking is a surprisingly strong and costly witness of those who did not—in spite of the imperial laws and societal expectations. "From the second century onward, and almost certainly from an earlier, less well-documented period, little groups of men and women, scattered among the Christian communities throughout the eastern Mediterranean and in the Near East, as far as the foothills of Iran, strove to render almost audible, by their 'singleness,' their studied isolation from marriage, the vast hush of the imminent end of the age."¹⁶ This was a vision of a life transformed, of eternity already present, in radically different life choices that claimed a different vision for the limits of

---

¹² Notably, however, the law did not require people to *stay* married. Divorce was easily achievable for either the husband or the wife (in contrast to Jewish society, where only the males had the right to divorce their wives). The ideal of a life-long marriage was certainly present, but, given the likelihood of widowhood or divorce, it was "by no means a legal requirement," Cooper, *Fall of the Roman Household*, 149. After the divorce, however, or after the death of a spouse, citizens were given a limited time to remarry before incurring penalties or restrictions, Ferguson, *Backgrounds*, 69. Similar penalties applied to those who were childless.

¹³ Dixon, *Roman Family*, 79. What is also notable is the link between Rome's greatness and Roman family values: the deterioration of the latter was presented as the reason why Rome was no longer as glorious as before. Such mythical past glory has interesting parallels to our modern West's imagined morality to be found in the presumed bliss of the nuclear family.

¹⁴ Tacitus, *Annals* 15:44, in Owen and Gildenhard, *Tacitus*.

¹⁵ *Diognetus* 5:6.

¹⁶ Brown, *Body and Society*, 85.

the body. The active role which women played in such a transformation of life is striking; already by the second century we have clear evidence of the vibrant life of the orders of virgins and widows, and "the persistent practice of female asceticism."[17]

By this point, asceticism and singleness had become inseparable. Under the influence of various Gnostic trends, resisting bodily urges and pleasures became an expression of the commitment to one's soul's yearning for communion with the divine. Such a stance became particularly associated with Encratite Christianity, which came to regard marriage and sex as simply incompatible with Christianity. For these Christians, the practice of *enkrateia*, or abstinence, became the focal point of their understanding of the Christian Way. *Enkrateia* included abstention from sexual relations, marriage, and procreation, but also meat and wine—all the elements that were associated with life after the fall and the exile from paradise. Abstinence, therefore, was about "[returning] to paradise and . . . regaining . . . the angelic condition of original creation."[18]

Encratite groups were especially prominent in early Syrian Christianity, where celibacy became the requirement for one's baptism.[19] Those who were already married were, obviously, too late to the virginity party, but were taught to embrace celibacy within marriage. In one of the texts which originated from among the Syrian churches, *The Acts of Thomas*, Jesus appears to a newly married couple in the bridal chamber and persuades them to "refrain from this filthy intercourse," to be free from the burden of raising children, and instead to trust that they will be blessed with spiritual children. The couple are convinced, and join "in a different marriage" of a spiritual kind.[20]

Even outside the Encratite tradition, commitment to virginity and chastity carried a strong eschatological message. This was a proclamation of the beginning of the end for "this world," and the beginning of eternal life. To control or deny the urges for sleep, food, and sex, typically associated with the mortality of the body, meant to experience some of that future transformation already in the present, and to prefigure what was to come. To renounce sex in particular was "to throw a switch located in the human person; and, by throwing that precise switch, it was believed possible to cut the current that sustained the sinister *perpetuum mobile* of life in 'the present age'."[21] As far as

---

[17] Salisbury, *Church Fathers*, 4.

[18] Shaw, "Sex and sexual renunciation," 365. See also Brown, *Body and Society*, 95.

[19] Vööbus, *Celibacy*.

[20] "Acts of Thomas," 12 and 14, in Ehrman, *Lost Scriptures*, 126–27. The practice of spiritual marriage would continue in church tradition, although attitudes towards such marriages varied considerably. See, e.g., Elliott, *Spiritual Marriage*.

[21] Brown, *Body and Society*, 85.

many ascetics were concerned, this was what it meant to be "like angels" (cf. Luke 20:34b–36). Notably, it was not so much a matter of "original condition," but something that one could actually "become": not only a calling of ever-virgins, but also to those who were married or widowed.[22]

Here, however, we ought to note a significant departure from an earlier emphasis of singleness as an expression of freedom in the age of the inbreaking kingdom of God—the emphasis we see in the New Testament writings. Jesus shocked his Jewish contemporaries by suggesting that a "eunuch life"—not a kind of life to be aspired to in Jewish culture—could be freely chosen "for the sake of the kingdom of heaven" (Matt 19:12, NRSV). In one of the key New Testament passages addressing abstention from marriage, 1 Corinthians 7, Paul also described unmarried life as one that focusses on "the affairs of the Lord," and marriage as something that can get in the way (1 Cor 7:32–34). In the light of the urgency of the time, single living was a "gift" and, as far as Paul was concerned, his preferred option (1 Cor 7:7). Yet Paul's preference for abstaining from marriage was not based on preserving sexual purity. Only later, under Gnostic and Neoplatonist influences, was the emphasis on sexual asceticism read into 1 Corinthians 7, so that it became a matter of a "choice between sexuality and spirituality."[23] As Cyprian put it, writing to the celibates, "That which we shall be, you have already begun to be. . . . You already possess the glory of the resurrection. . . . You pass through the world without contagion, like the angels of God."[24]

Remarkably, however, this path to heaven was now available to all Christians—including women. Any of them "could achieve reputations for sexual abstinence as stunning as those achieved by any cultivated male."[25] Thus, eschatological motivation apart, other factors also made virginity particularly attractive as a viable alternative to marriage from a woman's perspective. Freedom from marriage and sexual intercourse presented an opportunity for a woman to exercise much greater control over her own affairs, her own time, and her environment. It also meant control over her own body and freedom from such risks of marital life as pregnancy and childbirth. Women who did marry could still hope of finding such freedom later in life, after the death of their spouse, through embracing widowhood rather than remarrying. For a number of them, widowhood became the desired route. Just as the widows described in 1 Timothy 5:9–11, these women continued the tradition, taking the vow of chastity and embracing the duties of a Christian

---

[22] McNamara, *New Song*, 108–9.

[23] Deming, *Paul on Marriage*, 219.

[24] Cyprian, *On the Dress of Virgins* 22–23, in Osiek and Balch, *Families in the New Testament World*, 152.

[25] Brown, *Body and Society*, 61.

widow: visiting and nursing the sick, supporting the poor, instructing younger women, and, especially in the Eastern churches, serving as deaconesses. Overall, such a choice was viewed overwhelmingly positively by the rest of the church. Tertullian addressed the widows considering remarriage with the following passionate question: "Why do you reject the freedom that is given to you in returning to the bonds of matrimony?"[26]

Of course, the answer to this rhetorical question depended on the widow's social status and the support of the church. Many widows would have had very meagre resources; for them not remarrying carried a risk of extreme poverty. However, the increasing respect for the status of a widow and the care system organized by the church meant that, before too long, "a life as a widow was not only desirable; it was also rendered feasible."[27] And as far as the well-to-do widows were concerned, they often played an important role in enabling the work of theologians and entire churches. The fourth- and early fifth-century theologian, Jerome, is a particularly good example of a church leader who discussed the role of widows at great length while being funded by two ascetic widows, Marcella and Paula. The two women featured prominently in his correspondence and funded his projects, including the translation of the Bible into Latin.

For women, both virginity and widowhood enabled something otherwise impossible: namely, transcending the confines of gender and sexual difference. With masculinity regarded as the golden standard of humanity, these women, too, could now be described in masculine terms.[28] The very act of claiming power over one's body meant that these women were seen, and saw themselves, as more than women, or even no longer women. Some cut their hair; some left their husbands; and some adopted male clothing as a way of claiming equality in Christian ministry, in choirs, in teaching and assisting in baptizing other women, or the distribution of communion to women at home. Older celibate women, especially widows with property, were able to transform their own home into a celibate community of prayer, fasting, and sacred study. Ascetic transcendence of femininity offered a promise of being treated "no longer as subordinates or objects of male desire, but as potential equals, thus honorary men."[29]

It is not difficult to see why the Christian women's refusal to marry, and their aspirations for honorary masculinity, were met with such hostility by Roman society.[30] Yet before too long, the independence of such women also

---

[26] Tertullian, *Ad Uxorem* i:8, quoted in Nathan, *Family*, 45.

[27] Seim, *Double Message*, 235.

[28] Lee, *Pagans and Christians*, 261.

[29] Osiek and Balch, *Families in the New Testament World*, 153.

[30] Wiesner-Hanks, *Christianity and Sexuality*, 29.

made their own (male) church leadership increasingly uncomfortable. Some of these women were freely travelling and organizing their lives as they saw best fit for the purposes of serving the kingdom of God. Some virgins, while being committed to chastity, wore beautiful clothing and jewellery and attended baths and parties, creating yet another challenge to the perception of celibate womanhood.[31] Not surprisingly, a number of church fathers had a few things to say on the subject. In his tract named *On the Veiling of Virgins*, Tertullian insists that the virgins should not claim any of the privileges not available to married women of the time, "such as speaking in church, teaching, baptizing, or holding ecclesiastical offices."[32] At the Synod of Elvira, in the early fourth century, it was decided that both virgins and widows were required to "take public vows and wear prescribed, identifiable clothing."[33] In these rulings, we can recognize a much more regulated form of celibacy, which would eventually enclose the Christian virgin within the walls of a monastery.

As the status of Christianity changed from persecuted to tolerated to preferred, and finally to the only legitimate religion of the Empire, countless Christians continued to flock to uninhabited places, whether to live on their own or in a group of fellow monastics, seeking to recreate that original "singleness of heart" which they felt now was increasingly missing in the church at large.[34] Christendom itself became marked by a clear hierarchy of holiness: virginity at the top, followed by widowhood, and marriage representing the lowest category.[35] The moral supremacy of the single status would remain unchallenged until the times of the magisterial Reformation, which would finally set marriage at the centre of a good and godly society. Before that change occurred, however, there was another fascinating and significant development, resulting in a new way of living out one's Christian faith as a woman. It is to that development that we turn next.

Religious and Secular, Contemplative and Active: The Beguine Option

While the monastery and, in the case of men in the Western world, priesthood were the most obvious and permanent pathways of unmarried life, a surprisingly large proportion of lay people in late medieval Christendom were leading single lives. These included servants, weavers, spinsters,

---

[31] McNamara, *New Song*, 116–17.

[32] Salisbury, *Church Fathers*, 123.

[33] Salisbury, *Church Fathers*, 6.

[34] Brown, *Body and Society*, 226.

[35] Cyprian compares these to the thirty, sixty, and hundredfold harvest of Mark 4:20, see Cyprian, *On the Dress of Virgins* 21, in Osiek and Balch, *Families in the New Testament World*, 153. Cf. Tertullian, *Exhortation to Chastity* 1.

prostitutes, guild members, and other city dwellers engaged in a trade or service which either prohibited or was complicated by married life.[36] However, the focus of this section will be on a particular, deeply spiritual expression of lay female single living. In order to understand its emergence, a few words must be said about its context.

The twelfth and thirteenth centuries represent a particularly interesting period of medieval Europe. In terms of religious activity, it was marked by the rise of mysticism, especially among the monastics, but also the upsurge of popular piety, as many lay people looked for patterns and communities of apostolic life, and embraced the ideals of chastity, humility, poverty, and simplicity. Some of these expressions were eventually absorbed by the church, while others were vehemently opposed and suppressed. Catharism, with its deep roots in ancient Gnosticism, its belief in the corruption of all that was physical, and its requirement of complete sexual abstinence, is the most prominent example of the latter.[37] Countless wandering preachers and recluses were calling people to the *vita apostolica*—a way of life resembling that of the early church, as described in the Acts of the Apostles. Among the various lay sisterhoods and brotherhoods that sprang up, one of the most remarkable was the emergence and growth of *mulieres religiosae*—women who chose a life centred around religious devotion, but without becoming nuns. Before too long, many of them became known as "the beguines."[38]

Arising in the twelfth century, the beguine movement spread throughout the European towns, with the majority of beguines concentrated in modern-day Belgium and The Netherlands, Paris, southern Germany, and southern France. The beguine way was broad enough to incorporate the option of becoming an anchoress—a form of life that allowed one to devote oneself to contemplation and the spiritual guidance of others while remaining in an urban context.[39] However, most beguines formed their own communities, or

---

[36] The numbers vary from at least ten percent to nearly half of the adult population, depending on the specific period and location. See, e.g., Kowaleski, "Singlewomen." Even some peasant women—not the most likely category of singles—remained unmarried. Joan of Arc is, no doubt, best known among these, but an equally interesting, and different, story is that of a fourteenth-century English peasant, Cecilia Panifader of Brigstock, who made a decision to remain unmarried and ran her own household. Another important development, in Northern Europe at least, was the emergence of the European Marriage Pattern, which saw men and women marrying later, in their thirties and forties, once they had acquired necessary finances to set up a separate household. On this, see Hajnal, "European Marriage Patterns."

[37] For background on the Cathars, see Moore, *Origins of European Dissent*, 168–240.

[38] For an excellent introduction to the beguines, with a particular focus on the Low Countries, see Simons, *Cities of Ladies*.

[39] Simons, *Cities of Ladies*, 74–76.

beguinages, which united women from different strata of medieval society into a common life. Often resembling nuns in their appearance, but retaining their rights to personal property, moving freely between their home and the town, they typically engaged in manual work in the textile industry, teaching, or nursing.[40] Theirs was a fluid movement: there was no centre or leadership, and no particular Rule that all beguines followed or agreed upon. There were no vows to take; one generally became a beguine out of her own choice, and only for as long as she wanted.[41]

The beguines' life on the border of the secular and the sacred both fascinated and perturbed the cultural imagination of medieval Europe. How could these single women be both in the world and not of it? The words of the Franciscan friar, Gilbert of Tournai, writing in 1274, are often quoted to illustrate this ambivalence towards the beguines: "There are among us women whom we do not know what to call, religious or lay, because they live neither in the world nor removed from it."[42] Remaining "in the world," but also embracing a life of devotion to Christ, without a clear hierarchy or a unified practice, they defied categorization.[43]

Walter Simons suggests that in the beguines' own understanding of their calling this required freedom from the cares associated with marriage and a detachment from material possessions.[44] However, poverty was not their goal, in contrast to some other contemporary groups such as the early Franciscans.[45] Gaining income through one's labour, as well as possessing property, did not clash with beguine spirituality. As far as marriage was concerned, the crux of the matter was chastity, rather than virginity. Even a married woman could become a beguine, if, alongside her spouse, she chose to stay a virgin in her marriage. Such was the case of Marie of Oignies (1177–1213), one of the early

---

[40] Here is an illustration from the life in the Paris beguinage. If a beguine had bought a house in the beguinage, but later wished to leave, she could freely do so by selling the house to another beguine, as long one-third of the value of the sale went to the community itself. Miller, "What's in a name?" 69.

[41] The term "beguine" was at times applied to any woman who lived a life of devotion and service, regardless of whether or not she was officially linked to a beguine community. Deane, "'Beguines' Reconsidered."

[42] Gilbert of Tournai, *Collectio de Scandalis Ecclesiae*, quoted in Miller, "What's in a name?" 69.

[43] Deane, "'Beguines' Reconsidered."

[44] Simons, *Cities of Ladies*, 62. A number of beguinages, such as one in Marseilles, were able to accumulate considerable resources; however, as noted further, it was not a life of poverty, but rather one of service and devotion, that was at the center of the beguine relationship to material possessions.

[45] Simons, *Cities of Ladies*, 66–67.

models of medieval "holy women." Married at the age of fourteen, she persuaded her spouse to maintain a spiritual—that is, chaste—marriage, and both of them devoted their life to the service to the lepers of Willambroux, before Marie finally withdrew to a life of contemplation.[46]

Here we can recognize the aforementioned "hierarchy of holiness" and the link between sexual activity and sin, which was firmly established at the juncture of Christianity and Christendom. Surviving documents also suggest a strong motif of presenting beguine life as a (better) alternative to marriage,[47] but this must be considered alongside the fact that being a beguine did not involve a life-long vow, and thus a beguine was free, at any point, to leave the community for marriage (or, potentially, a convent).

Some of those holding power in the church were sympathetic, or at least tolerant, of the beguines' cause, especially in the early stages of the movement. The beguines' piety and humility were considered to be worthy of admiration, as was their general obedience to clerical authority in a climate marked by apprehension of lay dissidence.[48] Jacques de Vitry (d. 1240), a French preacher and later cardinal, is a particularly notable example because of his support for the cause of beguines in his sermons, as well as for being the confessor of Marie of Oignies, the account of whose life he himself produced.[49]

However, in the eyes of many, these single women were dangerously free from the direct control of the church. Of specific concern was the beguines' interest in scripture and theological literature. As Gilbert of Turnai had complained in regard to the Parisian beguines, "They have interpreted the mysteries of Scripture into French, although they are hardly understood by experts in Holy Scripture. They read them in common, irreverently, audaciously, in their little rooms, workshops, and in the public squares."[50] Given that this description has been offered by someone perturbed by the beguines' activities, it should be taken with a pinch of salt, but a number of beguines were known for their production of religious, and particularly mystical, literature—most notably in the vernacular. At least partly, this was a literary movement, too, and one that incorporated a variety of genres. Hadewijch, a Dutch beguine, wrote letters and recorded poems as well as visions. Mechthild of Magdeburg wrote *The Flowing Light of the Godhead*, which was a collection of prayers, dialogues, and reports of mystical encounters. Felipa of Porcelet, a Provençal beguine, is the most likely author

---

[46] See Mulder-Bakker, *Mary of Oignies*.

[47] Simons, *Cities of Ladies*, 71–72.

[48] Miller, "What's in a name?" 61.

[49] De Vitry, *Life of Marie d'Oignies*.

[50] Gilbert of Tournai, *Collectio de scandalis ecclesiae*, in Miller, "What's in a name?" 81.

of a *Life of the Blessed Saint Doucelina*—an account of the founder of the beguines of Marseilles.[51] The case of Marguerite Porete, a French mystic who was at least accused of being a beguine, is particularly illustrative. In 1310, Porete was burned at the stake as a heretic for refusing to recant and cease the circulation of her own book, *The Mirror of Simple Souls*—"the first female Christian mystic burned at the stake after authoring a book," which has fortunately survived.[52]

Shortly after Porete's burning at the stake, two decrees associated with the Council of Vienne addressed the concern regarding "certain women commonly known as beguines."[53] One of them, *Cum de quibusdam*, contained a perpetual prohibition of anyone adopting the beguine lifestyle, on the basis that beguines "neither promise obedience to anyone, nor renounce personal property, nor profess any approved rule." What was worse, perhaps, was that "some of them, as if having been led into insanity, dispute and preach about the highest Trinity and the divine essence and introduce opinions contrary to the catholic faith concerning the articles of the faith and the sacraments of the church."[54] Yet the decree ended with the following qualification: "Of course by the preceding we in no way intend to forbid any faithful women, whether or not they promise chastity, from living honestly in their dwellings, doing penance, and serving the Lord in a spirit of humility, this being allowed to them as the Lord inspires them."[55]

The seeming internal contradiction of the decree is an illustration of the varied use of the term "beguine": it could refer to those who were above any reproach as well as to those whose doctrine and practice were deemed to be heretical.[56] And, indeed, the evidence suggests the term was used in a variety of ways: from admiration for their courage even in the face of opposition, to praise for the depth of their faith and the devotion to the works of mercy, to accusations of arrogance and pride.[57]

Historians continue to argue over the dominant motivation behind the emergence and the remarkable flourishing of the beguine life: were the

---

[51] Field, *The Beguine*, 7.

[52] Field, *The Beguine*, 3. Some doubts have been expressed about whether Marguerite Porete was really a beguine, or whether being described as one added weight to the charges for her condemnation. However, that is precisely the point being made here: beguines were increasingly viewed as a "problem."

[53] As translated by Makowski, in *Pernicious Sort of Woman*, 23.

[54] As translated by Makowski, in *Pernicious Sort of Woman*, 23–24.

[55] As translated by Makowski, in *Pernicious Sort of Woman*, 24.

[56] This is the argument, e.g., of Tarrant in "Clementine Decrees," 306.

[57] Miller, "What's in a name?" 64.

motivations of these women primarily religious, or socio-economic? Were they simply would-be nuns, except that they did not manage to gain entry into a convent, or were they perhaps banding together because such a way of life made good economic and social sense?[58]

In some ways, the appearance of such female communities made perfect sense, particularly in late medieval northwestern European urban centres, where women outnumbered men.[59] Convents were often oversubscribed, and so they were not always an option, especially for the poor. Establishing a self-supporting life together with other women considerably strengthened one's economic security and wellbeing. In the words of Katherine Lynch, beguinage was "one of the most interesting and 'original' examples of lay efforts to construct artificial families and communities within an urban setting."[60]

However, there was also a distinct spiritual emphasis and a particular attention to *vita contemplativa* alongside the beguines' commitment to *vita activa*. Many were influenced by mysticism, and would live out their devotion "at mass and the daily hours, in devotional exercises, in song and dance, and in writing."[61] The incorporation of the body in one's spiritual experience, whether through mindful employment of the senses or through bodily movement such as dance, is a remarkable example of a medieval "physical performance of ... faith."[62] Or, in the striking words of Mechthild of Magdeburg, a thirteenth-century German beguine,

> The pull of God with which God drew the soul in the beginning to himself, has such great power that it awakens the soul so that she can taste God's sweetness. After that, it drives out all evil from the five senses . . .[63]

In their writings, the beguines embraced the allegorical appropriation of the Song of Songs recently popularized by Bernard of Clairvaux. However, they also employed the language of courtly love.[64] As Barbara Newman argues, this

---

[58] Simons, *Cities of Ladies*, x–xi.

[59] For the background, see, e.g., Kowaleski, "Singlewomen;" and Simons, *Cities of Ladies*, 8–9. Simons also points out to the high numbers of women from rural areas joining court beguinages, 115–16.

[60] Lynch, *Individuals*, 80.

[61] Simons, "On the Margins," 322; and McDonnell, *Beguines and Beghards*, 84–85.

[62] On the use of dance and dance-like sacred performance in the thirteenth-century beguine experience, see Van Oort, "Dancing in Body and Spirit."

[63] Quoted in Poor, "Transmission and Impact," 101.

[64] Newman, *From Virile Woman*, 138. The language of courtly love is also present in some of the writings about, and for, the beguines, such as in the late thirteenth-century document *Règle des Fins Amans*, extolling the ideal beguine as the one who "'keep(s) the commandments of her lover', 'go(es) often and willingly to her lover', and

embrace of the courtly language alongside the "nuptial mysticism" rooted in the Song of Songs is illustrative of the beguines' "[straddling of] the border between religious and secular life."[65] While the erotic self-representation as the bride of Christ is a feature shared with medieval monastic spirituality, the prominence of the "courtly self" is more surprising, particularly in light of the beguines' vulnerability to the accusations of not being properly sheltered from the pollutions of the world. But it is perhaps precisely because of their particular expression of the *vita mixta*—a combination of action and contemplation—that the beguines were sometimes seen as uniquely positioned to understand the depths of theological truths. A thirteenth-century document offers the following description of the essence of being a beguine:

> "We know to love God, to confess, to know God, the seven sacraments, to love our neighbours and to distinguish between the vices and virtues, to have humility without pride, love without hate, patience in tribulation, clear knowledge of God and the Holy Church, and are ready to suffer everything for God: all this is the beguinage." After the theologian heard the beguine's description of her way of life, he remarked, "Thus you know more about divinity than all the masters of Paris."[66]

Yet, as Marguerite Porete's case so vividly illustrates, mystical inclinations could also cause one sail too close to the wind of heresy to survive. After the Vienne decrees, the beguine life was accompanied by increasing indictments of heresy, sporadic persecution, and suppression. "Unenclosed" beguines, living an independent life of devotion without the protection of a beguinage, were particularly distrusted. In Porete's case, there is no mention of her relationship to any particular beguinage, and so it is very possible that the severity of her punishment had to do with her lack of being properly "regulated." Eventually, the beguinage became the only acceptable form of being a beguine.[67]

However, even enclosed beguines did not manage to receive recognition from the papacy as an official religious order. As Jennifer Deanne observes,

> as *single women*, beguines were deemed sexually and socially dangerous by ecclesiastical elites because of their proximity to male confessors and/or men in the secular sphere; beguine communities could thus become a highly-charged presence in the cities of northern Europe. As *Christian women*, moreover, whom the Church typically sought to channel into the irrevocable institutions of either

---

'receive(s) devotedly the jewels her lover sends, which are poverty, suffering, maladies, and tribulations'." Miller, "What's in a name?" 75.

[65] Newman, *From Virile Woman*, 139.

[66] Quoted in Miller, "What's in a name?" 77–78.

[67] Miller, "What's in a name?" 62 and 85.

marriage or monasticism, beguines represented to some an alarmingly unauthorized and disturbingly temporary way of life.[68]

Eventually, the name "beguine" itself became increasingly problematic.[69] Although there was a brief period of renewal and growth around the time of the Counter-Reformation, by and large the life of most beguine communities was cut short or reorganized into recognized monastic and mendicant orders. Some beguinages in the Low Countries, however, continued, until the nineteenth and twentieth centuries. Their buildings in places like Bruges, Leuven, and Amsterdam still stand as witnesses of the fascinating medieval worlds of these single women. The world's last traditional beguine died in 2013.[70]

Beguines have received considerable attention in recent years, not only in the scholarly world, but also among those seeking new forms of Christian living: from people exploring what the example of the beguines may contribute to the development of the new monasticism in the twenty-first century,[71] to contemporary beguine-inspired communities.[72]

Single Women and Their Faith: Past and Present

Drawing parallels to, or lessons from, other times in history must always be done with caution. Context matters, and it is always complex—considerably more complex than I have been able to explore here. However, a brief look at two important periods in which single Christian women blossomed is an important reminder of what may be possible in our days, and can also offer a few words of caution as well as encouragement.

First of all, we may wish to reflect on the enthusiastic embrace of singleness in the early Christian centuries. The eschatological meaning behind this choice, so prevalent at the time, has been largely ignored, particularly in our contemporary Christian culture which, if anything, considers marriage and/or sexual fulfilment as heavenly bliss. There is an urgent need for recovering that eschatological edge—the deep awareness that all our relationships, and all of our lives, are to be radically re-evaluated and reinterpreted in light of the

---

[68] Deane, "'Beguines' Reconsidered" (italics original).

[69] Simons, *Cities of Ladies*, 134–36.

[70] "Marcella Pattyn;" and Abbott, *History*, 119.

[71] E.g., Howard, "Beguine Option."

[72] E.g., the American Beguine Community is an ecumenical group of laywomen (single or married) seeking to fashion their life on that of the beguines ("American Beguine Community") or the "Cologne Beguines" in Germany ("Willkommen bei den Kölner Beginen!").

Christ event. In this, single women may be ahead of the rest of the church. Swimming against the current of the married norm of life, they are more likely to take up the challenge of truly *Christian* meaning-making— that is, making sense of life in light of the Christian story, rather than other cultural narratives. This is a task that more easily evades those lulled by the sense of meaning provided by getting married and raising a family "like everybody else." Being not "like everybody else" helps bring the radical nature of Jesus' message into a much sharper focus.

Thus, the single lives of women in early Christianity can offer a much-needed eschatological corrective to our present theology of marriage. However, what also must be borne in mind is the momentous shift from the New Testament emphasis on singleness as freedom to the subsequent focus on singleness as bodily purity. The virgins and the widows of those first Christian centuries affirmed abstention from marriage as a sign of being at the forefront of the new age of the kingdom of God—something that just made sense in light of the good news of Jesus. However, as illustrated by the wives turning to celibate marriages, the focus on bodily (and particularly sexual) purity became regarded as the shortest route to the heavenly life. With the benefit of hindsight, it is evident how much damage has been done by the link forged between sexuality and sin, to married and single people alike. The church of today has much work to do in constructing a better, more holistic, theology of the body as the locus of human spirituality.

In relation to this, the witness of the beguines offers an enriching example of working out a way of life that does not force a "forever" choice between devotion to Christian ministry and living out one's faith in the world. While, given the cultural and theological climate of the day, the beguines certainly had to embrace the requirement of sexual chastity, their singleness was more a reminder of the earlier New Testament emphasis on freedom from the cares of this world than a preoccupation with one's own bodily purity. Their mystical inclinations, and particularly the sense of the role their daily lives and their bodies played in their spiritual experiences, helped to bring some healing to the deeply dualistic anthropology of medieval Christianity.

Furthermore, the beguines present a powerful example of single women organizing themselves into a new, communal, impressively democratic and flexible form of life, and, by doing so, of carving out a surprising space between the rigid demarcations of the secular and the sacred. With their interest in reading scripture in their own languages, and in lay preaching and teaching, they ventured into exciting territories, even if it contributed to their eventual suppression. As the beguines inhabited the undefined space between the convent and the married house, a question may be asked about the kind of new, still undefined spaces that may be there for single women to create and inhabit in today's world.

Hopefully, these observations might be of inspiration to those who are single, and particularly single women, who at times experience their invisibility, or their second-class status, in their own faith communities. Both of these historical episodes offer creative approaches to forging new ways for "doing what one can." I would also hope, however, that the church as a whole may wake up not only to the presence of many single people in their midst, but also to what must be learned from and with those who are single. If there is a lesson for church leadership in this, it is the temptation and the danger of quashing single women's movements when they start threatening existing power structures. The regulation and enclosure of Christian virgins and widows, and the suppression and absorption of the beguine communities are a loss which, I would like to hope, today's church will seek to recompense.

Bibliography

Abbott, Elizabeth. *A History of Celibacy*. Cambridge: Lutterworth Press, 2001.
"American Beguine Community." https://beguine.org/
Andronovienė, Lina. *Transforming the Struggles of Tamars: Single Women and Baptistic Communities*. Eugene: Wipf & Stock, 2014.
Berger, Peter, *et al. Religious America, Secular Europe? A Theme and Variations*. Aldershot: Ashgate, 2008.
Brown, Peter. *The Body and Society: Men, Women and Sexual Renunciation in Early Christianity*. London: Faber & Faber, 1990.
Cahill, Lisa Sowle. "A Christian Social Perspective on the Family." *Mennonite Quarterly Review* 75.2 (2001) 161–71.
Chiu, Joyce. "A Single-Minded Church." Barna Group Report. https://www.barna.com/single-minded-church/
Cooper, Kate. *The Fall of the Roman Household*. Cambridge: Cambridge University Press, 2007.
De Vitry, Jacques. *The Life of Marie d'Oignies*. Translated by Margot H. King. In *Two Lives of Marie d'Oignies*. 4th ed. Peregrina Translations Series. Toronto: Peregrina, 1998.
Deane, Jennifer. "'Beguines' Reconsidered: Historiographical Problems and New Directions." Monastic Matrix (2008), Commentaria 3461. http://monasticmatrix.osu.edu/commentaria/beguines-reconsidered-historiographical-problems-and-new-directions
Deming, Will. Paul on Marriage and Celibacy: The Hellenistic Background of 1 Corinthians 7. 2nd ed. Grand Rapids: Eerdmans, 2004.
Diognetus. In *Ante-Nicene Fathers* Volume 1. Edited by Alexander Roberts *et al*. Translated by Alexander Roberts and James Donaldson. Buffalo: Christian Literature, 1885. Rev. and Edited by Kevin Knight. http://www.newad vent.org/fathers/0101.htm
Dixon, Suzanne. *The Roman Family*. Baltimore: The Johns Hopkins University Press, 1992.
Ehrman, Bart D., ed. *Lost Scriptures: Books that Did Not Make It into the New Testament*. Oxford: Oxford University Press, 2003.

Elliott, Dyan. *Spiritual Marriage: Sexual Abstinence in Medieval Wedlock.* Princeton: Princeton University Press, 1993.

Ferguson, Everett. *Backgrounds of Early Christianity.* 2nd ed. Grand Rapids: Eerdmans, 1993.

Field, Sean L. *The Beguine, the Angel, and the Inquisitor: The Trials of Marguerite Porete and Guiard of Cressonessart.* Notre Dame: University of Notre Dame Press, 2012.

Hajnal, John. "European Marriage Patterns in Perspective." In *Population in History: Essays in Historical Demography,* 101–43. Edited by David Glass and D.E.C. Eversley. Chicago: Aldine, 1965.

Howard, Evan B. "The Beguine Option: A Persistent Past and a Promising Future of Christian Monasticism." *Religions* 10(9).491 (2019) 1–24. https://www.mdpi.com/2077-1444/10/9/491

Kowaleski, Maryanne. "Singlewomen in Medieval and Early Modern Europe: The Demographic Perspective." In *Singlewomen in the European Past, 1250–1800,* 38–81. Edited by Judith Bennett and Amy Froide. Philadelphia: University of Pennsylvania Press, 1999.

Lee, A.D. *Pagans and Christians in Late Antiquity: A Sourcebook.* London: Routledge, 2000.

Lynch, Katherine A. *Individuals, Families, and Communities in Europe, 1200–1800: The Urban Foundations of Western Society.* Cambridge Studies in Population, Economy and Society in Past Time, 37. Cambridge: Cambridge University Press, 2003.

Makowski, Elizabeth. *A Pernicious Sort of Woman: Quasi-Religious Women and Canon Lawyers in the Later Middle Ages.* Studies in Medieval and Early Modern Canon Law, 6. Washington: Catholic University of America Press, 2005.

"Marcella Pattyn." Obituaries. *The Telegraph* 16 May 2013. https://www.telegraph.co.uk/news/obituaries/10062339/Marcella-Pattyn.html

McDonnell, Ernest W. *The Beguines and Beghards in Medieval Culture: With Special Emphasis on the Belgian Scene.* New Brunswick: Rutgers University Press, 1954.

McNamara, Jo Ann. *A New Song: Celibate Women in the First Three Christian Centuries.* New York: Haworth, 1983.

Miller, Tanya Stabler. "What's in a name? Clerical representations of Parisian beguines (1200–1328)." *Journal of Medieval History* 33.1 (2007) 60–86.

Moore, R.I. *The Origins of European Dissent.* Oxford: Basil Blackwell, 1985.

Mulder-Bakker, Anneke B. *Mary of Oignies: Mother of Salvation.* Medieval Women: Texts and Contexts, 7. Brepols: Turnhaut, 2006.

Nathan, Geoffrey S. *The Family in Late Antiquity: The Rise of Christianity and the Endurance of Tradition.* London: Routledge, 2000.

Newman, Barbara. *From Virile Woman to Womanchrist. Studies in Medieval Religion and Literature.* Philadelphia: University of Pennsylvania Press, 1995.

Osiek, Carolyn, and David L. Balch. *Families in the New Testament World: Households and House Churches.* Louisville: Westminster John Knox, 1997.

Owen, Mathew, and Ingo Gildenhard. *Tacitus, Annals, 15.20–23, 33–45: Latin Text, Study Aids with Vocabulary, and Commentary.* Cambridge: Open Book, 2013.

Poor, Sara S. "Transmission and Impact: Mechtild of Magdeburg's *Das Fliessende Licht der Gottheit*." In *A Companion to Mysticism and Devotion in Northern Germany in the Late Middle Ages,* 73–101. Edited by Elizabeth Andersen *et al.* Leiden: Brill, 2013.

Pullinger, David. "Where are all the men?—facts and stats." Single friendly Church, 24 March 2017. https://www.singlefriendlychurch.com/what-do-you-say-when/awhere-are-all-the-mena

"Research co-funded by Single Christians confirms that the church is not attracting enough single men into its pews." https://www.singlefriendly church.com/research/yougov

Salisbury, Joyce E., *Church Fathers, Independent Virgins.* London: Verso, 1991.

Seim, Turid Karlsen. *The Double Message: Patterns of Gender in Luke-Acts.* Edinburgh: T&T Clark, 1994.

Shaw, Theresa M. "Sex and sexual renunciation I." In *The Early Christian World*, 355–71. 2nd ed. Edited by Philip F. Esler. London: Routledge, 2017.

Simons, Walter. *Cities of Ladies: Beguine Communities in the Medieval Low Countries, 1200–1565.* Philadelphia: University of Pennsylvania Press, 2001.

Simons, Walter. "On the Margins of Religious Life: Hermits and Recluses, Penitents and Tertiaries, Beguines and Beghards." In *The Cambridge History of Christianity,* 309–23. Edited by Miri Rubin and Walter Simons. Cambridge: Cambridge University Press, 2009.

Stone, Lyman. "Sex Ratios in the Pews: Is There Really a Deficit of Men in American Churches?" *Institute for Family Studies* 12 August 2019. https://ifstudies.org/blog/sex-ratios-in-the-pews-is-there-really-a-deficit-of-men-in-american-churches.

Tarrant, Jacqueline. "The Clementine Decrees on the Beguines: Conciliar and Papal Versions." *Archivum Historiae Pontificiae* 12 (1974) 300–308.

Tertullian. *On Exhortation to Chastity.* Edited by Alexander Roberts *et al.* Translated by S. Thelwall. Revised and Edited by Kevin Knight. Buffalo: Christian Literature, 1885. https://www.newadvent.org/fathers/0405.htm

Toth, Lina. *Singleness and Marriage after Christendom: Being and Doing Family.* Oregon: Wipf & Stock, 2021.

United Nations, Department of Economic and Social Affairs, Population Division. "World Marriage Data 2019." https://population.un.org/Mar riageData/Index.html#/home

Van Oort, Jessica. "Dancing in Body and Spirit: Dance and Sacred Performance in Thirteenth-Century Beguine Texts." 2009. PhD diss., Temple University, 2009.

Vööbus, Arthur. *Celibacy, A Requirement for Admission to Baptism in the Early Syrian Church*. Stockholm: Papers of the Estonian Theological Society in Exile, 1951.

Wiesner-Hanks, Merry E. *Christianity and Sexuality in the Early Modern World: Regulating Desire, Reforming Practice*. London: Routledge, 1999.

"What do single Christians say about church." https://www.singlefriendly church.com/what-do-single-christians-say-about-church/what-do-single-christians-say-about-church

"Willkommen bei den Kölner Beginen!" https://beginen.koeln/

CHAPTER 10

More Light, Truth and Transitions?: Gender Dysphoria as a Moral Case Study for the "Further Light" Clause

Michael J. Peat

> Only by meditation on the witness of the past are we likely to recognise the ways that are being indicated to us for today and the years ahead. The "ways known" lead on—the Lord assisting us—to the "ways to be known."[1]

Further Light and Future Ways

It is tempting to assume that the phrases above in inverted commas, in both the title of this essay and its opening quote, need no introduction to a Baptist reader. The Covenant Prayer offered in the service for "Making and Renewing Covenant" in *Gathering for Worship* invites the gathered congregation to commit "to watch over each other and to walk together in ways known and still to be made known."[2] This line consciously echoes the 1606 covenant formed by the early Separatist congregation who gathered in the Nottinghamshire village of Scrooby.[3] Although perhaps less often sung now than it once was, George Rawson's hymn, reprinted in *Baptist Praise and*

---

[1] Payne, *Ways Known Made Known*, 8.

[2] Blyth and Ellis, *Gathering for Worship*, 98.

[3] As recalled by one member, William Bradford, the congregation "as the Lord's free people, joined themselves (by a covenant of the Lord) into a church estate, in the fellowship of the gospel, *to walk in all His ways made known, or to be made known unto them*, according to their best endeavours, whatsoever it should cost them, the Lord assisting them." William Bradford, *Of Plymouth Plantation*, 8, quoted in Cross, "'Through a Glass Darkly,'" 92 (italics added by Cross). Seeking the freedom to worship as their consciences led them, members of this congregation would emigrate to Amsterdam in 1608, along with others from the nearby congregation from Gainsborough, Lincolnshire, led by John Smyth and Thomas Helwys. In Amsterdam, Smyth led the first Baptist church. Cross, "'Through a Glass Darkly,'" 92–93.

Worship, includes this refrain, "The Lord has yet more light and truth to break forth from his word."[4] This alludes to the renowned words of John Robinson, who declared in his farewell sermon to the Scrooby congregation he had pastored, led to Leyden, and on 21 July 1620 saw onto the Mayflower, that

> he was very confident the Lord had more light and truth yet to break forth out of his Holy Word. . . . For though they [the Calvinists] were precious lights shining in their Times, yet God has not yet revealed his whole will to them; "and were they now living", saith he, "they would be as ready and wiling to embrace further light, as that they had received."[5]

Edward Winslow's account of this moment notes that Robinson then "put us in mind of our Church Covenant; at least that part of it whereby 'we promise and covenant with God and with one another to receive whatsoever light or truth shall be made known to us from his written Word.'"[6] Recalling these milestones in early Baptist history demonstrates that the connection between continually expecting new insight ("further *light*") and embracing its implications for action ("*walk* in . . . ways to be made known") has been an identifying mark of Baptists from their beginning.[7] Moreover, the significance of this connection for Baptist identity has been the focus of attention amongst contemporary Baptist scholars.[8] The covenantal view of theological enquiry that it shapes emphasizes the provisionality of our epistemological claims alongside a positive attitude towards hermeneutical diversity amongst interdependent believers.[9] Covenanted communities read scripture together in

---

[4] *Baptist Praise and Worship*, 156 (hymn number 107). Cross notes that it was B.R. White who coined the phrase "further light clause." White, *English Separatist Tradition*, 123, quoted in Cross, "'Through a Glass Darkly,'" 92.

[5] Burgess, *John Robinson*, 239–40, quoted in Winter, *More Light and Truth*, 5. The Mayflower was a ship bound for the Americas, where the congregation would form the Plymouth Colony.

[6] Burgess, *John Robinson*, 240, quoted in Winter, *More Light and Truth*, 6.

[7] This should not, of course, be taken to mean that anticipation of further revelation is an *exclusively* Baptist identifying mark. Quash, *Found Theology*, 1, speaks of a "specifically *English* tradition of theology" (he is thinking mainly of Anglicanism) for which the role of historical process in facilitating developments in human knowledge and corresponding action occupies a privileged position.

[8] Two examples of publications which focus explicitly on this are Winter, *More Light and Truth*; and Cross, "'Through a Glass Darkly.'"

[9] A sample of texts from contemporary Baptist scholars in which this constellation of themes is prominent, and to which this essay owes a particular debt, include Winter, *More Light and Truth* and "Persuading Friends;" Dare, *Always Way and Fray*; and Cross, "'Through a Glass Darkly.'"

a time whose penultimate character, from an eschatological perspective, calls on them to think with humility about their understanding of God's purposes and to act with an open mind about the ways God might be leading them in the future.[10]

This essay sets out to add to this growing body of reflection on the implications of these two interconnected claims: that as covenant communities of local churches and wider networks we commit to walk together in "ways known and still to be made known" believing that God will reveal to us "yet more light and truth" for this journey. This essay aims to complement the historical, ecclesiological and hermeneutical insights that these claims have already evoked, by underlining their relevance for that aspect of "walking together" called Christian Ethics. Here, we will engage with a particular bioethical challenge with the same sense of provisionality that others have recognized as essential for honouring the "further light" clause. The opening quote is taken from Ernest Payne's 1977 Baptist Union presidential address, *Ways Known and to be Made Known*, and encapsulates its theme. Under this rubric, Payne identified several priorities for Baptist life going forward. Some were internal denominational matters, others looked out towards wider social concerns. Among the latter, Payne observed that

> Hard thinking is needed about the new moral issues posed to humanity in the fields of energy and genetics. Like previous generations, we have to apply in an ailing and sometimes hostile society what we learn from Jesus of Nazareth, who clearly held no brief for established authorities, preached a gospel of liberation to the poor and oppressed, and yet cannot be described as a social revolutionary, as that phrase is currently used.[11]

Were Payne able to elaborate on the implications of his theme today, it is not hard to imagine him including transgender experiences among the list of issues meriting the "hard thinking" entailed in meditating on the witness of the past to discern ways for the present and future. For this is a sphere in which the church's contribution has at times, and with reason, been viewed with suspicion,[12] and in which talk of delivering liberation for those who feel oppressed is conspicuous. It may also be, as an increasing number of theological voices are suggesting, a sphere for which this hard thinking will

---

[10] In this regard, Grenz's comment, *Renewing the Center*, 343, is paradigmatic: "Theological reflection becomes an anticipatory act, for it entails a partial yet nevertheless valid participation in a 'knowing' that is ultimately eschatological. As a consequence, theological statements and doctrinal formulae always have a type of provisionality to them."

[11] Payne, *Ways Known Made Known*, 12–13.

[12] For detail, see Merritt, "3 Reasons Christians Lose Transgender Debate."

lend credence to fellow Baptist Henry Cook's insistence that there are times when

> Theological expressions that seemed all-sufficient are discovered by the light of later knowledge to be inadequate; not because Christ Himself has in any way changed, but because God by His Spirit has taught us to see in Him treasures of wisdom and power that our fathers did not discover.[13]

Demarcating the Moral Case Study

Our case study is a specific phenomenon from the array that fall within the compass of transgender experiences. In order to retain focus and to keep this essay to an appropriate length, the examination of it that follows will be necessarily selective in its treatment of associated issues. "Transgender experiences" covers a range of experiences and expressions of gender identity, and whether or not, or to what degree, people who identify as transgender feel unease about their experience similarly varies. "Gender dysphoria," the focus of this essay, refers more specifically to transgender experiences in which a belief that one's biological sex and gender identity are incongruent becomes the cause of suffering. As Christian psychologist Mark Yarhouse puts it,

> Dysphoria means being uneasy about or generally dissatisfied with something. . . . Specifically, gender dysphoria, is on the one hand the experience of being born male (biological sex) but feeling a psychological and emotional identity as female. Similarly, gender dysphoria is the experience of being born female (biological sex) but feeling a psychological or emotional identity as male. When a person experiences gender incongruence and it is causing them significant distress or impairment, they may meet criteria for the diagnosis of Gender Dysphoria.[14]

A number of pertinent details come to light in this quote, which will shape the content and scope of the discussion to follow. For a start, the definition of gender dysphoria draws on a distinction that has become commonplace since the 1970s: "sex" is generally used to refer to biological characteristics and functions that are associated with the physical aspect of being male or female (or, arguably, intersex), and "gender" points to psychological attributes and expression, shaped in some measure by cultural context, which are generally

---

[13] Cook, *What Baptists Stand For*, 28, quoted in Cross, "'Through a Glass Darkly,'" 112. I should add here the same caveat as does Cross, that Cook also insists that any claims to a revised understanding and, therefore, theological expression, must prove their coherence in principle with the New Testament witness to Christ.

[14] Yarhouse, *Understanding Gender Dysphoria*, chap. 1, "Background," Kindle.

associated with these biological categories.[15] That adding the word "generally" is advisable here is evinced by challenges to the understanding of "sex" and "gender." For some, this challenge takes the form of a plea to review the meaning of these two terms in the light of inconsistencies in their use, whereas for others enamoured by queer theory, the very distinction these terms claim to identify is brought into question.[16] Perhaps the most renowned advocate of the latter challenge is Judith Butler, who, in her book *Gender Trouble*, proposed that "this construct called 'sex' is as culturally constructed as gender; indeed, perhaps it was always already gender, with the consequence that the distinction between sex and gender turns out to be no distinction at all."[17]

There is not sufficient space here to engage further with either challenge, except to say that noting them here anticipates observations that will be significant later. Suffice to say, at this stage, that I do not believe one needs to share Butler's constructionist view of "sex" to recognize that specifying the biological constituents of any particular category of biological sex can be more complex and uncertain than it is often presumed to be. This points to an advantage of describing the surgical interventions undertaken to alleviate distress in some instances of gender dysphoria as "gender confirmation surgery" rather than "sex reassignment (or sex change) surgery." This is that the former's explicit goal of enabling the sufferer to feel their body is better aligned with their sense of gender is easier to verify than is the claim that she or he has actually changed their biological sex from one kind to another.[18] We

---

[15] Whereas the common determinants of "sex" are typically considered to include chromosomes, hormones, gonads and/or genitals, "gender" refers to one's "inner sense" of themself as male or female and their expression of this sense (usually in relation to social norms of "masculinity" and "femininity"). Beilby and Eddy, "Understanding Transgender Experiences and Identities," 5.

[16] See the discussion in Beilby and Eddy, "Understanding Transgender Experiences and Identities," 14–15.

[17] Butler, *Gender Trouble*, 9–10, quoted in Beilby and Eddy, "Understanding Transgender Experiences and Identities," 15. For Butler, sex, no less than gender, is constituted through our performance—the actions, reactions and cultural discourse within the social environment we inhabit.

[18] My account of this advantage is, however, rather different from the reason more often proposed for shifting to the language of "gender confirmation" surgery, which tends to be based on a claim that gender should be conceived as the more stable property for the person concerned, rather than on what is more verifiable post-surgery. E.g., the website www.healthline.com proposes that "Today, many transgender people prefer to use the term 'gender confirmation surgery,' because when we say something like gender 'reassignment' or 'sex change,' it implies that a person's gender changes when they have surgery. As many trans folks have noted, surgery doesn't change one's gender—it changes the body in which one experiences that gender." Clements, "What

can measure the extent to which a postoperative transsexual person feels that surgery has confirmed his or her gender (as well as concomitant improvements in mental wellbeing); whether it has really changed his or her sex is a more controversial question.[19] Oliver O'Donovan's account of two contrasting judicial rulings from the 1970s, from the UK and USA respectively, provides an illustration of the controversial nature of the latter question. Both rulings concerned whether marriage was a legally valid option for a couple which included a transsexual person whose assumed sex was different from the birth sex of their partner. In the UK case—*Corbett v Corbett* (1970)—the judge ruled such a marriage to be invalid on the grounds that "unambiguous biological sex must be determinative of a person's sexual status for the purposes of marriage."[20] In the American case—the New Jersey Superior Court in *MT v JT* (1976)—a ruling was given which gave greater weight to non-biological criteria. Here, it was decided that sexual identity be measured by "'sexual capacity,' which 'requires the coalescence of both the physical ability and the psychological and emotional orientation to engage in intercourse as either male or female'."[21] Furthermore, in this case the surgical changes that had effected the transition were a sufficiently significant factor that "The court, considering its result, simply had to give 'legal effect to a *fait*

---

to Expect from Gender Confirmation Surgery." The advantage that I suggest is not necessarily at odds with this reasoning, but exhibits a difference in emphasis.

[19] A brief endnote comment in O'Donovan's Grove booklet, *Transsexualism*, provides a telling example of the way clinicians have shown, and dealt with, this mismatch in confidence about a transsexual's gender identity on the one hand, and their post-operative sex on the other. O'Donovan endorses the practice of using the gender pronoun that corresponds to such a person's confirmed gender identity. However, he also observes that "many practitioners will shy away from asserting outright that this 'he' is a man or this 'she' is a woman. The letter of support carried by one female-to-male transsexual from his clinic is carefully worded, 'It is our recommendation that this patient be encouraged to establish himself in his chosen cross-gender as a male.'" O'Donovan, *Transsexualism*, 27–28. Pastoral guidance produced for Church of England clergy on using the Rite of Affirmation of Baptismal Faith in this context similarly encourages clergy to "identify the preference of a transgender person in respect of their name and gendered (or other) pronouns" and to recognize that "Some trans people may not wish their former name or gender to be mentioned." Church of England website, "Pastoral Guidance Affirmation Baptismal Faith," 1 and 4.

[20] O'Donovan, *Transsexualism*, 9. The judge in this case determined that the threshold for "unambiguous sex" appropriate to marriage required a configuration of chromosomes, gonads and genitalia in which these three biological markers all aligned with either typical male or female biological characteristics. Transsexual alterations did not outweigh birth characteristics in this judgement.

[21] O'Donovan, *Transsexualism*, 14.

accompli.'"[22] Juxtaposing these two cases indicates that the determination of "sex" is by no means straightforward, although O'Donovan's discussion makes clear his preference for the analytical rigour of the ruling in *Corbett v Corbett* (a ruling subsequently overturned by legal provision in the UK's Gender Recognition Act 2004).

Furthermore, to speak of postoperative alignment with gender sense as "easier to verify" is not to suggest that successful achievement of this goal is a dependable outcome of such surgery. Accounts of the success, or otherwise, of gender confirmation surgery vary; not surprisingly, this often reflects the moral conclusion for which the account is being offered in evidence. Justin Sabia-Tanis claims that pursuing hormone therapy and gender confirmation surgery to reduce suffering accords with Christian ethics because "Christians with gender dysphoria have the right to pursue treatment that offers the greatest possibility for their health and well-being."[23] This correlates with his insistence that "An increasing number of [long follow-up] studies demonstrate the effectiveness of these treatments in reducing gender dysphoria" (and *vice versa*).[24] Conversely, the assured claim of recent guidance from the Evangelical Alliance that "biological sex should reveal and determine gender"[25] is resourced by a brief allusion to evidence concerning outcomes of transitioning in the form of a handful of quotes. These quotes either strongly emphasize the limits of evidence or speak of negative outcomes in sensational terms.[26] I suspect that a more measured assessment of these outcomes, the conclusion of a lengthier overview than the previous two, is offered by Mark Yarhouse and Julia Sadusky, who judge that

> Until more research is available, the broad consensus is that medical and surgical interventions may be helpful in reducing gender dysphoria, at least in the short term, while not necessarily abating psychological distress for some individuals. We do not fully understand the long-term implications of HT [hormone therapy] and SRS [sex reassignment surgery], although financial strain from the need to maintain HT permanently, and other concerns such as infertility, medical complications, social consequences due to stigma, are noteworthy.[27]

---

[22] O'Donovan, *Transsexualism*, 14–15. For quotes from *MT v JT*, O'Donovan draws on Twardy, "Medicolegal Aspects of Transsexualism," 273–75.

[23] Sabia-Tanis, "Holy Creation, Wholly Creative," 204.

[24] Sabia-Tanis, "Holy Creation, Wholly Creative," 213. See the discussion in 213–14.

[25] Evangelical Alliance, *Trans Formed*, 11.

[26] Evangelical Alliance, *Trans Formed*, 18.

[27] Yarhouse and Sadusky, "Complexities of Gender Identity," 120.

For the remainder of this essay, I will continue differentiating "sex" and "gender" according to prevailing conventions, and proceed on the assumption that the former refers to a differentiated biological reality beyond sociolinguistic construction (albeit recognizing that specifying that differentiation is more easily said than done).

We noted earlier that the equivocal and inconsistent use of the terms "sex" and "gender" has been regarded as a shortcoming that needs clarification. However, this terminological fluidity brings to mind fluidity in the understanding of gender characteristics and roles which serves a more positive function in the context of this discussion. This positive function is illuminated by the writing of Baptists applying the ethos of the further light clause to consideration of men and women in ministry, such as we see in this proposal from Paul Fiddes:

> Christian theology may expect to find some "gender difference" in human existence, or distinct characteristics of personality and approach to life that can be called "male" and "female," beyond the basic biological differences. Theologians ought, however, to be open and questioning in discovering *what* these qualities are, and *how* they are to be connected with the particular functions of men and women in personal and social spheres.[28]

Ruth Gouldbourne, whose scholarship is being honoured by the Festschrift to which this essay is a contribution, likewise encourages a more supple understanding of the relationship between sex and behavioural characteristics. She emphasizes that "when God calls us to the service of the church in ministry it is as individuals, uniquely gifted and with the weaknesses that are ours as well. We are not called in categories, nor can we serve in such."[29]

An "open and questioning" attitude similarly opens a broader vista on our understanding of human being, as it calls for an attentive disposition to the testimony of those who experience sex, gender, and their relationship, in unusual ways. Megan DeFranza ponders a more radical version of this train of thought, asking whether it is possible to conceive of a society so sympathetic to the prospect of discovering more about God's creativity from "gender nonconforming people" that medical intervention seeking to harmonize sex and gender becomes superfluous.[30] An approach less vulnerable to pre-empting the future of gender dysphoria, or of what God's further light might reveal about the normative meaning of sex and gender, can still benefit from attentiveness in this regard. Such benefits, I suggest, are likely to include

---

[28] Fiddes, "Woman's Head is Man," 379 (italics original).

[29] Gouldbourne, "Do Women Complement Men in Ministry," quoted in Allison-Glenny, "That We Might See Ourselves," 109. See the discussion in Allison-Glenny, "That We Might See Ourselves," 107–10.

[30] DeFranza, "Good News for Gender Minorities," 236.

equipping us for receiving that light and helping further to lessen the stigma which Yarhouse and Sadusky (among others) have identified as a contributory factor to the suffering arising from gender dysphoria.[31]

These observations about gender notwithstanding, Yarhouse's explanation of gender dysphoria reveals the tendency of those who suffer from it to interpret their conflict in terms which presume that biological sex is binary. Hence, Yarhouse structures his explanation in the quote above with the twofold parallel which gives rise to the common subdivision of post-operative transexual people as "male to female" or "female to male" transsexuals (or "transwoman" and "transman"). Beilby and Eddy note that since people with gender dysphoria often express underlying binary assumptions, for example by articulating their distress as feeling "trapped" in the "wrong body," they have provoked antagonism amongst many trans activists towards gender confirmation interventions, precisely because these reinforce binary claims about sex.[32]

One further observation arising from Yarhouse's account of gender dysphoria helps to pinpoint the moral issue in view, as well as the allocation of attention in this essay to the various questions it raises. For Yarhouse indicates that "gender dysphoria" does not simply name a phenomenon but classifies a specific pathology with diagnostic criteria. This, seemingly obvious, point gains significance from the fact that "gender dysphoria" replaced "gender identity disorder" in the American Psychiatric Association's 2013 revision (fifth edition) to the *Diagnostic and Statistical Manual of Mental Disorders* (*DSM–5*). Whereas the classification of "gender identity disorder" in the earlier edition of *DSM* implied that transgender experiences themselves were pathological, the replacement of this with "gender dysphoria" pathologizes the *distress* (dysphoria) that can accompany certain transgender experiences rather than transgender experience as such. There is a political dimension to the change, influenced as it is by transgender activism which saw the depathologization of transgender experience *per se* as a vital step in fostering a view of transgenderism as essential to the proper diversity of human gender.[33] For our purposes here, the historical context emphasizes that selecting gender *dysphoria* as a case study entails focusing primarily on the scope of morally

---

[31] See also comments by Sabia-Tanis, "Holy Creation, Wholly Creative," 210–11, on research demonstrating "a link between nonacceptance and negative health outcomes" on the one hand, and the benefits of "supportive social interactions" on the other.

[32] Eddy and Beilby, "Understanding Transgender Experiences and Identities," 17–18.

[33] Eddy and Beilby, "Understanding Transgender Experiences and Identities," 26. Some transgender people consider "gender dysphoria" still to carry stigmatizing connotations.

defensible options to respond to the distress it causes. The question of how to conceptualize the sexual identity of a transsexual person for other moral purposes (e.g., marriage) has a secondary and, consequently, peripheral part to play in this essay. That, of course, should not be taken as a sign that this question is not significant, but simply as an acknowledgement that an enquiry focused on it would have different parameters. A number of Christian proponents of unreservedly affirming transgender experiences have been resourced by exegetical and historical perspectives that question a dimorphic view of sex, that is, one committed to "male" and "female" as the fundamental biological categories.[34] The reasons I will suggest for condoning a cautious endorsement of gender confirmation interventions, including surgery, in the more severe cases of gender dysphoria, neither requires nor refutes their reasoning. My argument can be advanced without disavowing the conventional binary understanding of sex more often presupposed in Christian thought, whatever the merits or otherwise of doing so may be.

Having demarcated the moral issue in view as a case study for the further light clause, we need now to identify sources of understanding relevant to theological enquiry into it according to whether they emerge from history as "ways known" or present themselves as prospective conduits for "ways to be made known." Before undertaking this task, however, I will draw on insights from Ben Quash's argument for what he calls "found" theology. Quash's outlook resonates strongly with the further light clause, but also brings an emphasis on maintaining reciprocity in the relationship between past and present discovery (*given* and *found*, as he puts it) which adds further weight to the conclusion I intend to offer.

Relating the Given to the Found

For Quash, the task of theology proceeds from a conviction that "the perfection of God's revelation in Christ is not compromised by—indeed, precisely implies—an ongoing historical dynamic whereby, in God, human beings are constantly invited to *relate the given to the found*."[35] Kinship between

---

[34] One notable example is Adrian Thatcher's appeal to the "one sex" theory propounded by Thomas Lacquer, according to which the conception of human beings belonging to one of two kinds of sex is a relatively modern contrivance that displaced an older assumption that men and women are two (admittedly unequal) variants of a single sex. Lacquer, *Making Sex*. Thatcher suggests that the biblical writers who refer to "male and female" would have been imbued with the "one sex" concept. This gives grounds for suggesting that such references can reasonably be understood as a dipolar continuum which, as such, is more capable of accommodating the various sex-gender configurations which cast empirical doubt on the conventional presumption that human sex is twofold. Thatcher, *Redeeming Gender*, 16, and 142–46.

[35] Quash, *Found Theology*, xiv (italics original).

this approach and that of Baptists engaging the covenant language of "walking together" in anticipation of "further light" becomes all the clearer as Quash elaborates on his vision using the metaphor of a journey that the Scrooby covenant drew on:

> The God who has "stocked our backpack for the journey", so to speak, also "places things in our path", up ahead of us. The presumption that the givens of Christian faith will help to order and illuminate newly encountered experiences or challenges can work the other way too: found things, conceived as gifts of the Holy Spirit who unfolds all the riches that are in Christ, can and must reconfigure, unlock and amplify what is already held true by the Church.[36]

As we have seen already with Baptist exponents of this emphasis on the past (ways known) and future (further light) as sources of divine revelation, Quash is keen to emphasize that found theology calls for an ethos of patience and provisionality. These correspond to an intellectual humility that befits recognition of its dependence on a historical trajectory which is still unfolding.[37] But what is equally evident in his account is that this humility is debased if, in practice, it morphs into reticence about the revelatory possibilities of emergent features of unfolding history. Disproportionate emphasis on "givens" can foster resistance to grasping those things which may have been left by the Spirit for us to find in this dynamic process. It risks foreclosing new learning opportunities, presumes our knowledge of what we have accepted as givens is sufficient, and proceeds as if God were removed from the movement of history, especially "those bits of our experience of the world that do not immediately seem to fit the 'story' we have inherited."[38]

Quash is clear that sources of theology, the witness of scripture and church tradition, no less than any other repository of wisdom, can be misappropriated by excessive attachment to what is presumed to be given within them. This point, too, finds an echo in recent Baptist reflection. Sean Winter observes that "There is always the need for vigilance, lest scripture is *elevated or demoted* to a place that distorts its overall role within the divine economy."[39] Winter and Quash are both alert to the risk that scripture and its exegesis easily

---

[36] Quash, *Found Theology*, xiv.

[37] Indeed, so committed is Quash, *Found Theology*, 283, to this ethos that the final chapter of *Found Theology* is entitled "Inconclusion" because "In the light of all that has been said in the preceding chapters about the continual call to finding which is generally the task of creatures and specifically the task of Christian theology, these closing remarks cannot in good conscience call themselves a Conclusion—not, at least, if a conclusion implies a final word."

[38] Quash, *Found Theology*, 1.

[39] Winter, "Persuading Friends," 270 (italics added).

become confused in practice, and point to different, albeit connected, givens of hermeneutical exploration.[40] Where Winter highlights the inevitability of interpretative diversity which premature adjudication is liable to sell short,[41] Quash recognizes that "sometimes holes are punched in our *exegeses* by encounters with the Spirit in Church and world as well as in scriptural study."[42] Needless to say, both insights need to be taken seriously by a theological enquiry into the moral questions that gender dysphoria gives rise to, as it does for any other challenge in which a moral dimension to relating given and found is to the fore. While scripture is central to the finding of revelatory truths about God and the world for Quash, he also makes a point of emphasizing that the "The *dynamic* relation between found and given must be genuinely *mutual* too. There is always a temptation 'to fear the Spirit's freedom and hold fast only to trusted images of Christ'."[43] A similar kind of mutuality is suggested by Stephen Fowl and Luke Gregory Jones, who emphasize the need for Christians to provide "readings of the world" from a vision shaped by "readings of the texts" (scripture) which should retain normative primacy for them. But important also is the need to allow the world to provide "readings" of us, not in such a way that the place of scripture is displaced, but so that we can become more alert to our own complicity with ungodly habits of thought and social organization, and more open to wisdom from other disciplines and "readings" of the world.[44]

An objection that Quash foresees to his approach is the mirror image of his resistance to an inhibiting over-dependence on givens. Enthusiasm for what might be found ahead risks lapsing into uncritical embrace of any new thing as Spirit-given, simply on the grounds that it *is* new—"confusing the good with the future,"[45] as O'Donovan puts it—and so warping the reciprocal shape of the relationship between given and found from the other direction.[46] Baptists across the centuries have been keen to insist on a christological test for any claim to further light illuminating new ways under the fallen conditions of the penultimate time. Similarly, Quash emphasizes that relating the given to the

---

[40] Winter, "More Light and Truth," 9–11; and Quash, *Found Theology*, 285.

[41] Winter, "Persuading Friends," 269. See the discussion of scriptural interpretation in a covenanted community of friends (257–67). See also his "More Light and Truth," 12–16; and Dare, *Always Way and Fray*, 23–26.

[42] Quash, *Found Theology*, 285 n.8 (italics original).

[43] Quash, *Found Theology*, 18 (italics original). Quash includes here a quote from Ochs, *Another Revelation*, 212.

[44] Fowl and Jones, *Reading in Communion*, 44–49.

[45] O'Donovan, *Conversation Waiting to Begin*, 88.

[46] Quash, *Found Theology*, 15–16.

found requires the integration of christology and pneumatology in order to make sense of this task as a truly human sharing in the economy of the trinitarian God.

> In the finding of the Spirit one realizes oneself as, in fact, caught up in a trinitarian dynamic, in which the Son who shows us the Father is redelivered to the Church by way of its active, imaginative engagement with the events of history. The provisionality and risk of error that attends this process is part of life in the Spirit; part of the call to responsibility that marks the human vocation. ... What seems to be found in the Spirit needs testing against what has been given in the Son: it is only in the interaction of both that revelation is constituted. ... Many of the found things in the world, many of its particularities, are sinful or sin-affected. My argument in this book for taking the "found" seriously has not been that every sinful act or effect we may encounter is God-given; it has been that all God-givenness comes to us in the form of history.[47]

Quash's nuanced emphasis on the *mutuality* of given and found brings to our consideration of "ways known" and "ways to be made known" a raised sensitivity to the truth that "neither old light nor new light is *full* light."[48] With it, we are better prepared to consider how insights from various disciplines, doctrine and ethics foremost amongst them, array themselves across these twin poles to facilitate a response to gender dysphoria.

Applying what is Known; Exploring what May be Known

A revealing portal through which we might enter the territory of "ways made known" which bear on responding to gender dysphoria can be found in earlier twentieth-century Catholic teaching on human sterilization. It need hardly be said that the two scenarios are different in various significant ways. Nonetheless, key building blocks of reasoning seen here rest on doctrinal foundations that are vital to Christian moral reflection on gender dysphoria across the ecumenical spectrum (albeit that the structures built upon these foundations may vary). *Casti Connubii* (*On Christian Marriage*), an encyclical from Pope Pius XI written in 1930, was produced at a time when policies of involuntary sterilization had been established in several countries, including Germany and the United States.[49] However, its instruction censuring induced sterility was not limited to those instances in which the practice was *enforced* by political regimes. Rather, the Pope's reasoning had a broader application,

---

[47] Quash, *Found Theology*, xvi, 17 and 288.

[48] Freeman, "More Light from the Word," 11 (italics added); also quoted by Cross, "'Through a Glass Darkly,'" 115–16 n.89.

[49] Jones, "Gender Reassignment Surgery," 325.

including elective sterilization interventions for contraceptive purposes no less than involuntary measures. This is because its grounds for moral discrimination concerned the meaning of bodily integrity rather than the author of decisions made in respect of it.

> ... Christian doctrine establishes, and the light of human reason makes it most clear, that private individuals have no other power over the members of their bodies than that which pertains to their natural ends; and they are not free to destroy or mutilate their members, or in any other way render themselves unfit for their natural functions, except when no other provision can be made for the good of the whole body.[50]

This instruction directs a maxim in Catholic teaching which has guided its thinking about the morality of surgery more generally to the specific question of induced removal of procreative function. This is the "principle of totality," drawn from Thomas Aquinas' writing, which legitimizes the removal of a bodily *part* if, *and only if*, retaining it in the *whole* body threatens serious harm to that whole.[51]

This privileging of a concept of bodily integrity which, on this view, surgical intervention actually underwrites by being ordered to the safeguarding of the whole, is in turn rooted in the doctrine of creation. Not, we must add, the bare fact of creation's being given by a creator, but that what is "given" here, which is the condition of medical practice of any kind, is a work of divine love structured and ordered to Christ as the one *in* whom, *through* whom and *for* whom "all things in heaven and on earth were created."[52] O'Donovan's well known account of this presupposition of Christian moral judgement is worth quoting from at length, for it encapsulates the significance of the revealed given of creation from which moral deliberation regarding gender dysphoria proceeds.

> In proclaiming the resurrection of Christ, the apostles proclaimed also the resurrection of mankind in Christ; and in proclaiming the resurrection of mankind, they proclaimed the renewal of all creation with him. The resurrection of Christ in isolation from mankind would not be a gospel message. The resurrection of mankind apart from creation would be a gospel of a sort, but of a

---

[50] Pius XI, *Casti Connubii*, n.71.

[51] "... a member of the human body is of itself useful to the good of the whole body, yet, accidentally it may happen to be hurtful, as when a decayed member is a source of corruption to the whole body. Accordingly, so long as a member is healthy and retains its natural disposition, it cannot be cut off without injury to the whole body." Aquinas, *Summa Theologiae* 2-2, q. 65, a. 1, co, quoted in Jones, "Gender Reassignment Surgery," 327.

[52] Col 1:16 (NRSV).

purely gnostic and world-denying sort which is far from the gospel that the apostles actually preached. So the resurrection of Christ directs our attention back to the creation which it vindicates. But we must understand "creation" not merely as the raw material out of which the world as we know it is composed, but as the order and coherence *in* which it is composed. To speak of the resurrection of creation would be meaningless if creation were no more than so much undifferentiated energy. Such a proclamation can have point only as it assures us that the very thing which God has made will continue and flourish. It is not created energy as such that is vindicated in the resurrection of Christ, but the order in which created energy was disposed by the hand of the Creator.[53]

For O'Donovan, to speak of creation as matter whose integrity is bound up with its inherent order is not to deny that this creation looks forward to future renewal beyond its current condition. Rather, the created order is the presupposition of the *restoration* of creation that is integral to, but does not exhaust the meaning of, its eschatological *transformation*. This change corresponds to Christ's *restoration* from the dead and *glorification* through ascension.[54] Consequently, Christian ethics is here described in a way that maps onto the interplay of "ways known" and "ways to be made known," because it "looks both backwards and forwards. ... It respects the natural structures of life in the world, while looking forward to their transformation."[55] Human creativity engages with a world *already* ordered, to which its creative contribution properly brings about an element of reconfiguration to the form of matter, in accordance with its delimited "plasticity."

> But in more complex organic structures there is also a degree of systemic differentiation which runs counter to plasticity. The body of a living animal is susceptible to moulding only at the cost of its systemic integrity; sealskins make excellent coats, but the decision to make coats out of them is the decision to kill seals. Respect for natural forms, then, must mean more than the exploitation of plastic possibilities. It implies sometimes the resolve not to exploit plasticity in order that more complex forms may retain their integrity.[56]

Official Catholic rejection of induced permanent sterility builds on the conviction that the deliberate loss of human procreative function, being a valuable and fundamental aspect of human embodiment, bears the excessive cost of compromising bodily integrity. This has been the basis for an emerging refusal of surgery that effects this loss of function as a response to gender

---

[53] O'Donovan, *Resurrection and Moral Order*, 31.

[54] O'Donovan, *Resurrection and Moral Order*, 56.

[55] O'Donovan, *Resurrection and Moral Order*, 58.

[56] O'Donovan, *Transsexualism*, 18.

dysphoria, albeit that this conclusion has its dissenters within Catholicism.[57] Other Christian ethicists convinced that gender confirmation surgery constitutes an intrinsic violation of bodily integrity argue that the systematic differentiation they regard as essential to human life, in particular our differentiation as biologically male and female, is inevitably undermined by this option.[58] About this conclusion, however, O'Donovan is more circumspect, although his treatment of the subject evinces considerable doubt about the propriety of significant surgical changes.[59] While, for him, such surgery is of "questionable appropriateness,"[60] the focus of his attention is on whether marriage between a transsexual person and a partner with the same birth sex is an appropriate expression of a Christian marriage. With not unsympathetic tones, he imagines the possibility of surgery as "merely a supportive factor in role-adoption," undertaken where there is good reason to think it will coordinate well with ongoing psychological support, and in the absence of effective corrective psychiatric interventions.[61] But O'Donovan is clear that any more ontological claim for the assumed sex of a postoperative transsexual person is delusional. For

> If I claim to have a "real sex," which may be at war with the sex of my body and is at least in a rather uncertain relationship to it, I am shrinking from the glad acceptance of myself as a physical as well as a spiritual being, and seeking self-knowledge in a kind of Gnostic withdrawal from material creation.[62]

---

[57] The only Vatican document to date to refer specifically to a surgical response to gender dysphoria states that "The physical integrity of a person cannot be impaired to cure an illness of psychic or spiritual origin ... And this is why the principle of totality cannot be correctly taken as a criterion for legitimizing anti-procreative sterilization, therapeutic abortion and transsexual medicine and surgery." Pontifical Council for Pastoral Assistance to Health Care Workers, *Charter for Healthcare Workers*, n.145, quoted in Jones "Gender Reassignment Surgery," 317. The reference to "transsexual medicine or surgery" in this quote from the 1995 edition of the *Charter* does not appear in the 2017 edition. See the discussion in Jones, "Gender Reassignment Surgery" for an analysis of Catholic arguments favouring and challenging this position.

[58] E.g., Strachan, "Transition or Transformation."

[59] Cornwall, *Sex and Uncertainty*, 114, does not do justice to O'Donovan's guarded tone when she claims that O'Donovan "insists that transgender surgery goes beyond the pale of the limits appropriate for human bodies. ... He also seems to view transsexual surgery as inherently cosmetic—and thus superfluous—rather than therapeutic."

[60] O'Donovan, *Transsexualism*, 4.

[61] O'Donovan, *Transsexualism*, 21.

[62] O'Donovan, *Transsexualism*, 13.

We should note that "realising my *real* sex" is not necessarily the self-perception of every person seeking transsexual surgery, and there is no indication that O'Donovan would disagree with this point.[63] However, as Susannah Cornwall observes, O'Donovan's challenge to gender dysphoria sufferers who do perceive their plight in these terms has its own rather uncertain relationship with an earlier claim he makes in the same essay. Faced with the "ambiguities" of people born with certain intersex conditions, he says, "we may be forced to resolve them *away from* the sex to which, had all gone well in gestation, the person would have developed."[64] Forced by what? By means of surgery? These questions gain further traction from reports of people operated on in early life. Some could not adjust to dissonance in their sexual identity in adult life. Others indicated that they would rather have lived with so-called "ambiguous" anatomical features rather than suffer postoperative scarring and poor sensation in the genitals that were fashioned for them.[65] To my mind, this discrepancy does not deal a fatal blow to O'Donovan's objection, at a conceptual level, to claims to have a "real" sex at odds with their biological sex. But I think it does point to a need to "read between the lines" of this claim, rather than simply decry it as an expression of ingratitude; to detect in it an attempt to articulate an enduring sense of dissonance between the sex the body appears to be and the sex that the sufferer apprehends. J. David Hester's observation about inconsistencies like this in the consideration of surgery for intersex conditions and gender dysphoria (which are by no means limited to O'Donovan) is telling: "Apparently, not having an *identifiable* sex [in the case of intersex conditions] is an emergency and something worth correcting, but having the "wrong" sex is not. . . . This looks to be a serious inconsistency . . . when what is at stake in both cases is gender assignment."[66] The word "identifiable" is significant here, for it signals that a predilection for what we can verify based on what is already known may underlie the discrepancy. In doing so, it takes us back to the overarching theme of this essay, and highlights the need to set what is "given—known" about sex alongside what might be "found—made known" in the claim to have a paradoxical "real" sex, namely that identifying sex is, in some cases, stubbornly elusive. A more sympathetic hearing of this claim may alert us to the possibility of further light in this case, albeit light that, again paradoxically,

---

[63] Note the example Jones, "Gender Reassignment Surgery," 335, gives of someone with gender dysphoria who concludes that, for all she might wish it, she cannot be a *ciswoman* [non-transgender woman] after surgery, but would have no hesitation in identifying herself as a *transwoman*.

[64] O'Donovan, *Transsexualism*, 8 (italics original).

[65] Cornwall, *Sex and Uncertainty*, 34–41.

[66] Hester, "Intersexes and the End of Gender," 216 (italics added), quoted in Cornwall, "Sex and Uncertainty," 115.

sensitizes us to the realistic possibility that a person's sex is sometimes opaque.[67] The connection between case study and theological methodology is brought out well by Quash.

> ... suffering experience, traumatic experience, in its resistance to easy assimilation, is in fact one of the key arguments in *favour* of a theology of the found. ... A cry can be the first signal that something is in need of repair, and *may* therefore be the first portent of that repair. Even "found suffering", in other words, may need to be embraced and learned from in order that the given may remain healthy.[68]

At this point, it might be thought that I am confusing the biological term "sex" with its perceptual counterpart "gender" having been keen to avoid doing so earlier. To the contrary, my purpose is to pave the way for a brief comment on recent scientific research which may augment such light as may be glimpsed through the "real sex" claim, research that has caused Megan DeFranza to declare, "Too many Christians who make a distinction between intersex people as 'born this way' and transgender people as those who 'choose' their identity fail to remember that the brain is part of the body."[69] The question of what causes gender dysphoria remains open and controversial. Indeed, the variety and complexity of contending theories—psychological and biological—may point to a multifactorial phenomenon whose constituents vary in different cases.[70] More recently, it seems that evidence and, consequently, scientific opinion, is gravitating towards recognizing that at least one significant cause is what has become known as the "Brain sex" or "intersex brain" theory.[71] Put simply, this suggests that, as a norm, some parts of the brain are sexually differentiated according to a broadly dimorphic (male/female) structure. In the rare instances of gender dysphoria, "a discrepancy may exist between prenatal genital differentiation and brain differentiation such that the external genitals develop, for example, as male

---

[67] To suggest that sex can be "opaque" is, of course, not of itself a claim that decries belief that human sex is dimorphic in favour of alternative accounts: this essay offers no judgement on this question.

[68] Quash, *Found Theology*, 18–19.

[69] DeFranza, "Good News for Gender Minorities," 156.

[70] Jones, "Gender Reassignment Surgery," 321; and Beilby and Eddy, "Understanding Transgender Experiences and Identities," 33. For a helpful overview of the various theories and associated evidence espoused about the causes of gender dysphoria, see Beilby and Eddy, "Understanding Transgender Experiences and Identities," 21–33.

[71] The latter term derives from Diamond, "Transsexualism as an Intersex condition."

while the brain develops as female."⁷² Although still contested, the evidence for this theory has grown stronger over time, and gives grounds for thinking that anomalous morphological traits in the brain are a significant feature of the causal factors of gender dysphoria.⁷³

Jones is right to question the assumption that knowledge of the origins of gender dysphoria is decisive in determining what counts as ethically acceptable treatment: even to identify a condition as fundamentally psychological is not to make the case for denying, on principle, that any form of surgery might be used to alleviate its symptoms.⁷⁴ The point here is to recognize that further light from a scientific source fortifies reasons to doubt the characterization of pleas for gender confirmation surgery as one more project contrived to indulge fantasies of autonomy by exploiting the body's plasticity. The suggestion that such pleas exemplify what Brian Brock calls "technological rationality," which contradicts our calling to "a form of life in which created order is neither worshipped nor dismissed," becomes more attenuated by the likelihood that gender dysphoria draws attention to physiological *as well as* psychological dissonance in personal identity.⁷⁵ In fact, the experience of dividedness that gender dysphoria presents may highlight limitations to the body's legibility in a creation that is both ordered and fallen.⁷⁶ Rather than characterizing gender confirmation surgery as "dismissing" the created order, there may be cause to ask whether outright rejection of it, whatever the severity of dysphoria it aims to address, is a better fit for complicity in "worshipping" creation (i.e., idolizing an uninterpreted biological entity just because it exists) rather than respecting it.⁷⁷

In order to avoid this error, it is important that we keep earlier observations clearly in view: that Christian ethics needs both to respect natural structures

---

⁷² Meston and Frohlich, "Gender Identity Disorder," quoted in Yarhouse and Sadusky, "Complexities of Gender Identity," 106.

⁷³ Yarhouse and Sadusky, "Complexities of Gender Identity," 106–8.

⁷⁴ Jones, "Gender Reassignment Surgery," 321.

⁷⁵ Brock, *Christian Ethics Technological Age*, 322.

⁷⁶ Song, "Ethics of Mutilation," 500, makes a similar comment in relation to another rare condition—body integrity identity disorder—which is likewise marked by dissonance between outward bodily characteristics and enduring perception, and which, like gender dysphoria, may be caused in part by neurological anomalies.

⁷⁷ It should be noted that Brock's own consideration of gender confirmation surgery as a response to gender dysphoria appear to be considerably more sceptical although, like O'Donovan, his attention rests on how such a theological critique of such surgery "fleshes out the theological mechanics of how marriage reveals the moral meaning of material order." Brock, *Christian Ethics Technological Age*, 331. See the discussion in 331–35.

and look to their future eschatological transformation (O'Donovan), and also that a suffering cry may signal the need for repair and so, *prima facie,* merit serious attention (Quash). To these observations we may add a third, which is that the created given of human personhood is, as the Judeo–Christian tradition has long insisted, a psychosomatic unity rather than just a biological organism. To put the matter in biblical terms, the human body certainly deserves respect as "a temple of the Holy Spirit" (1 Cor 6:19, NRSV), but the God of peace who brings about our sanctification is attentive to "spirit and soul and body" (1 Thess 5:23, NRSV). Both Catholic and Protestant ethicists have recognized that the whole person—body and mind—is the object of attention for the principle of totality that informs the morality of surgery, even if the significance of this is not always fully addressed.[78]

The importance of this for my conclusion comes to light in the following testimony from Abigail, a postoperative transwoman.

> Before I transitioned, I wanted to die—I remember looking longingly up at tall buildings. Only since my GRS [gender reassignment surgery] have I begun to appreciate my body—my thighs, fingertips, earlobes and eyelashes—and delight in it. . . . A paradox: I reach wholeness through mutilation. Yet though I could probably have fathered a child in the narrow sense of fertilising an ovum, while pretending to be a man I could not have formed relationships within a family and brought up that child.[79]

The presence of suicidal ideation in Abigail's case, and its consequent amelioration by surgery, demonstrates both the severity of threat that gender dysphoria can pose to the whole person and the role surgery can play in safeguarding that whole. This holds true even though the means of safeguarding are seemingly paradoxical, that is, removing a function which, as a norm, is considered a basic good. I think a persuasive case can be made for the relevance of double-effect in some cases of treating gender dysphoria via surgery, because the *intended* good of the whole person is served by alleviating a serious debilitating condition even though the *foreseeable* result of the means deployed is loss of procreative function.[80] Whether or not Abigail is correct in

---

[78] Jones, "Gender Reassignment Surgery," 329; and Song, "Ethics of Mutilation," 498–500.

[79] Beardsley and O'Brien, *This is My Body*, 153.

[80] The principle of double-effect has a long history in Christian moral thought. It refers to the idea that in respect of a single act, a moral distinction can be drawn between *intended* effects, and effects that may be *foreseen* but are not directly intended by the act in question. I am not persuaded by Jones' challenge to the application of double-effect to Gender Confirmation Surgery, which rests on the claim that the physical parts removed in this surgery is not actually the physical *cause* of the dysphoria (unlike lobotomy, which may be legitimate because "the brain relates to the whole person as a part to the whole"). Rather, these parts are the *object* of dysphoria whose

believing that she could not have formed family relationships conducive to bringing up a child is unanswerable and beside the point. What her comment about parenting points to is the inadequacy of aggrandizing procreative function in considering a vocation to parenthood in the light of gender dysphoria. In fact, in relation to procreation, the Christ event can be interpreted as itself a "found" revelation that casts a transforming light on what was hitherto considered to be "given" regarding God's purposes prior to his incarnation. The point is well made by Robert Song:

> The first *adam* may be created male and female, and thereby ordained and rendered able to procreate. But the last Adam, the one who unlike the first Adam does succeed in having all things placed under his feet, does not do so by procreation. Jesus Christ, in whom creation is being renewed (cf. Col 3:10–11), points the way to a different order in which marriage is to be fulfilled. . . . Unlike the old covenant, in which membership of the chosen community was determined by shared ancestral blood, membership in the new covenant is determined by sharing in the blood of Christ. Life in the community of the resurrection is life in which the hope of children is no longer intrinsic to the community's identity. Human flourishing has been given a profound reorientation; full humanity, full participation in the imaging of God, possible without marriage, without procreation, indeed without being sexually active.[81]

In the penultimate time between Christ's resurrection and new creation, procreation remains important as a witness to the created order. But with Christ's resurrection we are shown the first fruits of a renewed order which can be witnessed to in ways that are not procreative, and so, in some way or other, those who do not procreate can fully participate in this witness. It is with this in mind that I propose that gender confirmation surgery is morally acceptable in cases of severe and enduring cases of gender dysphoria that have

---

direct *cause* is the mental perception the sufferer has of these bodily parts and "because the intentional object of a mental state is not, per se, in a part-to-whole relation, the principle of totality is not available as a justification for harm to the body. . . . Surgery to remove or disguise the object of distress may be justifiable, but only if it would not cause serious and lasting harm to the body at the level of function." Jones, "Gender Reassignment Surgery," 330–31. It seems to me that this reasoning neglects to keep in view the *whole* person as the object of the principle of totality (despite Jones' claim to be doing so), whose perceptions arising from their mental state are a part of this whole in the same way that the brain and other organs, limbs, etc., are part of the bodily whole.

[81] Song, *Covenant and Calling*, 17–18. We need not be concerned here with whether witness to the eschatological order inaugurated by Christ limits sexual expression to marriage and celibacy or, as Song goes on to explore in the rest of this book, a "third vocation" involving sexually active non-procreative covenant partnerships in which partners need not necessarily be sexually differentiated.

proved resistant to other, less invasive, options for alleviation. Respect for the natural structures of biological life as integral to the form of the created order, gives grounds for maintaining this high threshold for surgical intervention. So, too, the impact of cultural habits of thought that shape our self-understanding and deliberation buttress this conclusion. Robert Song, whose conclusion regarding the morality of amputation surgery in response to cases of body integrity identity disorder echoes this conclusion about gender dysphoria (as well as some of its underlying reasoning), highlights a danger that applies to both conditions. This is the danger that once a diagnostic category has a name and a set of symptoms identified with it by a medical authority, it can acquire a kind of seductive power, drawing people into interpreting their personal experiences according to the category that stands before them. As Song puts it,

> because of the reciprocal, reflexive nature of the relation between people's self-interpretations and the diagnostic categories available to them, especially when mediated through support groups, internet blogs, information sites, and the like, such classifications may end up structuring the ways in which people perform their mental torment in ways that preclude alternative interpretations. ... It might leave them grasping onto their identity as sufferers from [body integrity identity disorder] as the deepest truth about themselves, clinging to the possibility of surgical intervention as their sole hope of salvation, and unable to ask even in principle whether there were any alternatives.[82]

These considerations emphasize the need for special vigilance in considering cases of gender dysphoria. They underline the importance of thorough assessment beforehand, of having reasonable confidence that surgery will bring about improvement, of exploring less-invasive therapies first, and of ensuring that comprehensive support is sustained before, during and long after surgery has occurred. But I do not believe they override support for gender confirmation surgery as an appropriate method of treatment for a limited range of cases of gender dysphoria.

Yet More Light...

This essay has been deliberately limited to considering the moral scope of medical interventions, especially surgery, that respond to gender dysphoria. Consequently, it offers only a limited conclusion. It leaves open questions regarding transsexual people in marital relationships. Should uncertainty regarding the sexual identity of a transsexual person give grounds for a "benefit of the doubt" approach to adopting their assumed sex in marriage? Is a "para-marital relationship" established as an exceptional pastoral accommodation

---

[82] Song, "Ethics of Mutilation," 501–2.

more suitable?[83] Or can we conceive of welcoming them into non-procreative covenant partnerships, of equal standing to marriage, for which sexual differentiation is not a prerequisite?[84] Questions like these, as well as what we might learn from the testimony of transsexual people about their sense of vocation, have an important part to play as we look in hope for the ways God is making known to us in the present and future.[85] Ruth Gouldbourne's observations about the value of counter-cultural ways of discernment— "Arguing slowly, carefully, with respect and with enough time and hope of finding a way forward together"[86]—are undoubtably apt here, as we look for yet more light and truth to break forth from God's word.

Bibliography

Allison-Glenny, Beth. "That We Might See Ourselves as We Could Be: Baptist Interpretations of Scripture on the Complementarity of Male and Female." In *Gathering Disciples: Essays in Honor of Christopher J. Ellis*, 90–111. Edited by Myra Blyth and Andy Goodliff. Eugene: Pickwick, 2017.

American Psychiatric Association. *Diagnostic and Statistical Manual of Mental Disorders*. Fifth Edition. Arlington: American Psychiatric Association, 2013.

Beardsley, Tina, and Michelle O'Brien, ed. *This is my Body: Hearing the Theology of Transgender Christians*. London: Darton, Longman and Todd, 2016.

Beilby, James K., and Paul R. Eddy, ed. *Understanding Transgender Experiences and Identities: Four Views*. Grand Rapids: Baker Academic, 2019.

Beilby, James K., and Paul R. Eddy. "Understanding Transgender Experiences and Identities: An Introduction." In *Understanding Transgender Experiences and Identities*, 1–54. Edited by Beilby and Eddy.

Blyth, Myra and Christopher J. Ellis, ed. *Gathering for Worship: Patterns and Prayers for the Community of Disciples*. Norwich: Canterbury, 2005.

Bradford, William. *Of Plymouth Plantation 1620–1647*. New York: The Modern Library, 1981.

Brock, Brian. *Christian Ethics in a Technological Age*. Grand Rapids: Eerdmans, 2010.

---

[83] O'Donovan, *Transsexualism*, 25.

[84] See the discussion in Song, *Covenant and Calling*, especially 81–92.

[85] Revealing testimonies in this regard can be found in Sabia-Tanis, "Holy Creation, Wholly Creative," 104; Beardsley and O'Brien, *This is My Body*; and Hunt, *Book of Queer Prophets*.

[86] Gouldbourne, "In Praise of Incompetence," 70.

Burgess, Walter H. *John Robinson, Pastor of the Pilgrim Fathers: A Study of His Life and Times*. London/New York: Williams and Norgate/Harcourt, Brace and Howe, 1920.

Butler, Judith. *Gender Trouble: Feminism and the Subversion of Identity*. New York: Routledge, 1990.

Church of England website. "Pastoral Guidance for use in Conjunction with the Affirmation of Baptismal Faith in the Context of Gender Transition." https://www.churchofengland.org/sites/default/files/2018–12/Pastoral%20Guidance-Affirmation-Baptismal-Faith.pdf, 2018

Clements, K.C. "What to Expect from Gender Confirmation Surgery." 2018. https://www.healthline.com/health/transgender/gender-confirmation-surgery#TOC_TITLE_HDR_1

Cook, Henry. *What Baptists Stand For*. London: Carey Kingsgate, 1964.

Cornwall, Susannah. *Sex and Uncertainty in the Body of Christ*. Oxford: Routledge, 2010.

Cross, Anthony, "'Through a Glass Darkly': The Further Light Clause in Baptist Thought." In *Questions of Identity: Studies in Honour of Brian Haymes*. Edited by Anthony R. Cross and Ruth Gouldbourne, 92–118. Oxford: Regent's Park College, 2011.

Dare, Helen J. *Always on the Way and in the Fray: Reading the Bible as Baptists*. The Whitley Lecture 2014. Oxford: Whitley, 2014.

Diamond, Milton. "Transsexualism as an Intersex Condition." In *Transsexuality in Theology and Neuroscience: Findings, Controversies, and Perspectives*, 43–53. Edited by Gerhard Schreiber. Boston: de Gruyter, 2016.

DeFranza, Megan K. "Good News for Gender Minorities." In *Understanding Transgender Experiences and Identities*, 147–93. Edited by Beilby and Eddy.

Evangelical Alliance. *Trans Formed: A Brief Biblical and Pastoral Introduction to Understanding Transgender in a Changing Culture*. London: Evangelical Alliance, 2018.

Fiddes, Paul S. "'Woman's Head is Man': A Doctrinal Reflection upon a Pauline Text." *Baptist Quarterly* 31.8 (1986) 370–83.

Freeman, Curtis W. "More Light from the Word." Paper presented to the North Carolina Alliance of Baptists at the Olin T. Binkley Baptist Church, Chapel Hill, North Carolina on 21 January 2005.

Fowl, Stephen E. and Jones, Luke G. *Reading in Communion*. Eugene: Wipf and Stock, 1998.

Gouldbourne, Ruth M.B. "In Praise of Incompetence." *Baptist Quarterly* 44.2 (2011) 68–85.

Grenz, Stanley J. *Renewing the Center: Evangelical Theology in a Post-Liberal Era*. Grand Rapids: Baker Academic, 2000.

Hester, J. David. "Intersexes and the End of Gender: Corporeal Ethics and Postgender Bodies." *Journal of Gender Studies* 13.3 (2004) 215–25.

Hunt, Ruth, ed. *The Book of Queer Prophets*. London: William Collins, 2020.

Jones, David A. "Gender Reassignment Surgery: A Catholic Bioethical Analysis." *Theological Studies* 79.2 (2018) 314–38.
Lacquer, Thomas. *Making Sex: Body and Gender from the Greeks to Freud.* Cambridge: Harvard University Press, 1990.
Merritt, Jonathan. "3 Reasons Conservative Christians will Lose the Transgender Debate." 2016. https://religionnews.com/2016/05/14/3-reasons-conservative-christians-will-lose-the-transgender-debate/
Meston, Cindy M., and Penny Frohlich, "Gender Identity Disorder." The Sexual Psychophysiology Laboratory. https://labs.la.utexas.edu/mestonlab/gender-identity-disorder/#:~:text=Meston%20&%20Penny%20Frohlich.%20The%20DSM-IV%20describes%20gender,if%20the%20symptoms%20produce%20marked%20distress%20or%20impairment
Ochs, Peter. *Another Revelation: Postliberal Christianity and the Jews.* Grand Rapids: Baker Academic, 2011.
O'Donovan, *A Conversation Waiting to Begin: The Churches and the Gay Controversy.* London: SCM, 2009.
———. *Resurrection and Moral Order: An Outline for Evangelical Ethics.* 2nd ed. Grand Rapids: Eerdmans, 1994.
———. *Transsexualism: Issues and Argument.* Cambridge: Grove, 1982.
Payne, Ernest. *Ways Known and to be Made Known.* London: The Baptist Union of Great Britain and Ireland, 1977.
Pius XI, *Casti Connubii.* 1930. https://w2.vatican.va/content/pius-xi/en/encyclicals/documents/hf_p-xi_enc_19301231_casti-connubii.html
Pontifical Council for Pastoral Assistance to Health Care Workers, *Charter for Healthcare Workers.* 1995. http://www.ewtn.com/library/curia/pcpaheal.htm
Quash, Ben. *Found Theology: History, Imagination and the Holy Spirit.* London: Bloomsbury T&T Clark, 2013.
Sabia-Tanis, Justin. "Holy Creation, Wholly Creative: God's Intention for Gender Diversity." In *Understanding Transgender Identities*, 195–233. Edited by Beilby and Eddy.
Song, Robert. "Body Integrity Identity Disorder and the Ethics of Mutilation." *Studies in Christian Ethics* 26.4 (2013) 487–503.
Thatcher, Adrian. *Redeeming Gender.* Oxford: Oxford University Press, 2016.
Twardy, S. "Medicolegal aspects of transsexualism." *Medical Trial Technique Quarterly* 26.3 (1980) 273–75.
White, Barry R. *The English Separatist Tradition: From the Marian Martyrs to the Pilgrim Fathers.* Oxford: Oxford University Press, 1971.
Winter, Sean F. *More Light and Truth? Biblical Interpretation in Covenantal Perspective.* The Whitley Lecture 2007. Oxford: Whitley, 2007.
———. "Persuading Friends: Friendship and Testimony in Baptist Interpretative Communities." In *The "Plainly Revealed Word of God?": Baptist Hermeneutics in Theory and Practice.* Edited by Helen Dare and Simon Woodman. Macon: Mercer University Press, 2011.

Yarhouse, Mark. *Understanding Gender Dysphoria: Navigating Transgender Issues in a Changing Culture*. Downers Grove: IVP Academic, 2015. Kindle Edition.

Yarhouse, Mark and Sadusky, Julia. "The Complexities of Gender Identity: Toward a More Nuanced Response to the Transgender Experience." In *Understanding Transgender Experiences and Identities*, 101–41. Edited by Beilby and Eddy.

Chapter 11

"Spend and be spent:"
The Nature of the Ministry

Anthony R. Cross

The Christian understanding of ministry must always begin with the mission of God,[1] and therefore with Jesus and his call to follow him.

> As Jesus walked beside the Sea of Galilee, he saw Simon and his brother Andrew casting a net into the lake, for they were fishermen. "Come, follow me," Jesus said, "and I will make you fishers of men and women." At once they left their nets and followed him.
> When he had gone a little farther, he saw James son of Zebedee and his brother John in a boat, preparing their nets. Without delay he called them, and they left their father Zebedee in the boat with the hired men and followed him. (Mark 1:16–20)[2]

But Jesus also

> called the crowd to him along with the disciples and said: "Those who would come after me must deny themselves and take up their cross and follow me. For those who want to save their lives will lose them, but those who lose their lives for me and for the gospel will save them. What good is it for you to gain the whole world, yet forfeit your soul?" (Mark 8:34–38)

As it was for our Lord, so it is for us as those called by God to, as Luke expresses it in Acts 6:4, "the ministry of the word".

The sacrificial nature of the ministry is not often spoken of, but as the way of the cross was for Christ, so it will be for those men and women called and gifted by God to serve him and his church as ministers of the gospel of Christ. In Matt 5:11–12, Jesus forewarned us: "'Blessed are you when people insult you, persecute you and falsely say all kinds of evil against you because of me. Rejoice and be glad [and that's counter-intuitive], because great is your reward

---

[1] Haymes, Gouldbourne and Cross, *On Being the Church*, e.g., 3–6 and 153 (cf. 152–79).

[2] Biblical quotations are from the *NIV*.

in heaven, for in the same way they persecuted the prophets who were before you.'" And yet, when it happens to us, it often comes as a complete shock. Sometimes it is a devastating blow, because, too often, it comes from God's own people, and has been the reason for many to walk away from the call of God on them. In Matt 7:13–14 Jesus also told us, "'Enter through the narrow gate. For wide is the gate and broad is the road that leads to destruction, and many enter through it. But small is the gate and narrow the road that leads to life, and only a few find it.'"

So what can we learn from the tradition of those who "were before" us?

Andrew Gifford (c.1641–1721), who after his death came to be known as "The Apostle of the West,"[3] was called to the ministry of the church in The Pithay, Bristol—now Cairns Road Baptist Church—which he served for nearly forty years,[4] having spent sixty of his eighty years in the ministry. During his pastorate there, The Pithay church endured three periods of severe persecution,[5] one result of which was that they were unable to support him, most likely because of the result of taxes and fines. Gifford, therefore, used up his own savings, as well as having some of his possessions constrained. Joseph Ivimey, himself an eminent minister, preacher, and historian, said of Gifford that his "ministry of the gospel was the very delight of his soul, and he could say with the Psalmist, The zeal of thy house hath eaten me up. He thought no pains too great which he took in the work of his Lord; that he might honour him, and promote the good of souls," and this despite his congregation being poor and, therefore, unable to support him financially.[6]

Three times Gifford was imprisoned in Bristol, and one final time in Gloucester,[7] nevertheless, William Bazley (d.1736),[8] co-minister at The Pithay, with Gifford's son, Emmanuel Gifford (d.1721),[9] stated, "His ministry was truly eminent." Though "he had not the advantage of several parts of learning which others enjoyed (and which he lamented) yet the want of this was abundantly supplied by the gracious assistance of the spirit of God; a quick apprehension; a solid judgment; and a very lively invention." His

---

[3] J.G. Fuller, *Rise and Progress*, 227.

[4] Ivimey, *History*, 2:551.

[5] See Ivimey, *History*, 1:412–15.

[6] Ivimey, *History*, 2:548–49, quoting Ps 69:9.

[7] See Ivimey, *History*, 1:413–15.

[8] On whom, see the few remarks in Ivimey, *History*, 2:547–48 and 551–52; 3:170; and 4:283.

[9] The church moved to The Pithay in 1699 during Andrew Gifford Sr's ministry, then later to King Street, and is now Cairns Road. Emmanuel Gifford became co-minister in 1705, and Bazley in 1723.

sermons were "full of flights of wit, and terms of art" and "abounded with sublime thought and substantial divinity." He neither indulged his congregation nor did he "please the fancy," but his aim was "to warm and affect the heart, and inform the judgment in the great and necessary things of salvation."[10] Crucially,

> The sum and substance of all his sermons were (as were the Apostles) *Repentance and Faith*. He desired to know nothing among his hearers, but *Jesus Christ and him crucified*; and at the close of his sermon . . . he would offer Christ to sinners, and invite them to embrace him as offered in the most affectionate and pathetic manner. The regard he had to the honour of his Lord and Master, and his affection to his fellow-creatures taught his tongue eloquence, and filled his mouth with the most nervous arguments: and he saw the effects of it in the conversion of multitudes; yea of many hundreds. As he was thus faithful, and skilful to win souls by his preaching; so he was most eminent in the discharge of his pastoral care; in visiting the sick; bearing the infirmities of the weak; comforting the disconsolate; encouraging the serious and the godly; gently reproving the forward, and those who opposed themselves to the good of the church. It may truly be said of him, that he was heartily willing to *spend and be spent* for his flock; neither did *he count his life dear to himself, so that he might finish his course with joy, and the ministry which he had received of the Lord Jesus, to testify the gospel of the grace of God.*

Bazley summed up this part of his tribute and linked it to the next, "The graces and virtues of the Holy Spirit shone in him with uncommon lustre."[11] The Baptist historian, Thomas Crosby (c.1685–1752), also noted the evangelistic nature of Gifford's preaching, when he remarked that "many hundreds were the feals of his miniftry," such that when he began his ministry at The Pithay in 1677[12] there were only forty members, but nearly 400 by his death.[13]

The focus of our attention, however, is not with the subjects that preoccupy the thoughts of most ministers, churches, Associations, and Baptists Together today—mission and growth—but the sacrificial nature of ministry. Remember Jesus' saying that "'Those who would come after me must deny themselves and take up their cross and follow me'" (Mark 8:34). The language of "to spend and be spent," of the sacrificial nature of the call to the ministry, encapsulates

---

[10] Ivimey, *History*, 2:548–49.

[11] Ivimey, *History*, 2:549–50 (italics original).

[12] He was ordained in London at the hands of Daniel Dyke, and Nehemiah Cox on "the 3rd of the 6 month, 1677, by laying on of the hands . . . , with prayer and fasting in the church," so Ivimey, *History*, 2:546.

[13] Crosby, *History*, 3:148; also Ivimey, *History*, 2:546.

this faithfulness, and appears particularly throughout the writings of Baptists in the long eighteenth century, that is c.1689–the early nineteenth century.

Addressing the Bristol Education Society in 1773, Hugh Evans (c.1713–81) maintained that God uses instruments, means, those whom he has called and gifted, as his agents of fulfilling his purposes in the church and the world. He stated unequivocally that only God

> can make able minifters of the new teftament. But as he is pleafed to make ufe of inftruments to effect his own purpofes, the honor you are ambitious of, is that of being employed by him, in the accomplifhment of the great and defirable work of raifing up able minifters of the gofpel. And there is the greater reafon for our being folicitous about this matter in the prefent day, as able minifters are much wanted. The harveft truly is plenteous, but able laborers very few. There are moreover many able and indefatigable adverfaries of the gofpel, and great need therefore of able and zealous minifters to vindicate and eftablish the truth as it is in Jefus.[14]

Whatever services ministers are called to, Hugh Evans believed that they should be attended to "with diligence and zeal,"[15] though he recognized that those ministers who were "zealous and faithful in the execution of their office" would often have "many adverfaries."[16]

This zeal was emphasized by Caleb Evans (1737–91) who noted that after his father's baptism he had "purfued his ftudies with redoubtable vigour, being desirous of ferving God in the gofpel of his fon," that he was "diligent in bufinefs, fervent in fpirit, ferving the Lord."[17]

Caleb Evans lauded his father's "foundness of ... underftanding," his "expanfive heaven illumin'd mind," noted that he was "directed by fervent piety and an ardent zeal for the glory of God and the happinefs of mankind,"[18] and that as a minister "He was not a flothful fervant, but truly active, zealous, laborious and unwearied in the fervice of his beloved mafter."[19] Indeed, he was "ready to fpend and be fpent" (2 Cor. 12:15).[20] Of his father, he believed that few "excelled him as a Tutor," in which he "labored affiduoufly ... not merely to form fubftantial fcholars, but as far as in him lay was defirous of being made

---

[14] H. Evans, *Able Minifter*, 4 (italics original).

[15] H. Evans, *Minifters defcribed*, 4.

[16] H. Evans, *Sermon*, 36.

[17] C. Evans, *Elisha's Exclamation!*, 27.

[18] C. Evans, *Elisha's Exclamation!*, 30–31.

[19] C. Evans, *Elisha's Exclamation!*, 37.

[20] H. Evans, *Able Minifter*, 37, and *Ministers defcribed*, 29.

an inftrument in God's hand of forming them able, evangelical, lively, zealous Minifters of the gofpel."[21]

Preaching at the ordination of William Belsher to Silver Street, Worcester, in 1796, John Ryland (1753–1825) made explicit the ongoing necessity that ministers must continue to study, to do theology, for without it they run dry— they run out of things to say. Ryland asserted that, since ministers must always be ready to preach, they

> must apply closely to study, and unite it with fervent prayer. Understanding is a well-spring of life to him that hath it; but this well is deep, and it is laborious work to draw up these living waters. Clearly to exhibit to our people the great truths of religion, and to point out their salutary tendency, to pacify the conscience, and purify the heart; keeping back nothing that is profitable; but defending the doctrines of the gospel against all opposers, and abusers of them, and guarding our hearers against error on either hand, is no trivial business, which may be performed without exertion or toil. Not only to produce in the pulpit things new and old, but continually to watch over them who are committed to our care, endeavouring, in truly pastoral visits, to water privately, what we have sown in public, requires our utmost diligence.[22]

Samuel Pearce (1766–99) was equally convinced that the minister's ongoing study is of the highest importance to preaching. In fact, the minister who "thinks lightly of its value, betrays an ignorance and indolence, which, if indulged, will eventually debase both his character and labours."

> A studious habit, as you have heard to-day, is essential to a stated minister. A lively imagination may serve an itinerant; but when a man becomes stationary, and preaches three or four times a week to the same people, unless he be industrious in furnishing his mind, his services will soon become insipid, void of solidity, fraught with tautology, and unfit for edification. And what is the result? Why, the thoughtful hearers must either abide with dissatisfaction, or in grief retire; whilst the ignorant are kept in their ignorance, and remain babes, when, under a judicious ministry, they might have become "fathers in Christ."[23]

As an aside, the third tutor who worked alongside Hugh and Caleb Evans at the Bristol Academy, James Newton (1733–90), expressed it, "May we be excited to greater activity in our ftations," and he looked forward to the pleasure that would come when the Lord approved faithful stewardship with "Well done good and faithful fervants! Let this fire our fouls with an holy

---

[21] C. Evans, *Elisha's Exclamation!*, 31. This phrase spoken about his father formed the foundation and goal of the Bristol Baptist College tradition. See, e.g., West, *Bristol Tradition*, [9]; and Cross, "Early Bristol Tradition."

[22] Ryland, "Charge," 26.

[23] Pearce, "Sermon," 51 (italics original).

zeal."[24] Addressing a former student, Thomas Dunscombe, at his ordination to the church at Coate near Oxford in August 1773, Caleb Evans fervently believed that God's "Well done good and faithful servant" was the minister's sufficient reward, concluding, "Surely the thought will revive and rouse you!"[25]

Thomas Steffe Crisp (1788–1868), Ryland's colleague then successor as Principal at Bristol Academy, maintained that one aspect of Christian love was its demand for efforts to be made "for the good of souls. Perhaps," he continued, "there has never been a period, since the age of the Apostles, in which there has been more genuine zeal than in the present day; zeal which calls forth combined and successful exertions for the instruction of the ignorant, the dissemination of divine truth, and the salvation of souls." What was needed, though, was for all Christians "seriously to consider, what part he is taking in the extensive operations of christian benevolence which are now carried on."[26] Crisp called his hearers to look "with delight" at

> the proofs with which we are furnished, both in the history of the past, and by what is still taking place around us, that the love of souls is a benign and vigorous principle, calling into exercise the most generous feelings, and prompting to acts of the most distinguished benevolence.

And he called them to consider the Apostle Paul's words from 1 Thessalonians 2:8, Romans 9:3, Acts 20:24, and, between the latter, 2 Corinthians 12:15's "'I am willing to spend and be spent for your souls.'"[27]

Think about William Carey (1761–1834), father of the Baptist Missionary Society (BMS, now BMS World Mission) and the modern missionary movement: pastor, preacher, teacher, evangelist, and Bible translator. It was seven years before he won his first convert, Krishna Pal (1764–1822), to Christ. Many churches today might well have got rid of Carey for his lack of success. Writing to the BMS on 11 November 1851, the Jamaican former slave, Joseph Jackson Fuller (1825–1908) appealed to the BMS not to abandon the Cameroon Mission. His pleas included the challenge, "has our society never laboured with no success for a longer period than they have laboured in Africa, and yet have you not continued? And why should you shrink for Africa? Think of the South Seas, and remember Africa." A little later he continued, "England has washed her hands from the abomination of slavery, and shall the evangelization of Africa fright you? Shall the blood of Africa be required at your hands? Think of this, and see if there are no young

---

[24] Newton, *Good Steward*, 29.

[25] C. Evans, *Charge*, 19 (italics original).

[26] Crisp, *Charity, or Christian Love*, 29. See his whole discussion of this, 29–34.

[27] Crisp, *Charity, or Christian Love*, 31.

men who will be willing to spend and be spent for God."[28] One young man who eventually did so was George Grenfell (1849–1906). Later in life, after heavy losses on the mission field, and though "overworked and spent," he ignored the order to return home and stayed in the Congo.[29]

Addressing this subject, the great preacher and church planter, Charles Haddon Spurgeon (1834–92), expressed the same opinion as Newton and Caleb Evans about a century earlier. While today so many ministers, Christians in general, and churches, associations, and Baptists Together, judge success by numbers in the church, that is "successful" mission, Spurgeon cautioned against doing so.

> Do not take an exaggerated view of what the Lord expects of you. He will not blame you for not doing that which is beyond your mental power or physical strength. You are required to be faithful, but you are not bound to be successful.[30]

Returning to the language of instrumentality and means, these were important to The Bristol Tradition and Baptist evangelicals at this time. Hugh Evans stated that "we alſo know he uſually works by means, and ſuch means as are ſuited to the end, and that we may hope therefore to be made uſe of, as inſtruments in his hand, to promote and carry on his great and important deſigns."[31] Similarly, he closed his sermon, *Ministers deſcribed*, stating that as God had raised up fathers in the past who were "ornaments to the church and the world," so he could "and we truſt will raiſe up a succeſſion of wife and able men, who ſhall, as inſtruments in his hand, ſucceſsfully carry on the ſame glorious cauſe in which their predecessors were employed; building up the temple of the Lord . . . ."[32]

Not long before Hugh Evans' death, "whilſt he was ſitting in the Lecture room with many of his pupils about him," his son said that his father, "with tears of joy" in his eyes, was "'happy to ſee theſe young men riſing up'" and he hoped for their "'great and eminent uſefulneſs in the Church of God.'"[33] Similarly, Caleb Evans declared that "it is the higheſt ambition of your Friends and Tutors indulge reſpecting you, to ſee you able, faithful, and ſucceſsful, Miniſters of the New Teſtament; ſo, by uniformly supporting this

---

[28] J.J. Fuller, "Africa. Bimbia," 186.

[29] Hawker, *Life of George Grenfell*, 2–3.

[30] Spurgeon, *Spurgeon: An All Round Ministry*, 214.

[31] H. Evans, *Able Miniſter*, 42 (italics original).

[32] H. Evans, *Ministers deſcribed*, 37.

[33] C. Evans, *Elisha's Exclamation!*, 31.

character, you will moſt effectually ſecure the peace of your own minds and the approbation of God."[34]

Many ministers today give up if they don't see the results they or their church expected, or when the going gets tough—as it will. As Spurgeon stated, we're called to be faithful, not successful as the world understands it.

Again of his father, Caleb Evans spoke how he laboured "in ſeaſon and out of ſeaſon for a long courſe of years" at Broadmead, but also that "his labors were extended far and wide all around him. He had the care of many churches lying upon him, and was indeed ready to ſpend and be ſpent."[35] At Thomas Dunscombe's ordination, Caleb Evans first reminded him that he had "received this miniſtry" from the Lord, who had given him the "abilities for it." He then asked the young man to "Conſider the nature and importance of the ſervice itſelf" to which Christ had called him. He was to "watch for ſouls," to be "an embaſſador for Chriſt, to beſeech poor ſinners, in Chriſt's ſtead, to be reconciled to God, and to build up his people in knowledge, faith, holineſs and comfort unto eternal life." Evans then brought together the themes that lie at the centre of the Baptist understanding of the ministry: calling, service, faithfulness, and the work of the gospel. He continued,

> You not only ſerve a good Maſter, who may well expect you to be willing to ſpend and be ſpent for him; but you are engaged in a good cauſe, the beſt cauſe in the world. You are called upon to be a worker together with God, in the fulfilment of his great purpoſes with reſpect to the ſalvation of ſinners. Your buſineſs is, as an inſtrument in God's hand, to *ſave the ſouls* of them that hear you. Should not then every power and faculty be moſt cheerfully exerted in the fulfilment of a miniſtry ſo important as this? How can your time, how can your talents, your health, yea your very life, be better employed and ſpent than in a ſervice of this nature?[36]

Speaking at the funeral of their friend, James Hartley (1722–80), the minister of the church at Haworth, Yorkshire, William Crabtree (1720–1811), who was the minister at Bradford and close friend of John Fawcett (1740–1817), said that, "As the ſervants and meſſangers of the Moſt High," ministers were to "make full proof of their miniſtry" by their willingness "to ſpend and be ſpent, for the good of immortal souls."[37] Fawcett similarly described John Parker (1726–93), minister of Barnoldswick, as one who loved Jesus "in whoſe ſervice he was willing to ſpend and be ſpent."[38] In 1786, Parker

---

[34] C. Evans, *Address to the Students*, 1:351 (italics original).

[35] C. Evans, *Elisha's Exclamation!*, 35.

[36] C. Evans, *A Charge*, 17–18 (italics original).

[37] Crabtree, "Chriſtian Miniſter's Farewell to his Flock," 89.

[38] Fawcett, "Sketch of the Life and Character of John Parker," 20.

had written to a fellow minister how one Sunday he had preached for over an hour but had been overtaken by "many painful feelings . . . one of my ſhivering fits, and with great laſſitude." He expressed his fears that he would not be able to continue to preach, but professed "I am as willing as ever to ſpend and be ſpent in that ſacred employ."[39] Three years later he wrote to another friend, thanking God for his providence in keeping him and his family safe from some unidentified peril. Feeling his age, he expressed his continued desire "to do good to precious ſouls; and though much weakneſs still attends me, both in mind and body, I find myſelf as willing as ever, to ſpend and be ſpent for the honour of Chriſt, and in earneſt endeavours to win poor ſinners to him . . . ."[40]

John Fawcett Jr wrote a memoir of his father, Dr John Fawcett, first minister at Wainsgate, then, when the church divided into two, at Hebden Bridge. The Wainsgate church was never able to provide adequately for their minister. Nevertheless, "his attachment to them was so deeply fixed, that he concluded, at once, to cast himself on Providence, and live and die with them." In describing his father's commitment, Fawcett Jr said,

> It shows a delicate and solemn sense of the duties of the pastoral office, not to be deserted, except for the most urgent and satisfactory reasons; steadiness of attachment, compassionate regard, and disinterested [selfless] love, where that love perhaps has seldom met with suitable returns.

Such "traits of character" he identified in the Apostle Paul's words in 2 Corinthians 12:15, "'I will very gladly spend and be spent for you; though the more abundantly I love you, the less I be loved.'"[41]

Around 1793, William Ward (1769–1823) was accepted by the BMS to join William Carey and to undertake the printing of the latter's translations of the scriptures. In a letter he wrote to Carey around 1793, Ward declared, "It is in my heart to live and die with you, to spend and be spent with you."[42] The fruitfulness of Carey, Marshman and Ward's labours required just that, coming at great sacrifice. Their supporters back home knew this. In his sermon in support of the BMS, and Carey, Marshman and Ward in particular, Robert Hall Jr focused on the success of all mission work being solely on the Holy Spirit's agency. He believed,

---

[39] Parker, Letter XXXVII, dated 1 November 1786, to the Rev. W.C., in Parker, *Letters to his Friends*, 177.

[40] Parker, Letter XLV, dated 22 December 1789, to Mrs. R., in Parker, *Letters to his Friends*, 190.

[41] Fawcett Jr, *Life, Ministry and Writings of John Fawcett*, 174.

[42] Ward letter to Carey, in J.C. Marshman, *Life and Times of Carey, Marshman, and Ward*, 1:98.

The Divine Being will not frustrate the design his Spirit has excited; he will not cause the holy agitations which have been felt to be in vain; he will not suffer those desires which have been excited in the minds of Carey and others to evaporate without being in some manner fulfilled. Great things have been effected by the instrumentality of those who have gone before us, and we are now employed in the same great work. How many thousands are pouring out their prayers and tears for the spiritual conversion of the heathen! There has been a spiritual movement of divine love whereby many have been rendered willing to spend and be spent, yea, to die for the conversion of the Gentile nations; . . . .[43]

Hugh Evans concluded his *The Able Miniſter* with what is effectively a prayer:

So may we hope, under a divine bleſſing, to ſee religion revive and lift up its drooping head, and the knowledge of God, of Chriſt and divine things, ſpread and cover the face of the earth, as the waters do the bottom of the ſeas. . . . Let us then cheerfully contribute all that is in our power to forward their delightful approach; leaving the event to HIM, of whom, and through whom are all things, and to whom belongs ALL THE GLORY![44]

If I may be more personal, I would like to revisit the ordination sermon Dr Morris West, Principal of Bristol Baptist College from 1972–1987, a sermon on 2 Corinthians 5:17—6:10, which includes the College's New Testament motto, "We are ambassadors for Christ" (2 Cor. 5:20). May I encourage you to record ordination and induction services, and, from time to time, listen back to them, for they are words from God, not just for the moment, but for your or your pastor's ministries. Nearing the end of the sermon, Dr West turned to John Bunyan's *The Pilgrim's Progress* (1678) and the figure of Valiant-for-Truth. At the end of his life, Valiant-for-Truth is called to cross the river, and before he leaves he calls for his friends and addresses them. I'm quoting a slightly longer passage than Dr West did. Valiant-for-Truth says, "I am going to my Father's; and though with great difficulty I have got hither, yet now I do not repent me of all the troubles I have been at to arrive where I am." And this is the passage Doctor quoted, as Valiant-for-Truth bequeaths his possessions to his friends who are to remain. "My sword I give to him that shall succeed me in my pilgrimage, and my courage and skill to him that can get it." But, he continues, "My marks and scars I carry with me, to be a witness for me that I have fought His battles who now will be my rewarder."[45] At the time, 18 March 1989, I had no idea how prophetic these words were,

---

[43] Hall, "Success of Missions depends upon the Agency of the Spirit," 6:242–43.

[44] H. Evans, *Able Miniſter*, 44.

[45] Bunyan, *Pilgrim's Progress*, 317.

for so it has proved to be. Throughout it all, I have not been able to let go of the calling which was confirmed at my ordination in my home church and induction to my first pastorate, and my wife Jackie has joined me in that. Paul's injunction to the Thessalonians has remained with me, "Hold on to the good" (1 Thess 5:21, NRSV "Hold fast to what is good").

Dr West's concluding words are, I believe, appropriate to us all who have received God's call and gifting to serve him and his church in the world, so I am quoting him in full.

> The scars of the ministry are the signs of the faithful minister. You will accept them and you will receive them and, please God, you will bear them, not always bravely—because none of us are always brave—but as best you can, knowing that God is with you and remembering the end of all these quotations: "Take up the cross and follow. Whoever gives up his life for my sake and the gospel's will find it". That is the great paradox of the Christian gospel and also the paradox of the Christian ministry: it is through the scars and the sufferings and through the sacrifice that one really discovers what it is all about. That is why through baptism we are buried with Christ and rise again. Beyond the scars is the whole Christian understanding of life. That is exactly what Paul says autobiographically. We are treated as imposters. Unknown? Well, yes, "yet well known; as dying, and behold we live; as punished, and yet not killed; as sorrowful, yet always rejoicing; as poor, yet making many rich", not in money but in the gospel. "Silver and gold have I none, but what I have I give unto you", said Peter and John to that man at the Beautiful Gate; "rise up and walk". There it is. These last words of [2 Cor. 6] verse 10 sustain me, and part of this autobiography of Paul is mine as well, though in a very pale reflection of his "as having nothing and yet possessing everything".
>
> That is the paradox of ministry. There is no life like it, and there is no other calling that in the end shows a lost world the way home. To that you have been called. Remember, not what I have said, but what the word of God, through the words of St Paul, has tried to say to us today: hold fast to that as you hold fast to Christ, and you will find that you may not have too much as the world judges it, but in fact you have everything to give and in the ministry you will find that you receive more blessing than you ever dreamed was possible, far beyond one's deserving. God bless you and bless us all.[46]

Bibliography

Bunyan, John. *The Pilgrim's Progress*. 1953. Reprint. London: Collins, 1982.
Crabtree, William. "The Chriſtian Miniſter's Farewell to his Flock. A Sermon occasioned by the Death of the Rev. James Hartley, Late of Haworth, Yorkshire." In *Reign of Death*, 40–100. By Fawcett and Crabtree.

---

[46] West, *Baptists Together*, 33–34.

Crisp, Thomas Steffe. *Charity, or Christian Love. A Sermon, delivered as a Monthly Lecture, at the Independent Chapel, Brunswick Square, Bristol, October 12th, 1837.* London: Thomas Ward, 1837.

Crosby, Thomas. *The History of the English Baptists, from The Reformation to the Beginning of the Reign of King George I.* 4 vols; London: For the Editor, 1738–40.

Cross, Anthony R. "The Early Bristol Tradition as a Seedbed for Evangelical Reception among British Baptists, c.1720–1770." In *Pathways and Patterns in History*, 50–77. Edited by Cross, Morden, and Randall.

Cross, Anthony R., Peter J. Morden, and Ian M. Randall, eds. *Pathways and Patterns in History: Essays on Baptists, Evangelicals, and the Modern World in Honour of David Bebbington*. 2015. Reprint. Eugene: Wipf and Stock, 2020.

Evans, Caleb. *An Address to the Students in the Academy at Bristol. April 12, 1770.* In *Baptist Annual Register*, 345–51. By Rippon.

———. "A Charge, &c." In *A Charge and Sermon*, 3–19. By C. Evans and H. Evans.

———. *Elisha's Exclamation! A Sermon, Occaſioned by the Death of The Rev. Hugh Evans, M.A. Who departed this Life, March 28, 1781, In the 69th Year of his Age. Preached at Broadmead, Bristol, April 8, 1781.* Bristol: W. Pine, 1781.

Evans, Caleb, and Hugh Evans. *A Charge and Sermon, delivered at the Ordination of the Rev. Thomas Dunscombe, At Coate, Oxon, Auguſt 4th, 1773, The Charge By Caleb Evans, M.A. The Sermon By Hugh Evans, M.A. Publiſhed at the requeſt of the Church.* Bristol: W. Pine, T. Cadell, M. Ward, &c. and J. Buckland, 1773.

Evans, Hugh. *The Able Miniſter: A Sermon, Preached in Broad-mead, before the Briſtol Education Society, August 18, 1773.* Bristol: W. Pine, T. Cadell, M. Ward, S. Edwards, &c.—and G. Keith, and J. Buckland, 1773.

———. *Miniſters deſcribed, under the Characters of Fathers and Prophets, and their Death improved. A Sermon Preached to the Miniſters and Meſſengers of ſeveral Associated Churches, At Bethesda, near Newport, In the County of Monmouth, The 9th of June, 1773.* Bristol: W. Pine, T. Cadell, M. Ward, S. Edwards, &c.—and G. Keith, and J. Buckland, 1773.

———. "A Sermon, &c." In *A Charge and Sermon*, 21–39. By C. Evans and H. Evans.

Fawcett, John. "A Sketch of the Life and Character of The late Mr. John Parker." In *Letters to his Friends, By the Rev. John Parker*, 3–48. By Parker.

Fawcett, John Jr. *An Account of The Life, Ministry and Writings of the late Rev. John Fawcett, D.D., who was the Minister of the Gospel Fifty-Four Years, First at Wainsgate, and Afterwards at Hebdenbridge, in the Parish of Halifax; Comprehending Many Particulars Relative to The Revival and Progress of Religion in Yorkshire and Lancashire; and Illustrated by Copius Extracts from the Diary of the Deceased, from his Extensive Correspondence, and other Documents.* London: Baldwin, Craddock, and Joy, 1818.

Fawcett, John, and William Crabtree. *The Reign of Death. A Poem. Occafioned by the Deceaſe of the Rev. James Hartley, late of Haworth. By John Fawcett. With a Funeral Sermon On the ſame Occaſion By William Crabtree*. Leeds: For the Authors, 1780.

Fuller, J.G. *The Rise and Progress of Dissent in Bristol; Chiefly in Relation to the Broadmead Church: with Brief Accounts of the Church Meeting in King Street and of the Community of Friends; Including Notices of the Early History of Castle Green, Bridge Street, and Lewin's Mead*. Bristol: Hamilton, Adams, 1840.

Fuller, J.J. "Africa. Bimbia." *Baptist Magazine* 44 (March 1852) 185–86.

Hall, Robert. "The Success of Missions depends upon the Agency of the Spirit [preached at the Baptist Missionary Meeting at Cambridge, October 6, 1819]." In *The Entire Works of the Rev. Robert Hall, M.A. with A Brief Memoir of his Life, and a Critical Estimate of his Character and Writings*, 215–47. Edited by Olinthus Gregory. 6 vols. London: Holdsworth and Ball, 1831–32.

Haymes, Brian, Ruth Gouldbourne and Anthony R. Cross. *On Being the Church: Revisioning Baptist Identity*. Studies in Baptist History and Thought, 21. Milton Keynes: Paternoster, 2008.

Hawker, George. *The Life of George Grenfell: Congo Missionary and Explorer. With Photogravure Portrait, Maps, and Illustrations from Photographs*. London: Religious Tract Society, 1909.

Ivimey, Joseph. *A History of the English Baptists: including an Investigation of the History of Baptism in England from the Earliest Period to which it can be traced to the close of the Seventeenth Century*. 4 vols; London: For the Author, 1811–30.

Marshman, John Clark. *The Life and Times of Carey, Marshman, and Ward: Embracing the History of the Serampore Mission*. 2 vols. London: Longman, Brown, Green, Longmans, & Roberts, 1859.

The Holy Bible: New International Version Inclusive Language Edition. London: Hodder & Stoughton, 1996

Newton, James. *The Good Steward. A Sermon, Preached at Broad-Mead, Bristol, before the Education Society, August 14, 1776*. Bristol: W. Pine, and M. Ward, n.d. [1776].

Parker, John. *Letters to his Friends, By the Rev. John Parker, Late Minister of the Gospel at Wainsgate, In Wadsworth, near Halifax. With a Sketch of his Life and Character*. Leeds: Thomas Wright, 1794.

Pearce, Samuel. "A Sermon, &c," 40–62. In *Duty of Miniſters*. By Ryland and Pearce.

Rippon, John. *The Baptist Annual Register, Including Sketches of the State of Religion among Different Denominations of Good Men at Home and Abroad*. 4 vols; s.l.: s.n., 1790–1802.

Ryland, John. "A Charge, &c," 16–39. In *Duty of Miniſters*. By Ryland and Pearce.

Ryland, John, and Samuel Pearce. *The Duty of Minifters to be nurfing Fathers to the Church; and the Duty of Churches to regard Minifters as the Gift of Chrift: A Charge, delivered by The Rev. John Ryland, D.D. of Briftol; and A Sermon delivered by The Rev. S. Pearce, M.A. of Birmingham; in the Dissenters Meeting-House, Angel-Street, Worcester; at the Ordination of The Rev. W. Belsher, To the Paftorate of the Baptift Church, meeting in Silver-Street, in the Same City: Together with An Introductory Addrefs, By the Rev. G. Osborn, and also Mr. Belfher's Declaration of religious Sentiments.* s.l.: s.n., [1796].

Spurgeon, C.H. *Spurgeon: An All Round Ministry.* s.l.: Banner of Truth Trust, 1960.

West, W.M.S. *Baptists Together: Papers Published in Memory of W.M.S. West, JP, MA, DTheol, Hon LLD, 1922–1999.* Edited by J.H.Y. Briggs and Faith Bowers. Didcot: Baptist Historical Society, 2000.

———. *The Bristol Tradition: Then and Now.* [Bristol: Bristol Baptist College, 1987].

CHAPTER 12

Pastoral Prayer

Brian Haymes

This is an essay about one small aspect of being a Baptist minister. I readily confess that any reader might be forgiven for thinking that the whole exercise is a personal, self-indulgent trip down memory lane. Please believe me when I claim that, in its intention, it is far from that. I make no profession to being an historian, Baptist or of any other kind, but I have read somewhere that among an historian's many important responsibilities is one to combat amnesia. If we are to walk in ways know and to be made known, then we need to know what those ways were, lest in forgetfulness we lose our way. Things do get forgotten, genuine beautiful things. Every new generation of Baptists meets the temptation eventually to believe that their own practises are the norm, especially in matters and ways of worship. We forget and discard what was done in the past, especially if we are keen to see "the inherited church" thrown over in our liturgical freedom. But forgetting our past, the practices we once engaged in as a matter of importance before God, leads to a dangerous loss of identity. It may come as a surprise to a rising generation to learn that it was not always as it is. We quickly get set in our ways and we can become careless about the power our shared culture has over us, shaping our common life, relationships and worship practices. Of course, times do change and so do contexts. New times call for new responses, but my introductory point is that in the responding some important, even essential patterns and practices may be forgotten. I am going to recall something about being a Baptist minister of years ago when I was ordained in 1965 and in this essay I shall, eventually, come to focus on what today probably seems a very incidental detail indeed. I suspect more modern ministers will feel that this is a waste of an opportunity to reflect on our present moving situation and as such I am simply showing my age, trapped as I may be in my past. But I offer it because I believe that deep down something really important has changed and is changing, and not for the better. We have forgotten something that once was important to our identity. So, to set the scene . . . .

British Baptists found themselves after the Second World War with important ecumenical challenges to face. In consequence they produced a significant document of self-explanation. *The Baptist Doctrine of the Church* was approved by the Council of the Baptist Union in March 1948. Since it was a response to an approach by the Church of England to all Free Churches, predictably, the response focussed on the nature and calling of the church, its structure and governance, the ministry, sacraments and the relation of church and state. The document remains, in my judgement, one of the most important theological descriptions of what it is to be a local Baptist church in membership with the denomination in relations with other Christians. Does anyone read it now? It was a good guideline document in the years after the war as we saw healthy growing Baptist churches, sharing gratefully the steady confidence of the nation. Some congregations had never had it so good. However, patterns of social life, convictions about manners, authority, good behaviour in and out of the church were all about to change, but the document remained important and provided clarity as the times were eventually to be described by some as the shaking of foundations, as if two World Wars had not been enough. Two more significant reports helped Baptists of those days in their reflections and practices concerning ministry. First came *The Meaning and Practice of Ordination among Baptists* (1957) and *The Doctrine of the Ministry* (1961).[1]

In the early 1960s there were those, like myself, coming to Baptist colleges (and other colleges) believing themselves "called to ministry." Not that there was then, or ever, an agreed understanding of ministry and ordination. Ruth Gouldbourne is quite correct when she points out that "The question of what a minister is, is a perennial among Baptists."[2] She asserts that we have argued about the role and location of ministers, whether they should be trained and in what, whether they receive ordination or recognition and by whom. We have come near to common agreement that ministers are needed, since they are the gifts of God to enable us to live out our shared ministry as the body of Christ (Eph 4:11–13), but we remain seriously confused as to whether being a minister is a divine vocation, a whole way of living, or being a practitioner of particular functions needing to be done in church. Ruth's lecture of 2010 stands as one of the sanest, theologically thoughtful, experientially realistic and gospel-orientated reflections on ministry by a Baptist in recent years.[3]

In context, Ruth's lecture was delivered during one of the English Baptists' periodic attempts at restructuring our life together. Much discussion had gone on about "ministerial competencies," but because the definition of "ministry" had become so wide the competencies argument became difficult to sustain.

---

[1] The texts of the reports can be found in Hayden, *Baptist Union Documents 1948–1977*, 56–95 and 12–54 respectively.

[2] Gouldbourne, "In Praise of Incompetence," 169.

[3] Ruth first delivered this as the Dr. G.R. Beasley-Murray Memorial Lecture of 2010 at the Baptist Assembly in Plymouth under the title of "In Praise of Incompetence: Ministerial Formation and the Development of a Rooted Person." It later appeared in Wright, ed., *Truth That Never Dies*, 168–84.

More papers followed from those responsible in the Union's life concerning ministry, such as a report under the title of *Ignite* (2015) and more recently *Marks of Ministry* (2020).[4] It is not my present purpose to engage in any study of these documents, their theology, or lack of it, when it comes to ministry, but I do note one quotation from *Marks of Ministry*. In its second paragraph, as it opens up its argument for the need for "ministry" that is now flexible and multi-faceted, it states that "Some ministers will occupy the traditional position of pastor and teacher within a church.[5] Others are evangelists or pioneers working primarily with those outside church membership. Others are children's, youth and families workers. Still others are chaplains in health, education, prison, work, leisure, or the armed forces. With such a breadth of ministry contexts . . . ."[6] As I read this, I recalled my experience of being at South Street Baptist Church, Exeter, in the 1970s. I was the minister, ordained, called by the church, so the members believed in the purposes of God. In the description of the *Marks of Ministry*, I was the pastor and teacher, but it is worth noting that within the membership of the church there were those with the gift of sharing the faith as evangelists, some of them members of the Baptist Student William Knibb Society. Others in membership believed their work as teachers was a calling, a vocation, as they worked both in schools, colleges, homes and the church. One member was a lay chaplain at a local college, another a senior prison officer who helped the church become a community placement for those prisoners on day release. These were some of the people Christ had called together in membership of that particular local church. Together we worked at ways of worship, drawing on past and present resources. What we all did, minister and members, we understood as living out our baptism, that crucial vocation of Christ to all into the life and mission of God. There was one ministry going on in church and world and that was Christ's. That was largely our self-understanding as a church. It was a privilege to be a church member, sharing this calling. This was all a long time ago, of course, pastor and people together in the calling of Christ.

At the time of my ordination, I think it was true to say that being a Baptist minister was fundamentally understood as being a local pastor which is why, for the purposes of this paper, I use the words pastor and minister interchangeably. Indeed, in those years there were rules about not becoming a full-time hospital or university chaplain until you had completed your probationary years in a local pastorate. Mostly, we ministers fulfilled our calling through a local church. At some time we had been introduced to the local church, often by the Area Superintendent, though there were other less

---

[4] See [Jump], *Ignite*; and Ministries Team, *Marks of Ministry*.

[5] This is one of the very few uses of the words "pastor" or "pastoral" in the document.

[6] Ministries Team, *Marks of Ministry*, 2.

public and open ways of seeking a pastorate being employed. You had met the deacons, led worship, preached, met members of the congregation. You were set on following a vocation, more than seeking a job and payment, so you, with the church, sought the will and way of Christ together. A church meeting issued, in the name of Christ, a "call," an invitation to the pastorate. So you came to be inducted.

Let me recall the service of induction of those days, of Superintendents, and Payne and Winward.[7] The order of "The Induction of a Minister" was used at many such services. One of the key questions put to the pastor being inducted was "Do you promise to execute your charge with all fidelity, to preach and teach the word of God from the Holy Scriptures, to lead the congregation in worship and administer the gospel sacraments, to tend the flock of Christ and to do the work of an evangelist?"[8]

That word "charge" always has fascinated me. It was not about being "in charge," but was essentially about responsibilities. At many inductions in the 1960s there were two sermons; a "charge" preached to the pastor and a "charge" to the church. Far from the induction being the joining of a local congregation to their "chaplain" here was the beginning of a new partnership in the gospel, a partnership between the local church, their God-given pastor, God in Trinity who called them to be a people for God's purposes for all people. Christ was putting a congregation into the hand of a pastor to enable them to be more fully the church.

Sometimes a form of words was used that underlined the intensity of what was happening, such as, "Have always therefore printed in your remembrance, how great a trust is committed to your charge. For they are the sheep of Christ, which he bought with his death and for whom he shed his blood."[9] Being a minister in pastoral charge was no light matter. One friend[10] always spoke of the calling, echoing the Apostle, as to "present everyone mature in Christ" (Col 1:28). The pastor, under Christ, had the care of this people. They were not just the church members. Caring for them meant knowing them, in their homes and at their work, having such a relationship that confessions were heard, secrets shared, doubts faced and faith built up. As pastor, you were one of the first to be told when there was good news, or tragedy, or accident and disaster, even if the call came in the middle of the night. Pastor and people, living and growing in the life of trust in God, answering that call to be the church, that important aspect of God's mission to the world, local, national and international.

---

[7] Payne and Winward, *Orders and Prayers for Church Worship*.

[8] Payne and Winward, *Orders and Prayers for Church Worship*, 197–201.

[9] From the liturgy of "Ordering of Priests."

[10] The Rev. David Runcorn of Trinity College, Bristol, with whom I taught Pastoral Theology courses in Bristol.

In this growing developing relationship pastor and people prayed for each other, listened for the word of God together and worshipped. Indeed, leading the people in worship was part of that essential pastoral task. So, the pastor preached, facing the people with the word of God. So, the pastor prayed, facing God and gathering up the longing for the kingdom, the joys and sorrows of the people in the world in prayer. So, the pastor led them as Christ called them to the table, to share communion, that most intense of pastoral tasks. So, the pastor would baptize the living and bury the dead, expressing in this ministry the care and love of God for whoever came the pastor's way. Of all the "positions" offered to Baptists in their denominational life that of being the local pastor is surely the most significant? Or so we once thought and practised.

I want to narrow this pastoral calling down even more in this way. The pastor with the deacons and the whole church, in fact, had responsibility to offer the worship of God. As a people without an agreed prayer book, or agreed doctrinal affirmations, Baptists have always been vulnerable to the whims and ways of strong personalities, eager for their own ways. This "freedom" has been a mixed blessing in history. Good congregations have been reduced to sectarian groups by poor ministry and the opposite is true, some growing very large numerically if not always growing in God. There is an integrity in ministry to which we should always give more attention than we do. It's why the preparation and pastoral care of pastors matters more than we realize. I have often pondered those words of Richard Baxter, "All the churches either rise or fall as the ministry doth rise and fall (not in riches or worldly grandeur) but in knowledge, zeal and ability for their work."[11]

Part of that work of pastoral ministry is the leading of the people in prayer. So, I come closer to my point of focus. I am not thinking in this instance of those hours ministers give to their own prayers for people in their care and beyond. I am thinking of that moment when, in the public worship of God, the pastor gives the invitation, "Let us pray." This leading of the congregation in prayer as part of public worship once was understood to be a crucial responsibility. What I am recalling is something at times quite wonderful, a people, led by the pastor, in prayer to God. Here I call on the support of Charles Haddon Spurgeon (1834–92).

In his *Lectures to my Students*, we can still read some of the teaching given at what was once called The Pastors' College.[12] As early as Lecture IV and *before* he comes to speak about preaching, Spurgeon teaches on "Our Public

---

[11] Baxter, *Reliquiæ Baxterianæ*, part 1:115. Baxter (1615–91) was an English Puritan with sympathy for the tradition of Dissent. One of his most famous and influential books is *The Reformed Pastor* (1656).

[12] The edition I shall be citing is that published in 1977. The series first began in 1875.

Prayer."[13] He clearly sees in any act of the public worship of God elements of praise, proclamation and prayer, and he resists drawing any sharp distinction between preaching and praying. At some point in the worship, the congregation is to be led in prayer to God. For Spurgeon "free prayer" is the way. He is at odds with the Established Church's practice of reading prayers from the official book. He calls for extempore prayer, led by the Spirit, but he knows this is no light matter. He even suggests that liturgies might have been designed because freedom in prayer was abused and slovenly, careless, lifeless talk was offered in worship.[14] He insists with his students that it is a tremendous pastoral responsibility to see that this time of prayer is fitting. We are after all praying *to God*. No vulgarities are to be permitted in choice words before the King.[15] No more is prayer to be reduced to a matter of peremptory demands made on God.[16] We are to remember that we are praying, not talking about praying with the congregation or ourselves.

All of which means that this part of the service of worship must be led by the most spiritually able member. Spurgeon even argued that such an "appointment" is more to be considered than preaching the sermon! He has a long section on language; no cant phrases, no tired repetitions. Spurgeon apologizes to the students for the length of this section of his lecture but he obviously feels the matter deeply. For him, this leading of a congregation to God in prayer was a great privilege. It required a personal deep relationship with God, a loving knowledge of the people and a desire for the coming kingdom, the returning King. So, it comes as no surprise that at the end of the lecture, although he has resisted resorting to reading prayers, he nonetheless lays great stress on preparation. No one should just stand up and pray because this entails being really open to the Spirit's guidance, to being led after a previous time of reflection on congregational and other human needs so that the prayer is not a collection of random thoughts of the moment. The best preparation for public prayer is a life of private prayer. Leading a congregation in prayer is a great matter, not to be taken lightly, casually, and certainly not without fear of the Lord.[17]

Spurgeon taught and ministered in the nineteenth century. I want now to proceed further in reflection on this one aspect of the pastoral calling and its being crucial for the church and shall do so by commenting on three more of those, known as preachers of high effect, each being a controversial blessing to the church. I have made the choice of these three because of the surprising

---

[13] Spurgeon, *Lectures to my Students*, 53–71.

[14] Spurgeon, *Lectures to my Students*, 53–55.

[15] Spurgeon, *Lectures to my Students*, 63 and 66, though cf. 61.

[16] Spurgeon, *Lectures to my Students*, 58.

[17] Spurgeon, *Lectures to my Students*, 59–60.

approach they took to this task of pastoral prayer and the way they stressed the values inherent in this work. All three had considerable pastoral experience of pastoring local churches in the twentieth century.

I begin with an American Baptist, Harry Emerson Fosdick (1878–1969). He is readily acknowledged as one of the most influential preachers of the twentieth century. His name will always be associated with the Riverside Church, New York, with controversy, and in my mind with prayer. He saw himself as one called to preach and teach, to pastor the church of Christ. His preaching has been described as a form of group counselling as he faced up to the need of people in war and peace.[18] He spent hours at the task of preparing sermons. He had pastoral skills used in arranged meetings with those who sought his help. He also maintained a considerable personal correspondence. If he is famed as a preacher he also deserves the title pastor.

The Riverside Church, of which he was the first pastor, is a magnificent cathedral type building in the Gothic style. The sanctuary reflects Chartres Cathedral. Fosdick placed an unashamed emphasis on excellence, in worship, music, and art. In his day and ever since the life of the church has developed in a wide variety of cultural ways. There were huge congregations for the main service, which was well prepared and traditional in its form.

He was controversial because he took sides on divisive issues in the church of his time. Without his knowledge a friend printed and distributed a sermon, preached before the Riverside years, under the title "Shall the Fundamentalists win?"[19] Fosdick engaged seriously with modern thought, science and the arts. He was himself an eirenic person, utterly dedicated to his work of preaching the gospel. He was more drawn into controversy by his courageous facing of the issues of his day. He was a pacifist through two world wars.

He deserves to be remembered for his thoughts and practices of prayer. One justification for this claim is his little book, first published in 1915 entitled *The Meaning of Prayer*.[20] The book was written after a near total breakdown crisis in Fosdick's own life. The form of the text is simple; a biblical passage, a theological reflection, and a prayer. It covers ten weeks if worked at systematically, each week ending with a short essay on the aspect of prayer worked at through the week. It remains a treasure of its kind, a simple, but searching manual of prayer.

However, it is another book, much less well known, to which I want to draw particular attention. Each Sunday in the carefully prepared worship

---

[18] Linn, *Preaching as Counselling*.

[19] Miller, *Harry Emerson Fosdick*, 115–17.

[20] Fosdick called this his most influential book. It was followed by *The Meaning of Faith* (1917) and *The Meaning of Service* (1920), each having wide sales. I secured a hard back copy of *The Meaning of Prayer* as a student and have often turned to its pages.

Fosdick would lead the congregation in the pastoral prayer. He was to retire from the pastorate of Riverside in 1946. In 1959, surprisingly and, as he admits under considerable pressure, he reluctantly published *A Book of Public Prayers*.[21] The contents of the book include some fifty-six written pastoral prayers, eighteen prayers for Christian festivals, and other important days in the Christian year, and thirteen litanies, responses of praise and prayer, all used at some time at Riverside.

Fosdick provided an introduction to the book, offering a justification for what he did and how he did it. He argued that the non-liturgical churches took a bold step when they abandoned the service books and entrusted the task of leading in prayer to the pastors. In Fosdick's judgment on the churches of his day this decision was a point of failure in Free Church worship. He wonders why spontaneity is the test of authenticity. Why is the Spirit assumed to be in the immediate and not in long term preparation, writing and preparation? For Fosdick, there is an art in leading people in worship. It requires preparation, deep thought, always relying on the Spirit. In the pastoral prayer, Fosdick suggests the pastor is trying to phrase the "soul's adoration, thanksgiving, penitence, petitions and intercessions" in such a way that the congregation may be caught up into prayer to God. To undertake this task well requires an awareness of human need, insight into the individual, social and international problems the people have brought with them to worship. All this before God's grace and mercy. Fosdick argues that preparation for such prayer is akin to preparing to preach a sermon.[22]

He reflects on the dangers that can face the Free Church minister. The assumed "needs" of the congregation may, in fact, be very narrow, self-centred and with little awareness of the world, its tragedies and sin. The prayer may be an exercise in generalities. Forgiveness may be asked for but without saying for what in particular. Blessings may be sought, without naming them. Because of lack of thought and preparation the prayers may become jumbled, the language repetitive, full of well-worn clichés, lacking freshness, radiance and challenge. Fosdick wrote this in the middle of the twentieth century. In the early twenty-first century, my experience is that such "free prayer" remains a serious weakness in much Free Church worship. I have been in services of worship devoid of any apparent awareness of what is happening in the world and lacking, in consequence, all prayers of intercession.

Week by week, Fosdick wrote these prayers. They average between 500–700 words in length. They clearly betray careful thought, a progression through aspects of prayer. Fosdick used mainly what could be called a series of "collects." The prayers are full of biblical quotations and evocations. Years

---

[21] Fosdick, *Book of Public Prayers*. One of Fosdick's successors, also published a book of prayers from Riverside, see Campbell, *Where Cross the Crowed*.

[22] Fosdick, *Book of Public Prayers*, 7–9.

later, we can still discern the specific nature of some of the intercessions. Sometimes the form is directly individual. Here, by way of illustration is a quotation from Prayer 21.

> Save us from our narrow interests and cares. Help us to live out our lives in other lives. Knowing that there is no good that comes to each that should not come to all, and no good that may come to all that should not be the care of each, knowing that we are members of one brotherhood, help us when we pray, as the Master said, Our—Our Father, our debts, our trespasses, our daily bread. Help us to take the common needs of every day and lift them up into the great fellowship of the human family. Cast down prejudice and across all barriers that ancient days have built of race, creed, class, and nation grant that our generosity and friendliness may flow to all the sons of men.
>
> Especially we seek thy benediction upon any lives here overthrown in anxiety, fear and sorrow. O God, in the quiet of our silent prayer may the Spirit move among this people and upon stricken hearts lay a healing, cooling hand. Let the fever subside. Let serenity, tranquillity, steadiness and peace come now into some life that sorely needs them. Throw the horizons of thy greatness around us and be our unseen Friend.[23]

When the book was published Fosdick's successor in the pastorate, Robert McCracken, stated that "A great part of the secret that drew worshippers in throngs to The Riverside Church year after year is here uncovered."[24] Fosdick developed a deep pastoral relationship with the congregation, with the people. He knew them. He had skills both as a preacher and pastoral counsellor, skills he constantly worked at and developed through his ministry. In this he cared for the flock of God which was his charge. And the large congregation grew. In many of his other books, notably *The Meaning of Prayer*, *The Meaning of Faith*, and *The Meaning of Service*, he draws on his wide knowledge of the treasury of Christian prayer. He quotes the prayers of others, but as the pastor he carefully wrote the pastoral prayer for the people in his own words. I still recognize an element of surprise in myself as I am faced by this notable preacher who took such care over the prayers.

I cannot resist a word of personal testimony here. For much of my ministry I too wrote the prayers, the pastoral prayer. Fosdick was an inspiring example. Later, when sometimes Sunday morning worship services had been uninspiring and poor in quality, I would take *A Book of Public Prayers* with me into a quiet place and I would read one or two of them. They led me into worship, into the practice of prayer, and they brought me again into the sense of life before and in God.

---

[23] Fosdick, *Book of Public Prayers*, 52–53. I have left the words as Fosdick wrote and prayed them, hence the lack of inclusive language.

[24] Quoted in Miller, *Harry Emerson Fosdick*, 235.

My second choice of a famous preacher is George MacLeod (1895–1991) and he too comes with a surprise in matters of prayer. The word often applied to this courageous controversial creative man is "prophet." He fought in the First World War and for ever after was a pacifist, maintaining a consistent argument against all nuclear weapons. He became a minister of the Church of Scotland and served a notable ministry in Govan, a parish in the poorer part of Glasgow. He was conservative in the content of his faith, but radical in its living. He believed in the doctrine of the incarnation and lived it among his people, refusing the manse for a flat among the people. He rejoiced in the doctrine of the Trinity, holding together, creation and salvation, transcendence and immanence, holy love and holy fear. His name will always be connected with Iona, that bold expression of hope and trust in Christ's longing to renew the church. George McLeod's glorious tumultuous life story is told with critical affection by Ronald Ferguson, a one-time leader of the Iona Community.[25] My particular recalling of this extraordinary inspiring man is because of his prayers.

Having come from a privileged background, educated at Winchester and Oxford, he came to be minister at Govan. One of the first things that struck him was the need to rewrite all his prayers. From the first he had this habit of drafting prayers to be used in worship. The language had to be appropriate to God and the particular people of the congregation. In an amazingly busy pastorate this rewriting was important work. In his own words,

> Let us be under no delusion that in these modern days [1930s]? pastors are expected to dissemble their profession. If they are good at games or can crack a passing joke, that is all well and good. But still what people look for—especially the non-church-goers—are men who are prepared to pray when they visit in their houses . . . .[26]

For all his radical politics, his focus in worship could be described as conservative. God was to be worshipped in holy love and fear. This conviction is best understood in the light of an experience MacLeod had on Easter Day 1933 in Jerusalem. He was there with his father, sharing a holiday after he had come near to breakdown in the Govan pastorate. He went to the early morning service of the Russian Orthodox Church. He was overwhelmed by the proclamation and celebration—*Christ is risen!* He wrote later, "For sheer worship I have never seen anything like it—nor shall see again on earth—we can never touch it in the West—not even Rome could do it. It was the devotional presentation of the New Life, beyond 'Acting' and beyond 'Lesson'—simply worship."[27] The God of Creation and Salvation, Lord of this

---

[25] Ferguson, *George MacLeod*.

[26] Ferguson, *George MacLeod*, 104.

[27] Ferguson, *George MacLeod*, 110.

sacramental world, God of bodies, flesh and blood and spirit was the heart of MacLeod's spirituality, ministry and politics. Christ is risen—all things were made through him and without him was not anything made that was made (John 1:3, RSV). Whatever he had "seen" before, MacLeod now lived with the conviction that the whole earth is full of God's glory![28]

In the National Library of Scotland, among the MacLeod files are folders with papers giving evidence of MacLeod's prayers They are not in any specific order, but they are well worked over. On his ninetieth birthday, the Iona Community published a collection of these prayers. Thirty of them are printed along with some stunning photographs. They appear in polished form, but this can betray the reality in the original folders which suggests that hours went into the shaping of these public prayers. The texts are worked over, new words written in, the order changed. Clearly this was an important aspect of ministry for MacLeod. The prayers reveal deep reverence for the Holy God, an immeasurable compassion for human beings in their need, indeed for all creation. There is evidence of MacLeod's constant prophetic struggle with all forms of injustice and the failure which is war. Ronald Ferguson affirms that "Preparation for Worship has always been, and remains, fundamental for George MacLeod, as all who have shared in leading worship with him will testify. Five hours preparation for a five minute prayer is by no means unusual."[29]

MacLeod's language in the prayers is not literary as if he was consciously trying to impress anyone with his prose. But the language is living, vibrant, engaging, surprising. He knew there was a difference between talking to the people about God in preaching and speaking to and with God in prayer. The vitality expressed the theology, urgent, prophetic, anticipating a different world where God's people had refused to come to terms with unjust economic and social structures, nor had accepted that they will simply have to live with the bomb, but faced the call to repent and follow Christ the Lord. MacLeod loved God and God's people under whatever name they lived. His prayers tell us that. Sometimes the phrases have a startling, courageous character, such as, when he challenges our self-justifying acceptance of the church in its disunity; Presbyterians, Catholics and Anglicans all are identified in their sin,[30] and in the same prayer comes rejoicing at the signs of some, lowly of heart, coming to acknowledge the rule of Christ. MacLeod, with the Iona Community, was unashamedly ecumenical. The prayers rejoice in creation, not just in its beauty, but in its greyness, its storms, its cloud and rain, God in all things, nurturing and caring for the earth. One quotation, striking in its language and imagery, reflects the deep pastoral heart MacLeod showed in Govan and on

---

[28] MacLeod, *Whole Earth Shall Cry Glory*. See the article by Gordon, "Prayer."

[29] MacLeod, *Whole Earth Shall Cry Glory*, 6.

[30] MacLeod, *Whole Earth Shall Cry Glory*, 49–50.

the island with a changing community, all marked by serious human needs. He prayed, "And You are love: uncalculating love. When we kick You in the teeth, Your sole concern in [*sic*] whether we have stubbed our toes."[31] Deeply sacramental, cruciform, christocentric, these are the prayers of a pastor longing for the people, with himself, to grow in trust and service of the trinitarian God, longing for the kingdom, God's will done on earth. To be led in prayer by such a pastor was a rich, sometimes disturbing, blessing. And it too remains a surprise that in the midst of such busyness he took such time to prepare to lead others in prayer.

For my third example, we travel back across the Atlantic Ocean. Reinhold Niebuhr (1892–1971) was one of America's leading theologians for a large part of the twentieth century. US Presidents made reference to the significance of his work in their lives. He taught in the field of social and political ethics, but he thought of himself fundamentally as a preacher and pastor: "we preachers" was the way he would address ministers.

A son of the manse, he began his ministry in 1915 at Bethel Evangelical Church, Detroit, Michigan. This city was undergoing change by industrialization led by Henry Ford. Social and moral developments meant that economic and political injustices were brought to light. What would salvation look like? What would Christian discipleship entail? What was the church called to be? And what of the calling of the pastor? In times of war and social disruption, how was the church to pray? Niebuhr kept a "diary" of reflections on ministry which he eventually published under the title *Leaves from the Notebook of a Tamed Cynic*.[32] These acute penetrating observations on pastoral ministry remain a classic and, of course, they touch on the pastoral prayer.

Nine years into the pastorate and following a summer in Europe, he reflected on worship.[33] He had been struck by liturgy, its beauty and meaning which might be developed within a Free Church tradition like his own, free from Anglican rubrics. Through his life and ministry, Niebuhr grew to appreciate the significance of the church, its worship, the beauty of its liturgy and the sacraments. That all this could become an end in itself, frustrating the gospel, he had no doubt, but the real thing was glorious and essential.

> The idea that a formless service is more spontaneous and therefore more religious than a formal one is disproved in my own experience. Only a very few men have really put me in a mood of prayer by their 'pastoral prayers'. On the

---

[31] MacLeod, *Whole Earth Shall Cry Glory*, 38.

[32] A recent republication of this and other Niebuhr works appears in *Reinhold Niebuhr: Major Works on Religion and Politics*, Edited by Elisabeth Sifton, and published in 2015. See Niebuhr, *Leaves*, 9–133.

[33] Niebuhr, *Leaves*, 47.

other hand, a really beautiful worship service actually gives me a mystic sense of the divine.

Niebuhr went on to be a notable seminary and university teacher, but he never lost an appreciation of the pastoral calling, in spite of the fact that he was sometimes acutely aware of the moral ambiguity it often faced.

> Having both entered and left the parish ministry against my inclinations, I pay tribute to the calling, firm in the conviction that it offers greater opportunities for both moral adventure and social usefulness than any other calling if it is entered with open eyes and a consciousness of the hazards to virtue which lurk in it. I make no apology for being critical of what I love. No one wants a love which is based upon illusions, and there is no reason why we should not love a profession and yet be critical of it.[34]

Given this comment on "the pastoral prayer," why do I still remember Niebuhr in this essay? There are two reasons, the first of which is simply a prayer. Niebuhr is the author of what is called *The Serenity Prayer*. He wrote it in 1943. It has been adopted and adapted by various groups and organizations, notably Alcoholics Anonymous, often wrongly attributed and distorted. Elizabeth Sifton, Niebuhr's daughter, has written a splendid book on the prayer, setting it and the author in the context of its times.[35] The prayer reads

> God, give us grace to accept with serenity the things that cannot be changed, courage to change the things that should be changed, and the wisdom to distinguish the one from the other.[36]

The realism, honesty, verbal astringency of the prayer is obvious. He was asked for the prayer after a service he led at a summer preaching engagement and so it was given to a friend who shared it with others. It is typical of Niebuhr's prayers.

The second reason owes much to Ursula Niebuhr. She came to Union Seminary as an English student with a "first" in Theology from Oxford. She and Reinhold married in 1931. Ursula wanted Reinhold's sermons and especially his prayers to be more available significantly because she feared that in her husband's reputation in the fields of political and social ethics the religious context of his concerns might be overlooked. She knew he was a Christian minister.

So, she began to gather together the scripts of Niebuhr's sermons and prayers with a view to possible publication. She thereby brought to light what

---

[34] Niebuhr, *Leaves*, 7.

[35] Sifton, *Serenity Prayer*.

[36] Sifton, *Serenity Prayer*, 7.

can strike us as a surprise. She asserts in the "Preface" that Niebuhr never wrote out his sermons, but he did write all his prayers.[37] It prompts the question, why this difference? He preached regularly and some of his sermons were recorded electronically or by stenographers. Later they were published and some found their way, via Niebuhr's development, into volumes of "sermonic essays," such as *Beyond Tragedy* which, it may be argued, offers one of the best introductions to Niebuhr's thought. Many of the prayers were written as he led prayers in the daily morning college services.

The thoughtful "Introduction" to the book Ursula wrote is revealing. In it she recognizes Niebuhr's love of preaching, but he had come to believe over the years that the Free Churches he knew and served could become too dependent on the sermon. What happens when it fails? A good liturgy will still carry the worshipper through the whole drama of the faith. The pastoral task of leading, shaping, acceptable worship abides as essential to ministerial calling.[38] Such a pastoral task takes careful preparation, "requires a high measure of discipline. The discipline is necessary because the temptation is to forget and to neglect the basic and common and perennial needs of all men when the prayer is not carefully prepared."[39] Niebuhr was quick to raid the tradition, reading the prayers of the past, even if the words were not used in his prayers. Triviality, superficiality, not taking seriously our own humanity, full of grief and glory, these attitude and convictions drew his direct criticism. Idealism, sentimentality, served up by pastors who like to be liked, who may even have ambitions to be seen at the Royal Court (Amos 7:10–17), were besetting temptations in the liberal and evangelical church he knew. Simple moralism in preaching and teaching he dismissed for its error. There are no pat answers to ultimate questions. Let our prayers respect that and they will have integrity.

In his prayers, creation and redemption are held together, as are disclosure and mystery. Those who shout their certainties about God only reveal their ignorance. "Nothing is more insufferable than a professional holy man in a pulpit who pretends to all the Christian virtues."[40] I have come to share this conviction of Niebuhr:

> The older I grow in the ministry, the more I am impressed by good pastors who do not necessarily specialize in the word of God from the pulpit. That is a hit-

---

[37] Ursula Niebuhr, "Preface" to Niebuhr, *Justice and Mercy*, ix.

[38] One might wonder if the praise band, the singing group, the choir, the drama group, haven't sometimes taken the critical place of the over-blown sermon?

[39] Ursula Niebuhr, "Introduction" to Niebuhr, *Justice and Mercy*, 1–2.

[40] Niebuhr, *Justice and Mercy*, 131. The quotation comes from the final chapter in the book entitled "Hazards and Difficulties of the Christian Ministry," 128–37. It is a humbling and helpful read.

or-miss affair in any event, because it has to deal with the severity and the goodness of God, and you have to distinguish somewhat between those who must be broken before they can be rebuilt, and those who are broken and must be rebuilt; between justice and mercy. That is the pastoral task and only a man of great humility and charity can help all these wandering and confused people. The scattering shot of the pulpit is not nearly as valuable as the pastoral work with individual souls.[41]

These three, Fosdick, MacLeod, and Niebuhr, for all their fame as preachers, clearly took with great care their responsibility of leading people in public prayer, as being pastors. They worked hard at their task, thinking, praying and writing. As ministers of the gospel, they understood that this was a crucial aspect of their calling, leading a congregation, for whom they had accepted pastoral charge under Christ. Their pastoral prayers were labours of love, love for God, for God was always the one to whom the prayer was addressed, love and longing for the kingdom and love for the people they were called to care for in the gospel. Blessed are the people who have such pastors.

Each one of the three were different, not the least in their theologies. That showed in their prayers as a mark of their personal integrity; not that they wrote prayers as theological essays, nor offered streams of consciousness as theological reflections, too full of themselves. But the theological emphases are there. With Fosdick we are in the world of persons, liberty of conscience and the excitement of intellectual discovery. With MacLeod we share the wonder of creation with Christ in all things, not least in the call to seek justice, to love mercy and to walk humbly with God in the sanctuary and the high street. In the prayers of Niebuhr we confront realism, modesty, a world full of grace and glory, the fact of sin and the deep consciousness of how easily we religious folk are able to deceive ourselves. But for all these differences of emphases they are together in their christological focus and trinitarian convictions. All three were ministers of the gospel.

There is something fundamental about God's calling of those God will give as pastors to the congregation. Theirs is a mixed life, involving great joy and costly sorrow. The pastor tries to help this group of individuals become the body of Christ in the world. The calling can take the pastor into realms of glory, of this world transfigured. But it always means a sharing in the sufferings of Christ. Pastors can laugh uproariously. But they can have their hearts broken. And all the time, the care of the people of God entrusted to their charge must go on, sometimes a frustration, sometimes a delight. I have focused in detail upon leading the pastoral prayer, one factor only in the pastoral task. I sense that it may be being downplayed at present among British Baptists in favour of less demanding forms of being ministers—or do I

---

[41] Niebuhr, *Justice and Mercy*, 134.

mean "leaders"? What can compare with the calling to build up the congregation, the local expression of the body of Christ, to be a pastor?

The Apostle Paul offers us a vivid picture of the pastor minister. "We are treated as impostors, and yet are true; as unknown, and yet are well known; as dying, and see—we are alive; as punished, and yet not killed; as sorrowful, yet always rejoicing; as poor, yet making many rich; as having nothing, and yet possessing everything" (2 Cor 6:1–10). The minister embodies the drama of our redemption; the nobody who lives in the public eye, who is assumed to be an imposter but who dares speak the truth, not least the truth the church often does not want to hear. Yet God known in Jesus only ever comes near to us in embodied weak human flesh, vulnerable, despised, open to betraying and being betrayed. The treasure is in earthen vessels.[42] Our calling as pastors is not to be a success in the world, not even to make a name for ourselves in the church, but faithfully to embody and proclaim with the whole church that gift of life that bears the cross and still cries glory because Christ is the hope and salvation of the world.

Now this by way of concluding, a kind of postscript. I have known what it is to be ministered to by Ruth, in college and church. It has been obvious to the worshippers that she has not come with sheaves of paper from which to read to us, but with a prepared mind and heart to share with us and lead us. Simon Perry characterized her intercessory prayers as biblical shrapnel, "incisive, heartfelt, politically engaged and sensitive to the present."[43] To be led in worship by Ruth is to be blessed, to be loved and cared for, to be taken deeper into God. She is a pastor.

One of those who knew her ministry at Bloomsbury offered me this picture of part of the morning service of worship.

> The sermon is preached, the hymn is sung and all are seated. It is Ruth's turn to lead us in prayer. She stands up. She takes a small step forward. Quietly and firmly she says to the congregation, "Let us pray". She folds her hands together, closes her eyes and tilts her head upwards. There is silence. Then she opens her mouth and we together are taken into this extraordinary experience of talking with God.[44]

Bibliography

Baxter, Baxter. *Reliquiæ Baxterianæ*. London: T. Parkhurst, J. Robinson, J. Lawrence, and J. Dunton, 1696.

---

[42] I have long valued the chapter by Neville Clark, "Servants of the Servants of God," especially the final paragraph when he likens the calling of the minister to that of court-jester, 52.

[43] For this quotation, see Derek Murray's chapter in this volume.

[44] Personal information from notes from a confidential conversation.

Campbell, Ernest T. *Where Cross the Crowded Ways*. 1973. Rev. ed. Grand Rapids: Eerdmans. 2005.

Clark, Neville. "Servants of the Servants of God." In *Ministry in Question*, 28–52. Edited by Alec Gilmore. London: Darton, Longman and Todd, 1971.

Ferguson, Ronald. *George MacLeod; Founder of the Iona Community*. London: Collins, 1990.

Fosdick, Harry Emerson. *A Book of Public Prayers*. New York: Harper and Brothers, 1959.

———. *The Meaning of Faith*. Philadelphia: American Baptist Publication Society, 1917.

———. *The Meaning of Prayer*. London: SCM, 1915.

———. *The Meaning of Service*. Philadelphia: Presbyterian Board of Publication and Sabbath School Work, 1920.

Gordon, James. "Prayer: When the 'Whole Thing' Becomes 'the Whole Blessed Thing'—Perspectives on George MacLeod and the Founding of the Iona Community." *Theology in Scotland* 16.1 (2009) 29–38.

Gouldbourne, Ruth M.B. "In Praise of Incompetence: Ministerial Formation and the Development of a Rooted Person." In *Truth That Never Dies. The Dr. G.R. Beasley-Murray Memorial Lectures 2002–2012*, 168–84. Edited by Nigel G. Wright. Eugene: Pickwick, 2015.

Hayden, Roger, *Baptist Union Documents 1948–1977*. London: Baptist Historical Society, 1980.

[Jump, Phil]. *Ignite: Final Report*. Didcot: Baptist Union of Great Britain, 2015.

Linn, Edmund Holt. *Preaching as Counselling: The Unique Method of Harry Emerson Fosdick*. Valley Forge: Judson, 1966.

MacLeod, George F. *The Whole Earth Shall Cry Glory: Iona Prayers by Rev George F. MacLeod*. Iona: Wild Goose Publications, 1985.

Ministries Team. *Marks of Ministry*. Didcot: Baptist Union of Great Britain, 2020.

Miller, Robert Moats. *Harry Emerson Fosdick; Preacher, Pastor, Prophet*. New York: Oxford University Press, 1985.

Niebuhr, Reinhold. *Beyond Tragedy: Essays on the Christian Interpretation of History*. London: Nisbet, 1938.

———. *Justice and Mercy*. Edited by Ursula M. Niebuhr. New York: Harper and Row, 1974.

———. *Major Works on Religion and Politics*. Edited by Elisabeth Sifton. New York: The Library of America, 2015.

"The Ordering of Priests: The Form and Manner of Ordering Priests." In *Book of Common Prayer, The*. https://www.churchofengland.org/prayer-and-worship/worship-texts-and-resources/book-common-prayer/ordaining-and-consecrating-0

Payne, Ernest A. and Winward, Stephen F. *Orders and Prayers for Church Worship: A Manual for Ministers*. London: Carey Kingsgate, 1960.

Sifton, Elisabeth. *The Serenity Prayer: Faith and Politics in Times of Peace and War.* New York: W.W. Norton, 2003.
Spurgeon, Charles Haddon. *Lectures to my Students.* Grand Rapids: Baker Book House, 1977.

CHAPTER 13

"I Have a Vision:"
Assessing the Impact of Martin Luther King Preaching at Bloomsbury Central Baptist Church

Simon Woodman

A significant feature in the defining mythology of Bloomsbury Central Baptist Church is "that Martin Luther King, Jr preached there once." It's mentioned proudly in the church history, and six decades later is still remembered and recounted by people who were there at the time. Newcomers to the church are swiftly inducted into this story, and it is often used as an example of "the kind of church" that Bloomsbury is (or aspires to be). Isabella Sandwell comments on the relationship between preacher and congregation, noting that preachers need "people to hear and respond to the messages they preach . . . if they [are] not just to speak into empty air and in vain."[1] The question, therefore, is to what extent has Dr King's ministry at Bloomsbury affected the later ministry of the church? Bloomsbury historian Faith Bowers tells the story of how his visit impacted the then minister, Howard Williams.

> Some of Williams's finest sermons dealt with matters on people's minds that week, like a mining disaster, the Coal Strike, and the deaths of Steve Biko and Martin Luther King, who had preached to a packed morning congregation at Bloomsbury on 29 October 1961. Dr Williams *remembered* him "being astonished that he could do so without being surrounded by security guards."[2]

The concern for King's safety was not unfounded. *The New York Times* reports his speaking engagement for the next day (30 October) at a meeting in Methodist Central Hall organized by Christian Action, a British group opposed to Apartheid in South Africa. King's hour-long address, "Progress in the Area of Race Relations," was heckled during a minute of silent prayer with shouts of "keep Britain white" and "go back to your own country," with the

---

[1] Lyons and Sandwell, *Delivering the Word*, 2. Throughout quotations follow the original, and isn't to be taken in any way as endorsing gender exclusive language.

[2] Bowers, *Bold Experiment*, 388.

hecklers being escorted from the meeting.[3] His friend and advisor, Stanley D. Levinson, wrote to him a couple of days later commenting,

> I was happy to know you returned safely. The New York Times in a small item reported you were heckled by a small group, and knowing that many of the British bigots are derived from facist [sic] elements, I was concerned about a possible use of violence against you. It was bizarre enough to have you attacked in the North by a Negro; it would be worse to have you injured in England by a hoodlum with a British accent.[4]

Bloomsbury minister, the Welshman, H. Howard Williams, was present for King's address at Central Hall, and afterwards wrote in the *Baptist Times* reflecting, as one preacher on the work of another, on King's oratorical style.

> The words came singing from him with all the sadness and desperate hope of a Negro spiritual. The audience was overwhelmed by this torrent of controlled speech and it must be many a day since the spoken word in this country was given with such power. As I sat and listened I tried to analyse the man's power. It is not simply the speech, for often this becomes clumsy and Dr. King's love for the sonorous word reveals the peril which could lead to the way of the demagogue. English people love to hear their language sound good even when it is murdered. I suspect that Martin Luther King is aware of the danger of intoxication and it is only this and his own humble walk with God which can prevent his powers being spoiled by the flattery of those who value his reputation more than his work. His real power lies in that he speaks for his people. He speaks for justice and righteousness from a situation where those things are often denied. It is the strength of Moses that is in him and it is in the name of the living God that he cries, "Let my people go." But there is also his understanding that God is a loving God and because God is like that, we must be loving too. There is no hate in him and he believes passionately in the power of love to heal and redeem. This is the way of hope for him and the only way for the saving of men.[5]

---

[3] "Britons Taunt Dr. King; Hecklers Ejected During Talk by Anti-Segregationist," *New York Times* 31 October 1961, quoted in Carson and Armstrong, *To Save the Soul of America*, 7:640. See also Anon., "Hecklers Escorted out of Meeting."

[4] Carson and Armstrong, *To Save the Soul of America*, 7:318.

[5] Williams, "This Man Martin Luther King." The analogy with Moses that Williams drew here was echoed in a lecture given by Dr Kenneth Slack, MBE, at Bloomsbury in 1978, as reported in the *Bloomsbury Magazine*: "He could have avoided casting in his lot with the real negro poor against the injustice which, to some extent, all negroes feel in America and, for that matter, in the western world. But, like Moses, he heard and felt the cry, 'Let My people go!'" Bloomsbury Central Baptist Church, "Dr Martin Luther King, Report of a Lecture by Dr Kenneth Slack," 12.

The sermon King delivered at Bloomsbury, "The Three Dimensions of a Complete Life," used the image of the new Jerusalem from the Book of Revelation to call people to a life of equal length, breadth, and height.[6] By his exegesis, a "long" life is one where a person's talents are harnessed and developed to the full, a "broad" life has an outgoing concern for the welfare of others, and a life of "height" intentionally includes God as the pinnacle of a complete life, recognizing that personal and humanitarian concerns are too small without this third dimension. As King himself put it in the sermon,

> This is my faith. And I choose to go on through my days with this faith. I tell you if you catch it, you will be able to rise from the fatigue of despair to the buoyancy of hope (Yes). Love yourself, you are commanded to do that (Well). That is the length of life (Well). Love your neighbor as you love yourself (Oh Yeah), you are commanded to do that. That's the breadth of life (Well, Oh yes). But never forget that there is a first and even greater commandment. Love the Lord thy God with all thy heart (Oh yes), with all thy soul (Yes), and with all thy mind (Yes). That is the height of life. And when you do this, you'll live the complete life. Thank God for John who, centuries ago, out on a lonely obscure island, caught vision of the new Jerusalem. And God grant to those of us who are left to live life, who have kept the vision (Oh yes), and decide to move toward that city of complete life in which the length, and the breadth (Oh yes), and the height are equal (Oh yes, Yes, Amen, My Lord).[7]

This sermon was one which King re-used over many years, having been the first sermon his wife heard him give. She commented in her biography that, "it had a special meaning for me, because it was . . . the first sermon I had ever heard him preach on a Sunday long ago in a little church at Roxbury, Massachusetts."[8] He later delivered the sermon on 24 January 1954 as his "preach with a view" to the pastorate at Dexter Avenue Baptist Church in Montgomery, Alabama; a church he was to serve as pastor until 1960, and from which he organized the Montgomery Bus Boycott of 1955–56.[9] He returned to "The Three Dimensions" for his inaugural sermon at Ebenezer Baptist Church, Atlanta, Georgia, in 1960, where he was to minister

---

[6] The timeline of King's visit to the UK, including the sermon title and place of delivery, can be found in Carson and Armstrong, *To Save the Soul of America*, 7:61.

[7] This is taken from a transcript of King preaching the sermon a year earlier, and includes the congregational responses. King Jr, "Three Dimensions of a Complete Life . . . 1960."

[8] Scott King, *My Life with Martin Luther King*, 6.

[9] For a transcript of this delivery of the sermon, including a scan of the first page of King's handwritten script, see King Jr, "Dimensions of a Complete Life . . . 1954."

alongside his father until his assassination in 1968,[10] and he also delivered it for his Evensong sermon at St Paul's Cathedral in 1964.[11] Comparison of various instances of him delivering the sermon would suggest that he worked from a script, with the more "exegetical" sections earlier in the sermon repeated almost verbatim each time, followed by an "application" section which was more varied, before returning to a set conclusion.[12] Coretta Scott King said of his delivery at St Paul's Cathedral that "as always, Martin took the theme and adapted it to his audience, adding new insights, changing it in accordance with the times and elaborating upon it extemporaneously."[13] Regrettably, no direct record of him preaching at Bloomsbury is known to have survived, but those who were there remember the sermon well. The late Eleanor Bowers wrote a note at the time on the theme of the sermon:

> The vision given to John on Patmos of the new Jerusalem, the city whose dimensions were equal in length, breadth and height, leapt into contemporary terms as he spoke on the three dimensions of a complete life. The length—harnessing and developing given talents to the full; the breadth . . . of outgoing concern for the welfare of others . . . the need to include God as the height in this vision of a complete life—to recognize him in every situation and to realize that personal and humanitarian plans without this third dimension are too small.[14]

---

[10] Martin Luther King Jr. Research and Education Institute, "Ebenezer Baptist Church (Atlanta, Georgia);" and Muir, "Martin Luther King in London, 1964."

[11] There are not many Baptists who have preached at St Paul's Cathedral, but three Bloomsbury ministers are known to have done so: Howard Williams (1958–86) did so in 1969 giving a sermon which echoed King's theme, "Speaking on 'Evangelism Today' at St Paul's in January 1969, he expounded the Gospel as a three-way relationship: not just 'God and me' but 'God, me and my neighbour,'" see Bowers, *Bold Experiment*, 386; Brian Haymes (2000–2005) preached there for a City University Service; and Simon Woodman (2012–) gave the sermon for the Morning Sung Eucharist on the first Sunday in Lent 2017.

[12] An audio recording of King delivering the sermon on 14 January 1962 at Battell Chapel, Yale University, can be found at King Jr, "Dimensions of a Complete Life." Further details relating to this recording can be found at Pacifica Radio Archives, "Dimensions of a Complete Life/Martin Luther King."

[13] Scott King, *My Life with Martin Luther King*, 6. She also compared her experience of the sermon in different locations, 59. "The first time I heard him, he chose 'Three Dimensions of a Complete Life,' the sermon he later gave at St. Paul's in London. Of course, it was somewhat different from the London sermon, not as polished, nor oriented to British understanding. Yet, even in its original form, 'Three Dimensions' was a tremendously inspiring message. I was deeply impressed."

[14] Bowers, *Bold Experiment*, 388.

The definitive version of "The Three Dimensions of the Complete Life" was published at the family's request some years after King's death in *A Gift of Love*, a revision of King's 1963 sermon collection *Strength to Love*.[15] This provides an edited version of the sermon, based on his delivery of it at the New Covenant Baptist Church in Chicago on 9 April 1967. For the 2013 re-release of the volume, the Rev. Dr Raphael Warnock, senior pastor of King's former church, Ebenezer, Atlanta, says of the sermon,

> Herein is the clarion call of a spiritual genius and sober-minded sentinel who insists that we pray with our lips and our feet, and work with our heads, hearts, and hands for the beloved community, faithfully pushing against the tide of what he often called "the triplet evils of racism, materialism and militarism." In a divided world and amid religious and political pronouncements in our public discourse that erroneously divide the self, we still need that message.[16]

Clearly, for King this sermon offered an enduring message which bore repetition throughout his ministry, communicating the essence of his vision for the African-American civil rights movement, so it is perhaps unsurprising that he should have used it for his first preaching engagement in London.

The invitation to preach at Bloomsbury had been issued by Howard Williams only three weeks earlier, with King travelling to London for the weekend to fulfil a variety of other engagements.[17] His timeline for the weekend was fast-paced: having delivered a keynote address at Colombia University on 27 October, he had departing for London arriving at Heathrow on the morning of Saturday 28 October.[18] King went straight from the airport to the London studio of the artist Feliks Topolski, who drew his portrait for use as the title sequence of the special live transmission of the BBC "Face to Face" interview programme on the Sunday afternoon.[19] Topolski later recalled

---

[15] King Jr., *Gift of Love*.

[16] Warnock, "Forword," in King Jr., *Gift of Love*, xiii.

[17] Williams' letter of invitation to King is now in the "Martin Luther King, Jr., Papers, 1954–1968" Archive at Boston University, with a copy at the "Martin Luther King, Jr. Papers Project" at Stanford University. Interestingly, the letter has marginal comments by King, and is tagged "The Three Dimensions of a Complete Life." It has not been possible to obtain a copy of the letter, so we can only speculate as to whether Williams specifically requested this sermon, or whether King noted on the letter the sermon he had chosen for delivery. Williams, "Letter to Martin Luther King, Jr."

[18] The chronology of the visit to London is recorded in Carson and Armstrong, *To Save the Soul of America*, 7:61. A famous photograph of King is of him arriving at Heathrow, and this can be viewed at Getty Images, "Civil Rights Movement—Martin Luther King—Heathrow Airport, London."

[19] A photograph of King in Topolski's studio, talking with Hugh Burnett the producer of "Face to Face," can be viewed at Radio 4 and 4 Extra Blog, "Ten

King's visit, "Martin Luther King arrived in London ... [and] was taken to my house (14 Hanover Terrace), not the studio, went to sleep in Daniel's bed, had lunch with us—and I drew him on until he was fetched. There was plenty of easily flowing simple talk; however, with such a singular anointed gospeller, it never left his apostolic theme." Teresa Topolski, the artist's daughter, also writes of her memory of "a drowsy (just off the plane) Martin Luther King sitting at our kitchen table."[20]

On Sunday morning King preached at Bloomsbury, and afterward went back to the manse for lunch with Howard Williams and his family. Faith Bowers records, "King remembered that his parents had worshipped in Bloomsbury in 1955, and he enjoyed a meal at the manse, feeling 'at home' among four children."[21] Howard Williams's son recalls being told by his parents that, aged fifteen months, he sat on King's lap for a group photograph; however, despite Williams's request at the time to be sent a copy, that photograph has not yet been located.[22] The *Bloomsbury Magazine* for December 1961 records Howard Williams's memory of the event, originally published in the *Baptist Times*,

> He came as a quiet man with a reputation. One might have expected that he would be big, loud and assertive. But he was gentle, quiet in conversation and persuasive in his public speaking. He had been to Britain before but this was the

---

Remarkable Guests from John Freeman's Face to Face." Topolski's drawing of King, along with other "Face to Face" portraits can be viewed at Mike Lynch Cartoons, "Face to Face Portraits by Feliks Topolski."

[20] It seems Feliks Topolski's memory of the occasion may be somewhat conflated, as the full quote states, "Martin Luther King arrived in London on the morning of his late afternoon programme 29th October, 1961, was taken to my house ... ," whereas the evidence from King's official chronology is that he arrived in London on Saturday 28th and went to Topolski's studio to have his portrait drawn, before being recorded by the BBC on the afternoon of the following day. See Abbott and Holder, "11. Martin Luther King (1929–1968)."

[21] Bowers, *Bold Experiment*, 389.

[22] Enquiries with the Press Association and the BBC Photo Archive have revealed some information about the source of the known photographs from that weekend. The picture of King in front of the aircraft arriving at Heathrow is credited to the Press Association, and their practice at that time was to have an "airport photographer" on standby to catch people of note on arrival. The photograph of King in Topolski's studio is one of a series of photographs taken by a BBC photographer, now available through the BBC Picture Archive, which track his time both with Topolski on the Saturday, and in the BBC studio on the Sunday evening. However, the BBC archive does not contain any images of him at either Bloomsbury or the manse. Additionally, there are photographs of King speaking at Westminster Central Hall the next day available at ReportDigital.

first time for him to make public appearances. I am glad to think that his first sermon in this country was given at Bloomsbury. It was all authentic autobiography—"This one thing I know . . . ." He was clearly delighted to recall that his mother and father had worshipped at Bloomsbury when the Baptist World Alliance met at London in 1955.[23]

Sunday evening saw King interviewed by John Freeman, editor of the *New Statesman*, for a live transmission of "Face to Face" on the BBC. The recording of this interview is available from the BBC website, and offers a fascinating insight into King's motivation and concerns at this point in his life.[24] The conversation mostly focusses on King's personal experience of segregation and violence, and, with an eye to the wide viewership afforded by the programme, he is guarded in relating his campaign for equal rights to his personal faith. However, towards the end of the interview he says,

> in the final analysis, even in moments of loneliness, something ultimately came to remind me that this struggle is basically right, because it is a thrust forward to achieve something not just for negro people, but something that will save the whole of mankind, and when I have come to see these things I always felt a sense of cosmic companionship.

It is clear that for King, even when addressing a secular audience, faith is an integral part of his motivation and sustenance for the struggle.

After his broadcast for the BBC, King was recorded for the Granada TV programme "Protest" in an interview with Bill Grundy (whose notoriety was eventually assured by his 1976 interview with the Sex Pistols). The next day, Monday 30 October, King spoke at Methodist Central Hall, Westminster, where he was heckled, and afterwards attended a reception sponsored by the Afro Asia West Indian Community at Africa Unity House. He left London for New York the following day.

It was in the midst of this busy weekend of engagements, at only three weeks' notice, King made time to preach on the new Jerusalem from the Book of Revelation at Bloomsbury Central Baptist Church. It is worth spending some time understanding his exegesis of this text, before turning to its application and impact. Justifying his choice of text, King comments in the sermon,

> For many of us the Book of Revelation is a difficult book, puzzling to decode, and we tend to think of it as something of a great enigma wrapped in mystery, and I guess if you look at the Book of Revelation as a record of actual historical occurrences it is a difficult book shrouded with impenetrable mysteries. But if

---

[23] Bloomsbury Central Baptist Church, "Dr Martin Luther King," 3; and Williams, "This Man Martin Luther King."

[24] BBC, "Face to Face with Martin Luther King, Jr."

you will look beneath the peculiar jargon of vocabulary of the author and [what theologians call] the prevailing [apocalyptic] symbolism, you will see in the Book of Revelation many eternal truths which forever challenge us.[25]

For King, the Book of Revelation does not describe a sequence of events to be played out in the course of human history, but rather offers a symbolic world which speaks to each generation with fresh challenge and insight. This exegetical methodology is exemplified in the way he uses the image of the new Jerusalem. While for many interpreters the new Jerusalem offers an eschatological image, a vision of an idealized and longed-for future, for King it is an image of the church in the here-and-now, and of the individuals that comprise it.

In Revelation 21:9–27, John adopts and adapts Ezekiel's postexilic vision of a restored temple (Ezek 40–44), describing the new Jerusalem as the "bride of the Lamb," depicted as a massive cuboid city inhabited by the children of God. Like the holy of holies in the first temple, the new Jerusalem has a height equal to its length and its width (see 1 Kgs 6:19–20), suggesting that within the christological community, the presence of God is with the people of God, rather than distanced from them in a separated holy place. It is this three-dimensional aspect of the new Jerusalem that gives King his hook for the sermon:

> what John is really saying is this: that life at its best and life as it should be is three-dimensional; it's complete on all sides. So there are three dimensions of any complete life, for which we can certainly give the words of this text: length, breadth, and height.[26]

Within the first few sentences, King deftly moves his congregation away from futurist interpretations of Revelation, offering them instead a memorable "three points" on which he can build the rhetoric of conviction and the challenge to change which will follow. He repeatedly emphasizes the threefold mantra of "length, breadth, and height" through the early part of the sermon, using a variety of synonyms: "inward, outward, and upward," "the individual person, other persons, and the supreme infinite person," all building to his clear challenge, "the complete life is the three-dimensional life."

---

[25] King Jr, "Three Dimensions of a Complete Life ... Pasadena, February 1960." The bracketed additions to this quote are from a separate version of the sermon given later the same year, and are included here to clarify his exegetical methodology. See Martin Luther King Jr, "Three Dimensions of a Complete Life ... Germantown, December 1960."

[26] King Jr, "Three Dimensions of a Complete Life ... Germantown, December 1960," 572.

The exegetical section of the sermon then addresses each of these three in turn, beginning with the "length" of life which for King is "that dimension of life ... in which the individual is concerned with developing his inner powers."[27] King's experience as the community organizer behind the Montgomery Bus Boycott is demonstrated here as he deploys the language of "self-interest."[28] He asserts that "there is such a thing as rational, healthy, and moral self-interest. If an individual is not concerned about himself, he cannot really be concerned about other selves."[29] The bedrock of community organizing is the discovery of a person's self-interest, and King shows that he is adept at marshalling this as the motivation for encouraging individuals to become concerned for the welfare of others. In the seminal work on community organizing from 1946, *Reveille for Radicals*, the Chicago-based sociologist and community organizer Saul Alinsky (1909–72) spoke fearlessly and frequently of harnessing self-interest for the wider cause of radical social transformation:

> The radical with full recognition that many of our people are warped by the kind of society which they are products will realize that in the initial stages of organization he must deal with these qualities of ambition and self-interest as realities. Only a fool would step into a community dominated by materialistic standards and self-interest and begin to preach ideals.[30]

This tactic of appealing to self-interest is evident in the first of King's three points in the sermon. His call to the "length" of life, to a life lived well and with purpose, is compelling and motivating. He spells it out,

> Once we discover what we are made for, what we are called to do in life, we must set out to do it with all of the strength and all of the power that we can muster up ... as something with cosmic significance; no matter how small it happens to be, or no matter how insignificant we tend to feel it is. ... So to carry it to one extreme, if it falls one's lot to be a street sweeper, he should at that moment seek to sweep streets like Michelangelo carved marble, like Rafael painted pictures. He should seek to sweep streets like Beethoven composed the music or like Shakespeare wrote poetry. He should seek to sweep streets so well that all the hosts of heaven and earth will have to pause and say, "Here lived a

---

[27] King Jr, "Three Dimensions of a Complete Life ... Germantown, December 1960," 572.

[28] King trained in Community Organizing along with Rosa Parks at the Highlander Folk School (f.1932). See Highlander Research and Education Center, "Highlander's Mission and Work."

[29] King Jr, "Three Dimensions of a Complete Life ... Germantown, December 1960," 572.

[30] Alinsky, *Reveille*, 107.

great street sweeper, [who] swept [their] job well."³¹ [Have you altered the language in square brackets to be gender inclusive? If so, return to original as you're quoting MLK not correcting him.]

However, Alinsky is clear that discovery of self-interest is only the first step for radicalization of the individual or the community. He says,

> The Radical recognizes that in order to work with people he must first approach them on a basis of common understanding. It is as simple and essential as learning to talk the language of those with whom one is trying to converse. The procedures or tactics that follow from here on should be understood in those terms.³²

Neither does King leave it there: the discovery of a life lived with purpose for the "length" of days that it has available to it is only the starting point. The discovery of self-interest should initiate the discovery of shared responsibility, and this is what King refers to as the "breadth" of life. He asserts that a person without breadth to their life will live a selfish life, love with a utilitarian love, and serve only their own self-interest. But a person who learns to be concerned for the interests of others "can rise above the narrow confines of . . . individualistic concerns to the broader concerns of all humanity."³³ King suggests that the main reason people refrain from taking this active concern for the welfare of others is fear, and he relates this directly to the unwillingness of white people to speak out on the issue of race relations. He says that too many "are concerned merely about the length of life rather than the breadth of life, concerned about their so-called way of life, concerned about perpetuating a preferred economic position, concerned about preserving a sort of political status and power, concerned about preserving a so-called social status."³⁴ In this, again, he echoes Alinsky's analysis of fear as the friend of the oppressive status quo:

> Our democratic way of life is permeated by man's fear of man. The powerful few fear the many, and the many distrust each other. . . . It is difficult to find the faintest flicker of faith in man whether one scours the Democrats from the southern racist poll taxers to their northern corrupt city machines or scrutinizes the decayed reactionaries of the Republicans. On the contrary, it will be found

---

[31] King Jr, "Three Dimensions of a Complete Life . . . Germantown, December 1960," 572–73.

[32] Alinsky, *Reveille*, 108.

[33] King Jr, "Three Dimensions of a Complete Life . . . Germantown, December 1960," 573.

[34] King Jr, "Three Dimensions of a Complete Life . . . Germantown, December 1960," 575.

that with few exceptions all of these leaders, regardless of their party labels or affiliations, share in common a deep fear and suspicion of the masses of people. Let the masses remain inert, unthinking; do not disturb them, do not arouse them; do not get them moving, for if you do you are an agitator, a trouble maker, a Red! You are un-American, you are a Radical![35]

The role of the community organizer, as both Alinsky and King demonstrate it, is to wake people from their fear-induced torpor and rouse them to action, paying the cost if necessary. And for both, nonviolence is key. King asserts that "those of us who have been on the oppressed end of the old order have as much responsibility to be concerned about breadth as anybody else. This is why I believe so firmly in nonviolence."[36] While Alinsky similarly posits that "if Radicals are stormy and fighting on the outside, inside they possess a rare inner peace. It is that tranquility [sic.] that can come only from consistency of conscience and conduct. The first part of the Prayer of St. Francis of Assisi expresses to a large extent the Radical's hopes, aspirations, dreams, and philosophy: *Lord, make me. [sic.] an instrument of Thy peace.*"[37]

An unswerving commitment to nonviolence is one of King's most well-known doctrines (he was awarded the Nobel Peace Prize in 1964), and here in this sermon his nonviolence can be seen to arise directly from his concern for the "breadth" of life. If a person has a genuine concern for the welfare of others, rather than a narrow concern merely for their own self-interest, they will recognize that their self-interest will never be truly served by doing violence to the other. King is not interested in replacing one oppressor with another, but with freeing people of all creeds and colours from the narratives of violence that enslave them. He says,

> This is why I disagree so firmly with any philosophy of black supremacy, for I am absolutely convinced that God is not interested merely in the freedom of black men and brown men and yellow men. But God is interested in the freedom of the whole human race, the creation of a society where all men will live together as brothers and every man will respect the dignity and worth of all human personality. And a doctrine of white supremacy is concerned merely about the length of life, not the breadth of life. So the aim of the Negro [should] never be to defeat or humiliate the white man but to win his friendship and understanding.[38]

---

[35] Alinsky, *Reveille*, 209.

[36] King Jr, "Three Dimensions of a Complete Life ... Germantown, December 1960," 575.

[37] Alinsky, *Reveille*, 25–26 (italics original).

[38] King Jr, "Three Dimensions of a Complete Life ... Germantown, December 1960," 576.

It is this widening of the issue of race relations to include a universal understanding of the common good of humanity, rather than simply focusing on the good of the oppressed black population, that allows King to locate the root of the problem away from any one set of persons. He observes,

> The tension which we face in America today, not so much a tension between black men and white men, but it's a tension between justice and injustice, a struggle between the forces of light and the forces of darkness. And, if there is a victory, it will be a victory not merely for seventeen or eighteen million Negroes. It will be a victory for democracy, a victory for justice, a victory for freedom.[39]

The question then, for King, becomes one of how to motivate not only the oppressed black population, but also the privileged white population to work together, peacefully, in the cause of justice. The problem of privileged lethargy is one that Alinsky wrestled with too, commenting,

> Since there are always at least two sides to every question and all justice on one side involves a certain degree of injustice to the other side, Liberals are hesitant to act. Their opinions are studded with "but on the other hand." Caught on the horns of this dilemma they are paralyzed into immobility.[40]

King's antidote to such lethargy is to appeal not just to a person's social conscience, but to their sense of innate humanity before God. It is noteworthy that King's message in this regard remained consistent whether preaching to a predominantly white congregation in Central London, or to predominantly black congregations in the United States: his call to black nonviolent resistance to white supremacy is matched by his call for white people to rise from their inactivity and join the struggle for equal rights. And it is here that King turns to his third dimension, the "height" to which a person must aspire if they are to live a complete life.

When King's life and contribution are summarized, much is made of his commitment to nonviolence and of his philosophy of equal rights for all, however the religious basis for these is often downplayed. For example, the citation on the Nobel Prize website makes no mention of his ordination to the Baptist ministry, nor of the theological basis for his convictions. Instead, his nonviolence is ascribed to the inspiration of Ghandi, and his life's work is cast in terms of his contribution to the civil rights struggle.[41] It is as if the third dimension that he spoke of in his sermon, and to which aspired in his life, is of little significance to his legacy. King certainly did not see it this way.

---

[39] King Jr, "Three Dimensions of a Complete Life ... Germantown, December 1960," 576.

[40] Alinsky, *Reveille*, 28.

[41] The Nobel Prize, "Martin Luther King Jr. Facts."

We must not stop with length and breadth. There is another dimension. Now some people never get beyond the first two. They are brilliant people, and in many instances they love humanity. They have active social concerns. They stop right there, so they seek to live life without a sky. They live only on the horizontal plane with no real concern for the vertical.[42]

For King, the church could, and should, be the cradle of the movement he was seeking to create; and when it wasn't it betrayed his call for people of faith to live "complete" lives. In a press conference the day after giving his sermon at Bloomsbury, he spoke about the lack of support he had received from white ministers in the southern USA, commenting that, "One of the great tragedies was the fact that the church often stood behind rather than leading the way. It was an echo instead of a voice."[43] Just as the Alabama Bus Boycott was organized from his church in Montgomery, so other churches and communities of faith could inspire social transformation in the cause of justice. However, King was not blind to the complicity of churches in injustice, damningly observing that "the church has too often been that institution that serves to crystallize the patterns of society through often evil patterns. How often in the church have we had a high blood pressure of creeds and an anemia of deeds?"[44] But he remained convinced that if they can recover the third dimension of "height" in their community life together, churches can become the agents of change rather than obstacles to it. It is this recovery of confidence of faith in God which, for King, will be the ultimate source of community transformation. To this end he exhorted his listeners,

> So let us go out with a cultivation of the third dimension, for it can give life new meaning. It can give life new zest, and I can speak of this out of personal experience. Over the last few years, circumstances have made it necessary for me to stand so often amid the surging of life's restless sea. Moments of frustration, the chilly winds of adversity all around, but there was always something deep down within that could keep me going, a strange feeling that you are not alone in this struggle, that the struggle for the good life is a struggle in which the individual has cosmic companionship. For so many times I have been able with my people to walk and never get weary because I am convinced that there is a great camp meeting in the promised land of God's universe. Maybe St.

---

[42] King Jr, "Three Dimensions of a Complete Life ... Germantown, December 1960," 577.

[43] Anon., "Africa's Effect on U.S. Colour Bar," 5.

[44] King Jr, "Three Dimensions of a Complete Life ... Germantown, December 1960," 578.

Augustine was right: we were made for God; we will be restless until we find rest in him.[45]

This focus on the communities and practices of faith as the strength and sustenance for works of selfless struggle in the cause of justice is also at the heart of Alinsky's model of community organizing. He is aware that churches represent organized communities which have the potential to work together for justice, but, like King, he is alert to the capacity of such institutions to oppose change and defend the status quo.[46] Alinsky does not see community transformation occurring primarily through the transformation of individuals, but rather through the transformation of communities. His vision of a People's Organization intentionally embraces churches, along with other civic groups, and he suggests that "it include all of the churches, civic, social, athletic, recreational, labor, nationality, and service organizations."[47]

The Community Organizing networks of twenty-first-century Britain and North America are the direct descendants of the work of early organizers such as Alinsky and King, and draw both methodology and inspiration from them. The North American Industrial Areas Foundation (IAF) was founded by Alinsky in 1940, and describes itself as "the nation's largest and longest-standing network of local faith and community-based organizations ... [working] with thousands of religious congregations, non-profits, civic organizations and unions, in more than sixty-five cities."[48] It's UK Affiliate similarly describes itself: "Citizens UK organises communities to act together for power, social justice and the common good. . . . Our members are schools, churches, mosques, synagogues, parents groups, health practices and other diverse institutions."[49] Bloomsbury Central Baptist Church, where King preached his call to a complete life in 1961, is a founder member of the Westminster Citizens Alliance, part of Citizens UK. Bloomsbury's current minister, Simon Woodman, is on the leadership team for West London Citizens, and observes,

> The context for community organising in Westminster and the West End of London is unusual—many of institutions that might come into membership are attended by people who live most of their lives outside Westminster, people who

---

[45] King Jr, "Three Dimensions of a Complete Life ... Germantown, December 1960," 579.

[46] Alinsky, *Reveille*, 107, notes that "it can be safely assumed that a great many of these agencies will be antagonistic toward the development of a People's Organization."

[47] Alinsky, *Reveille*, 71.

[48] IAF, "Homepage."

[49] Citizens UK, "About Us."

come into the West End for worship, play, or work from elsewhere in London. Yet it is also an area with the potential for organising to have an effect far beyond just the local—with the headquarters of many national organisations, including government itself, literally on our doorstep.[50]

The vision which King presented before Bloomsbury sixty years ago remains part of the mission of the church: a community focused not only on helping individuals to live well, but on fostering a concern for others, a desire to participate non-violently in the transformation of society, and a commitment to doing so in the name of God. As the American philosopher, political activist, and anti-racism campaigner, Cornel West, commented in 2018, "King's radical legacy remains primarily among the awakening youth and militant citizens who choose to be extremists of love, justice, courage and freedom, even if our chances to win are that of a snowball in hell!"[51]

For the fiftieth anniversary of King's assassination in 2018, a special screening took place at Bloomsbury of the rarely seen documentary, "From Montgomery to Memphis."[52] This three-hour film was created in 1970 to mark the second anniversary of his death, and was screened across America for one night only before being withdrawn; despite this, it was nominated for an Academy Award.[53] The screening at Bloomsbury was followed by a panel discussion with leading contributors from a range of backgrounds reflecting on the scope and impact of King's theology and activism.[54] One of the key strands to emerge from the discussion was the relationship between King's faith and his activism, as the following quotes illustrate:[55]

---

[50] Woodman, "Westminster Citizens: Forging a New Alliance."

[51] West, "Martin Luther King Jr Was a Radical."

[52] This event was organized by Tipping Point North South in association with #MLKGlobal. See MLKGlobal, "Screening of 'King, a Filmed Record' at Bloomsbury Baptist Church London." Both video and audio recordings of the post-screening discussion are available from https://youtu.be/wcG1UNwkI6k and https://soundcloud.com/bloomsbury-1/martin-luther-king-legacy-and-relevance-panel-discussion

[53] Kino Lorber Experience Cinema, "King: A Filmed Record."

[54] The contributors to this discussion were Dr David Muir, political scientist and theologian; Dionne Gravesande, corporate lead on ecumenical relations for Christian Aid; Richard Reddie, author, broadcaster, community activist and biographer of Martin Luther King, Jr; Neil Jameson, CBE, UK Founder and Former Executive Director of Citizens UK; Selina Stone, Tutor and Lecturer in Political Theology at St Mellitus College; and Eleasah Louis, academic researcher and facilitator of Black Consciousness and Christian Faith.

[55] All the following quotes are from my transcription of the audio recordings mentioned above in n.52.

I run a programme which is a bridge between churches and people who have left the church, have left Christianity, because they can't see how Jesus and the church speaks to their blackness, speaks to their suffering in Britain, speaks to their racial injustice. . . . It was so powerful to watch such a man [as Martin Luther King] contextualise his blackness through his faith, and through his community.—Eleasah Louis

My interest is about activism and organising within churches, and how we develop a culture of action so that we link our belief in the kingdom of God and our belief in the gospel with what that means in the practice of our ministry, our mission, and in our local communities.—Selina Stone

In terms of the church, Dr King was atypical. You sometimes get the impression that the church in that time was very radical—it wasn't, it was very conservative. And the fact is King ended up leaving the NBC [Northern Baptist Convention] and setting up his own denomination [the Progressive National Baptist Convention in September 1961] because they didn't like the idea of him mixing politics with religion.[56]—Richard Reddie

Dr King brought together what is essentially a human rights agenda but through a faith-based lens. These two things are [not] in conflict: [it is often assumed that] a set of faith based values somehow do not speak to a human rights agenda. Dr King politicises his theology, and so it's not an either/or, it's a both/and; and that hugely inspires me as a Christian, but it also inspires me as an activist.—Dionne Gravesande

A vital part of the whole [civil rights] movement was the church tradition . . . and Martin Luther King and Saul Alinsky have taught us that organising institutions is a quick way of finding organised people. . . . We need to touch the soul, but so often we're afraid to touch the soul in case it's embarrassing.—Neil Jameson

The third dimension from King's sermon, the necessity of active faith for the living of a "complete life," was something that he embodied. It was the source of his activism, because it was the source of his desire to live his life to the best of his ability and in the service of others; and he firmly believed that if others were to join him in his struggle for justice, they too would need to ensure that they lived in the love of God, not neglecting the third dimension of the complete life.

---

[56] For a summary of the conflicts King found himself engaged in within the NBC, see The Martin Luther King Jr. Research and Education Institute, "National Baptist Convention." The King Encyclopedia notes that the founding of PNBC "demonstrated the hostility of the NBC's leadership to the use of nonviolent direct action tactics," the Martin Luther King Jr. Research and Education Institute, "Progressive National Baptist Convention."

Assessing the Impact of Martin Luther King Preaching at Bloomsbury 253

As this analysis of his sermon preached at Bloomsbury draws towards its conclusion, it is worth reflecting on whether this fusion of equal love of self, the other, and God, remains a driving force for social transformation within the church. As a congregation, Bloomsbury has continued to engage in issues of justice and inclusion. For example, it was the first Baptist church in the UK to conduct a same sex wedding in December 2016, and has taken overt (and controversial) decisions of inclusion on issues of gender and sexuality. Bloomsbury is also an active member of West London Citizens, directly aligning itself with the community organizing tradition that inspired both King and Alinsky. The church continues to find ways of engaging the needs of the vulnerable, homeless, and disenfranchised within the city of London, through the activities of its Communities Minister, the Rev. Dawn Cole-Savidge, and through a variety of partnerships with other institutions and charities. Those who comprise the church are also aware of how much there still is to do—the congregation remains predominantly white and middle class, and the challenges of exclusion and injustice are ever before us. Bloomsbury is not yet who Bloomsbury aspires to be. So the call to live equally the three dimensions of a complete life, to embody the fullness of the vision of the church that King drew from his text of the new Jerusalem in the Book of Revelation, remains ever before those who seek to walk in his footsteps.

Perhaps it is fitting that the last word should go to Ruth Gouldbourne who, in her twelve years of ministry at Bloomsbury, continually called the church back to the heart of its faith. Echoing the words of Martin Luther King, she frequently sought to remind the congregation that in the midst of all their activism, all their efforts to bring about a new world, they must learn to live in the love of God, to abide in God, that God may abide in them. The closing words of her final sermon to the church, at the conclusion of her ministry there on 29 April 2018, were as follows:

> If we abide, if we live who we truly are; then fruit will flourish, and the kingdom will be glimpsed, and resurrection will make sense, and we will know what to do, and we will know how to do it. There is a joke among preachers that we all of us have a signature sermon. And for some of us, we not only have a signature sermon, we actually have only one sermon and we dress it up in different words for different passages. Ten thousand thousand are her texts, but all her sermons one. Well it's true, and I probably do have only one sermon, and it's this: "God loves you, get over it, and live as if it's true." The letter of John puts it much better: "God is love, and those who abide in love abide in God, and God abides in them." That is who you are as a church. That is who you are called to be. May

the grace of God incarnate this truth in you, now and for the years to come. Amen.[57]

Bibliography

Abbott and Holder. "11. Martin Luther King (1929–1968)." http://www.abbottandholder-thelist.co.uk/feliks-topol ski-2017/
Anon. "Africa's Effect on U.S. Colour Bar." *The Times* 31 October 1961, 5.
Anon. "Hecklers Escorted out of Meeting." *The Times* 31 October 1961, 13.
Alinsky, Saul. *Reveille for Radicals*. Chicago: University of Chicago Press, 1946.
BBC. "Face to Face with Martin Luther King, Jr." https://www.bbc.co.uk/iplayer/episode/p00lgzyl/face-to-face-martin-luther-king.
Bloomsbury Central Baptist Church. "Dr Martin Luther King." *Bloomsbury Magazine* December 1961, 3.
———. "Dr Martin Luther King, Report of a Lecture on Wednesday Evening 22nd February by Dr Kenneth Slack." *Bloomsbury Magazine* Summer 1978, 12–13.
Bowers, Faith. *A Bold Experiment*. Rev. ed. London: Bloomsbury Central Baptist Church, 2016.
Carson, Clayborne, and Tenisha Armstrong, eds. *To Save the Soul of America, January 1961—August 1962*. Volume 7. The Papers of Martin Luther King, Jr. Oakland: University of California Press, 2014.
Citizens UK. "About Us." https://www.citizensuk.org/about_us
Getty Images, "Civil Rights Movement—Martin Luther King—Heathrow Airport, London."
Highlander Research and Education Center. "Highlander's Mission and Work." https://www.highlandercenter.org/about-us/
IAF. "Homepage." http://www.industrialareasfoundation.org/
King Jr, Martin Luther. "The Dimensions of a Complete Life." https://youtu.be/JlvFpmkAAkM
———. "The Dimensions of a Complete Life, Sermon at Dexter Avenue Baptist Church, Montgomery Alabama, 24 January 1954." Stanford University Martin Luther King Jr. Papers Project. https://stanford.app.box.com/s/pstod2mchrngzrd2zuidbtjho0995umr
———. *A Gift of Love: Sermons from Strength to Love and Other Preachings*. Penguin Modern Classics. Kindle Edition: Penguin Books, 1981.
———. "The Three Dimensions of a Complete Life, Sermon Delivered at the Friendship Baptist Church, Pasadena, California, 28 February 1960."

---

[57] Ruth Gouldbourne preaching at Bloomsbury Central Baptist Church, 29 April 2018. Taken from a transcript made by the author, https://soundcloud.com/bloomsbury-1/2018-04-29-ruth-gouldbourne

http://okra.stanford.edu/transcription/document_images/Vol06Scans/28F eb1960TheThreeDimensionsofaCompleteLife.pdf; http://okra.stanford.ed u/en/permalink/document600228–001

———. "The Three Dimensions of the Complete Life, Delivered at the Unitarian Church of Germantown on 11 December 1960." Stanford University Martin Luther King, Jr. Papers Project. https://king institute.stanford.edu/king-papers/documents/three-dimensionscom plete-life-sermon-delivered-unitarian-church-germantown

Kino Lorber Experience Cinema. "King: A Filmed Record . . . Montgomery to Memphis." https://www.kinolorber.com/film/view/id/1288.

Lyons, William John, and Isabella Sandwell, ed. *Delivering the Word: Preaching and Exegesis in the Western Christian Tradition*. BibleWorld. London: Equinox, 2012.

Martin Luther King Jr. Research and Education Institute, The. "Ebenezer Baptist Church (Atlanta, Georgia)." Stanford University. https://kingin stitute.stanford.edu/encyclopedia/ebenezer-baptist-church-atlanta-georgia

———. "Letter to Martin Luther King, Jr." Stanford University. http://okra.stanford. edu/en/permalink/document611007–000

———. "National Baptist Convention." https://kinginstitute.stanford. edu/encyclopedia/national-baptist-convention-nbc

———. "Progressive National Baptist Convention." https://kinginstitute. stanford.edu/encyclopedia/progressive-national-baptist-convention-pnbc

Nobel Prize, The. "Martin Luther King Jr. Facts." https://www.nobel prize.org/prizes/peace/1964/king/facts/

Mike Lynch Cartoons. "Face to Face Portraits by Feliks Topolski." http:// mikelynchcartoons.blogspot.com/2017/11/face-to-face-portraits-by-feliks. html

MLKGlobal. "Screening of 'King, a Filmed Record' at Bloomsbury Baptist Church London." https://mlkglobal.org/2018/06/28/screening-of-king-a-filmed-record-at-bloomsbury-baptist-church-london/

Muir, Hugh. "Martin Luther King in London, 1964: Reflections on a Landmark Visit." *The Guardian* https://www.theguardian.com/us-news/20 14/dec/02/martin-luther-king-in-london-1964-reflections-on-a-landmark -visit

Pacifica Radio Archives. "The Dimensions of a Complete Life/Martin Luther King." https://www.pacificaradioarchives.org/recording/bb3438

Radio 4 and 4 Extra Blog. "Ten Remarkable Guests from John Freeman's Face to Face." http://www.bbc.co.uk/blogs/radio4/2011/02/face_to_face _john_freeman_and_his_remarkable_guests.html

ReportDigital. https://www.reportdigital.co.uk/archive-photos/1960s/martin-luther-king-westminster-central-hall-1961.html.

Scott King, Coretta. *My Life with Martin Luther King, Jr.* New York: Holt, Rinehart and Winston, 1969.

Warnock, Raphael. "Foreword." In *Gift of Love*, ix–xiii. By King Jr.

West, Cornel. "Martin Luther King Jr Was a Radical. We Must Not Sterilize His Legacy." *The Guardian*. https://www.theguardian.com/commentisfree/2018/apr/04/martin-luther-king-cornel-west-legacy.

Williams, H. Howard. "This Man Martin Luther King." *The Baptist Times* 9 November 1961, 8.

———. "Letter to Martin Luther King, Jr." In Stanford University, The Martin Luther King Jr. Research and Education Institute. http://okra.stanford.edu/en/permalink/document611007–000

Woodman, Simon. "Westminster Citizens: Forging a New Alliance." Citizens UK. https://www.citizensuk.org/westminster_newalliance

CHAPTER 14

Shakespeare and Spirituality

Paul S. Fiddes

A Spirituality of "More Things"

"There are more things in heaven and earth, Horatio / Than are dreamt of in your philosophy."[1] The "more things" which Hamlet urges his friend to consider, are not in some other world, in some other context of being than the one in which we—the audience of the play—are living. Despite the popular use of the text to commend an other-worldly and dualistic spirituality, Hamlet is commending an openness of mind, a willingness to break with accepted dogma in facing the strange and unfamiliar in the *midst* of life. The spirituality we can discern in Shakespeare's work is, in general, the capacity to look beneath the surface of things and to find "an extraordinary world of value."[2] As Ewan Fernie suggests in his collection *Spiritual Shakespeares*, a Shakespearian kind of spirituality is an openness to what is "other," which challenges any making ultimate of materialism and power, and which encourages a "radical materialism" in finding the true values embodied in the physical world.[3]

These are the "more things" or "excess" that we often fail to dream about. In the words of the theologian Jean-Luc Marion, as we explore the phenomena of the world, there is always "more, indeed immeasurably more" to be given to us.[4] But this does not *oppose* the spiritual to the empirical, as some who repeat Hamlet's phrase like to do. While these "more things" can never be reduced to physical existence or exhausted into it, their transcendence is always "immanent," always present in bodies and especially in relations between bodies, imbedded into them, and only *knowable* by means of them. Any actor and playwright who deals in the movement and interaction of bodies on the stage, like Shakespeare, knows this. From a Christian

---

[1] *Hamlet*, 1.1.155–6. All quotations from Shakespeare's plays are from *The Arden Shakespeare, Third Series*.

[2] Fernie, *Spiritual Shakespeares*, 9.

[3] Fernie, *Spiritual Shakespeares*, 8, cf. 8–10.

[4] Marion, *Being Given*, 196–99.

theological point of view, these values beyond superficial appearances are a way of life that comes from participation in a God who is fully relational, and fully committed to physical creation—that is, a triune God. Shakespeare is not as theological as this account of the "more things," but his spirituality is a foundation from which such a theology can be shaped and made.

Shakespeare himself appears to be developing a spirituality which is not closely tied to any particular set of doctrines. In fact, the religious situation of his time gives him special opportunity for developing what I would call a "general spirituality." Historians of the period have recently become inclined to the view that there were blurred boundaries between confessional stances. While theologians of the different parties, and politicians who wished to exploit differences, might make sharp distinctions in belief and church polity, for most ordinary people "their daily experience would have usually led them to understand that they had more in common than not."[5] A good deal of confusion about religious identity must have been prevalent in the pews since in the space of twenty-five years they, or their parents, had experienced a movement from Catholicism to Protestantism, a counter-movement back to Catholicism and then a reversal once again back to a Protestant faith. This was a situation, I suggest, of which Shakespeare could take advantage. I mean that Shakespeare can be quite relaxed about referring to the Bible, Christian doctrine, the liturgy and other ecclesial practices as stuff—and especially a mine of metaphor—for making poetry and drama. He need feel no obligation to draw on this material for any particular polemical purpose. He need not fear that he will be recruited to one camp or another, or claimed by them, on the basis of references he makes. He can thus exploit ambiguities, even muddles in his audiences' minds, to ransack the riches of texts in the interests of nothing but a playful imagination. On this basis, Shakespeare also has a freedom to develop a kind of "general spirituality" devoid of any specific dogma. He is working across open boundaries.

I have chosen this theme with which to honour my good friend Ruth Gouldbourne, and not only because she has herself been engaged in research on the relation between Shakespeare's plays and the Christian liturgy. More widely, in her remarkable blending of academic and pastoral aspects in her ministry, she has always been sensitive to the "more things" that lie at the heart of creation. The variety of essays in this book, written in a tribute to her, bear witness to her humane breadth of interest and her prophetic insight penetrating beneath the surface, and I hope that my own essay will do no less.

---

[5] Kastan, *Will to Believe*, 75; he appeals for support to Marsh, *Popular Religion in Sixteenth-Century England*. Also see Shuger, "Protesting Catholic Puritan," 587–630; White, "The *via media*," 211–30; and Haigh, "Continuity of Catholicism," 176–208.

A Spirituality of Love

As we read Shakespeare's plays, his spirituality becomes concrete in a number of sub-themes, which he constantly supports through an intertextuality with the Bible and other religious texts.[6] First, the priority of love means a challenge to established conventions of society and traditions of culture. For example, in *Anthony and Cleopatra*, Anthony claims an intuitive vision of his love with Cleopatra in Egypt:

> Let Rome in Tiber melt, and the wide arch
> Of the ranged empire fall! Here is my space!
> Kingdoms are clay! Our dungy earth alike
> Feeds beast as man; the nobleness of life
> Is to do thus . . . (1.1.34–8)

Probably drawing on at least two biblical references—the kingdom portrayed as a figure with feet of iron and clay in Daniel 2:42 ("partly strong and partly broken") and the "dung of the earth" in Psalm 83:12—Anthony asserts that his love runs counter to the political values of Rome.[7] A few lines earlier, to the suggestion that any limit could be set to his love, he had claimed, "Then must thou needs find our new heaven, new earth" (1.1.7), echoing Revelation 21:1, "I saw a new heaven and a new earth," and evoking the sense that his love is always characterized by "more" than daily experience. Similarly, Romeo finds in the new world of his intense love for Juliet that the social norms of a feud between two families are of no significance, and turns away Tybalt's insults with the soft answer, "[I] love thee better than thou canst devise."[8] Othello and Desdemona, too, overturn the conventions of white, Venetian society by a love that challenges race and class so strongly that Iago can call it "Foul disproportion; thoughts unnatural,"[9] and even persuade Othello himself, in the throes of jealousy, that this must be the case. It is, in fact, their tragedy that Othello, along with Anthony and Romeo, all fail to hold faithfully to the vision of love they perceive at times, but this failure does not invalidate the supreme value of love in society as Shakespeare presents it.

In *A Midsummer Night's Dream*, Helena celebrates the power of love to contest prevailing conventions:

---

[6] I identify the same elements of spirituality in Fiddes, *"More Things in Heaven and Earth,"* but with different discussion.

[7] So Naseem, *Biblical References*, 644–45, who also tentatively suggests Eccl 3:18–20 for "feeds beast as man" and Eccl 3:12, 13, 22 for "The nobleness of life / Is to do thus."

[8] *Romeo and Juliet*, 3.1.69.

[9] *Othello*, 3.3.237.

> Love looks not with the *eyes*, but with the *mind*,
> and therefore is wing'd Cupid painted blind. (1.1.234–5)

In Renaissance iconography, Cupid was depicted wearing a blindfold, because love's sight does not depend upon the senses;[10] there is a kind of seeing, a kind of perception which transcends the evidence of the senses and reason, and even seems to contradict it at times. Egeus, a prominent citizen of Athens, wants to marry his daughter Hermia to a young man Demetrius, but she is refusing because she is in love with Lysander, who is not favoured by her Father. Egeus requests Duke Theseus to give judgement, that either she must obey him or by the laws of Athens must die. Hermia pleads, "I would my Father look'd but with my eyes" (1.1.56). The Duke replies in similar terms: "Rather your eyes must with his judgement look," but as she cries later to Lysander, "O Hell! to choose love by another's eyes" (1.1.140). It is clear right from the outset that this is a play about seeing properly, which means seeing with the eyes of love and not merely cold reason or social privilege.

Later, the workman Bottom is to mis-quote St Paul hilariously on the subject of seeing. Where the Apostle had written, "eye hath not seen, neither ear hath heard, neither hath come into man's heart [what] God hath prepared for them that love him,"[11] Bottom can only describe the wonder of an enchanted night spent as the lover of the Fairy Queen with the words, "The eye of man hath not *heard*, the ear of man hath not *seen*, man's hand is not able to *taste*, his tongue to conceive, nor his heart to report what my dream was" (4.1.209–12). Bottom is right to think his dream is a deep one. Somehow he feels that the confusions of his dream have had ultimate meaning, if only he could work out what it was. He does not relate his experience of love to God, but Shakespeare knows the whole quotation.

The Merchant of Venice begins with alternative exegeses of a passage in the Book of Genesis describing Jacob's method of breeding sheep and goats (Gen 30:37–43). While Shylock interprets the act of his ancestor as being a multiplication of his assets, Antonio reads the text as narrating a "hazard" to which Jacob exposes himself—and in the background there is the story of Jacob's love for Rachel. These different readings thus set up a contrast in the play between hazarding, or risking all for the sake of love on the one hand, as Antonio does in entering the fatal flesh-bond to raise money for Bassanio's voyage of love, and on the other the calculations of commerce, supported by a legalism by which Shylock insists on the strict letter of his bond. In this dialectic, Shylock is not condemned by the play for his ethnicity, but for an attitude of legalism, of which the Christians are shown to be equally guilty. Nor is the contrast simply between the "old" and the "new" covenant but

---

[10] See Wind, *Pagan Mysteries*, 53 and 80.

[11] 1 Cor 2:9–10. All quotations from the Bible are from the Geneva *Bible and Holy Scriptures*.

between the new covenant of love and the old covenant read *in a certain way*, ignoring its elements of mercy and lovingkindness. The action of the play alternates almost scene by scene between two places—Venice and Belmont, one a place of law and commerce, and the other a setting for the love which challenges those social conventions. If Venice typifies the making of bonds which are sanctioned by law, Belmont is the place in which the bonds of love and marriage are made and consummated. While Shylock insists that "I stand here for law" (4.1.141), Portia declares "I stand for sacrifice" (3.2.57). By this she means in the first place that she is the sacrifice of her father's will, but the word has wider resonances of sacrificial love: as Hamlin suggests, "Shylock and Portia 'stand' for opposed values of Justice versus Mercy."[12]

In the game of three caskets devised by Portia's deceased father, the lead casket containing Portia's portrait and the reward of marriage to her carries the threatening slogan, "who chooseth me, must give and hazard all he hath." Portia assures Bassanio that "if you do love me, you will find me out" (3.2.41), but at the same time she tells him that he must "hazard" and "venture" for her (3.2.2, 10), using terms that occur eighteen times in the play. No source for the play has yet been discovered which links the three caskets story to the wooing of a lady of Belmont;[13] this original move by Shakespeare has enabled him to build a contrast between, on the one side, law, regard for outer appearances and a literal reading of a text, and, on the other side, love, risky self-giving, and a regard for the inner spirit and open meaning of a text. This is the spiritual approach to life that Shakespeare's play commends, and it is the theme that Shakespeare carries through into the climax of the judgement before the Duke of Venice.

A Spirituality of Death

The life which love illuminates must, second, be lived in continual awareness of the boundary of death that awaits us all. Characters, as we have seen, often come to a sense of self-identity as they speak in soliloquies in which they face death. So Macbeth muses,

> To-morrow, and to-morrow, and to-morrow,
> Creeps in this petty pace from day to day,
> To the last syllable of recorded time,
> And all our yesterdays, have lighted fools
> The way to dusty death. Out, out, brief candle.
> Life's but a walking shadow . . . (5.5.19–24)

---

[12] Hamlin, *Bible in Shakespeare*, 107. Similarly, Klause, "Catholic and Protestant," 182.

[13] Brown, *Merchant of Venice*, xxix–xxx, dismisses the theory that a lost play, called *The Jew* (c. 1579), had already combined the caskets story with the plot of *Il Pecorone*.

The inevitable approach of death is sounded in three images woven densely together, as the passing of time is compared to a slow but inexorable treading of feet, to the reading of the pages of a book of words to the last syllable, and finally a funeral procession. Biblical resonances are there in the book of judgement, the dust to which all must return, the snuffing out of a candle and life as a shadow.[14]

Hamlet, drawing on the established association of sleep and death, is troubled by the vague worry "in that sleep what dreams may come." The spiritual gain of remembering death is an awakening of conscience ("conscience does make cowards"),[15] a "self-knowledge" that for the Reformation mind was an awareness of standing before the judgement of God.[16] Hamlet shows considerable uncertainty about what form that judgement might take, if it exists at all, since death is

> The undiscovered country, from whose bourn
> No traveller returns (3.1.78–9)

in order to inform us about it. The non-return has scriptural authority, the assertion that one does not travel back from death's other country being repeated three times in the Book of Job: "Before I go and shall not return, even to the land of darkness and shadow of death" (10:21–2, cf. 16:22, 7:9–10; also Wisdom 2:1).[17] Shakespeare capitalizes on the confusion in the minds of his audience about their destiny after death, arising from the different versions offered by Catholicism and the Reformation. We see this doctrinal hesitation played out in the blurred identity of the ghost: although Hamlet describes death as the land from which there is no return, he is still uncertain about whether the ghost is really the spirit of his dead father, or whether it is the devil assuming the shape of his father in order to trick him into an action—murder—that will damn him eternally:

> The Spirit that I have seen
> May be a de'il [devil], and the de'il hath power
> T'assume a pleasing shape. (2.2.537)

---

[14] For the "last syllable," see Dan 7:10, Rev 20:12. For "dusty death," see Ps 22:15 ("the dust of death"), Gen 3:19 and the Burial Service, "Ashes to ashes, dust to dust." For "out, brief candle," see Job 18:6 ("his candle shall be put out") and Job 21:17. For "walking shadow," see Ps 39:7 (v.6 Geneva *Bible*) "Man walketh in a vain shadow" and the Burial Service "he fleeth as it were a shadow." The Burial Service is in the *Booke of Common Prayer* (1559), U.i–iv.

[15] *Hamlet*, 3.1.65, 82.

[16] Calvin, *Institutes*, 3.19.15; 4.10.3. See Bradbury, "Non-Conformist Conscience?" 32–35.

[17] Sheehan, *Biblical References*, 547–48.

The Catholic doctrine of purgatory would allow the ghost really to be the dead Hamlet (while not ensuring it), but the Protestant denial of purgatory and insistence that a soul goes immediately to either heaven or hell would mean the ghost must be a demonic impersonation. Shakespeare's refusal to endorse either version of the post-mortem state is demonstrated vividly in the scene where Hamlet fails to take the opportunity to kill Claudius when he finds him alone, praying. Hamlet's reasoning is that while he is at prayer, Claudius is in a state of grace: if he killed him while praying, Hamlet thinks, his soul would go straight to heaven. In this extraordinary piece of theological drama, Hamlet's desired revenge on Claudius is motivated by the ghost's lament that he is suffering in the flames of purgatory but can escape for a brief moment in order to speak with him, consistent with a Catholic imagination. But Hamlet appears to be manifesting a Protestant conviction that repentance and faith before death will ensure an *immediate* transit to heaven or hell, since in the Protestant view there *is* no purgatory. In Hamlet's words, Claudius by praying is here and now "*purging* his soul" (3.3.85, italics added). Hamlet's actions seem to require a Catholic belief in purgatory and a Protestant belief in the efficacy of personal repentance simultaneously.

The result of Shakespeare's refusal to commit to a particular doctrinal view of his time leaves death as a greater unknown, and so a more sinister threat to life, than would be the case if one believed in a particular scenario to follow. As Hamlet puts it in a dying pun, "the rest is silence," meaning that no more can be said, but also hinting that in the "rest" of death there is only silence. There is an echo here of Psalm 115:17, "The dead praise not thee, O Lord; neither all they that go down into the silence" (Coverdale).[18]

If it is a mark of Shakespeare's spirituality to live each day under the horizon of death, a third element is made by putting the first two marks together. We must be warned that "All lovers young, all lovers must / Consign to thee and come to dust,"[19] but nevertheless love has the power to overcome death, though *how* can hardly be defined. When Cleopatra exults that "I have immortal longings in me," and defuses the sting of death by comparing it to a "lover's pinch, that hurts and is desired,"[20] and when Romeo seals with his kiss a "dateless bargain to engrossing death,"[21] we believe that even death cannot extinguish love. But there remains a mystery about the way that love outlasts even death, which exceeds any rational explanation.

---

[18] Coverdale's translation of the Psalms in *Booke of Common Prayer*. So Sheehan, *Biblical References*, 563.

[19] *Cymbeline*, 4.2.274.

[20] *Anthony and Cleopatra*, 5.2.279–80, 294–95.

[21] *Romeo and Juliet*, 5.3.115.

We find this dramatized at the end of King Lear, when we are bidden by him to "look" upon a kind of secula *pieta*.[22] In place of Mary holding the dead Jesus in her lap, Lear is holding his dead daughter, Cordelia. In this almost unbearable ending to a tragedy, Lear is a man who has been reduced to zero. Following ironically upon his assertion to Cordelia at the beginning of the play that "nothing will come of nothing," Lear has been stripped bare of all he has, and taken the journey to nothingness. As the Fool tells him early on, "Now thou art an O without a figure," that is, a zero with no number in front of it to give it value: "Thou art nothing" (1.4.183–5). When he finally commands the audience to "look here," he is inviting us to contemplate humanity at its lowest point, "the thing itself (3.4.105)," and the "nothing" is accompanied by two other negatives, "no" and "never;" with the body of Cordelia in his arms, he laments,

> And my poor fool is hanged. No, no, no life!
> Why should a dog, a horse, a rat, have life
> And thou no breath at all? O thou'lt come no more,
> Never, never, never, never, never. (5.3.304–7)

Yet it is open to the audience to think with the Reformers that something can still come of nothing. In Reformation theology, humanity is reduced to nothingness in judgement as a prelude to justification by grace through faith alone, and not by human actions. As Luther puts it, "God destroys all things and makes us out of nothing and *then* justifies us."[23] Calvin writes similarly, commenting on the Pauline text "God . . . who calleth those things which be not, as if they were" (Rom 4:17), that "when we are called by God we arise out of nothing . . . those who are nothing begin by his power to become something."[24] Shakespeare himself does not portray this movement from nothing to "something"—it is a step that only the audience can take for itself—but he does give a hint of what the "something" might be.

For transfusing the nothingness is Cordelia's love for Lear and his for her in the face of death. It is love with no reconciliation to come, no eternal happiness as promised in conventional dogma. This is love in the face of bare mortality; yet humankind reduced to zero can still learn to love. Shakespeare's spirituality is to encourage hope in the potential of the power of love to survive and transform even death, though no details of this conquest can be given. This is the something "more" which the nothingness provokes us to hope for, and which finally proves Lear wrong with his anti-creation dictum, "Nothing will come of nothing." Instead, there are "more things in heaven and earth"

---

[22] So Gardner, *King Lear*, 27–28.

[23] Luther, *Die zweite Disputationen*, 470; cf. Jüngel, "The world as possibility," 107.

[24] Calvin, *Epistles of Paul the Apostle*, 96.

than are dreamed of in his philosophy of strict remuneration. Thus we are presented with the final *pieta* of Lear with Cordelia dead upon his lap. It is a pose of faithful love. This is the "something" that comes of nothing. "My poor fool," says Lear, "look on her lips," and this is not a hopeless delusion that she is breathing, but a command that awakens all the echoes of love songs we have known where lips are the place for the kiss of love.[25]

A Spirituality of Forgiveness and Mercy

This life, limited by death and yet unlimited by love, is morally frail and marred by errors, so that mutual forgiveness is essential in living together. This fourth element of spirituality is reinforced by many echoes in Shakespeare of the phrase in the Lord's Prayer, which in the Prayer Book version runs, "Forgive us our trespasses as we forgive them that trespass against us." Laertes with his dying breath asks Hamlet to "exchange forgiveness" with him, and similarly the dying Edmund in *King Lear* offers forgiveness to Edgar before Edgar asks him to "exchange charity."[26] The condemned Buckingham tells Sir Thomas Lovell that "I as free forgive you / As I would be forgiven," in a passage from *Henry VIII* that has been argued to be Shakespeare's composition.[27] The word "mercy" can carry the sense, like forgiveness, of a restoring of personal relations, and reference is made to the same petition of the Lord's Prayer when Portia first asks Shylock, "how shalt thou hope for mercy, rend'ring none?" (4.1.88) and then urges him,

> . . . therefore Jew,
> Though justice be thy plea, consider this,
> That in the course of justice, none of us
> Should see salvation: we do pray for mercy,
> *And that same prayer*, doth teach us all to render
> The deeds of mercy . . . (4.1.193–8, italics added.)

As well as reference to the petition of forgiveness from the Lord's Prayer, Portia is paraphrasing St Paul on the nature of justification by grace and condemnation by the law (Rom 3:20–21), but it is consistent with Shakespeare's "general spirituality" that there is no explicit mention of the Christian story of the cross of Jesus. This is apt, because *both* Christian and Jewish believers can be urged to read their scriptures as witness to a God of grace and not a God of strict legalism.

---

[25] Cf. Knight, *Wheel of Fire*, 176.

[26] *Hamlet*, 5.2.313; and *King Lear*, 5.3.164.

[27] *Henry VIII*, 2.1.82–3. See McMullan, *King Henry VIII*, 266n.

Other plays add more layers to this essential element of forgiveness in human life, and again it is built on reference to the biblical text and Christian ideas, but is generalized into a wider spirituality. Forgiveness becomes an overt theme in the "Last Romances," and in *The Winter's Tale* it is presented as no instant matter but as a long and painful process for both the one who forgives and the one who is forgiven. After sixteen years of Leontes' daily act of repentance for causing the death of his son and, as he thinks, his daughter and his queen, his courtiers are anxious to assure him of divine forgiveness:

> Sir, you have done enough, and have performed
> A saint-like sorrow. No fault could you make
> Which you have not redeemed; indeed paid down
> More penitence than done trespass. At the last
> Do as the heavens have done, forget your evil;
> With them, forgive yourself. (5.1.1–6)

There are several resonances in this speech to both the Prayer Book and scripture, in the words "penitence," "forget," and the forgiveness of heaven.[28] The Absolution in Morning Prayer gives the minister the authority "To declare and pronounce to his people being *penitent*, the absolution and remission of their sins . . . ," and the first opening sentence of the service offers the promise "At what time soeuer a sinner doth repent him of his sinne from the bottom of his heart; I will put all his wickednesse out of my *remembrance*, saith the Lord." This is a quotation from Ezekiel 18:21–3, and similar is Jeremiah 31:34, "I will forgive their inequity, and will *remember* their sins no more." However, Leontes is not satisfied with these assurances, and, prompted by the remorseless Paulina, cannot simply "forget." In this Leontes is truer to the intent of scripture than those who simply quote it to him. The Hebrew word for "remember" (*zakar*) can also mean "to act," so that God is promising not to act as the sin deserves. The point is that God does not "remember" in the sense of holding sin against human beings, bringing it up against them, or carrying out penalties. Shakespeare himself is probably reacting to the text intuitively, when he dramatizes here the fact that forgiveness cannot be an easy matter of forgetting. Neither for Shakespeare, nor for scripture, does it have the nature of a transaction ("paid down")—so much forgiveness for so much repentance—as his courtiers suppose. Love, as we have learnt from *The Merchant of Venice* and *King Lear*, is not a matter of commerce.

The theological idea of the forgiveness of "heaven" is thus generalized into a painful human journey of forgiveness, in which both the offender and the person hurt must face the truth and enter into the feelings of the other. This is

---

[28] See Sheehan, *Biblical References*, 731–2. Cf. *King Lear* 5.1.77, "forget and forgive."

portrayed in the scene where Hermione's supposed statue stirs gradually into life, matching the long process of sixteen years' repentance by Leontes. Not strictly a resurrection, it is a renewal of life, celebrated in the play through the symbol of "Great Creating Nature," and the renewal comes through forgiveness requiring time and memory. Before the climactic event, Paulina conjures up the image of Hermione as a ghost, bidding "remember mine [my eyes],"[29] and Leontes recognizes that Paulina has always held "the memory of Hermione . . . in honour."[30] While the restored Hermione embraces Leontes, she speaks to her daughter, but not yet to him. Time will be needed for the journey of forgiveness to find its destination, which Leontes himself acknowledges by calling for a period when each can tell her or his story to the other:

> Lead us from hence, where we may leisurely
> Each one demand and answer to his part
> Performed in this wide gap of time since first
> We were dissevered. (*Winter's Tale* 5.2.152–55.)

If the "dissevering" is to be overcome in forgiveness, there must be a "leisurely" process of retrieving, with mutual sympathy, what has been done during the passing of long time.

The Tempest shows us another aspect of forgiveness, that the one who wants to forgive will always be vulnerable to the freedom of the other to respond or not. Shakespeare builds up the sense of Prospero as a man in total control of all outward circumstances on his island, using a series of images which effectively compare Prospero's power over nature with Christ's, as reported in the Gospels. Prospero, for instance, claims that "graves at my command / Have waked their sleepers, ope'd, and let 'em forth / By my so potent art (5.1.48–50). While the influence of Medea's speech in Ovid's *Metamorphoses*, book 7, is frequently noted here, the stronger resonance is surely with the passage in the Fourth Gospel about the raising of Lazarus from the tomb, when Jesus commands "Come forth!" (John 11:43)—compare here, "let 'em forth." Similar is John 5:25–29, where Christ claims, "the hour shall come in the which all that are in the graves, shall hear his voice. And they shall come forth . . . ." Like Christ in this passage, Prospero also has his "hour" for judgement: "At this hour," he exults, "lies at my mercy all my enemies" (4.1.262). Sebastian associates Prospero with Christ when he exclaims, "The devil speaks in him" (5.1.128), recalling the Pharisees' accusation that Jesus "has a demon."[31] Prospero is not a "Christ-figure": echoes from the Gospels

---

[29] *Winter's Tale*, 5.1.67.

[30] *Winter's Tale* 5.1.50–51.

[31] Luke 11:18; John 7:20, 8:48, 8:52 and 10:20.

are invoked simply to underline his sovereignty over natural forces. Yet this power for Prospero does not extend to being able to compel his enemies to accept the forgiveness which he freely offers towards the end of the play.

Prospero resolves that "the rarer action is / In virtue than in vengeance" (5.1.25–32), the "virtue" here being forgiveness or mercy,[32] and shortly Prospero is to say clearly, "I do forgive thee, / Unnatural though thou art" (78–99). Nevertheless, two of the three nobles implicated in the ousting of Prospero from his dukedom, to whom this forgiveness is extended, appear to reject it. This continuing hostility, together with Prospero's general sense of the hazards of existence once he has renounced his magic and left the little globe of his island, underlines his vulnerability which has been exposed. Shakespeare makes the audience realize its own vulnerability too, facing the tempest of existence, recognizing "the baseless fabric of this vision," and knowing that "we are such stuff / As dreams are made on" (4.1.151–7).

We feel the weakness of our human situation with Prospero as, remarkably, he retains his dramatic identity in the epilogue, asking for our prayers to assist him back to Milan now his "charms are all o'erthrown." Thus the boundaries between theatre and life dissolve. In the light of our own human crisis, we hear once again the Gospel prayer to forgive as we are forgiven: "As you from crimes would pardon'd be, / Let your indulgence set me free." For hearers who envisage Christ only as a world-sovereign, the reduction of even his lesser image Prospero to a beggar is shocking. Shakespeare's general spirituality would seem to conflict with a theology which promises power. But those who understand the "folly" of God in the cross (1 Cor 1:23) will recall that, announcing forgiveness of sins unconditionally, Christ made himself vulnerable to human hostility. Echoing scripture, Shakespeare is creating a general spirituality in which the weakness of human nature makes forgiveness essential, while that very nature is made still more fragile by forgiveness itself.

The practice of reciprocal forgiveness thus has an intertextuality with phrases from the Bible, although it does not require any dogmatic belief in the mercy of God. This is also the case with a fifth element of Shakespeare's spirituality, which takes up the more forensic dimension of "mercy." The imperfections of human *justice* mean that mercy will always be required. The play that most extensively explores this theme is *Measure for Measure*, where Isabella goes to Angelo to plead for her brother's life, condemned by a harsh law that makes sexual relations outside marriage a capital offence, but finds Angelo obdurate. To his blunt statement, "Your brother is a forfeit of the law" (2.2.75), she responds with the most explicit reference to the atonement in Christ, the "remedy" that God "found out":

> Alas, alas!
> Why, all the souls that were, were forfeit once,

---

[32] So Vaughan and Vaughan, *The Tempest*, 286.

> And He that might the vantage best have took
> Found out the remedy. How would you be
> If He, which is the top of judgement, should
> But judge you as you are? O, think on that,
> And mercy then will breathe within your lips,
> Like man new made. (2.2.73–8)

This speech is full of echoes from Paul's Letter to the Romans, with its promise of a new humanity ("man new made") and yet also its realistic psychology of a continuing struggle between the old man and the new man, a conflict between the old Adam and the man in Christ (Rom 7:14–25).[33] "what I would, that do I not; but what I hate, that I do," confesses Paul, and it was a fundamental tenet of Reformation thought that the new man was "at the same time justified and a sinner" (*simul justus et peccator*). Angelo, however, fails to recognize his own frailty and sinfulness, and stands under Paul's accusation, "in that thou judgest another, thou condemnest thy self: for thou that judgest, doest the same things" (Rom 2:1, Geneva).

The values held by Isabella ("More than our brother is our chastity," 2.4.184) make this what has been called "a problem play."[34] But the whole situation of applying law and justice in a fallen world is a "problem" of conflicting values that has no neat solution. What *is* the "*lawful mercy*" to which Isabella appeals? (2.4.112). There is no easy resolution. There is thus in this play no *direct* application to human law-making of the act of pardon shown by God in the cross of Christ, despite attempts by critics and theologians to make the play an allegory of atonement,[35] with the Duke as a symbol for God or Christ.[36] In the quotation above, there is the clearest reference to God's initiative in atonement in any Shakespearean text ("He ... found out the remedy") and many biblical texts that deal with human fallenness and redemption are intertexts (in Romans alone, 3:23–25, 6:23, 5:8–10). Nevertheless, the spiritual principle that no human law can be absolute, that mercy is essential, and so a merciful character needs to be developed, emerges without any need for doctrine. The image of God as

---

[33] So Berman, "Shakespeare and the Law," 142–43 and 145–46.

[34] Schanzer, *Problem Plays of Shakespeare*, 100; cf. Muir, *Shakespeare's Comic Sequence*, 136–37. But Schafer, *Theatre and Christianity*, 19, insists that "within [a] layered religious context, Isabella embarks on a staggering spiritual journey."

[35] Coghill, "Comic Form in *Measure for Measure*," 14–27. Nuttall, *Shakespeare the Thinker*, 262–76, finds an allegory of substitutionary atonement, but a "gnostic" version in which the appeased Father (the Duke) is an evil creator.

[36] Knight, *Wheel of Fire*, 82–96. But Shuger, *Political Theologies*, 54, points out that language of divinity (5.1.364–68) refers to the Duke's status as a sacral ruler, and Groves, *Texts and Traditions*, 155–57, finds deliberate reference to James I.

supreme Judge need not be explicitly invoked to urge the tempering of law by mercy.

A Spirituality of Authority

Just as no human law can be absolute, nor can any political or even monarchical authority. A sixth spiritual principle we can discern is that values of living together in community outweigh the right of a ruler to exert power when he or she is abusing power to the detriment of society as a whole. With an Elizabethan view of the created world, Shakespeare was, in principle, horrified at the consequences that flow from loss of order in the concentric circles of personal life, society and cosmos, and he sees disorder in any one of these spheres as having a consequent effect on the other. A kind of definition of order is offered by Ulysses in *Troilus and Cressida* under the label of "degree":

> O, when degree is shaked,
> Which is the ladder to all high designs,
> The enterprise is sick . . .
> Take but degree away, untune that string,
> and mark what discord follows . . .
>   The bounded waters
> Should lift their bosoms higher than the shores . . .
> And the rude son should strike his father dead. (1.3.101–15)

Ulysses' speech on degree has in fact an intertextual relation to at least two of the homilies from the Book of Homilies.[37] The Homily "Concerning Good Order, and Obedience to Rulers and Magistrates" links "perfect ordre" in "heaven, the earth, and waters" to Kings and Princes "in all good and necessary ordre,"[38] just as Ulysses conjoins "crowns and sceptres" with "the bounded waters," and the exclamation "Take but degree away" echoes the Homily's "Take away . . . ordre . . . there must nedes folowe all mischief."[39] Ulysses warns that degree lost "the rude son should strike his father dead," echoing The Homily "Against Disobedience and Will-full Rebellion" with its warning "the brother to seeke, and often to worke the death of his brother, the sonne of the father, the father to seeke or procure the death of his sons."[40]

---

[37] See Shaheen, *Biblical References*, 567.

[38] *Homilies I*, R.iii/3.

[39] *Homilies I*, R.iii/4, "Take awaye Kynges, Princes, Rulers, Magistrates, Iudges, and suche states of Gods ordre."

[40] *Homilies II*, 580.

Shakespeare is, then, in favour of order, but he seems sensitive to what *true* order might actually be, and does not *inevitably* equate it with the established order of the existing hierarchy. In listening to Ulysses' speech we must not forget that this character is portrayed by Shakespeare as unscrupulously using his rhetoric to manipulate his superiors and to goad the reluctant Achilles into action. We glean from the plays the message that no human order is absolute, and that injustice can be resisted, even in a consecrated monarch. Shakespeare has an ambivalent, even ironic, approach to order, and in echoing the notion of order in the Prayer Book he thus touches not only state power but also church authority.

In *Richard II*, for example, Richard claims an exaggerated version of the divine right of kings, insisting that

> Not all the water in the rough rude sea
> Can wash the balm off from an anointed king;
> The breath of worldly men cannot depose
> The deputy elected by the Lord.
> For every man that Bolingbroke hath pressed
> To lift shrewd steel against our golden crown,
> God for His Richard hath in heavenly pay
> A glorious angel. Then if angels fight,
> Weak men must fall, for heaven still guards the right. (3.2.54–62)

These lines begin with scriptural and theological resonances that appear to support Richard's viewpoint. The Hebrew Bible often uses the phrase "the Lord's anointed" of the Davidic kingship, and the office of David was transferred to the English king in the Anglican theology of the period, by, for example, Richard Hooker.[41] Romans 13:4 refers to the ruler as the "minister of God," a term used in parallel with "deputy" by John of Gaunt in 1.2.38–41, who articulates the typical Tudor doctrine of unconditional obedience to the sovereign. Even if, he declares, the "deputy anointed in His sight" has done wrong, "Let heaven revenge, for I may never lift / An angry arm against his minister." This echoes the homily "An Exhortation to Good Order and Obedience," which warns that even in the case of wicked rulers and magistrates "we may not in any wyse withstand violently, or rebel agaynst rulers, or make any insurrection ... agaynst the anoynted of the Lorde ... referring the iudgement of our cause onely to God."[42] Richard, significantly, appeals to the case of Christ in order to underline this dogma. Asserting, that as anointed king, he would be guarded by angels, he recalls the promise in

---

[41] Hooker, *Laws of Ecclesiastical Polity*, 2: 6.1.3–4 (237); 7.6.7 (354); 7.15.6 (410); 8.1.1 (483).

[42] *Homilies I*, T.i/1. The proof-text for the instruction is Rom 13, "the powers that be, be ordeyned of God," *Homilies I*, S.ii/1.

Psalm 91:11, "he shall give his angels charge over thee: to keep thee in all thy ways," and evokes Christ's own claim that if he prayed to God his Father, God would "cause to stand by me more than twelve legions of Angels" (Matt 26:53).

But it is Richard's implicit comparison of himself with Christ that makes us suspect that the whole speech is a falsely based confidence. While Christ's words appear to be the supreme instance of the Lord's anointed, the Messiah, guarded by angels, according to the Gospel text Christ actually *refused* the aid of angels to keep him from harm. When Peter in the garden of Gethsemane draws a sword to defend Jesus, and Jesus asks, "Thinkest thou, that I can not now pray to my Father; and he will give me more then twelve legions of Angels?" (Matt 26:53), the point is that he is *not* going to do so and so Peter also should not use violence on his behalf.

Richard in fact has given away his identity as a true king. By leasing out the land of England to pay for his wars, he has become—as the dying Gaunt declares—"Landlord of England . . . not king." No wonder that in his passion story, desposed by Bolingbroke, Richard confesses that "[I] know not now what name to call myself" (4.1.259). He has, in effect, disqualified himself, and here Shakespeare seems to have approximated to Calvin's exegesis of Romans 13 in the final section of the *Institutes*, where he argues that disobedience against rulers is allowed if they cease to act as God's minister.[43] But Shakespeare's "spirituality of authority" does not need this dogmatic basis. In the ambiguities of Richard's deposition the health and well-being of the community take precedence over any doctrinal view of God-given rights of rulers, as is demonstrated by the allegory of the garden, "our commonwealth" (3.4.35). The gardeners lament that the land is "full of weeds, her fairest flowers choked up, / Her fruit trees all unpruned, her hedges ruined" (3.4.44–45), echoing the prophetic lament over the people of Israel as a ruined vineyard (Isa 5:1–6). The garden episode features two Adams—the gardener who faithfully tends the commonwealth, and the Adam who has proudly asserted his right to power and whose fall is presaged (3.4.72–78).

In *Richard II*, scripture is used both to illustrate and to deconstruct Richard's claim to be a sacral person in the image of Christ himself. In *King John* it is used to support the transfer of sacral kingship from John to another claimant altogether—the young Arthur. John has disabled himself from kingship by pursing the idol of "commodity," or self-interest. In opposition to Shakespeare's sources for the play, which compare John to Christ,[44] christological imagery is used to enhance the sympathetic portrayal of Arthur instead, as in the scene where Hubert (at John's instigation) intends to blind

---

[43] Calvin, *Institutes*, 2: 4.20.34.

[44] E.g., Anon., *The Troublesome Raigne of King John*, 15.98–101; cit. Groves, *Texts and Contexts*, 95.

Arthur, and the boy refers to himself in the biblical language of a sacrificial lamb: "I will not struggle, I will stand stone-still/ ... I will sit as quiet as a lamb." Beatrice Groves has convincingly proposed that this scene has strong resonances of the Mystery Plays which depicted the sacrifice of Isaac;[45] these substituted a lamb for the "ram caught in a thicket" of Genesis 22:13 which took Isaac's place as a sacrifice. The use of a lamb in the performance of the Mysteries underlined the typological reference from Isaac to Christ, the lamb of God, of whom the words of Isaiah 53:7 were seen as a prediction in the New Testament: "he was led as a sheep to the slaughter; and like a lamb dumb before his shearers, so opened he not his mouth" (Acts 8:32–5).

In his own time, when the monarchy was in a perpetual state of insecurity, Shakespeare was navigating a skilful passage between respect for the sacred office of kingship, and scepticism about a dogma of unconditional obedience. In *Richard II*, a subtle use of scriptural texts about Adam and Christ—recalling that in the New Testament Adam is a type of Christ—supports a general spirituality about the health of the community. In *King John*, a similar concern is expressed by transferring sacral identity from an anointed king to a vulnerable and un-anointed child.

The Quest for a Story

The seventh and final element of spirituality to which I want to draw attention gathers together the rest. Shakespeare's characters are in quest of a story to make sense of their lives, giving priority to love, living in awareness of death, confident that love remains in face of death, making room for forgiveness in personal relations and for mercy in legal settings, and sensitive to ambiguities in the maintaining of order. Characters in Shakespeare's plays seek for a story, or fail to make a story, or are awarded a story by survivors. Enobarbus in *Anthony and Cleopatra*, for example, is content to stay with his general, Anthony, even though he has growing doubts about the loyalty of Cleopatra, as long as he believes there is a story to be inhabited:

> Yet he that can endure
> To follow with allegiance a fallen lord
> Does conquer him that did his master conquer,
> And earns a place i'th' story. (3.13.44–48)

Hamlet, on the brink of death, bids Horatio to remain alive "And in this harsh world draw thy breath in pain / To tell my story" (5.2.332–33). Just before he kills himself Othello tells a little story of his past nobleness of heart

---

[45] Groves, *Texts and Contexts*, 110–15. Roy Battenhouse and Sandra Billington had already compared this scene to the sacrifice of Isaac in the mystery plays, see Battenhouse, "Religion in *King John*," 146–47; and Billington, "Response," 290–92.

("Set you down this, / . . . that in Aleppo once . . ."), and commands his hearers to "relate" the events of "one who loved not wisely, but too well" (5.2.342), although Gratiano immediately doubts Othello's version of the story, commenting: "All that's spoke is marred." Romeo and Juliet are to be remembered less ambiguously: "never was a story of more woe / Than this of Juliet and her Romeo" (5.3.309–10), and Juliet is to be awarded a gold statue, evoking the story of one who was "true and faithful." On the eve of their deaths (only half-aware of the danger), Lear proposes that he and Cordelia, celebrating their renewed love, will tell tales from a God's-eye point of view:

> . . . so we'll live,
> And pray, and sing, and tell old tales, and laugh . . .
> And take upon's the mystery of things
> As if we were God's spies . . . (5.1.10–17)

Telling their story on the brink of death, or making a story out of their deaths, Shakespeare's tragic heroes are allowed to recapitulate a vision of love and virtue that they had glimpsed during their lives, which had set them at odds with their society, and which they had failed to hold faithfully. In Shakespeare's tragedies this brings just a shaft of light into the darkness of loss and waste. Anthony and Cleopatra, while betraying their love for each other in life, attain fidelity to each other in death: now, claims Cleopatra,

> I am marble-constant: now the fleeting moon
> No planet is of mine . . .
> The stroke of death is as a lover's pinch
> Which hurts, and is desir'd. (5.2.238–39, 294)

Truly, if it were not for death's coming the hero might betray the vision again; Cleopatra would again "pack cards with Caesar," Othello would let jealousy "perplex" his reason, and Lear would demand a mathematical computation of love. But this is just the point: since death *has* come, it can be used to fix the vision into a monument of art which will survive death itself.

Macbeth seems an exception: he appears to have lost all sense of what his story might be: "It is a tale / Told by an idiot, full of sound and fury, / signifying nothing" (5.5.25–7). We can hear echoes in Macbeth's despair of several biblical texts, such as the Psalter version of Psalm 90:9, cited in the Burial Service, "we bring our years to an end, as it were a tale that is told," and the Geneva version of Ecclesiasticus 20:18, "A man without grace is as a foolish tale which is oft told." Yet if he had never had a vision of what kingship might genuinely be, we would not find his fate to be a tragedy at all.

Some stories, such as those in Shakespeare's last romances, are frankly fabulous, and—as Paulina tells us—"should be hooted at / Like an old tale." But they still seem to offer clues to the story we seek for ourselves, for as

Paulina continues, "it appears she lives."[46] Moreover, it is important at the end of a comedy for the participants who have lived through the confusing events to tell each other—usually off-stage—all the details of the story they may have missed. Malvolio, though apparently excluded from the happy ending of *Twelfth Night*, must be pursued because there are wrinkles in the fabric of the story that only he can unfold: "He hath not told us of the captain yet" (5.1.374). Dark shadows that remain witness to an incompleteness of the story, and we see that—as with light at the end of a tragedy—Shakespeare is always writing tragi-comedy. Although there has been a denouement and truth has been exposed, this is never enough, and there is a sense that the story continues even as it is being told.

This is the "more" to which Hamlet bids Horatio be open. Shakespeare's spirituality is to explore always what the "more" in the story—of the characters, of the audience—might be. He draws upon scripture, on the Prayer Book, and on contemporary doctrine in order to launch himself towards the inexhaustible "more." Those who read scripture superficially might think that at times his spirituality is in conflict with the texts to which he alludes, but those who read according to the spirit and not the letter will disagree. It is certainly true that the values he displays, of love, justice, mercy, and forgiveness, are presented in a general way that does not *require* dogma to make them valid, but the deep roots are always visible.

Bibliography

Battenhouse, Roy. "Religion in *King John*: Shakespeare's View." *Connotations* 1.2 (1991) 146–47.

Berman, Ronald. "Shakespeare and the Law." *Shakespeare Quarterly* 18.2 (1967) 141–50.

The Bible and Holy Scriptures conteyned in the Olde and Newe Testament ... Geneva: Printed by Rouland Hall, 1560.

Billington, Sandra. "A Response to Roy Battenhouse." *Connotations* 1.3 (1991) 290–92.

Booke of Common Prayer, and Administracion of the Sacramentes ..., The. London: Richard Iugge & Iohannis Cawood, 1559.

Bradbury, John P. "Non-Conformist Conscience? Individual Conscience and the Authority of the Church from John Calvin to the Present." *Ecclesiology* 10 (2014) 32–52.

Brown, John Russell, ed. *William Shakespeare: The Merchant of Venice.* Arden Shakespeare Second Series. London: Methuen, 1955.

Calvin, John. *Epistles of Paul the Apostle to the Romans and to the Thessalonians.* Translated by Ross Mackenzie. Edinburgh: St Andrew Press, 1972.

---

[46] *The Winter's Tale*, 5.3.116–17.

———. *Institutes of the Christian Religion*. Edited by John T. McNeill, translated by Ford Lewis Battles. 2 Volumes. London: SCM, 1961.

Coghill, Neville. "Comic Form in *Measure for Measure*." In *Shakespeare Survey* 8, 14–27. Edited by Allardyce Nicoll. Cambridge: Cambridge University Press, 1955.

Fernie, Ewan, ed. *Spiritual Shakespeares*. London: Routledge, 2005.

Fiddes, Paul S. *"More Things in Heaven and Earth": Shakespeare, Theology, and the Interplay of Texts*. Charlottesville: University of Virginia Press, 2021.

Gardner, Helen. *King Lear. The John Coffin Memorial Lecture 1966*. London: Athlone Press, 1967.

Groves, Beatrice. *Texts and Traditions: Religion in Shakespeare 1592–1604*. Oxford: Oxford University Press, 2007.

Haigh, Christopher. "The Continuity of Catholicism in the English Reformation". In *The English Reformation Revised*, 176–208. Edited by Christopher Haigh. Cambridge: Cambridge University Press, 1987.

Hamlin, Hannibal. *The Bible in Shakespeare*. Oxford: Oxford University Press, 2013.

Homilies I = Certayne Sermons, or Homilies . . . London: Edward Whitchurche, 1547.

Homilies II = The Second Tome of Homilees . . . London: Richard Iugge and Iohn Cawood, 1571.

Hooker, Richard. *Of the Laws of Ecclesiastical Polity*. In *The Works of . . . Mr Richard Hooker*. 2 Volumes. Oxford: Clarendon Press, 1885.

Jüngel, Eberhard. "The World as Possibility and Actuality. The Ontology of the Doctrine of Justification." In Eberhard Jüngel, *Theological Essays*. Translated and edited by John Webster. Edinburgh: T. & T. Clark, 1989.

Kastan, David Scott. *A Will to Believe: Shakespeare and Religion*. Oxford: Oxford University Press, 2014.

Klause, John. "Catholic and Protestant, Jesuit and Jew: Historical Religion in The Merchant of Venice." *Shakespeare and the Culture of Christianity in Early Modern England*, 180–221. Edited by Dennis Taylor and David Beauregard. New York: Fordham University Press, 2003.

Knight, G. Wilson. *The Wheel of Fire: Interpretations of Shakespearian Tragedy*. Revised edition. London: Methuen, 1965.

Luther, Martin. *Die zweite Disputationen gegen die Antinomer*. In *Disputationen 1535–38, D. Martin Luthers Werke* 39.1. Weimar: H. Bohlaus Nachfolger, 1883–1929.

Marion, Jean-Luc. *Being Given: Towards a Phenomenology of Givenness*. Translated by Jeffrey L. Kossky. Stanford: Stanford University Press, 2002.

Marsh, Christopher. *Popular Religion in Sixteenth-Century England: Holding their Peace*. Basingstoke: Macmillan, 1993.

McMullan, Gordon, ed. *Shakespeare: King Henry VIII*. Arden Shakespeare Third Series. London: Bloomsbury, 2009.

Muir, Kenneth. *Shakespeare's Comic Sequence.* Liverpool: Liverpool University Press, 1979.
Nuttall, A.D. *Shakespeare the Thinker.* New Haven: Yale University Press, 2007.
Schafer, Elizabeth. *Theatre and Christianity.* London: Red Globe, 2019.
Schanzer, Ernest. *The Problem Plays of Shakespeare.* London: Routledge, 1963.
Shaheen, Naseeb. *Biblical References in Shakespeare's Plays.* Newark: University of Delaware Press, 2011.
Shakespeare, William. *The Arden Shakespeare.* Third Series. 40 Volumes. London: Bloomsbury, 1995–2020.
Shuger, Deborah K. *Political Theologies in Shakespeare's England: The Sacred and the State in "Measure for Measure."* New York: Palgrave, 2001.
———. "A Protesting Catholic Puritan in Elizabethan England." *Journal of British Studies* 48 (2009) 587–630.
Vaughan, Virginia Mason, and Alden T. Vaughan. *Shakesperare: The Tempest.* Arden Shakespeare Third Series. London: Bloomsbury, 2011.
White, Peter. "The *via media* in the Early Stuart Church." In *The Early Stuart Church, 1603–1642*, 211–30. Edited by Kenneth Fincham. Stanford: Stanford University Press, 1993.
Wind, Edgar. *Pagan Mysteries in the Renaissance.* Rev. ed. Harmondsworth: Penguin, 1967.

CHAPTER 15

Intimations of Transcendence:
A Legacy of "The Scottish Colourists"

Richard L. Kidd

The "Iona" pictures of Francis Cadell and Samuel Peploe can still pack a gallery, and they can still leave viewers spell-bound by their visual magic. How much is this down to a place, the Island of Iona, and how much to their artful handling of form and colour? I am in little doubt that it is *both* the Island *and* the skill of these remarkable painters, two of "The Scottish Colourists," still combining to produce such an impact a full century after their creation. For many of us, both the Island of Iona and exposure to the work of The Colourists awaken in us what I call here, "intimations of transcendence." In this chapter, I am keen to explore what it is about the place, Iona, and about the painterly style of The Scottish Colourists, that arouses in so many viewers an uplifting sense of God as Creator, a transcendent One in whom all this wildness and rugged beauty are grounded. I am also interested to know how this might connect with a phrase, much-used in contemporary spiritual writings, "finding God in all things"?

My reflection finds its focus in the term "palette," familiar from the world of painters and painting. In the hands of an artist, a palette can simply be a temporary platform on which to support their colours. As the descriptor of a creative imagination, it can denote a particular range of colours, ones that an artist most typically loads onto a palette. More generally, it can describe the whole constellation of factors that together determine the style of a particular painter. In this paper, the "palette" will become a unifying metaphor holding together its various themes. Our personal choice of palette can be crucial, not only for how others see us and what we do, but also for how we ourselves are ready-primed to see and interpret others and the world in a particular way.

It is the palette of notes that helps us "spot the composer," sometimes only seconds after turning on a radio. It is the palette of colours that enables us to identify an artist responsible for a particular painting. It might be a picture that we have never seen before but, no matter, often we can recognize the artist almost as soon as we enter a gallery. It is the subtle difference in linguistic palettes that makes it possible for us to tell which New Testament Gospel is being read, without seeing the text or its title. It is also how we recognize poets, novelists and theologians, having seen no more than a few sentences in a brief quotation. It is, you might say, right at the heart of the way we experience and interpret our lives in the world. It provides, I would add, a paradigmatic example of hermeneutical processes in action.

As I write, Ruth Gouldbourne, to whom this book is dedicated, repeatedly comes to mind. I trust she will understand that I am not singling her out for special treatment, when I say that Ruth has her own distinctive array of palettes. More than that, she herself *is* a palette, and a unique one at that. I would recognize Ruth in a crowd—as I also recognize others—for a whole constellation of reasons that conspire to make identification possible. Ruth's palette of *personae* includes historian, minister of word and sacrament, Baptist Christian, trained counsellor, prophetic voice for justice, and more besides. All of these, she puts to work with characteristic enthusiasm and care. She is a palette that comes ready-primed with many artistic and spiritual sensitivities, that determine, for example, the way she leads Christian worship. Somewhere among her palettes is a gentle, engaging, Scottish accent; as well as a wardrobe, I hazard a guess, that suggests colour preferences biased towards those also preferred by The Scottish Colourists—but I am racing ahead of myself.

Every intellectual and practical discipline comes with its own distinctive palette. Reading and writing theology require palettes of theological words and concepts. Listening to and playing music need palettes of notes that can be sequenced into melodies and stacked into chords. Seeing art and the act of painting demand palettes of colours, and it is the selection and juxtaposition of these colours, among other things, that determine the unique style of a particular painter. Most of us come to our creative activities equipped with more than one palette: theologian, musician, painter, and so on. It is especially important that some, like Ruth, include the palette of historian, because palettes themselves change over time. They each have their own history, and there is always a backstory that deserves further historical research.

Painters and Their Palettes

The paint on the palettes of actual painters has changed greatly over time. This has not merely been a matter of cost—although there have been times when the price of *lapis lazuli* put it well-beyond the reach of most painters. Much of the change has been prompted by developing technologies. Crucially, the range of pigments and mediums mixed to create their paints has increased in leaps and bounds. Long ago, cave painters worked with very limited palettes: mainly "earth colours," including red and yellow ochres, and lamp black. At the time, these were the only materials to hand. Millennia later, one of the most dramatic developments in Western art only became after the discovery of oil as a cost-effective medium. Rembrandt van Rijn (1606–69), for example, was able to use oil-colours in ways unimaginable, even to medieval painters just a few centuries earlier. Less than three centuries later, the explosion of colour that marked another artistic revolution around the turn of the twentieth century also depended on the availability of a new generation of vibrant pigments and versatile mediums. Despite these major developments, however, there has been massive continuity over thousands of years. Creative artists have always managed to make use of materials available at the time, their specialist skills enabling them to produce amazing images, seemingly out of very little. Cave paintings dating back nearly 60,000 years, discovered in some parts of modern Australia, demonstrate skills not at all dissimilar from those still coveted by artists in the early twenty-first century.

Each colour has its own fascinating history. Significant factors include: the availability of pigments; the symbolic significance of particular colours in different cultures around the world; and how individual colours have been used in colour-combinations for the purpose of decoration and design. There are many indicators of ever-shifting trends in colour-preferences. A good example is the changing designs of wallpaper, ever since its first appearance as a decorative lining for storerooms and cupboards in the sixteenth century. In England, my parents' generation, in the mid-twentieth century, predominantly chose subdued colours and unobtrusive designs. By the time that I and my life-partner were making our first home, we and our contemporaries were choosing more intense colours and preferring much bolder patterns.

Over time, painters settle on a particular selection of colours, as also they tend to settle on a memorable layout for their colours on their palette. This does, of course, evolve as an individual style develops but, at any one time, the choice of palette has a very significant impact on the kind of work that an artist produces. I am fascinated when, particularly in self-portraits, we catch a glimpse of an artist holding a palette. Vincent van Gogh (1853–90) has a famous self-portrait in which his palette can be seen very clearly.[1] In Van Gogh's case, his choice of palette changed radically mid-career. This was one of the signs that a major psychological re-orientation was taking place. From the beginning of his short career as a full-time artist in the early 1880s through to 1887–88, his colours were largely dark and subdued. "The Potato Eaters" (1885),[2] a picture I have found to be an excellent starting point for theological reflection on Vincent's *oeuvre*, is famously described as if crafted using soil in which the potatoes had been grown, its colours clearly symbolic of the lives endured by peasant communities in The Borinage where the potatoes had been harvested. There is an extreme contrast with "Sunflowers" (1889).[3] From that time, through to his untimely death, little more than a year

---

[1] See https://www.vangoghmuseum.nl/en/collection/s0022V1962

[2] See https://www.vangoghmuseum.nl/en/collection/s0005V1962

[3] See https://www.vangoghmuseum.nl/en/collection/s0031V1962

later, Van Gogh's colours intensified, increasingly prioritizing yellows, especially Naples Yellow, and a rich spectrum of bluey-purples.

Some painters have been much more consistent in their choice of palette across a lifetime of work as an artist. Pierre-Auguste Renoir (1841–1919), it would seem, never lost his early penchant for mauves and purples, something that would almost certainly have been reflected in the "normal" configuration of his palette.[4] Mark Rothko (1903–70), however, predominantly favoured maroons and dark greys—in unusually large quantities.[5] Once an artist has developed a recognizable style, deviations from "the normal palette" often come as a shock to a viewer: a pleasant surprise perhaps in an otherwise unmemorable exhibition. Some painters choose to load their palettes with only a very limited selection of colours. Others litter them with numerous ready-mixed hues. It is, of course, possible to create any colour that is visible to the human eye, simply by mixing three "primary" colours. This can be simply red, yellow and blue, but other carefully chosen trios work equally well. Whatever the choice of primaries, there is always an infinity of possible mixes. Even among greys, often thought to be lifeless and dull, there is an infinite range of possibilities. I now realize that my own childhood experience of simply mixing black and white to make grey was a serious insult to the hidden potential awaiting me in "colourful" greys. Most artists typically settle on six or seven "staple" colours, only adding extras for particular projects. As I noted, each painter tends to arrange the colours in a consistent pattern as they prime an empty palette, the juxtapositions corresponding to common colour-combinations, another key to their distinctive style.

Many painters, as a matter of financial necessity, largely conform to popular taste and local trends when it comes to their choice of colours. Wassily Kandinsky (1866–1944), in his ground-breaking, *Concerning the Spiritual in Art*, provided a now widely quoted explanation for this phenomenon.[6] According to Kandinsky, the lamentable reality is that a majority of artists largely conform to public expectations, and rarely experiment beyond modest variations on themes they first learnt from their teachers. In the late nineteenth century, this meant continuing to produce near-photographic landscapes and portraits, in traditions established over many generations and perpetuated in respected art colleges all around Europe. A crisis was building, however, in the still relatively new "age of the camera," and a revolution was long overdue. According to Kandinsky's analysis, there will always be a small number of artists, prophetic spirits, non-conformist pioneers who push over

---

[4] See, e.g., "Au bord de l'eau" (1885). https://www.simondickinson.com/2016/02/26/renoir1885/

[5] See, e.g., https://www.tate.org.uk/whats-on/tate-modern/display/mark-rothko

[6] This appears in Kandinsky, *Concerning the Spiritual in Art*, 6–9, and is part of a section exploring how revolutionary cultural changes can come about in artistic taste.

the existing boundaries. Eventually such break-throughs can effect a paradigm shift, and a consequence is that, even more years later, their innovative practice becomes the "new normal." Unfortunately, being a pioneer is a thankless role. When Edvard Munch (1863–1944) pioneered one such revolution in Norway, and when Claude Monet (1840–1926) led the advance into Impressionism in France, neither painter received much by way of affirmation, and certainly they received little remuneration as reward for their innovative creativity. Instead, their reward was predominantly one of verbal ridicule and abuse. One hundred years later, of course, the gallery-going public is full of gratitude for their gritty determination and resilience.[7] Today we rush to gallery websites, making advanced bookings for their retrospective exhibitions, queueing around the streets to guarantee entry.

Introducing "The Scottish Colourists"

In the early years of the twentieth century, four notable artists—Francis Campbell Boileau Cadell (1883–1937), John Duncan Fergusson (1874–1967), George Leslie Hunter (1877–1931) and Samuel John Peploe (1871–1925)—emerged as the leading figures in one such pioneering movement that would have a long-term impact on art in Scotland. They themselves had been massively influenced by contemporary artists in Paris and the South of France. Eventually, they would become known as "The Scottish Colourists," although that term that would not be used with reference to all four of them until 1948, by which time three of them had long-since died. I will not rehearse the biographies of these four artists. There are more than enough monographs and critical studies already in print, and my own research does not equip me to add to existing studies. Here I will be drawing largely on existing resources. My own aim is to explore new possibilities for making inter-disciplinary connections, and to enable a creative process of theological reflection. A significant point of reference for much of my reflection has been the extensive catalogue, *The Scottish Colourists 1900–1930*, that accompanied major exhibitions in both Edinburgh and London, as recently as the year 2000.[8]

Amid the ferment of ideas circulating at the turn of the twentieth century, the writings of the philosopher Henri Bergson (1859–1941) was a major influence on the arts across continental Europe. In Bergson, the revolutionary artists, known collectively as the "Fauves," found an inspirational ally, and The Colourists would in time come to be seen as a uniquely Scottish incarnation of continental fauvism. Bergson had proposed a philosophical model that pushed

---

[7] I describe this phenomenon in my chapter on Edvard Munch in Kidd and Sparkes, *God and the Art of Seeing*, 8–9.

[8] Long with Cumming, *The Scottish Colourists 1900–1930*. See also the catalogue that accompanied a more recent exhibition, *The Scottish Colourists Festival Exhibition*.

beyond a simple division between realist and idealist ways of thinking about the world. It had all the dynamic energy of post-Darwinian evolutionary ideas, and it affirmed both material and spiritual realities in the unifying concept of an *élan vitale*, a "life force."[9] On a fauvist palette this appeared as vibrant colours, often straight from the tube, liberally applied to the canvas. This was Post-Impressionism, before Roger Fry gave the label its *début* in Britain. The Fauves consolidated a break with Representation, already well underway. Using areas of bold colour, loosely applied, they saw themselves as creating energetic expressions of meaning, far in excess of the simple materiality of the paint. This was one version of Expressionism in action, finding spiritual energy in the rawness of colour and the juxtaposition of complimentary colours, often highlighted by a strong use of line defining the boundaries between colours.

Leading the way in France in the first decade of the twentieth century, were Henri Matisse (1869–1954) and André Derain (1880–1954). Wassily Kandinsky, who would collaborate with the German *Blau Reiter* artists in the following decade,[10] was already providing a theoretical justification for the spiritual significance of line and colour, Bergson providing a unifying interpretation of their combined impact. Kandinsky's text on "point, line and plane" provided a unique way of framing Bergsonian ideas for a new generation of painters.[11] This was the cultural context that greeted Fergusson and Peploe, who were the first of the four to settle in France in 1907 and 1910 respectively, and to become part of the intellectual *café*-communities of pre-war Paris. A significant number of artists were already gathering under the label "Rhythmists," and Fergusson would come to play a major role in editing a publication to broadcast their ideas. It was this fauvist/rhythmist spirit that he and Peploe brought back to the more sober art world of Edinburgh on their eventual return.

It is no surprise that the work of Fergusson and Peploe did not receive an entirely enthusiastic reception back in their Scottish homeland, but their names were not lost in France where they were known as *"Les Peintres de l'Ecosse Moderne,"* the Scottish "fauves," as it were. Cadell and Hunter had reached similar convictions by different routes: Hunter in the United States, and Cadell in Munich from 1906–8. My focus of interest is on Cadell and Peploe, who took these ideas and practices on painting tours: first to France, later to the West Coast of Scotland, and especially to the Island of Iona.

---

[9] The primary text was Bergson, *Creative Evolution*, but Bergson, *Matter and Memory*, is also significant for the ideas circulating among the "Fauves" of Paris.

[10] Kandinsky and Marc, *Blaue Reiter Almanac*.

[11] Kandinsky, *Point and Line to Plane*, published in 1926, was a mature development of his earlier *Concerning the Spiritual in Art*. It became hugely influential in providing foundational principles for non-Representational painting.

These "*fauves écosses*" brought a previously unknown palette and style to their island landscapes and seascapes, and the results continue to catch the imagination of viewers all these years later.

Unlike their predecessors, they were not bound by literal approaches to "local colour"—strictly re-presenting the original colours on the canvas—nor by the limitations of form as conceived by photographic realists. William McTaggart (1835–1910) had in measure led the way, but it was Peploe and Cadell who inaugurated a new era. Their work, while clearly inspired by the visual world around them, was also in the full spirit of abstraction, the definitive signature of a new art in Europe. Without losing touch with the rugged geology and wild meteorology of the Island of Iona, their innovative use of line and colour was far removed from literal representation. In fact, in their hands, the colours of Iona marble, the moorland heathers, and the wild waves communicated an inspirational depth rarely achieved with oil on canvas.

Why an Emphasis on Colour?

The complexity of colour perception is not widely appreciated, even amongst those for whom colour is a source of great enjoyment. The experience of colour results from a confluence of inter-connected factors.[12] These include: the molecular structure of pigments, their reflective and refractive properties; the impact of wavelength on the way that each colour of light travels through gases and translucent solids; the long evolutionary history of the human eye; the physiology of the optical nerve and the neurological structure of the brain; the cognitive lenses peculiar to the psychological history of each individual's brain as it shapes its interpretation of data; the cultural lenses peculiar to different societies and communities; and so on. Given such complexity, it is a wonder, you might say, that colour makes any sense to us at all. It is, I would say, an even greater wonder that colour does actually make sense to us, and functions powerfully and effectively helping us to map our way through the world around us.

Here are some specific examples of how the factors listed above help us to enjoy the mysterious pathways that painters daily negotiate as part of their trade. I have already alluded to the history of pigments, but a related question is how each pigment makes its unique colour known in the surrounding environment. Imagine a luscious "sap green," the kind everywhere present in temperate climates on account of chlorophyl in the abundance of leaves. Perceived "green-ness" originates as molecules of chlorophyl reflect back certain parts of the green spectrum of light that fall on it. This is a consequence of its unique molecular structure, a fascinating area of study in its own right. From the perspective of trees and plants, the light that is absorbed

---

[12] Much of what follows, I first encountered reading Lamb and Bourriau, *Colour, Art and Science*.

is far more significant than the light reflected back for us to see—all the colours, that is, in the visible spectrum "other than green." These are the colours, the ones we do not see, that are absorbed by green leaves, the ones that transfer their energy, using the chemistry of chlorophyl, to become the life-building chemicals that enable trees and plants to grow and flourish. Many of these plants and their fruits are then eaten by humans, providing energy that fuels eyes and brains. The circle is completed as these eyes, brains and human minds enable us to see the colour green—including the green light that was never actually used in the process at all. Is that not an occasion for wonder?

What, then, about the ongoing transmission of visible light? Staying with chlorophyl-green, its perceived colour finds itself modified in a variety of ways. Imagine, for example, that our green light passes through a shard of what we think of as blue glass. We only see the glass as blue because of its ability selectively to transmit blue light. This means, of course, that the non-blue parts of the spectrum must have been reflected back on meeting the first surface. Now, as every child in primary school should know, green is a simple mixture of blue and yellow. The transmitted light, as seen from inside a building, might well be vibrant blue. The reflected light, however, as seen from outside a building, is likely to be a dull yellowey-grey. This, of course, is why such different skills are needed by painters working with light reflected back (as a result of addition) from pigments on canvas, and by artists working with light transmitted (after subtraction) through stained glass. Wonders will never cease!

It will come as no surprise to find that the physiology of eyes and brains is also immensely complex. Let us stay with the yellow light that has just been reflected back from the green light landing on a "blue" glass surface—seen as it were from the "wrong" side. On entering the eye, it might be reasonable to assume that it would stimulate a yellow receptor. There is, however, no such thing. All we have in our eyes are three kinds of light-sensitive "cones," responsive to reds, greens and blues respectively. Our cerebral software, then, must be operating not unlike a basic computer that uses its programmes to analyse colours using their RGB (red, green, blue) values—with a little additional help from our "rods" that take into account levels of light intensity. The brain in some way re-integrates the proportions of red, green and blue to distinguish each particular colour.

The complexity, however, does not end there. Artists have long been aware of additional visual phenomena, physiologically rooted, that produce other striking effects. Vincent van Gogh, as a result of careful observation and artistic practice, began to exploit the juxtaposition of certain colours, especially so-called "complementary" colours, in radically new ways. The classic "complementary" pairings are blue/orange, red/green and yellow/purple. The Pointillists were already onto these phenomena in good measure too. George-Pierre Seurat (1859–91) painted whole pictures using a multitude of coloured dots, carefully documenting the perceptual outcomes. More recently, Brigit Riley (b.1931) has used areas of colour in carefully crafted combinations of lines and patches. If we go close-up to a Seurat or a Riley, isolating a small area of colour for detailed inspection, we can see the "local colour" undistorted by its neighbours. In Brigit Riley's "Silvered 2" (1981),[13] for example, try looking at the individual colours in a blown-up image, and then "stand back" and look at their combined effect. The result is almost impossible to predict. The only thing of which we can be certain is that the combined result will be significantly different from any of the individual components. The colours become changed and, for many viewers, there is even an energetic vibrating effect that can generate a sense of movement.

What, then, about individual psychological histories? For most of us, for most of the time, yellow reminds us of sunlight, and the pleasurable memories evoked by it. In my own life, one persistent memory continues to produce a striking counter-effect. Around the age of six, I succumbed to one of many childhood illnesses, and was prescribed a bright yellow liquid. Unfortunately, every time I tried to take my medicine, I was horribly sick. Similar yellows still bring that memory forcibly back to mind. My guess is that everyone will have their own stories, some good and some bad, about particular colours. In the transcript of a very moving letter, in a book that gathers a correspondence between John Berger and John Christie, Berger recalls the impact of an arrangement of cadmium red carnations at a crematorium funeral.[14] Encounters with specific colours can lay down very powerful memories.

At societal and cultural levels, the symbolic resonances invoked by colours vary greatly around the world, and they are also susceptible to local variations. Staying with "sap green," there is a widely held view that greens have a calming effect on the human spirit. Long ago, I recall a short meditation by Michel Quoist—remember Quoist?—entitled "Green Blackboards," reflecting on green-ness as powerfully pleasing to the eye.[15] Looking at it again fifty years later, I am now struck by its cultural specificity—something that would not have occurred to me in the 1970s. The symbolic calm of green-ness is unlikely to be as universal as I once assumed. It belongs very much to the temperate climates to which I referred earlier. Inuit people do not get to see much green, and nor do nomadic communities in sub-Saharan Africa. Hopefully, they are calmed by other colours instead.

All this suggests to me that it is well-worth pursuing the power of colour to elicit a response. Colour plays a powerful role across the board in human experience, and it is core to a great deal of our inter-personal communications.

---

[13] See https://www.tate.org.uk/art/artworks/riley-silvered-2-p11564

[14] Berger and Christie, *I Send You This Cadmium Red*, in the letter dated 25 February 1997.

[15] Quoist *Prayers of Life*, 16.

The Scottish Colourists, learning from and building on the insights of their continental contemporaries and recent predecessors, knew their way around colours as well as any of the revolutionary painters working in the early decades of the twentieth century.

The Colours of the Western Isles

We now look in more detail at some of colour sketches and oils that Francis Cadell and Samuel Peploe completed during lengthy summer stays on Iona and other Western Islands of Scotland, especially in the second decade of the twentieth century, before the disruption of the Great War in Europe. There is no substitute for looking at representative pictures for ourselves—and where better than on some of the current websites of Scottish Art Galleries.[16] Immediately we are struck by the frequency of certain colours and their related tones, many of which will be familiar from photographs, perhaps our own, taken on similar locations: the blues and whites of sky and sea, clouds and waves; the greens and earth colours of moorland heather, sheep-mown grasses and exposed peat bogs; the sandy tones and pinks of wind-swept beaches and ancient marble outcrops. In the work of these four artists, however, there are other less-expected appearances of mauvy-purples, bright patches of yellow and red, that catch the eye and bring a special quality to their images, quite unlike the majority of photographs. They seem to bring an extra vitality even to pictures that were quite clearly painted on the dullest of days. There are many examples of those deliberate juxtapositions associated with Van Gogh and Seurat: splashes of red colliding as it were with larger areas of greens, and flashes of yellow and orange butting-up to patches of blue.

It is these energetic meetings between "colour and colour" that bring these scenes to life: making waves to move, spray to sparkle, and invigorating island weathers that lash out from the canvas. The Colourists also exploited the visual impact of various dark lines, those for example that out-line the profile of rocks, producing effects beyond the scope of any un-manipulated photograph. One of the surprises, certainly for me, is that these lines do not intrude or appear artificial—as perhaps they might in an unskilled painting of a house or a stylized face. These artists really did know what they were doing with their lines and colours. They knew a great deal about the complex interactions that take place in every human "act of seeing": how local colours stimulate the human eye, how they are processed in the human brain and, perhaps more importantly, how they awaken inspired and inspiring images in

---

[16] A good place to start is on the site of the National Galleries Scotland at https://www.nationalgalleries.org/art-and-artists/glossary-terms/scottish-colourists. A list of many galleries holding pictures by The Colourists, along with links to their websites, can be found at http://www.scottishcolourists.co.uk/the-collections/

the minds of their viewers. The Colourists knew how to launch their viewers on unexpected journeys of "seeing" and potentially thrilling "reflection."

Francis Cadell and Samuel Peploe

All the reports of Francis Cadell on the Island of Iona suggest that he was a gregarious, eccentric figure, well known by islanders as a result of his many long summers painting around the island. Cadell arrived for the first time in 1912, then in his late twenties and, although his style would include recognizable consistencies, there would be developments over time. His work was certainly influenced by the arrival of his older companion, Peploe, who did not join him on the island for almost a decade. Cadell almost always worked *en plein air*, using either watercolour or oil. His normal practice was to work at speed, usually finishing a picture in a single sitting, there being very little evidence of alterations made at a later time.

Cadell, at one time or another, painted almost everywhere around the coast of Iona, but I am choosing here two pictures painted near the northern end of the island.[17] This will facilitate comparisons with Peploe, who clearly favoured the north end. It also plays into my own prejudice, having camped with a young family for fifteen summers on North End surviving everything the weather could throw at us. My first choice of a picture is Cadell's "Iona. East Bay—the Little Island and Mull," painted on the shore of the East Bay, known as The White Strand.[18] This particular view looks roughly North East, the Island of Eilean Annraidh with its very distinctive little beach in the middle ground, and the Island of Mull in the distance. I have chosen it because it clearly illustrates some of the distinctive elements in Cadell's style. There can be little doubting a Fauvist-like influence on the rocks in the foreground. Viewed in detail as local colours layered on the canvas, the dark reds, yellows and bright blues of the rocks are far from the natural colours immediately visible to the painter from his easel. Remarkably, however, there is no sense in which they appear inappropriate or out of place. In fact, they communicate very clearly an authentic "Iona-moment," a mood that those of us who have walked the same shore, standing on a similar spot, recognize very well. The second picture, simply titled "Ben More," again shows Eileen Annraidh looking from further north, with Mull's Ben More in the background.[19] Ben More, the highest point on Mull, rising to 996m, features in a many of The Colourists' paintings. I chose this particular image because

---

[17] For a comprehensive collection of Cadell's work, see https://www.francis-campbell-boileau-cadell.org/the-complete-works.html?pageno=1

[18] See https://www.wikigallery.org/wiki/painting_334159/Francis-Campbell-Boileau-Cadell/Iona.-East-Bay---The-Little-Island-And-Mull

[19] See http://www.battlefieldframers.co.uk/?page_id=7953

of the way it illustrates how Cadell typically allows a natural boundary to define the meeting of different colours, without any substantial use of dividing lines.

Samuel Peploe was almost fifty years old when he first accompanied Cadell on a painting trip to the Island of Iona, having already achieved a more recognizable style. Peploe's work would eventually win the greater attention, Peploe being widely recognized as the leader among his companion-Colourists. Unlike Cadell, Peploe worked almost exclusively in oil, although the difficulty of handling this medium in challenging weather did not prevent him from also working quickly, making only minor alterations on return to shelter. His more reserved character is perhaps reflected in the absence of almost all figuration. From Peploe's extensive gallery of Iona images,[20] I have chosen a view from The White Strand, entitled "Iona, Sunny Waters," because it clearly demonstrates his characteristic use of strong dark lines outlining patches of colour.[21] To accompany this, I have chosen Peploe's view of Ben More, painted from almost the same spot as Cadell's.[22] It also shows his use of line, as well as his technique of using flat areas of colour, boldly applied. As I noted, Peploe's paintings were almost all done towards the north end of the island, and they include multiple images from the same location in a variety of weathers.

A Matter of Theological and Spiritual Perception

I suggest that rich resources for theological reflection, and indeed the beginnings of reflection itself, have been circulating just below the surface from almost the first sentence of this chapter. Immediately, we were encountering the same hermeneutical principles that today have become the bread and butter of biblical scholarship, and they are now the basis for a prophetic de-construction and re-construction of theological perspectives. We soon began to see in action a guiding principle that now pervades a wide range of critical studies, spanning the interests of artists, scientists and theologians alike. As the story of The Scottish Colourists started to unfold, we repeatedly came upon examples of a fundamental polarity that exists between raw human sensations and the complex processes by which we make sense of them. Phenomenologists would identify this as an intrinsic polarity between subjectivity and objectivity, a universal characteristic of human experience. In similar vein, today's historians typically draw attention to a polarity between

---

[20] For a comprehensive gallery of Peploe's work, see https://www.wikigallery.org/wiki/artist41380/Samuel-John-Peploe/page-1

[21] See http://www.duncanmiller.com/archive/item/387/7349/iona_sunny_waters

[22] See https://artuk.org/shop/image-library/gallery-product/poster/ben-more-from-iona-124879/posterid/124879.html

facts and interpretations. Artists are concerned about polar relationships between "the viewer" and "the viewed." In the paintings of the Cadell and Peploe we have a particular example of the relationship between the physicality of landscapes and seascapes of a Scottish Island, and the creative imagination of skilled artists. This, I suggest, is fuel for a focused theological reflection on how immersion in a tradition, a tradition of faith for example, profoundly shapes the way we interpret the world we encounter. Critically for a theologian it probes a question about what it means for God to make Godself known in the awesome beauty of the natural world.

I myself am greatly indebted to the writings of the phenomenologist, Maurice Merleau-Ponty, who has enabled me to recognize how significantly a work of art, specifically an oil on canvas, can be understood as paradigmatic of the relationship between an "objective" artifact and its significantly "subjective" creator and viewer.[23] It is this relationship that underpins a visual artifact's capacity to disclose hidden layers of meaning to a sensitive observer. I do not doubt that the same can be said about every artifact, and not merely paintings. In the language of hermeneutics, every work of art functions as a text, regardless of its medium. I am particularly interested here, however, to explore how this works out in the case of imaginative painting, especially a painting of Iona either by Cadell or Peploe. I find myself thoroughly convinced by the phenomenological argument that every human cognitive event has, in some measure, both subjective and objective dimensions. Some human knowledge, no doubt, is significantly objectively secure—but never, I suggest, a full one hundred percent. There will always be subjective dimensions that, thankfully, ensures an appropriate residual element of provisionality. The other way around, one hundred percent subjective knowledge is barely a credible concept at all. Even the most abstract visual image has roots connecting it into something, if nothing else, the medium with which it has been formed. In her book, *The Question of Painting: Rethinking Thought with Merleau-Ponty*, Jorella Andrews writes,

> Specific meanings are not created by us *ex nihilo* and superimposed upon a supposedly unintelligible perceptual world, nor are they uncovered by us, as if they exist, in themselves, in an unambiguous form beneath or beyond the flux of appearances. They are the consequence of a reciprocal interaction between embodied perceiver and the perceived. We experience meaning as coming to birth for us within the context of our perceptual explorations of the world. If we will continue to observe and describe, we witness its inexhaustible unfolding before us. Thus, perception always occurs within contexts that are both spatial and temporal.[24]

---

[23] See Merleau-Ponty, *Phenomenology of Perception*.

[24] Andrews, *Question of Painting*, Kindle Location 2625.

In this short paragraph, Andrews pushes home the central role of embodiment in Merleau-Ponty's phenomenological epistemology: an embodied painter, an embodied viewer and, bringing them together in an epistemological event, the materiality of oil and canvas—for example, a painting by one of The Scottish Colourists. In his writings, Merleau-Ponty most commonly illustrated his point using the paintings of Paul Cézanne, but his methodology works no less well with Cadell and Peploe.

An actual painting, a careful organization of pigments on a stretched canvas, is a text in which both objective and subjective dimension of reality are fused in a single artifact. The painting becomes the material locus of an "event of knowing," the result of both intended and accidental sedimentation, making accessible in one place many moments from a complex creative process. It would be wrong, however, ever to think of this process as complete. Every apparently finished artifact immediately becomes the starting point for ongoing conversations and further disclosures of meaning. Andrews chose these words of Merleau-Ponty as an introductory quotation inside the cover of her book: "There is a pictorial rationality as there is a rationality of a painter's work, rationality not of completion but of 'investigation'."[25] This, I suggest, is exactly what is happening when I am moved by and inspired by a Colourist image of Iona.

In any one of Peploe's paintings of Iona, there is *both* something rooted in an original setting—the wind whipping up waves, the sand repeatedly relocated with every incoming tide, a million-year geological story of rocks and their formation—*and* there is a skilfully presented deposit of an artist's physical, intellectual, emotional and spiritual response to a personal encounter. All this is present in the single painting, and it comes to life again in my presence as an observer. This, I suggest, has enormous historical, spiritual and theological significance.

Cadell, Peploe, and "Objectivity"

No-one could pretend that The Colourists' paintings of Ben More can replace the high degree of objectivity provided by a photograph, a geological survey, or a mountain walker's guide to mountain safety. There is good evidence, however, that for all their subjectivity, Cadell's and Peploe's paintings of the Iona shoreline have proved themselves to be an important source of objective evidence for a certain kind of historical investigation. I have in mind here an exceptional study undertaken by Philip MacLeod Coupe (1944–2013). His name is not as yet widely known, but his life and work have impacted my own reflections in quite unexpected ways.

Unfortunately, Philip and I never met. My partner, Rosemary, came to know Philip McLeod Coupe—painter, historian and lute-maker—meeting

---

[25] Andrews, *Question of Painting*, inside cover.

him on more than one occasion, while retreating on the Island of Iona. She was captivated by their conversations over breakfasts and, after each occasion, returned enthusiastic that I should meet him too. Sadly, it was not to be. Philip died quite suddenly during a year, between visits to Iona. Among our treasured possessions is now a signed print of one of his pictures, "Ben More from Iona,"[26] and also a what has become a cherished limited edition (Number 101/500) of his book, *Paintings of Iona: Cadell and Peploe*, published soon after his untimely death. Not least this book brings together in one volume a remarkable collection of Iona paintings, accompanied by photographs of Cadell and Peploe at work, and also photographs taken as nearly as possible from the locations at which the artists once worked at their easels. MacLeod Coupe was not only deeply attracted to the work of The Colourists, but developed his own painterly style very much in their tradition.[27] The main purpose of MacLeod Coupe's book—the dimension that helps me to home in on the more objective significance of these painters' images—was to map the changes that have occurred around the shores of Iona as a result of shifting sand, moved by the tides over the span of the last century. This is a historical study of much more than archival significance. A record of the impact from strong tidal forces on a coastal profile makes an important scientific contribution to future predictions concerning the impact of global warming on weather and sea levels in coming decades. MacLeod Coupe in an unassuming and delightful way has put his multi-disciplinary skills to work and has made a lasting contribution of understanding the past, present and future of the Island of Iona and its coastal environs.

Iona—A "Thin" Place?

Taking now a more subjective approach, what can we also learn from Cadell and Peploe about the spiritual and theological significance of Iona, both as a place of great beauty, and also as an historic destination for pilgrimage? A shift towards what I have called the subjective pole, enables us to probe a little further into the hearts and minds of Cadell and Peploe as visual artists. We are compelled to ask how it is that some places can become so widely valued as spiritual venues, becoming places where pilgrims bear testimony to living encounters with a deep level of reality that they come to associate with God.

I first met the term "thin place" on the Island of Iona in the 1970s, where it was introduced as an early Celtic description much used by George MacLeod, the Founder of the Iona Community. Fifty years later MacLeod's words

---

[26] See http://www.ionagallery.com/Limited%20Edition%20Pages/lep_pmc1%20Ben%20More.htm

[27] E.g., http://www.ionagallery.com/Iona%20Paintings%20contemporary%20pages/pmc%20LochnaKeal.htm

describing the Island as "a very thin place where only a tissue paper separating the material from the spiritual realm" are quoted seemingly everywhere on the internet. According to Rosemary Power,[28] however, the description of Iona as a "thin place" or a place "where the veil is thin" may date back to the 1930s, and might actually have originated with the writer George MacDonald. The biblical allusion is to the "veil" in the Jerusalem Temple, shielding the people from God's awesome presence. Sadly, like so many fertile metaphors, "thin place" has begun to suffer death by continual repetition, and these days I myself only use it sparingly. When I first heard it, however, I was in no doubt at all about what it was intended to convey, and it is a phrase to which I have returned many times over years. Today, I prefer a much older term, *genius loci*, the spirit of a place, which has similar implications: that there are certain places that can come to mean something very special indeed in our lives. Iona was one such place for myself, my life-partner and our family. It evidently went deep, as our children and grandchildren are still drawn there with a strange lure that has not as yet lost its appeal. Some places—again Iona is one of them—become "special" for very large numbers of people. There is something extra special about them that seems to tap into a larger social phenomenon. On Iona, like others, I too have wondered how much this might be linked to a special quality of light, peculiar to small offshore islands exposed to Atlantic airflows, and surrounded by highly reflective, often turbulent waters. I still suspect that this is an important part of the story, but there is more to Iona's lure than that too. I have come to associate it within a larger story of transcendence and its occurrence as a significant dimension of human perception. It is not that transcendence is more concentrated in some places than others, but long histories of human testimony to experiences of transcendence gradually build as it were a reservoir, that can be tapped by later generations as they too immerse themselves in a particular story; indeed, becoming part of that story themselves. The attraction of Iona for me was also connected with reading the stories of Columba and early Celtic missionaries: monks reciting The Psalms, up to their necks in the icy water of Iona Sound; repetitive liturgical rituals of prayer hammering away, making their marks on the very marble that is core to the island's existence; and stories of martyrs risking everything for the sake of the transcendent One, whose call they believed to be shaping their lives.

I have written elsewhere about another artist with a peculiar fascination for the *genius loci*, Paul Nash (1889–1946), English landscape painter and two-times War Artist.[29] From early life, Nash began to accumulate what he called special places, many of them associated with trees: a garden in which embryonic experiences of strangeness and presence were first encountered;

---

[28] Power, "Place of Community."

[29] Kidd, "Perceiving an Absent Presence."

sites of iron-age hillforts, now sporting clusters of trees like beacons broadcasting an ominous presence for miles around. He also warmed to some of England's more famous stone circles: Stonehenge is the best known, but for Nash nothing ever quite matched the impact of Avebury Ring in Wiltshire. These are places that featured time and again in his paintings, as if he were striving to anchor the meaning of their specialness for others to share too. I was one who was susceptible to the lure of Nash's places, visiting many of his favourite sites, and becoming part of their story myself too. I went on from there to discover places uniquely my own, and I continue to do so in parts of rural Derbyshire, especially the White Peak, where I now live. Their appeal is hard to pin down, but one common feature, the one I and my co-authors highlighted in our book, *Communion, Covenant and Creativity*, is human stories that in some measure are encapsulated by artists in wood or stone, and linger as graphic memories, now inseparable from their original locations. In my own writing about Nash, I make connections with the Christian idea of The Communion of Saints—these are places where I become entwined with the stories of my forebears, some of whom I know in part, others who exist in my imagination as little more than a hazy dream.

I find myself coming back, however, to the issue of light. In the spirit of a Merleau-Ponty analysis, I find myself attracted to the idea that painters of the *genius loci*, use light to bring together in their pictures something of the myriad traditions associated with special places, strangely and wonderfully sedimenting what they themselves one experienced, now in the physicality of colourful paint. Each artist brings to the task something of their own "genius," rooted in a special grasp of painterly techniques and, not least, a palette of colours. Nash certainly did this in a distinctive way, capturing something quite extraordinary in his images of Wittenham Clumps, an Iron Age site near Oxford.[30] Cadell and Peploe achieved something similar as they painted on Iona. Mere representation (or re-presentation), photographic realism alone, is unlikely ever to capture it. Just as the experience of transcendence recalled by pilgrims to Iona cannot be "bottled" and brought home, so the capacity of a painting to evoke transcendence cannot be identified simply "in" the paint. There is something about constellations of effects conspiring together to communicate something "more than" simply "normal" communication. My growing conviction is that it is significantly triggered by particular palettes of colour, particular distributions of paint—be they dots, patches or sweeping strokes—and by lines introduced by an artist to encourage our minds into a visual space comparable with their own.

Theologically, there are evident connections with the contemplative idea of "finding God in all things," a phrase that inspired the title of Gerard Hughes

---

[30] See, e.g., Paul Nash's "Landscape of the Summer Solstice" (1943) at https://www.ngv.vic.gov.au/explore/collection/work/4210/

highly acclaimed book, *God in All Things*.[31] The concept of "God in all things" is, of course, no less metaphorical than any other attempt to pin down the idea of God's transcendence, and to understand how God becomes known immanently in human experience. The idea of "finding God in all things" is, I suggest, a useful way into understanding more about the subtleties of the relationship between transcendence and immanence. I no longer expect, for example, to find "intimations of transcendence" other than in immanent material encounters; and I do not expect there to be any material reality that is entirely devoid of a capacity to intimate transcendence. Hughes urges his readers to reach beyond an over-simplified split between the immanent and the transcendent, something he believes comes back to life in the practice of contemplative prayer. He commends it as a way of thinking about God's relationship with the world, deep-rooted in a Christian understanding of incarnation. Additionally, in my own thinking, it sits especially well with those philosophical models of thinking about God and the world that are gathered under the broad umbrella of Process Theology, which provides models of reality that can have a strong appeal to people who come to visual arts with a scientific background like my own—but that is another story.[32]

I have also always found Paul Tillich's use of the metaphor of "depth" hard to beat when it comes to a description of God's relationship with the world.[33] A typical Tillichian way of expressing this would be say that transcendence is universally immanent because every "being" has its ultimate ground in "Being Itself." If Tillich was right about this, and I think he was, then it is hardly surprising that constellations of materiality, comprising no more than oil and canvas, can uncover and disclose depth with such notable effect—some, of course, more effectively than others.

In commending the Iona Paintings of Francis Cadell and Samuel Peploe, then, I am drawing attention to artifacts that, because of their peculiar constellations of form and colour, do remarkable justice to the island, in much the same way as those who have chosen to call it a "thin place" and those who visit expecting to find "God in all things." I have tried to identify how simple elements of form, such as patches of uniform colour and heavy dark lines, conspire with a carefully chosen palette of colours to work this unpredictable magic. I have tried to show how their own unique styles owe much to radical techniques simultaneously explored by many of their contemporaries on the continent of Europe. In the legacy of The Scottish Colourists, then, I am not at all surprised to find strong "intimations of transcendence."

---

[31] Hughes, *God in All Things*.

[32] An example of how these ideas come together in Process Theology is explored in my chapter Kidd, "Memory and Communion," especially 38–44.

[33] See especially Tillich's sermon, "The Depth of Existence" in his *Shaking of the Foundations*, 59–70.

Bibliography

Andrews, Jorella. *The Question of Painting*. London: Bloomsbury, 2018. Kindle edition.
Berger, John, and John Christie. *I Send You This Cadmium Red*. Barcelona: ACTAR, 1999.
Bergson, Henri. *Creative Evolution*. Translated by Arthur Mitchell. London: Macmillan, 1911.
Bergson, Henri. *Matter and Memory*. Translated by Nancy Margaret Paul and W. Scott Palmer. London: Macmillan, 1911.
Fiddes, Paul S., Brian Haymes, and Richard Kidd. *Baptists and the Communion of Saints: A Theology of Covenanted Disciples*. Waco: Baylor University Press, 2014.
Fiddes, Paul S., Brian Haymes and Richard L. Kidd. *Communion, Covenant and Creativity: An Approach to the Communion of Saints through the Arts*. Oregon: Wipf & Stock, 2020.
Hughes, Gerard. *God in All Things*. London: Hodder & Stoughton, 2003.
Kandinsky, Wassily. *Point and Line to Plane*. New York: Dover, 1979.
Kandinsky, Wassily. *Concerning the Spiritual in Art*. London: Tate, 2006.
Kandinsky, Wassily, and Marc, Franz. *The Blaue Reiter Almanac*. London: Tate, 2006.
Kidd, Richard. "Perceiving an Absent Presence: The Visual World of Paul Nash." In *Communion, Covenant and Creativity*, 23–50. By Fiddes, Haymes and Kidd.
Kidd, Richard. "Memory and Communion." In *Baptists and the Communion of Saints*, 31–53. By Fiddes, Haymes and Kidd.
Kidd, Richard, and Graham Sparkes. *God and the Art of Seeing: Visual Resources for a Journey of Faith*. Regent's Study Guides, 11. Oxford: Regent's Park College, 2003.
Lamb, Trevor, and Bourriau, Janine. *Colour, Art and Science*. Cambridge: Cambridge University Press, 1995.
Long, Philip, with Elizabeth Cumming. *The Scottish Colourists 1900–1930*. Edinburgh: National Galleries of Scotland, 2001.
MacLeod Coupe, Philip. *Paintings of Iona: Cadell and Peploe*. s.l.: privately published for the Heirs of Philip MacLeod Coupe, 2014.
Merleau-Ponty, Maurice. *Phenomenology of Perception*. Translated by Donald A. Landes. Abingdon: Routledge, 2012.
Power, Rosemary, "A Place of Community: 'Celtic' Iona and Institutional Religion." *Folklore* 117 (2006) 33–53.
Quoist, Michel. *Prayers of Life*. Dublin: M.H. Gill & Son, 1963.
The Scottish Colourists Festival Exhibition. Edinburgh: Scottish Gallery, 2016.
Tillich, Paul. *The Shaking of the Foundations*. Harmondsworth: Penguin Books, 1949.

Select Bibliography
of the Writings of Ruth Gouldbourne

Allison-Glenny, Beth, Andy Goodliff, Ruth Gouldbourne, Steve Holmes, David Kerrigan, and Glen Marshall. "The Courage to be Baptist: A Statement on Baptist Ecclesiology and Human Sexuality." *Baptist Quarterly* 48.1 (2017) 2–10.

"Balthasar Hubmaier (1480–1528)," and "Menno Simons (1496–1561)." In *Biographical Dictionary of Evangelicals*, 314–15 and 424–26. Edited by Timothy Larsen. Leicester: Inter-Varsity Press, 2003.

"Baptists, Women, and Ministry." *Feminist Theology* 26.1 (2017) 59–68.

"The Depressed Donkey," "The Haughty Camel," "The House-proud Cow," and "The Sheep's Story." In *Gathering up the Crumbs: Celebrating a Century of Accredited, Ordained, Baptist Women in Ministry in the UK*, 91–94, 94–96, 97–100, and 100–103. Edited by Catriona Gorton, Claire Nicholls, Ruth Gouldbourne, *et al*. London: Baptist Union of Great Britain, 2020.

"Desert island books." *Baptist Minister's Journal* 327 (July 2015) 5–7.

"Do Women Complement Men in Ministry?" *Ministry Today* 17 (October, 1999), https://www.ministrytoday.org.uk/magazine/issues/17/97/

"Ecclesiology and Gender: Radical Reformation, Baptist Beginnings, and Baptists Today." The Hughey Lectures 1998, delivered at The International Baptist Theological Seminary, Prague, November 1998. https://www.ibts.eu/research/hughey-lectures

"Encountering Christ: Zwingli, Signs and Baptists around the Table." In *For the Sake of the Church: Essays in Honour of Paul S. Fiddes*, 78–90. Edited by A.J. Clarke. Centre for Baptist History and Heritage Studies, 3. Oxford: Regent's Park College, 2014.

"Episcope without Episcopacy: Baptist Attitudes to the Bishops in Seventeenth-Century England." In *Interfaces: Baptists and Others*, 29–46. Edited by David W. Bebbington, and Martin Sutherland. Studies in Baptist History and Thought. Milton Keynes: Paternoster, 2013.

The Flesh and the Feminine: Gender and Theology in the Writings of Caspar Schwenckfeld. Studies in Christian History and Thought. Milton Keynes: Paternoster, 2006.

"Identity and Pain: Women's Consultations 1987–92." *Baptist Ministers' Journal* 243 (July 1993) 8–10.

"In Praise of Incompetence: Ministerial Formation and the Development of a Rooted Person." In *Truth That Never Dies: The Dr. G.R. Beasley-Murray Memorial Lectures 2002–2012*, 168–84. Edited by Nigel G. Wright. Eugene: Pickwick Publications, 2014.

"Kissing Cousins: Theatre and Pulpit in Seventeenth-Century London." MA diss, King's College London, 2017.

"Liturgical Identity Carriers for Ecclesial Transformation." *American Baptist Quarterly* 31.4 (2012) 379–91.

"Messengers: Do They Have a Message for Us?" In *Translocal Ministry: "equipping the churches for mission*," 24–32. Edited by Stuart Murray. Didcot: Baptist Union of Great Britain, 2004.

"Not just a Disembodied Voice: Towards an Understanding of Preaching as an Embodied Practice." *Baptistic Theologies* 5.1 (2013) 53–67.

"Praise and Prayer." *Baptist Quarterly* 35.2 (1993) 90–94

"Reflecting on Ministry (3)." 3 July 2014. andygoodliff: church, world and the Christian life. https://andygoodliff.typepad.com/my_weblog/ministry// Gouldbourne

Reinventing the Wheel: Women and Ministry in English Baptist Life. The Whitley Lecture 1997–1998. Oxford: Whitley Publications, 1997.

"A short history of Baptist women in ministry." *Baptists Together* (Spring 2019), 6–8.

"Story-telling, Sacraments, and Sexuality." In *Questions of Identity*, 239–52. Edited by Cross and Gouldbourne.

"Theology and Gender in the Writings of Caspar Schwenckfeld." PhD diss., University of London, 2000.

"'This Sad Work': Scandal in Broadmead." *Baptist Quarterly* 39.3 (2001) 146–52.

"Voices." *Baptist Ministers' Journal* 268 (1999) 6–9.

"'We are Gathered with the Millions': Celebrating the Communion of Saints." In *Gathering Disciples: Essays in Honor of Christopher J. Ellis*, 173–84. Edited by Myra Blyth and Andy Goodliff. Eugene: Pickwick, 2017.

"What makes the Anabaptists so Annoying?" In *Coming Home: Stories of Anabaptists in Britain and Ireland*, 61–62. Edited by Alan Kreider and Stuart Murray. Kitchener: Pandora, 2000.

"When we meet to worship you . . ." In *Prayers of the People,* 150. Edited by Karen E. Smith and Simon P. Woodman. Centre for Baptist History and Heritage Studies and South Wales Baptist College. Oxford: Regent's Park, 2011.

Cross, Anthony R., and Ruth Gouldbourne, eds. *Questions of Identity: Studies in Honour of Brian Haymes*. Centre for Baptist History and Heritage Studies, 6. Oxford: Regent's Park College, 2011.

Haymes, Brian, Ruth Gouldbourne and Anthony R. Cross. *On Being the Church: Revisioning Baptist Identity*. Studies in Baptist History and Thought, 21. Milton Keynes: Paternoster, 2008.

General Index

Abigail 198–99
Adcock, R. 72
Albright, W.F. 35
Alinsky, S. 245–48, 250
Andrews, J. 290–91

Baptist Magazine 124–38
Baptist Missionary Society (BMS) 73
Baptist Women's League (BWL) 74
Baptist Zenana Mission (BZM) 71, 73, 75, 78
Bartlett, A. 52
Baxter, R. 223
Bazley, W. 206
Bellis, A.O. 32, 45
Bergson, H. 283
Blenskinsopp, J. 31
Bloomsbury Central Baptist Church, 18, 96, 234, 237, 250, 253
Booth, C. 58, 64
Boström, G. 30
Bourne, H. 55–56
Bowers, F. 237
Brenner, Athalya 32, 42, 45
Brock, B. 197
Burns, C.C. 76–78
Butler, J. 183

Cadell, F.C.B. 278, 282–95
Calvin, J. 58–64, 272
"Capable" Women 39–44
Camp, C. 34, 37–39, 42
Carey, W. 70, 210
Carey Hall, 110
Cartwright, C. 68
Casti Connubii, 191
Chidley, K. 54
Church League for Women's Sufferage (CLWS) 67–68
Church Meeting 18
Clifford, J. 84–85
Clifford, R.J. 30–31, 36
Colour, 284–95
Cook, H. 182
Cornwall, S. 195
Coupe, P. MacL. 292–93
Covenant 180
Crawford, E. 67
Crawford, P. 128
Crisp, T.S. 210

Crosby, T. 207

deaconess 73–74, 89
Deanne, J. 172
DeFranza, M. 186,196
Derain, H. 283
Dods, M. 106–7

Embodiment 13
Encratite Christianity, 163–64
Evangelical Alliance, 185
Evans C. 208–9, 210, 212
Evans, H. 208, 211, 214

Family Prayers 132–34
Farrer, E. 78–79
Fawcett, J. 212–13
Felipa of Porcelet 169
Fell, M. 54
Ferguson, R. 228–29
Fergusson, J.D. 282–95
Fernie, E. 257
Fiddes, P.S. 12, 186
"Forbidden" Woman 30–34
Fosdick, H.E. 225–27
Foucault, M. 18
Fox, N.V. 34, 36, 37, 43
Free Church League for Women's Suffrage (FCLWS) 68
Freeman, C. 72
Freeman, J. 243
Furcha, E.J. 2

Gender Dysphoria 180
Gilbert of Tournai 168, 169
Gifford, A. 206–7
Giles, K. 50
Gouldbourne, I. xiii–xvii
Gouldbourne, R.M.B. ix–xxi, 18, 48, 69, 159, 201, 220, 234, 253, 258, 279
Gravesande, D. 252
Grenfell, G. 211
Groves, B. 273

Hadewijch, 169
Hall Jr. R. 213–14
Hays, R. 7
Heath, J. 8–9
Henry, M. 58, 60–62

Hester, J.D. 195
Hooker, R. 271
Hunter, G.L. 282–95
Hughes, G. 295

Inductions 222
Iona, 378, 284, 287–89, 292–95

Jameson, N. 252
Jones, D.A. 197

Kandinsky, W. 281
Katvel, I. 140–56
Kayatz, C. 35
Kemp, E.G. 79–82, 95–120
King, C.S. 240
King Jr, M.L. 237
Knox, W.L. 35

Laqueur, T. 62–63
Letter and Spirit 3–14
Levinson, S.D. 238
Listening 19–28
Louis, E. 252
Luther, M. 19, 27, 264

MacLeod, G. 228–30, 292
Marchal, J. 14
Marie of Oignies, 168–69
Marion, J-L. 257
Martin, D. 14
Martin, G. ix
Masenya, M. 42
Matisse, H. 283
McCracken, R. 227
McTaggart, W. 284
Mechthild of Magdeburg, 169, 171
Merleau-Ponty, M. 290–91
Mill, J.S. 70
Ministry 206–15
Monet, C. 282
Morgan, R. 11
Munch, E. 282

Narva Evangelical Christian Free Church, 143, 145
Nash, P. 293–94
Newman, B. 171–72
Newton, J. 209
Niebuhr, R. 230–33
Niebuhr, U. 231–32

O'Donovan, O. 184–85, 190, 194–95
Otwell, J.H. 37

Palettes 279–82
Palmer, P. 57–58, 64
Parker, J. 212–13
Pascal 51
Pastoral Prayer 219–34
Paul, apostle 2–14, 260, 264, 265, 269
Payne, E.A. 68, 181
Pearce, S. 209
Peploe, S. 278, 282–95
Perry S. 234
Personified Wisdom, 34–39
Pigott, T.W. 99–104
Poiesis 24–28
Porete, M. 170, 172
Praying for Children 130–32
Proverbs, 29–45

Quash, B. 188–91, 196
Quoist, M. 286

Reddie, R. 252
Reinventing the Wheel 48
Renoir, P-A. 281
Riley, B. 286
Robinson, J. 180
Rothko, M. 281
Ryland, J. 209

Sabia-Tanis, J. 185
Sanders, K. 67
Schwenckfeld, C. xxv–xxvii, 1–2
Scott, R.B.Y. 42
"Scottish Colourists" 282–95
Serenity Prayer 231
Seurat, P. 285
Shakespeare, W. 257–75
    Authority 270–75
    Forgiveness and Mercy 265–70
    Spirituality of Death 261–65
    Spirituality of Love 259–61
Sifton, E. 231
Single people, 159–75
Sinnott, A.M. 36
Snowden, E. 82–84
Song, R. 199–200
Spurgeon, C.H. 135–36, 211, 223–24
Stone, S. 252
Story 273–75
Sufferage 75–78

Summerville College Chapel 95–96, 114–20

Tallinn 154
Temperance 75–78
Tertullion 166
Thomas, S. 129–30, 133
Tillich, P. 295
Topolski, F. 241–42
Tosh, J. 128

Unanswered prayer, 129

Valler, S. 42
Van Gogh, V. 280
Van Leenwen, R.C. 45

Ward, W. 214
Warner, M. 14
Warnock, R. 241
Watson, F. 10
Weeks, S. 34
Wesley, J. 54
West, C. 251
West, W.M.S. 214–15
Whybray, R.N. 36
Williams, H. 237, 238, 241–42
Winslow, E. 180
Winter, S. 189
Wollstonecraft, M.70
Wolters, AI. 40–41
Women Deacons, 86–88
Wright, C.J.H. 31
Wright, N.T. 18, 21

Yarhouse, M. 182, 185, 187
Yee, G.A. 32
Yoder, C.R. 42

www.ingramcontent.com/pod-product-compliance
Ingram Content Group UK Ltd.
Pitfield, Milton Keynes, MK11 3LW, UK
UKHW022000220326
11408UKWH00003B/390